The Holy Spirit and Christian Ethics in the Theology of Klaus Bockmuehl

The Holy Spirit and Christian Ethics in the Theology of Klaus Bockmuehl

ANNETTE M. GLAW

◆PICKWICK *Publications* · Eugene, Oregon

THE HOLY SPIRIT AND CHRISTIAN ETHICS IN THE
THEOLOGY OF KLAUS BOCKMUEHL

Copyright © 2013 Annette M. Glaw. All rights reserved. Except for brief quotations in critical publications or reviews, no part of this book may be reproduced in any manner without prior written permission from the publisher. Write: Permissions, Wipf and Stock Publishers, 199 W. 8th Ave., Suite 3, Eugene, OR 97401.

Pickwick Publications
An Imprint of Wipf and Stock Publishers
199 W. 8th Ave., Suite 3
Eugene, OR 97401

www.wipfandstock.com

ISBN 13: 978-1-62032-401-1

Cataloguing-in-Publication data:

Glaw, Annette M.

The Holy Spirit and Christian ethics in the theology of Klaus Bockmuehl / Annette M. Glaw.

xiv + 302 pp. ; 23 cm. Includes bibliographical references and indexes.

ISBN 13: 978-1-62032-401-1

1. Bockmühl, Klaus, 1931–1989. 2. Holy Spirit. 3. Christian ethics. I. Title.

BT121 G5 2013

Manufactured in the U.S.A.

All scripture quotations, unless otherwise indicated, are taken from the Holy Bible, New International Version®, NIV®. Copyright ©1973, 1978, 1984, 2011 by Biblica, Inc.™ Used by permission of Zondervan. All rights reserved worldwide. www.zondervan.com The "NIV" and "New International Version" are trademarks registered in the United States Patent and Trademark Office by Biblica, Inc.™
www.wipfandstock.com

Contents

Foreword by Graham McFarlane   *vii*
Acknowledgments   ix
Abbreviations   xi

Introduction   1

Part One: Bockmuehl's Theological Work

1   Theological and Spiritual Influences on Bockmuehl   25

2   Bockmuehl's Main Theological Concerns   90

Part Two: The Holy Spirit and Christian Ethics in the Theology of Klaus Bockmuehl

3   The Neglect of the Holy Spirit in the History of Christian Ethics and Bockmuehl's Response   109

4   Bockmuehl's Understanding of Christian Ethics   137

Part Three: A Critical Appraisal of and a Response to Bockmuehl's Concept of the Spirit's Role in Christian Ethics

5   A Critical Appraisal of Bockmuehl's Concept of the Holy Spirit and Christian Ethics   187

6   A Response: Spirit as the Loving Presence of God—Toward a Relational Concept of the Spirit in Christian Ethics   201

Conclusion   237

Bibliography   239
Author Index   287
Subject Index   291

Foreword

WITHOUT DOUBT THE CONTEMPORARY Christian scene is becoming dominated by interest in all things Pneumatic—anything to do with the Spirit of God is a crowd-puller and pleaser. This is a good thing: we are increasingly becoming interested not only in *what* the Spirit does but *how* he goes about it. However, most attention is given to what the Spirit does in our gatherings at the expense of individual spirituality. What is needed, today, is a theology of the Spirit that engages with basic questions of Christian existence, at a very practical level. What does this activity look like? How does it "work"?

Enter the prophetic perspective of Klaus Bockmuehl, a theologian who saw this need at a time when things of the Spirit were perceived a "niche" realm of the seminary. Precocious and sometimes marginalized his insights regarding the Spirit's agency in Christian ethics, and therefore in our daily Christian experiences, have renewed import, now. At last, someone who saw the connection between Law (the framework of Scripture—not rules and regulations) and Spirit. Without Spirit, Law only leads to legalism and its antinomian reactions. And they are rife in the contemporary church. And this plays itself out in our ethics, of course.

What Annette Glaw does in this exposition of Bockmuehl's analysis of the Spirit in Christian Ethics is to extend his thinking into a more relational context. By building on Bockmuehl's functional view of the Spirit Glaw argues that a more relational approach to Christian Ethics would enable us to think of the Spirit as drawing people into a love relationship with the Father. As such, a Christian ethic is better understood as union and communion with the living God through loving relationships with God, neighbor and self. And this only happens when the Spirit moves and empowers.

This is an exceptional book—it introduces us for the first time to a much-neglected thinker. It also equips us with an understanding of how the church can live ethically in power—through its love relationship with

Foreword

the Father. In both respects it has much to offer its reader and the wider contemporary church.

Graham McFarlane
London School of Theology

Acknowledgments

WRITING A BOOK ABOUT the Holy Spirit and Christian ethics is not an easy task, and I was only able to reach this stage of submission by learning to depend on God's and other people's love and support.

I want to first of all thank my PhD supervisor, Graham McFarlane, for his encouragement and support throughout the long years of research. His theology, especially his concept of atonement with its emphasis on the primacy of God's love, has been truly inspiring and life-changing for me. Moreover, without his understanding and affirmation of my personal journey toward the discovery of God's love I would not have been able to finish this thesis.

The same is particularly true for Sue Sainsbury (and her husband John), whose truly unconditional, constant, and caring love has been life-transforming since it enabled me to "take the beautiful risk," "a leap into the wild spaces of love, a dance of faith,"[1] and thereby discover a love more gracious and healing than I thought possible—God's own love.

I want to thank my friends, particularly Gabi, Martina, Kesia, Amy, and Shivali for "journeying together" with me toward the "miracle of love . . . no demands, no judgments—being respected, received, affirmed, and blessed. To show oneself as the person we are—wounded, blemished, hurting, longing—and to feel welcomed and accepted is to experience grace."[2] I am, furthermore, grateful to Julia Arnold and my housemates for their encouragement and support, and for providing me with a temporary "home." Particular thanks goes to my parents and sister for their love and support, and for their appreciation of and prayers for my research.

I want to mention especially Volker Rabens whose research on *The Holy Spirit and Ethics in Paul: Transformation and Empowering for Religious-Ethical Life* (published 2010) was the inspiration for my own topic. It has been encouraging to have a fellow-researcher also emphasizing the

---

1. Olthuis, *Beautiful Risk*, 14, 237.
2. Ibid., 66, 207.

Acknowledgments

relational work of the Holy Spirit in Christian ethics and to have a friend in him and his wife who share the journey toward the discovery of God's love and a deeper intimacy with God.

I would also like to express my gratitude to Elisabeth Bockmuehl, who supported me in many ways, not least in taking time to answer my questions concerning her husband and entrusting me her keys for the Bockmuehl-archives during my visit at St. Chrischona.

I am similarly grateful to Werner Neuer who took time to read the early parts of my PhD. Special thanks also to my three very capable, helpful, and flexible proof-readers, Sue Sainsbury, Helen Shephard, and Volker Rabens, and to Julia Arnold for answering my many questions regarding the English language.

Without the financial support from the Laing Trust, the *Arbeitskreis für evangelikale Theologie*, as well as from family and friends I could not have done my research.

I would also like to thank Chris Spinks of Pickwick Publications for his helpful assistance throughout the publication process.

My greatest thanks, however, goes to God for loving me just as I am—no matter what, for giving me friends who reflect his love and for helping me to discover that "the Spirit truly is the divine love guiding us home. Through the Spirit we come 'home' to the divine life the Father intends for us—and freely shares with us—in the Son."[3]

---

3. Grenz, "Holy Spirit," 12.

Abbreviations

Bockmuehl's Works

CaL	*Conservation and Lifestyle.* Translated by Bruce N. Kaye. Bramcote: Grove, 1977.
CM	*The Challenge of Marxism: A Christian Response.* Downers Grove: IVP, 1980
CW	*The Christian Way of Living: An Ethics of the Ten Commandments.* Vancouver: Regent College Bookstore, 1994.
DH	*Denken im Horizont der Wirklichkeit Gottes. Schriften zur Dogmatik und Theologiegeschichte.* Edited by Rainer Mayer. BWA 2/1. Giessen, Germany: Brunnen, 1999.
GG	*Gesetz und Geist. Eine kritische Würdigung des Erbes protestantischer Ethik.* Vol. I, *Die Ethik der reformatorischen Bekenntnisschriften.* Giessen, Germany: Brunnen, 1987.
gh	*glauben und handeln. Beiträge zur Begründung evangelischer Ethik (Gesammelte Aufsätze).* Giessen, Germany: Brunnen, 1975.
GiE	*Gott im Exil? Zur Kritik der "Neuen Moral."* Wuppertal, Germany: Aussaat, 1975.
LbG	*Living by the Gospel: Christian Roots of Confidence and Purpose.* Colorado Springs: Helmers & Howard, 1986.
LG	*Listening to the God who speaks. Reflections on God's Guidance from the Scripture and the Lives of God's People.* Colorado Springs: Helmers & Howard, 1990.
LuG	*Leiblichkeit und Gesellschaft. Studien zur Religionskritik und Anthropologie im Frühwerk von Ludwig Feuerbach und Karl Marx.* 2nd rev. ed. with new epilogue. Giessen, Germany: Brunnen, 1980.

Abbreviations

LWG	*Leben nach dem Willen Gottes. Schriften zur Materialethik.* Edited by Rainer Mayer. BWA 2/3. Giessen, Germany: Brunnen, 2006.
SU	*Sinn und Unsinn der neuen Moral: Kritik und Selbstkritik.* TuD 1. 2nd ed. Giessen, Germany: Brunnen, 1974
TuL	*Theologie und Lebensführung. Gesammelte Aufsätze 2.* Giessen, Germany: Brunnen, 1982.
UG	*The Unreal God of Modern Theology. Bultmann, Barth, and the Theology of Atheism: a Call to Recovering the Truth of God's Reality.* Translated by Geoffrey W. Bromiley. Colorado Springs: Helmers & Howard, 1988.
VG	*Verantwortung des Glaubens im Wandel der Zeit. Protestantische Theologie im 19. und 20. Jahrhundert.* Edited by Helmut Burkhardt. BWA 3/3. Giessen, Germany: Brunnen, 2001.
WM	*Was heißt heute Mission? Entscheidungsfragen der neueren Missionstheologie.* Edited by Helmut Egelkraut. BWA 1/3. Giessen, Germany: Brunnen, 2000.

General

AfeT	Arbeitskreis für evangelikale Theologie
AGORA	Krelinger Studentenrundbrief, GRZ Krelingen, Walsrode
BSac	Bibliotheca Sacra
BuG	Bibel und Gemeinde. Berlin: Bibelbund
BWA	Bockmuehl-Werk-Ausgabe
CVJM	Christlicher Verein junger Männer/Menschen
Crux	Crux: a quarterly journal of Christian thought and opinion; Vancouver: Regent College
dran	dran. Witten: Bundes-Verlag GmbH (magazine)
ELThG	*Evangelisches Lexikon für Theologie und Gemeinde.* Edited by H. Burkhardt and U. Swarat. Wuppertal, Germany: Brockhaus, 1992–1994
EvTh	Evangelische Theologie, Munich: Kaiser
ERT	Evangelical Review of Theology
idea-Doku	*idea-Dokumentation.* Evangelische Nachrichtenagentur, Wetzlar: idea

Abbreviations

idea-Spektrum	Nachrichten und Meinungen aus der evangelischen Welt, edited by Informationsdienst der Evangelischen Allianz e.V., Wetzlar: idea
IVP	InterVarsity Press
JETh	Jahrbuch für Evangelikale Theologie, Wuppertal, Germany: Brockhaus, 1987–
JTS	Journal of Theological Studies
KiZ	Kirche in der Zeit, Evangelische Kirchenzeitung, Düsseldorf: Postverlagsort
LW	*Luther's Works: American Edition*. Edited by Jaroslav Pelikan and Helmut T. Lehmann.
MPTh	Monatsschrift für Pastoraltheologie
MRA	Moral Re-Armament
OJC	Offensive Junger Christen
OJC Frbrief	Anstiftungen zu gemeinsamem Christenleben, Freundesbrief der Ökumenischen Kommunität Offensive Junger Christen in Reichelsheim im Odenwald und Greifswald. Reichelsheim: Christen in der Offensive e.V., 1968–.
Porta	Journal of the student mission in Germany; Marburg: Studenten Mission Deutschland
RefR	The Reformed Review
SJT	Scottish Journal of Theology
SMD	Studenten Mission Deutschland (student mission in Germany)
ThBeitr	Theologische Beiträge. Wuppertal: Brockhaus, 1970–.
ThLZ	Theologische Literaturzeitung
TuD	Theologie und Dienst (series)
ThZ	Theologische Zeitschrift, edited by the theological faculty of the University Basel, Basel: Friedrich Reinhardt AG
TRE	Theologische Realenzyklopädie, edited by G. Krause and G. Müller, 1976–
VF	Verkündigung und Forschung, Munich: Kaiser
VLM	Verlag der Liebenzeller Mission

xiii

Introduction

MANY YEARS AGO I came across the devotional book *Listening to the God Who Speaks* by Klaus Bockmuehl and was fascinated to find that here was a German theologian who had written many outstanding theological as well as ethical works of research and yet emphasized that we can actually *experience* God's transforming reality through the work of the Spirit. Moreover, here was a German theologian who not only wrote about spiritual issues such as the *guidance* of the Holy Spirit but for whom the latter was a daily experience. This kindled my interest and motivated me to delve into other books by Bockmuehl such as his excellent appraisal of the heritage of Protestant ethics entitled *Law and Spirit (Gesetz und Geist)*. The more I read, the more I discovered that here was a theologian addressing central questions of practical relevance: How do we know what God's will is in a particular situation? Does God still speak today? Does he speak only through Scripture or in a more direct way? What role does the Holy Spirit play in our daily lives, in our decision-making, in our transformation from the "old" to the "new" person etc.?

This led me to embark on a study of Bockmuehl's understanding of Holy Spirit and Christian ethics since "[t]he significance of the Holy Spirit for ethics was a central concern of Klaus Bockmuehl's theological work."[1] However, due to the fact that Bockmuehl was "often ignored within Protestant theology"[2] and is therefore not well-known, I realised that it was necessary to first give an introduction to Bockmuehl's life and overall work before focusing on his Christian ethics and the role the Holy Spirit played in the latter.

Hence, this book begins with a biographical overview of Bockmuehl's life before setting out which theologians and spiritual leaders as well as theological and spiritual traditions played a part in molding Bockmuehl's

---

1. Liebschner, "Bedeutung," 342 (citing from the English summary at the end of the German article).
2. Neuer, "Bockmühl, Klaus," 288.

theology and particularly his understanding of the Holy Spirit and Christian ethics. This is followed by a summary of his main theological concerns such as his passion for the reality of God and his will (Part One).

Part Two, which focuses on Bockmuehl's concept of the Holy Spirit and Christian ethics, examines first of all three concepts of Christian ethics that Bockmuehl considered to be very influential and to be responsible for the pneumatological weakness in ethics during his lifetime. This is followed by an outline of his understanding of Christian ethics, revealing Bockmuehl's answers to relevant questions such as the following: Is the law still valid for Christians or do Christians now only live by the Spirit? Does something like a natural law exist? Does a Christian ethic differ from a non-Christian one? How important is it for Christians to take social action and conserve the environment? Or should they mainly focus on evangelizing and preaching? I will also explore how, according to Bockmuehl, inner transformation can happen that leads to a changed life and if topics such as love for God, spirituality, and guidance by the Spirit should be dealt within a Christian ethic.

In the third and concluding part, I offer a critical appraisal of Bockmuehl's concept of the Holy Spirit and Christian ethics and attempt to answer the following questions: Is Bockmuehl's double principle of Christian ethics—law and Spirit—truly the answer to all our ethical questions and dilemmas? Is it more important to know God's will or to know God's nature? What is the correct balance between Christian activism and contemplation?

Following this critical appraisal, I offer a response to Bockmuehl by building upon Bockmuehl's insights with regard to the Holy Spirit and Christian ethics, weaving them together with a relational concept of the Spirit as the loving presence of God in Christian ethics. Why is it that being a Christian and knowing about God's love not always "automatically translate[s] into a changed life"?[3] What obstacles might hinder us in living and growing in loving relationship with God, self, and others? If the Holy Spirit is first and foremost the loving presence of God, what implications does this have for Christian ethics, for our relationships? These are some of the questions I explore in the final chapters of this book.

My hope is that this first in-depth study on Bockmuehl might in some way remedy the fact that Bockmuehl, as Neuer laments, "did on the whole not receive much attention within Protestant theology,"[4] despite his

---

3. Chan, *Spiritual Theology*, 79–80.
4. Neuer, "Bockmühl, Klaus," 288.

Introduction

theology being both biblical and topically relevant. However, it is encouraging that "none other than the former *Cardinal Ratzinger* and the present Pope Benedict XVI acknowledged Klaus Bockmuehl . . . to be a 'spiritual well digger.'"[5] Furthermore, my hope is that this book might be an aid on our journey toward discovering that "the Spirit truly is the divine love guiding us home. Through the Spirit we come 'home' to the divine life the Father intends for us—and freely shares with us—in the Son."[6]

Bockmuehl's Life

Childhood and Youth (1931–1951)

Klaus Erich Bockmuehl was born in Essen/Ruhr on 6 May 1931. He was the only son of Erich Bockmuehl, a mechanical engineer, and Hanna, née Ihlo. When looking at his spiritual background, we discover that, apart from his grandmother, no one in the family regularly attended church, even though his mother officially belonged to it.[7]

A significant factor in his childhood was the rise and fall of the National Socialists under Hitler and the Second World War. While attending the Helmholtz-Gymnasium in Essen, the whole school had to be evacuated to Austria (Sölden, Ötztal) in 1942–45 because of air raids on German cities. After his return to Essen, he witnessed the social misery of the majority of people, particularly among the working class in the Ruhr region, as the rebuilding of the economy was very slow. Furthermore, it is worth mentioning that after the war Germany was ideologically torn between two divergent systems: torn between democratic freedom in the West and the dictatorship of the USSR in the East. Not surprisingly, therefore, Bockmuehl started to deal with social and political topics such as Marxism, socialism, the "new man," and capitalism early on in life.[8]

Not long after returning to Germany, Bockmuehl, like most Protestant children, was confirmed in the Evangelical Church of the Rhineland. Even though the confirmation was no more than a traditional rite to him, he was, nevertheless, disappointed that his father did not attend this event.[9]

---

5. Neuer, "Weite," 5. On February 28, 2013 Benedict XVI resigned as Pope.
6. Grenz, "Holy Spirit," 12.
7. Thomas, "Spirituality of Klaus Bockmuehl: Part One," 3.
8. Bockmuehl, "The Marxist New Man," 53; cf. Hofmann, "Revolutionär," 17–18.
9. Cf. Thomas, "Spirituality of Klaus Bockmuehl: Part One," 3.

Concerning Bockmuehl's spiritual life, it was of great importance that he started to attend weekly youth services led by Pastor Wilhelm Busch in the "Weigle House," Essen, in 1947. There he experienced Christianity, more precisely German Pietism, in a lively, attractive form. In the summer of 1947 he took part in a retreat, organized by Wilhelm Busch. One day, while talking to his friend Karl Sundermeier and at the same time making a wooden cross, a stranger appeared suddenly and started an argument about the Christian faith attacking the person of Jesus. This incident disturbed Bockmuehl greatly since he felt that the devil himself was trying to hold him back from Jesus. Aware of the fact that, unlike Sundermeier, he had not yet committed his life to Christ, he decided as a result of this encounter to follow Jesus uncompromisingly. The wooden cross he had made during this decisive hour served him as a reminder of his conversion, and he hung it up in every office wherever he lived.[10]

In November 1948, Bockmuehl had the chance of watching a play called "The Forgotten Factor," written by Alan Thornhill, a former lecturer at Oxford and co-worker of Frank Buchman.[11] It was performed in Essen near the ruined Krupp works and later in the whole Ruhr region. Such was the attraction that more than 100,000 people saw it over a two-year period. Even Minister-President Karl Arnold and the Lord Mayor of Essen, Dr. Gustav Heinemann,[12] supported the play. Due to the fact that the latter belonged to Busch's church and was a personal friend of the Weigle-House, Busch encouraged young "Weigle-House-men," among them Bockmuehl, to help the team of about fifty international Christians, belonging to a movement called "Moral Re-Armament," prepare the play. The message of the play was to bring spiritual hope to a hopeless world by addressing the conflicts between different social and racial classes, and those within families. Beyond this, the play pointed to the uniting and transforming factor—the living God and what he had to say to people—since attitudes can only be changed through listening and obeying.[13]

While traveling around and helping the team, Bockmuehl seized the opportunity to take part in regular prayer times and witnessed a dynamic lifestyle. There he discovered that the creativity of the group and

---

10. Cf. Thomas, "Spirituality of Klaus Bockmuehl: Part One," 4; Hofmann, "Revolutionär," 19.

11. Cf. T. Spoerri, *Dynamic out of Silence*, 136–7.

12. From 1969 to 1974 he was President (*Bundespräsident*) of the Federal Republic of Germany.

13. Cf. Lean, *On the Tail of a Comet*, 293, 359; Hofmann, "Revolutionär," 22; Thomas, "Spirituality of Klaus Bockmuehl: Part One," 6. Mayer, "Einführung," *DH*, xx.

Introduction

its commitment to the devastated Ruhr-region sprang from listening to God and obeying him. As a result, Bockmuehl was convinced that MRA offered a real Christian alternative to Marxism and started to identify himself with the group.[14]

Owing to his involvement in the play, Bockmuehl was invited to attend a World Conference of MRA in 1949 at its main center at Caux, Switzerland, where he met its founder Frank N. Buchman for the first time. It was, however, his roommate who had a great impact on Bockmuehl by sharing his insights gained during his quiet time. For instance, one day after finishing his work, the roommate suggested to Bockmuehl that he might use his spare time to listen to God. It was during this time that Bockmuehl received a call from God to study theology instead of becoming a chemical engineer in the Ruhr industry as he had originally planned. The fact that many of the leading co-workers of MRA were theologians who were trying to help others to live an authentic and socially transforming Christian life certainly played a role in the process of decision-making. In the light of this experience, it was not surprising that Bockmuehl decided to go back to Caux one year later in order to take part in the recently founded "College of the good road." This new kind of Summer Training Course, led by Roger Higgs in collaboration with Theophil Spoerri, the principal of the University of Zürich, dealt with topics such as "The Ideology of Moral Re-Armament," "How to live your Ideology," "The Art of Study," "The Art and Romance of Life-Changing," "The Full Dimension of Change" and "How to change a Marxist." When looking at Bockmuehl's journal entries taken at that time, it is striking how often he reminded himself to keep the four absolutes (absolute honesty, purity, unselfishness, and love) foundational to MRA.[15] Considering this and the fact that Bockmuehl adopted the daily practice of listening to God in the morning from that summer onward, it is rather startling to discover that Bockmuehl lost contact with MRA over the next eight years.[16]

At Easter in 1950, Toyohito Kagawa, a Japanese Christian and Social Reformer well-known in Germany at that time, visited Essen at the invitation of Busch. It was characteristic of him that he drew the attention of his listeners to the necessity of taking up one's cross as a follower of Jesus, even

---

14. Cf. Hofmann, "Revolutionär," 22.

15. The year of attendance (1950) is based on Bockmuehl's "Journals" (cf. the entry on July 17, 1950) and on the comments made by the principal in Bockmuehl's "Reifezeugnis" (equivalent to A-levels) from 1951, in which he mentions that Bockmuehl had gone to Caux for 6 weeks the previous summer.

16. Cf. Hofmann, "Revolutionär," 23.

if this included giving up one's own life, since the way of love would never be an easy one. According to his friend Karl Sundermeier, Kagawa's visit left Bockmuehl with a passion for world mission.[17]

With regard to German literature, he took great pleasure in reading Thomas Mann, as he was inspired by the content as well as the style. In fact, he was so fascinated by the latter that, later in life, he often went back to the works of Thomas Mann before starting his own writing.[18]

Theological Training and Research (1951–1961)

After passing his "Reifezeugnis" (equivalent to A-levels) in 1951,[19] Bockmuehl started theological and philosophical studies in Wuppertal and later in Tübingen (1953/54), Göttingen (1954/55), and Basel (1955). He acquired a thorough grounding in biblical exegesis under famous professors such as Hans-Walter Wolff (Wuppertal), Walther Eichrodt (Basel, both OT), D. Otto Michel (Tübingen), and Joachim Jeremias[20] (Göttingen, both NT). Bockmuehl also decided to study sociology as a subsidiary subject while in Göttingen after gaining experience working in industry during his holidays and after attending guest lectures given by a French sociologist.[21] Furthermore, due to the fact that he was granted a scholarship, he attended lectures at the London School of Economics in 1955/56.[22] At the same time, he continued his theological and philosophical studies at

17. Cf. Hofmann, "Revolutionär," 19; Reininghaus, *Toyohiko Kagawa*, 12–13. It is interesting to discover that Kagawa practiced a quiet time early in the morning, which included listening to God and decision-making. Cf. Reininghaus, *Toyohiko Kagawa*, 14.

18. Elisabeth Bockmuehl (Klaus Bockmuehl's widow), interview by Annette Glaw, Sept. 10/11, 1999, St. Chrischona. We should be hardly surprised to discover that Bockmuehl even cites Thomas Mann in one of his theological books; cf. Bockmuehl, *LbG*, 24–25, 37. See also Bockmuehl, "Macht und Ohnmacht," 153; *CaL*, 13; Bockmuehl, "Quiet Holidays," n.p.; Bockmuehl, "Überlegungen," 109.

19. Cf. Bockmuehl, "Reifezeugnis."

20. Cf. Bockmuehl, "Predigt: Lukas 15," 5.

21. Cf. Bockmuehl, "Kirche," 142. Bockmuehl very much emphasizes the importance of a connection between theology and sociology, mainly inspired by lectures given by Helmuth Plessner in Göttingen. Cf. Bockmuehl, "Lebenslauf Klaus Erich Bockmuehl," 1. It is also worth mentioning that during one of his "work holidays" he stayed at Arthur Richter's house who was a personnel manager and at the same time the leader of the "Marburg Circle," originally initiated by MRA in Germany. Bockmuehl remained in personal contact with Richter for a long time (E. Bockmuehl, interview).

22. Cf. "Certificate of attendance," issued June 19, 1956.

Introduction

King's College, London,[23] and even started to write his doctoral thesis on "Corporeality and Society, Religious Criticism and the Idea of Man in the Early Writings of Ludwig Feuerbach and Karl Marx"[24] with the University of Basel under the supervision of the Dutch professor Hendrik van Oyen. After coming back to Basel in 1956 and while completing his PhD, he attended Karl Barth's select seminar in Systematic Theology and had the privilege of getting to know Barth personally. Their private conversations throughout the years would often focus on the current developments in theology, ethics, and the church.[25]

In 1957/58, Bockmuehl spent most of his time preparing for his first theological exam of the Evangelical Church of the Rhineland, which he passed in October 1958. As a result of gaining good marks, he was offered and he accepted the post of teaching assistant to professor Jürgen Moltmann at the Church University of Wuppertal. Only a year later he sat his exams for his doctorate degree at Basel University, which he passed with the highest possible grade of "summa cum laude."[26]

While in Wuppertal Bockmuehl realized that he did not have adequate answers to the problems faced by the students for whom he bore responsibility. In order to find solutions, he decided to get involved with MRA again, although by now he had theological reservations about the movement.[27] In 1959, he attended a World Conference of MRA at Caux to find out how "Christian" MRA was and, to his own surprise, received a positive answer:

> The conference focussed on the play called "The Ladder"; it challenged all its viewers unequivocally with the alternative between the striving for power, money, pleasure, and career (the ladder) which characterizes our time, and the carrying of the Cross, life lived as a follower of the Crucified, putting one's loyalty to God above all other claims of allegiance.

---

23. Cf. "Curriculum vitae," 1959.

24. Bockmuehl's own translation of his doctoral thesis in a "Curriculum Vitae," 1977. German title: *Leiblichkeit und Gesellschaft. Studien zur Religionskritik und Anthropologie im Frühwerk von Ludwig Feuerbach und Karl Marx*.

25. Cf. Hofmann, "Revolutionär," 21; Bockmuehl, "Lebenslauf Klaus Erich Bockmuehl," 1.

26. Cf. "Curriculum Vitae," 1959; "Curriculum Vitae," 1977; E. Bockmuehl, interview.

27. Cf. Hofmann, "Revolutionär," 20. 23; Thomas, "Spirituality of Klaus Bockmuehl: Part One," 6–7.

At the same time "The Hurricane" was staged, a play that deals with the racial conflicts in present-day Africa. It clearly shows that these conflicts are based on human pride and hatred, and are therefore nothing other than sin. From that the playwright concludes that there is but *one* way that can lead to a new order. The climax of the drama puts it into these words: Not the blood of slain whites will free the continent from all its evils, but "the blood of Jesus Christ, God's Son, that will cleanse us from all sin."[28]

Moreover, while staying at Caux, he sensed that God was asking *him* how Christian he himself was; during a quiet time he began to recognize his own career ambitions and his rivalry with Moltmann. In order to understand the latter we need to know that, since Bockmuehl disagreed with Moltmann's theology, he had found satisfaction in undermining Moltmann's position during seminars. He sensed that God was calling him to write a letter to Moltmann apologizing for his wrong attitude and disloyalty to him. On his return to Wuppertal, he discovered that Moltmann had not yet received the letter, which meant he had to apologize to him personally. From then on, instead of demolishing Moltmann's position, he started to support him. He also stopped caring about his career and instead trusted God that he would provide for him.[29]

It was during his time in Wuppertal that he got to know Elisabeth Becker, a fellow student also belonging to the Evangelical Church of the Rhineland and fell in love with her. It is interesting to discover that she, like Bockmuehl, was an only child and did not have Christian parents.[30] Because her religious education teacher was a committed Christian, she was converted in her late teens. It was, however, through getting to know Bockmuehl's spiritual background that she came to value Pietism and MRA.[31]

Elisabeth and Klaus were married on March 4, 1961, in the Castle Church of Linnep in North Rhine-Westphalia. They had three children: Markus, Anne-Ruth, and Christoph.

---

28. Bockmuehl, "Frank Buchman's Message," 1.
29. Cf. Thomas, "Spirituality of Klaus Bockmuehl: Part One," 6–7.
30. Cf. Houston, "Memory," 2.
31. Cf. Thomas, "Spirituality of Klaus Bockmuehl: Part One," 6.

Introduction

Pastor, Researcher, and Lecturer (1961–1977)

In 1961, Bockmuehl passed the second church exam of the Evangelical Church of the Rhineland and was ordained on August 1, 1961. He went on to serve for a year as an assistant pastor in a Reformed Church in Düren/Rhineland before accepting an invitation from professor Hendrik van Oyen to become his research fellow at the University of Basel (1962–65). It is of interest for our study that van Oyen gave lectures on Christian ethics and had published books in this area. In fact, van Oyen's first volume of Christian ethics was entitled: "The Fundamentals. The Advocacy of the Spirit" and even included a chapter on "Holy Spirit and Ethics."[32] It is likely that Bockmuehl's interest in the Holy Spirit and ethics was deepened by his close contact with van Oyen during his time in Basel. During these years he concentrated on the research into the history of Christian ethics. At the same time Bockmuehl started to write a postdoctoral dissertation (*Habilitation*) on "Regeneration and New Creation,"[33] a prerequisite for a professorship in some parts of Europe. Unfortunately, before Bockmuehl was able to finish, the university declared him "persona non grata" on account of his active involvement in a controversy about homosexuality. As a consequence, from 1963 onward the church government would not allow him to continue preaching once a month at the church of St. Martin's in Basel as had been his custom. Even the door to the position of a professorship at the University of Basel closed in 1965.[34]

In order to understand this development, we need to look more closely at the circumstances that brought about this disappointment. When in 1963 a dispute started in parliament about changing social and criminal law, the churches in Europe were forced to discuss the validity of divine commandments. In the course of time, Bockmuehl recognized that more and more theologians questioned the heritage of the Reformation and Pietism, particularly their concept of the validity of the law for ethics. This had direct implications for sexual ethical issues such as homosexuality. Despite this development, Busch challenged Bockmuehl to keep close to the biblical position even in ethical matters.[35] When in

32. Oyen, *Evangelische Ethik*, title of first volume and ch. 1.
33. Bockmuehl, "Wiedergeburt und Neuschöpfung."
34. Cf. letter from H. Schäfer to Bockmuehl, Nov. 19, 1963; letter from Bockmuehl to Mr. Halfenberg, Dec. 19, 1963.
35. Cf. Hofmann, "Revolutionär," 20. In his article on "Homosexuality," Bockmuehl refers to two of his professors, W. Eichrodt (p. 13) and K. Barth (p. 17), who also took a stand against homosexuality.

1962/63 Theodor Bovet, a famous Swiss marriage guidance counselor, professed publicly that homosexuality is as biologically natural as heterosexuality and even encouraged the church government to allow homosexual marriages, Bockmuehl and two pastors in Basel, both friends of Bovet, felt compelled to point out the unbiblical nature of his view; they were convinced that "homosexuality goes against the law of God and of nature."[36] Their first step was to speak privately with Bovet, who had once been closely connected with MRA, asking him to retract his suggestion of the promotion of homosexual practices. However, contrary to their plea, Bovet even recommended that the church set up marriage counseling for homosexual partners. When they learned that Bovet had been officially invited to speak at the first Swiss-German *Kirchentag* (church convention) in 1963, they pleaded with Bovet not to accept the offer; Bovet declined to do so. As a result, Bockmuehl supported the two pastors in writing an official petition to the Church government in Basel. Having shown that, according to the Bible, sexual relationships should only be lived out in heterosexual marriages, they urged the responsible Church leaders to prevent Bovet from accomplishing his plans. No sooner had it become public that Bockmuehl had taken a stand against Bovet in this matter, then the faculty in Basel distanced itself from him.[37] It is significant that because of his involvement in an *ethical* debate Bockmuehl was not allowed to hand in his postdoctoral dissertation (*Habilitation*) at Basel University at that time.[38]

This biographical incident shows very clearly that Bockmuehl not only publicly confronted doctrines that he considered to be contrary to the Bible but was indeed willing to accept the consequences such as sacrificing his anticipated career if necessary.[39] In fact, he defended the fundamental assumption that Scripture provided the norm for theology and Christian ethics throughout his whole life.

---

36. Bockmuehl, "Homosexuality," 13.

37. Cf. Bockmuehl, "Homosexuality," 13; Bockmuehl, "Die Diskussion über Homosexualität," 243–244, 247–251; Thomas, "Spirituality of Klaus Bockmuehl: Part Two," 31; Hofmann, "Revolutionär," 24; letter from Bockmuehl to Mr. Halfenberg, Dec. 19, 1963. Particularly interesting is a letter that Bockmuehl wrote to the professors and lecturers at the theological faculty in Basel on Sept. 28, 1963, in which he tried to gain their confidence.

38. Three years later Hendrik van Oyen told Bockmuehl that the situation at Basel University had changed and that the faculty would be open to him submitting his habilitation dissertation a year later (cf. letter from Oyen to Bockmuehl, July 6, 1968).

39. Cf. Bockmuehl, *Grundlagen christlicher Sexualethik*, 8–14. M. Bockmuehl and Burkhardt, "Preface," 7.

Introduction

In 1964, Bockmuehl assisted professor van Oyen in founding the European society for research in ethics, the "Societas Ethica." Bockmuehl was the first secretary until 1968 and worked alongside professor van Oyen who was the first president. One major task of their assignment was to invite leading Protestant and Catholic ethicists to discuss important ethical questions. There can be little doubt that this furnished Bockmuehl with a broad overview of contemporary developments in social and sexual ethics.

In 1964, the Protestant Sisterhood of Mary (*Evangelische Marienschwesternschaft*), situated in Darmstadt, with whom Bockmuehl kept in regular contact, asked him to give a lecture on the spiritual situation in Germany with special reference to the theological roots. Many spiritual leaders from all over the country listened to Bockmuehl's lecture in which he traced the current decay of ethics back to the reduction of Christian dogmatics in the nineteenth century. In the ensuing discussion about practical steps to improve the present situation, Bockmuehl shared with the others what he had written down in his quiet time that same morning.[40] He, for instance, told them that they had the task "to describe the line of battle between flesh and Spirit" to everyone.[41] He also reminded them that the expansion of the Kingdom of God had never happened without confrontation and that renewal was only possible through repentance. He then went on to stress that they had the duty of proclaiming the Gospel in a language intelligible to the world and "to fight together out of CONCERN FOR GERMANY!"[42] This last phrase became the keyword for the people present; some of them started a project of the same name soon afterwards with the purpose of evoking a movement of repentance and influencing the legislation process. Unfortunately, this did not happen to the extent hoped for, even though many people, including Bockmuehl, supported this project.[43]

In 1965, bishop Heidland of the Evangelical church of Baden inquired whether Bockmuehl would be willing to work as a student pastor at the University of Heidelberg. Only after accepting the offer did Bockmuehl

---

40. Cf. Hofmann, "Revolutionär," 26-27.

41. Bockmuehl, "Klaus Bockmühl," 28.

42. German phrase: "SORGE UM DEUTSCHLAND." Bockmuehl, "Klaus Bockmühl," 28.

43. Cf. Hofmann, "Revolutionär," 27–28. In 1968, the group supportive of this project organized a student conference out of which grew the ecumenical community "Offensive Junger Christen" (English name: "The Reichenberg Fellowship") situated in Reichelsheim/Odenwald and led by Bockmuehl's close friend Horst-Klaus Hofmann, which still exists today. Cf. ibid, 28; OJC, "Our Roots," n.p.

realize how invaluable his knowledge of different ideologies such as Marxism, Socialism etc. was for his work. During his time in Heidelberg, the student revolts took place and even students belonging to the Protestant student community sympathized with Marxism. Naturally, they were somewhat annoyed when they discovered that Bockmuehl was publicly criticizing Marxism. In fact, he had a debate with some of his fellow workers in January 1968 about the aim of the Protestant student community. "The point at issue was the thesis of one of the student leaders that 'in an age of crisis' (in university politics, domestic politics, and the whole structure of society) 'the question of God must be put on ice for a while.'"[44] Not surprisingly, Bockmuehl resolutely rejected this claim as being, what he called, temporary atheism induced by social problems. As a consequence, the student leaders of the Marxist movement urged Bockmuehl to resign. It is interesting to learn of his response to this rather hostile request. He merely told them that he would ask the Lord for guidance in this matter. After a day of praying he came to the conclusion that he should not resign and informed the students accordingly. As the students did not accept his resolution to stay on, the conflict came to a head on January 24, 1968. It was during a plenary assembly of the Protestant student community that the students brought charges against Bockmuehl in order to destroy his career hoping that the journalists present would advocate their view. However, unexpectedly, students of the SMD (student mission in Germany),[45] who had not been involved in political issues up until then, began to defend Bockmuehl. In fact, the true purpose of the assembly came to light so that, in the end, even the newspapers supported Bockmuehl's stance.[46]

After this controversy Bockmuehl felt uneasy about continuing his work as a minister and counselor to students who distrusted him. It was, however, not before inquiring after God's will that he finally decided to resign.[47] In order to demonstrate his sympathy with Bockmuehl, the bishop wanted him to become a pastor of a well-known church in Heidelberg. At

44. *UG*, 134. The original German edition was published in 1969, one year after the debate.

45. Similar to the Christian Unions of UCCF (Universities and Colleges Christian Fellowship).

46. Cf. Thomas, "Spirituality of Klaus Bockmuehl: Part Two," 31; Hofmann, "Revolutionär," 24–25.

47. Bockmuehl may have thought of his time in Heidelberg when he mentions in his last book: "This instruction as we have seen, sometimes means leaving a city because of, or staying in a city in spite of, mounting resistance . . . Neither persecution nor success, in human eyes, are decisive; only the instructions received from the Lord." *LG*, 80.

Introduction

the same time, various theological seminaries or Bible schools in Germany and abroad offered Bockmuehl lecturing posts. However, in spite of these excellent offers, Bockmuehl asked for a small parish as this would give him the opportunity to continue with further theological research. Thus, while ministering in Schmieheim/Black Forest in 1968–1971, he completed one of his most famous books on the theology of atheism entitled *Atheism in Christendom*.[48]

In addition to his work at Heidelberg and Schmieheim during the years 1965–71, Bockmuehl accepted an offer to teach part-time at the pietistic theological seminary and Bible school St. Chrischona situated near Basel.[49]

On account of his reputation for being a skillful theologian who did not hesitate to take decisive action in the current ideological and theological debate on Marxism, the chairman of the Albrecht-Bengel-Haus (ABH) association asked Bockmuehl at the end of 1969 to accept the post as director of the ABH in Tübingen. Before turning to Bockmuehl's response, let us take a closer look at the main aims of the ABH association. The general aim was to help theology students who were studying in a time of theological confusion; this they viewed as necessary since many lecturers at the university rejected the Bible as God's word and as the only foundation for proclamation in the church. The ABH sought to nurture the spiritual development of theology students, offering assistance with their studies and preparing them for future pastoral ministry. Bockmuehl was, indeed, open to the invitation and a correspondence started with professor Peter Beyerhaus from the University of Tübingen, the honorary director designate of the ABH. In the course of time Beyerhaus, due to his reservations with regard to MRA, required of Bockmuehl that, if he accepted the offer, he should refrain from discussing MRA and their principles with the students and from taking them to Caux as he had previously done in Heidelberg.[50] These were, however, Beyerhaus's personal concerns, since the ABH association committee affirmed their request for co-operation

48. German title: *Atheismus in der Christenheit*. This book was published in English in 1988 as *The Unreal God of Modern Theology*. Cf. letter from Bockmuehl to Michael Herwig, March 23, 1968. Bockmuel notes that before making the final decision which of the offers to accept he spent a quiet day with some of his friends (cf. ibid).

49. "Prediger- und Missionsseminar"; nowadays called "Theologisches Seminar St. Chrischona." See also Bockmuehl, "Curriculum vitae," 1959; "Curriculum Vitae," 1977.

50. Cf. Bockmuehl, "Eindrücke von der Arbeit." Bockmuehl summarizes the impact MRA had made on the theology students as follows: "They discovered the totality and directness of the guidance by the Holy Spirit" (ibid).

with Bockmuehl without laying down any conditions. Bockmuehl, then, wrote them a letter stating that "[i]f he (the regional bishop Heidland) believes that it is right for me to come to you and he sends me, then I will consider this way to be the right one."[51] After consultation with the bishop, Bockmuehl eventually declined the offer in April 1970.[52]

In Spring 1970, Bockmuehl, instead, seized the opportunity to visit India, first, attending a MRA conference in Panchgani near Bombay and, secondly, taking part in a conference of all Protestant churches in Shillong/north-east India. While there, Bockmuehl discovered parallels between the development of the Christian churches in Europe and those of India. In both cases the church initially seemed to raise civil and cultural standards, but after a while their influence on public life seemed to decline, and other ideologies, some even contrary to the Christian faith, began to determine social and political decisions. With regard to India, there was a tragic case where a Christian tribe accepted weapons and money from the Chinese in order to fight against the Indian government. For Bockmuehl, this incident clearly showed the need for experiencing reconciliation and honesty in a world ruled by bitterness, strife, self-centeredness, and corruption. However, the experience of restored relationships can only be brought about by personal change. Bockmuehl was convinced that to achieve this change and to bridge the gap between social life and private devoutness the practice of listening to God in a quiet time and the guidance of the Holy Spirit was absolutely indispensable.[53]

It was, furthermore, while traveling through India that he felt a deep desire to work among theology students in Europe. Consequently, after his return he intensified his work among them by lecturing regularly at summer schools for theology students (1967–76).[54] Rainer Riesner remarks that apart from Bockmuehl's theological knowledge it was his intensive relationship with God that made a deep impression on the students so that many felt theologically and spiritually challenged and encouraged by

---

51. Letter from Bockmuehl to H. Eißler, the chairman of the ABH-Association, March 13, 1970.

52. Cf. Hofmann, "Revolutionär," 25; Pfander, "Vorgeschichte und Anfangsjahre," 184.

53. Bockmuehl points out: "To bridge the gulf between theory and practice, individual piety and social life you need the secret of guidance, the Holy Spirit whose task it is to take the answer into all places and all situations" ("India Report," 4).

54. Ibid.; cf. Hofmann, "Revolutionär," 31; Haacker et al., "In Memoriam Klaus Bockmühl," 169.

Introduction

him.⁵⁵ In 1971, he became a full-time lecturer at the theological seminary St. Chrischona where he taught Ethics, Dogmatics and History of Theology. The students there appreciated the opportunity of a closer acquaintance with him over a longer period of time.

One incident in 1973 is worth mentioning, since it reveals Bockmuehl's deep concern for the world as well as his awareness of God's supremacy and his prophetic insight. In a lecture on Marxism he asked his students: "Gentlemen, what do we have to offer when communism comes to an end in 20 years time?"⁵⁶ However, the prophetic quality of this question was only unveiled some 15 years later with the collapse of the socialist system. Bockmuehl was convinced that Christians would be able to offer solutions to the problems of the world if they took time to listen to God.

Besides his work as a lecturer, Bockmuehl also helped to found and edit the seminary's theological literature program, *Theology and Service* (*Theologie und Dienst*), in 1973. The purpose of this series was to provide spiritual nourishment, to broaden theological knowledge, and to help discern current theological and ethical developments in the church. Bockmuehl, who undertook the task of writing the first book in this series, examined therefore the usefulness and uselessness of the "new morality" in comparison to the "old morality." It is worth mentioning that the topic of *Law and Spirit* already played a major role in this early publication. Bockmuehl, in fact, even devoted a whole chapter to "[t]he question concerning the work of the Holy Spirit in Ethics."⁵⁷

As Bockmuehl held written work in high esteem, it seems natural that he was publishing articles and reviews, mainly on ethical topics, in different magazines or journals such as *Christianity Today* (until 1982) or *Theologische Beiträge*. From 1973 onward he was also a member of the editorial board of the latter, who remembered him as a "dedicated advisor" and "one of their most prominent authors," completely devoted to the task of renewing theology and church throughout his whole life.⁵⁸ Furthermore, from 1976/1978–1980 Bockmuehl was a member of the Theological Commission of the "World Evangelical Fellowship" (WEF) and the editor of the serial publication of WEF called "Outreach and Identity."⁵⁹

55. Cf. Riesner, "Militia Christi und Militia Caesaris," 49.
56. Cited in Hofmann, "Nachfolge Christi," 143; cf. idea, "Theologische Woche," 13.
57. Chapter 3.2. in Bockmuehl, *SU*, 30–35.
58. Haacker, "In Memoriam," 169.
59. Cf. Nicholls, "The WEFT Theological Commission," 14; Hofmann, "Revolutionär," 29.

In 1975, he published a number of books on ethics, dealing with the foundations of evangelical ethics, evangelical social ethics, and environmental ethics besides investigating the problem of "new morality" at great length in his book *God in Exile? Regarding the critique of the "new morality."*[60] Two years later he published another significant book, *The Challenge of Marxism*, which received a number of favorable reviews even in non-Christian periodicals.[61] By now Bockmuehl had addressed systematically the three main issues that he had identified as early as 1967 to be jeopardizing the church: "1. The atheism of the new theology, 2. The sexual liberalism of the 'new morality,' 3. the attempt to make Christianity a tool of Marxism."[62]

A New Horizon—Professor in Canada (1977-1989)

Unexpectedly, Dr. James Houston, the principal of Regent College Vancouver, Canada, phoned Bockmuehl in Dec 1976 on John Stott's recommendation to enquire if Bockmuehl was interested in becoming a professor at the newly founded College. For two months Bockmuehl sought guidance on this matter through listening prayer. A journal entry gives insight into Bockmuehl's feelings at the time: "I do not disengage lightly from Chrischona. It is necessary to be thrown out of the Evangelical milieu in a small party sense. A tentative yes to Vancouver. There will be full clarity. Never expect God to speak on command . . . Everywhere, Abraham first built an altar. We need an altar in our lives. Obedience for departure . . . I seek the will of the Father."[63]

On account of the fact that the invitation would entail moving to a new country with a different culture and language, not only for Klaus Bockmuehl himself but also for his whole family, it was no easy decision for him.

While visiting Regent College in February 1977, for the purpose of meeting the staff, he was offered the position of professorship of systematic

---

60. German title: *Gott im Exil? Zur Kritik der "neuen Moral."* Regarding the foundations of evangelical ethics, see *glauben und handeln*; regarding evangelical social ethics: *Evangelicals and Social Ethics*; regarding environmental ethics: *Conservation and Lifestyle*.

61. Cf. Bibliography, Reviews on *Herausforderungen des Marxismus/The Challenge of Marxism* (1977/1980).

62. Letter from Bockmuehl to Rainer Klein, Dec. 9, 1967.

63. Cited in Thomas, "Spirituality of Klaus Bockmuehl: Part Two," 32.

Introduction

theology for the same year. For Bockmuehl, this was another confirmation alongside his discernment through his personal quiet time that God wanted him to accept the offer. It is worth mentioning in this context that whenever Bockmuehl had made a decision following prayer, he would "kill the alternative" and encouraged others to do likewise.[64]

During his time at Regent College Bockmuehl always started his lectures on systematics and ethics by sharing insights gained during his quiet time early in the morning.[65] Bockmuehl also incorporated into his publications many notes written during his devotional time. As this also applies to his theological books, there is little doubt that Bockmuehl was very much concerned about the unity of theology and spirituality. In fact, the endeavor to hold both together can be viewed as being a consistent thread running through his whole life. Bockmuehl even took the initiative in 1979 to found the "Gomaringen Circle"; this was an informal union of a small group of young Protestant theologians who not only discussed theological issues but also supported one another spiritually.[66] Furthermore, their main concern was to promote a "renewal of Protestant theology on the basis of the authority of Scripture."[67] One way of achieving this was, for instance, to publish a book in 1988 on the present-day relevance of Adolf Schlatter's theology with contributions by members of the "Gomaringen Group." It fell to Bockmuehl to edit the book and write a foreword. The purpose of the book, published exactly 50 years after Adolf Schlatter's death, was, first, to express gratitude for his contribution to theology as a great exegete and an outstanding systematician and, secondly, to inspire the readers to study his works in depth.[68]

A few years earlier, in time for the 350th anniversary of the birthday of Philipp Jakob Spener, Bockmuehl had written a book about the current relevance of pietism. The intention of this book was to challenge contemporary Christians to consider the characteristic topics of pietism

---

64. E. Bockmuehl, interview; Thomas, "Spirituality of Klaus Bockmuehl: Part Two," 32;

65. Thomas, "Spirituality of Klaus Bockmuehl: Part Two," 32.

66. The theologians are Helmut Burkhardt (lecturer at the theological seminary St. Chrischona), Rainer Riesner (Professor at Dortmund University), Werner Neuer (lecturer at the theological seminary St. Chrischona), Wolfgang J. Bittner (freelance theologian among other things). It is noteworthy that several of these theologians became lecturers and professors like Bockmuehl, accepting responsibility for a new generation of theology students.

67. Bockmuehl, "Vorwort des Herausgebers," 1. Cf. Hofmann, "Revolutionär," 31.

68. Bockmuehl, "Vorwort des Herausgebers," 1.

such as "concentration on Jesus," "sanctification," "pietism and mission," and "pietism and social ethics."[69] Bockmuehl, moreover, argued that by rejecting pietism and its spiritual concerns the church had lost much of its identity. Consequently, the greatest desire of pietism should be to strive for a spiritual revival in theology, church, and society. And indeed, Bockmuehl not only urged others to live for this purpose, but he endeavored to set a good example in his own life. According to his friend Horst-Klaus Hofmann, Bockmuehl considered himself not only to be a teacher but also a "shepherd" and spiritual "nurturer."[70]

In 1985, Bockmuehl was asked to take on an endowed professorship at Basel University, supported by the donations of evangelical Christians. It seems remarkable that twenty years after the door to a professorship at Basel University had been closed it should open again in such a way. While on the way to Europe for the purpose of presenting a lecture at Basel University, Bockmuehl received an urgent message telling him to immediately return to Canada for an operation for cancer of the esophagus. As a consequence, he not only had to cancel his lecture, but he also had to refuse the offer of the endowed professorship due to his illness.[71]

The surgery in June was fairly successful so that he was able to give some lectures and lead seminars at Regent College, and even to travel to Europe in 1987.[72] During that journey he presented a lecture at Basel University, which many students and lecturers from Basel, St. Chrischona, and Tübingen attended, and also at Bern, Bienenberg, and finally, at Caux.[73] In the same year, he completed an extensive study investigating and evaluating the heritage of Protestant ethics with regard to the topic law and spirit, which also included the issue of guidance by the Holy Spirit.[74] One year after the publication of this outstanding work of research entitled *Law and Spirit: A Critical Appraisal of the Heritage of Protestant Ethics*,[75] he

69. Cf. Bockmuehl, "Die Aktualität des Pietismus," 291–333.

70. Cf. Hofmann, "Nachfolge," 147.

71. Cf. circular letter written by Bockmuehl June 29, 1985; Thomas, "Spirituality of Klaus Bockmuehl: Part Two," 33.

72. As his lectures on ethics had previously been recorded on video, he initially only had to answer questions for half an hour. Cf. circular letter written by Bockmuehl in Jan. 1986.

73. In Bern, he delivered an address on "Serving with Christ" at the "Diakonia-Kongreß" at Bern, Switzerland, on July 3, 1987. Cf. Mayer, "Einführung," in *LWG*, xxv; Bockmuehl, "Serving with Christ," 1.

74. *GG*, 233–48, 416–39; Cf. Hofmann, "Revolutionär," 29.

75. German title: *Gesetz und Geist. Eine kritische Würdigung des Erbes protestantischer Ethik*; cf. Thomas, "Spirituality of Klaus Bockmuehl: Part One," 10.

Introduction

was awarded the "Johann-Tobias-Beck-Award." This gives evidence to the profundity and significance of his contribution. Due to his illness he was unfortunately not able to receive the award in person.[76] Notwithstanding the fact that the doctor had diagnosed terminal cancer in October 1988, he decided to start writing a book about *Listening to the God who speaks* rather than to continue with his "Introduction to Christian Ethics," as originally planned.[77] As James Houston, a colleague of Bockmuehl, pointed out in the foreword of what turned out to be Bockmuehl's final publication: "This book is very much a last will and testimony to the church from one of its most faithful and obedient sons . . . For twelve years he told me regularly—and in the last months of his life daily—what he was hearing from the Word of God to help him direct his steps day by day. No one who knew him could ever question that he practiced what he preaches in this book."[78]

For Bockmuehl, it was due to spending time listening to God that he was able to write the book and to continue teaching at Regent College. Yet, he was also aware that he depended on the prayer support of his friends as much as he needed food. He asked them to pray for him, first of all, that he "might once more become fit to do some *teaching* at the College," secondly, that he "might still find time, strength, and insight to *write*" and complete his last book, and, finally, that he "constantly might be given the strength for *intercession* and prayer generally, and the certainty of the sustaining and comforting presence of Christ."[79] Bockmuehl was, indeed, able to complete the manuscript of *Listening to the God who speaks* shortly before his death.[80]

During the last months of his life he experienced his deepest spiritual friendship, apart from that with his wife, with James Houston, professor of Spiritual Theology at Regent College. Previously his workload had been too demanding to leave time for a friendship on this deep level. One day Houston gave Bockmuehl a hazelnut to remind him of God's love. They were both acquainted with the visions of Julian of Norwich recorded in *Revelations of Divine Love*. In one of them God showed her something like a hazelnut in her hand representing the whole of creation. For her the

---

76. Cf. Burkhardt, "Zur Einführung," 5; idea, "Für biblische Erneuerung der Theologie," 8.
77. Cf. Thomas, "Spirituality of Klaus Bockmuehl: Part Two," 33.
78. Houston, "Foreword," ix.
79. Circular letter written by Bockmuehl Dec. 5, 1988.
80. Cf. Houston, "Foreword," ix.

hazelnut symbolized that "God made it," "God loves it," and "God keeps it."[81] Bockmuehl valued the hazelnut to the last as it reminded him that God held him in his loving hands.[82]

In spite of his fears and the pain caused by the illness he focused more than ever on God's love for humanity; he recorded in his journal on December 11, 1988: "[M]oment by moment I'm kept in his love"; and on December 23: "Knowing God's will is knowing God's love, because His will is His loving will for us. To go on living so that others might benefit from my communion with Christ." His own relationship with God was molded by a desire to love God more and more. On February 17, 1989 he wrote in his journal: "I still need to creep out of the chrysalis of my former theological existence and take on the wings of love of God and love of neighbor, gifts of the Holy Spirit." Since he was convinced that "[l]istening to God is the first step towards loving God,"[83] it is not surprising that Bockmuehl reminded himself time and again of the importance of a "[q]uiet pursuit of prayer and LGS [listening to the God who speaks]; simplify your life for these."[84] Furthermore, since his illness did not allow him to continue with his busy life as a lecturer and speaker, he became aware of the dangers of Christian activism. He admitted in his last talk entitled "Let us be listeners": "Now, in the past, if someone had called me a workaholic, I would secretly have responded: 'Of course, what else?' A workaholic in the Kingdom of God, that was a title of honour! I saw my Christian and human dignity, my self-confidence and reason for self-respect in being a 'worker' in God's vineyard. But Jesus said: 'No longer do I call you servants' (John 15:15). The sum-total of Christianity, love of Christ, following the Master, is not primarily a labour relationship."[85]

Thus, late in life Bockmuehl insisted on the primacy of nurturing our friendship with Christ by praying and listening. He considered this to be more important than following the commission without, however, neglecting the latter. Even though he had already in his early publications drawn attention to the necessity of rediscovering the active guidance of the Holy Spirit, including the practice of listening, he emphasized more

---

81. Julian of Norwich, *Revelation of Divine Love*, 67 (ch. 5); cf. Thomas, "Spirituality of Klaus Bockmuehl: Part Two," 34; Houston, *The Heart's Desire*, 40.

82. Cf. Bockmuehl, "Journals," Dec. 23, 1988; Thomas, "Spirituality of Klaus Bockmuehl: Part Two," 34.

83. Bockmuehl, "Listeners," 5.

84. Bockmuehl, "Journals," Feb. 6, 1989; cf. ibid., Jan. 10, 1989 and Feb. 5, 1989.

85. Bockmuehl, "Listeners," 4; cf. Bockmuehl, "Journals," Jan. 24, 1989.

Introduction

and more the pre-eminence of a friendship with Christ, not only as a goal toward the end of receiving instructions but for its own sake.[86]

Likewise, when looking at the relationship of theology and spirituality, Bockmuehl's statement, recorded in his journal on February 10, 1989, that "[s]pirituality is the crown of theology" seems like a culmination of his theological life and work. Just how much both were tied up together can be seen in a journal entry from February 14, 1989: "Utter gratefulness that I have been a theol. teacher, to pass God's truth on to a younger generation, at least to some extent, and I can still do it, through letter and LGS [listening to the God who speaks]."

His last official address, given at the Nineteenth Convocation at Regent College on May 15, 1989, from which we quoted earlier, was entitled "Let us be listeners." Since he was already very weak by that time and had to sit in a wheelchair while reading part of the talk, it was an unforgettable experience for the audience.[87]

Bockmuehl died on June 10, 1989 at the age of 58. Some of his last words reveal what was close to his heart and what he wanted succeeding generations to remember: "[H]old Jesus dear," "act out of being quiet," and "listen . . . to the God who speaks."[88]

---

86. Compare Bockmuehl, "Frank Buchman's Message," 32–38, with his final book *LG*.
87. Cf. Packer, "Klaus Bockmuehl's Rich Legacy," 9; Burkhardt, "Zur Einführung," 5.
88. Houston, "Memory," 2.

Part One

Bockmuehl's Theological Work

1

Theological and Spiritual Influences on Bockmuehl

WHICH THEOLOGIANS AND SPIRITUAL leaders as well as theological and spiritual traditions played a part in molding Bockmuehl's theology and particularly his understanding of the Holy Spirit and Christian ethics? For instance, who does Bockmuehl draw on for support when expounding his key concept of the guidance by the Spirit? These and similar questions we shall explore in this chapter.

The influences on Bockmuehl are catalogued in chronological order as it would be difficult, and somewhat arbitrary, to arrange this chapter according to the importance of the different influences upon him. Furthermore, I will outline not only direct influences but also affinities and casual parallels to Bockmuehl's thought. In fact, similarities cannot always be traced back far enough in order to decide with certainty if there was a direct influence or just a casual parallel. In either case, however, this gives us valuable information about Bockmuehl's theological and spiritual background.

It is characteristic of Bockmuehl that we have to deal with a variety of influences.[1] As well as encountering a number of spiritual leaders and theologians in person, he invested time in reading and examining spiritual and theological traditions. Even though he benefited greatly from several traditions, he was at the same time aware of their limitedness as the following statement by him shows: "In theology (and in the church in general) it is always imperative never to accept anybody's teaching unexamined,

1. It should be noted that the influences we are going to examine in this chapter were not his only ones, though they were the most significant.

PART ONE—Bockmuehl's Theological Work

never to become anyone's unconditional disciple. All human theology is but a broken, or partial, reflection of God's truth, like a mirror with blind spots, or defects, unevennesses or curvatures which enlarge one part of the mirrored object, and unduly reduce others. In short, theology always gives a rendering that in some way is either defective or out of proportion."[2]

We may, therefore, conclude that Bockmuehl strove to arrive at his theological stance by testing the various different views according to 1 Thessalonians 5:21: "Test everything. Hold on to the good."[3]

In turning now to the different influences upon Bockmuehl, we will focus primarily on the main issues that are distinctive in his thought, above all, Christian ethics and the Holy Spirit.

The Church Fathers and Medieval Theologians/Saints

When reading Bockmuehl, it is striking how often he refers to the Church Fathers and medieval theologians/saints. Bockmuehl was clearly influenced by them, particularly with regard to spirituality, including the topics of *love for God* and *guidance by the Holy Spirit*.

When repudiating Luther's contention that *love for God* should be expressed by way of loving one's neighbor, Bockmuehl draws on such Church Fathers and medieval theologians as St. Augustine, Thomas Aquinas, and Bernard of Clairvaux for support. In them he finds advocates for his conviction that the double commandment of love, first and foremost direct love for God, yet also love for one's neighbor, should be the central theme of ethics.[4] When looking at the motivation for doing good works, Bockmuehl refers to Bernard's exposition of the three stances, each representing a different motivation: the slave works out of fear, the mercenary works to gain a reward, and the son acts out of love for his father. He uses the illustration of the son, which he sees reflected in Jesus' own life, to picture the kind of attitude we should have toward God's commission.[5]

---

2. Bockmuehl, "Karl Barth," 32.

3. Cf. Bockmuehl, "Introduction," 103.

4. Cf. *GG*, 84, 272, 515. It is striking, when looking at the name index, how often Bockmuehl refers to these three theologians in his book *Gesetz und Geist*; cf. 533–37. See also M. Bockmuehl, "To Love God," 45–46.

5. *LbG*, 29. Bockmuehl, furthermore, agrees with Bernard that the command to love God will always be opposed by some, if not verbally, then by their way of living. Cf. *GG*, 515.

Theological and Spiritual Influences on Bockmuehl

The second point we observe is that Bockmuehl's last book, *Listening to the God who Speaks*, in particular, reveals his great indebtedness to the Church Fathers and medieval theologians/saints regarding the topic of *guidance by the Holy Spirit*. Thus, in order to show that God speaks and guides directly through the Holy Spirit, he not only refers to Scripture but also to the "Luminaries in Church History," such as Augustine, Bernard of Clairvaux, Francis of Assisi, Patrick, Ansgar, Thomas à Kempis and Johannes Tauler.[6] Besides examining their writings with regard to guidance, Bockmuehl particularly draws attention to the fact that the lives of these Church Fathers, saints, and missionaries illustrate the variety of ways in which God gives guidance, either through an external voice (e.g., Augustine, Patrick), a dream (e.g., Augustine's mother), a vision (e.g., Francis of Assisi, Patrick, Ansgar), or, most commonly, through an inner voice. An important witness to this inner guidance is Augustine, who Bockmuehl describes as "perhaps the greatest theologian and teacher in the history of the Christian church after apostolic times."[7] In his Confessions, for instance, Augustine reflects upon his experience of inner guidance: "You have walked everywhere at my side, O Truth, teaching me what to seek and what to avoid, whenever I laid before you the things that I was able to see in this world below and asked you to counsel me . . . [F]or you, the Truth, are the unfailing Light from which I sought counsel upon all these things, asking whether they were, what they were, and how they were to be valued. But I heard you teaching me and I heard the commands you gave."[8] Bockmuehl not only refers to this text in his last book *Listening to the God who Speaks*, but he also uses it in the final chapter of *Law and Spirit* (*Gesetz und Geist*) as evidence for his conviction that God still speaks today.[9] Similarly, he draws directly on Augustine's interpretation of Galatians 5:18 for support when linking Christian freedom with the guidance of the Spirit.[10]

The other main advocate he mentions with regard to guidance by the Spirit is Bernard of Clairvaux, whom Bockmuehl held in high esteem and whom he considered to have made an invaluable contribution to Christian spirituality. According to Bockmuehl, Bernard regarded the concept of the "inward testimony of the Holy Spirit [*testimonium Spiritus sancti*

---

6. *LG*, 101–17; cf. Dietz, "Mystik ist alles," 81–82.

7. *LG*, 103.

8. Augustine, *Confessions* 10.40 (pp. 248–49); cf. Augustine, *Confessions* 11.3 (p. 256); *LG*, 105.

9. Cf. *GG*, 517–18. See also *GG*, 245, 374.

10. Cf. *GG*, 526.

PART ONE—Bockmuehl's Theological Work

internum]"[11] to be crucial for the Christian life. He agrees with Bernard that the internal witness of the Holy Spirit is, first of all, the source for the illumination of Scripture by making it personal as well as making it individually relevant and, secondly, the source acting alongside Scripture for concrete, individual commission or instruction concerning our way of living. It is, therefore, rather unfortunate, in Bockmuehl's opinion, that the Reformers reduced the internal witness of the Holy Spirit only to the first source.[12] Consequently, he pleads for a rediscovery of the direct inspiration of the Holy Spirit alongside Scripture consonant with Augustine and Bernard.[13] At the same time, however, he is aware of the danger of overemphasizing the personal inspiration at the expense of Scripture. Significantly, when illustrating the right balance between Scripture and Holy Spirit, Bockmuehl twice cites these words by Augustine with approval: "How we are to please not men, but God, I am being told by Him, from Whom all healthy admonition derives, be they found in Scripture or perceived in the innermost soul."[14] Bockmuehl concludes from this quote that Augustine was aware that these two sources for moral guidance, Scripture and the soul, which Bockmuehl identifies with divine, personal inspiration, do not contradict each other. As a matter of fact, to be "steeped in Scripture"[15] seemed to be an indispensable precondition for the medieval theologians/saints in order to legitimate the received insight and to experience the personal guidance.[16]

---

11. *LG*, 107. However, this term is probably only mentioned explicitly from the time of Protestant orthodox theology onward, though the issue itself can be found much earlier. David Hollatz, for instance, mentions several times "internum Spiritus Sancti testimonium" in his chapter on Holy Scripture. (Hollatz, *Examen theologicum acroamaticum*, Q 28, p. 161, Q. 31, pp. 173, 178.) See also references to Johann Gerhard regarding the inner testimony of the Holy Spirit in Kirste, *Das Zeugnis des Geistes*, 203–4.

12. Cf. *GG*, 245 (Luther); 374–77 (Calvin).

13. Cf. *GG*, 242–5, 417–8; *LG*, 107–9.

14. Augustine, *Letters of Saint Augustine* 22.2.8, as cited by Bockmuehl in *LG*, 106, 147; cf. *GG*, 243.

15. *LG*, 111; cf. ibid., 106 (Augustine), 113 (Patrick), 116 (Thomas à Kempis). Particularly interesting is the fact that Bockmuehl, while lecturing at St. Chrischona, regularly met with one of his friends to read a thorough biography on Augustine and looked up many of the references given. Moreover, he tried to read a passage from Bernard's book *opera omnia* daily during the last ten years of his life. At the same time, he loved to read biographies of saints such as Francis of Assisi or Teresa of Avila. (E. Bockmuehl, interview.)

16. Cf. *LG*, 106, 147; *GG* 243.

Theological and Spiritual Influences on Bockmuehl

When we turn now to the issue of the works of supererogation (*opera supererogationis*), i.e., works that "go beyond the call of duty and commandment,"[17] it is by no means surprising to learn that Bockmuehl frequently draws on Church Fathers such as Ambrosius, Chrysostomos, and Augustine for support, since his concern is to recover this concept after it had been abandoned by the Reformers.[18] It is, furthermore, striking that Bockmuehl outlines the distinct concept of Clement of Alexandria in length, since he agrees with Clement that there are two stages in ethics that can be characterized by the terms "servant" and "friend," or "law" and "Spirit." Contrary to most Church Fathers and medieval theologians, whom Bockmuehl criticizes accordingly, Clement does not identify the two stages with two different groups of Christians but wants to see both stages applied in every Christian's life.[19] Bockmuehl, furthermore, stresses the importance of Clement's concept because it not only includes tasks related to the sustaining of life but also those related to church-building activities.[20]

When writing on *ethical topics*, Bockmuehl also refers several times to various Church Fathers and medieval theologians.[21] His article on the assessment of abortion in the early church, in which he outlines the biblical perspective as well as the testimony of the Church Fathers, is rather uncommon for Protestant ethics. Regarding the view of the Church Fathers, Bockmuehl states that the majority judged abortion to be murder. Only if the life of the mother was in danger did they allow abortion.[22] Bockmuehl's reasoning shows that the testimony of the Church Fathers had normative relevance for him as long as it did not contradict the Bible. Thus, he valued it as a spiritual legacy.

The Reformers

That Bockmuehl pastored a Protestant church for several years itself suggests that the theology of the Reformers entered his theology in some way or other. In this context, it is particularly interesting to discover that the

17. Bockmuehl, "Recovering Vocation," 96.
18. Cf. *GG*, 292–94, 304, 308.
19. Cf. *GG*, 201–94, 294–96.
20. Cf. *GG*, 296.
21. See, e.g., *CW*, 11–15; Bockmuehl, "On Wealth and Stewardship," 50.
22. Cf. Bockmuehl, "Die Beurteilung der Abtreibung," 63–75; Bockmuehl, "Dogmatisches zur Tauffrage," 10; *CW*, 97.

Part One—Bockmuehl's Theological Work

Evangelical Church of the Rhineland as well as the Evangelical Church of Baden, in which he served for several years, unites Lutheran and Reformed churches, unlike some other church dioceses in Germany.[23] Thus, Arthur D. Thomas correctly draws attention to the fact that Bockmuehl "claimed both Martin Luther and John Calvin as theological models for his life."[24] And yet, this does not exclude a clear preference for the Reformed tradition, which can be seen by his request that he made in 1961 to be placed in a Reformed church while serving as an assistant pastor.[25]

Besides this biographical evidence, Bockmuehl's theological work gives further indication of the Reformers' influence upon him. Throughout great parts of his life Bockmuehl was engaged in a study of the writings of the Reformers and the implications of their theology for today. In December 1979, Bockmuehl explicitly mentioned in a circular letter to his friends that he had spent most of the summer of 1978 reading a variety of books written by Luther in order to collect material for a detailed analysis and critical appreciation of the heritage of Protestant ethics.[26] He completed this project in 1987 by publishing the aforementioned profound and voluminous treatise *Law and Spirit: A Critical Appreciation of the Heritage of Protestant Ethics*.

When comparing this late work to some of his earlier articles, for example, "Regarding the Question of the Ethical Authority of the Bible"[27] as well as "Concerning the Validity of the Ten Commandments for Today,"[28] it is apparent that Bockmuehl became increasingly critical toward the Reformers even though he continued to appreciate their contribution. For instance, in 1966, Bockmuehl still traced the lack of a sound pneumatology in Protestantism—particularly in connection with Christian ethics—back to "specific developments within the second generation of the Reformation,"[29] referring to Lutheran Orthodox theologians in particular. Conversely, in his book *Law and Spirit*, he suggests that the origin of the

---

23. Some provinces belonging to the Evangelical Church in Germany are still purely Lutheran or Reformed. Cf. Hanacek, "Archive," n.p.

24. Thomas, "Spirituality of Klaus Bockmuehl: Part One," 2.

25. E. Bockmuehl, interview.

26. Cf. circular letter written by Bockmuehl Dec. 26, 1979, 2.

27. German title: "Zur Frage nach der Maßgeblichkeit der Bibel für die Ethik." This article is a revised version of a paper that Bockmuehl presented at a conference in Dortmund/Germany in 1966.

28. German title: "Über die Geltung der Zehn Gebote heute." The first draft of this article is based on a sermon that Bockmuehl preached on Nov. 12, 1966 in Heidelberg.

29. Bockmuehl, "Zur Frage nach der Maßgeblichkeit," 48.

Theological and Spiritual Influences on Bockmuehl

deficiency can, to a great extent, already be found in the theology of the Reformers.³⁰ Nevertheless, Bockmuehl often refers to the Reformers, in particular to Luther, as his advocate on many different issues.³¹ Yet, concerning his references to Luther, he admits that those citations are not always necessarily Luther's main thrust. Furthermore, he makes it very plain when he differs from Luther or Calvin. This reveals, on the one hand, his enormous admiration for the Reformers and, on the other hand, his recognition of their humanness, i.e., their fallibility. Bockmuehl thus calls for a critical evaluation of one's own confessional position in the light of the biblical text, in order to avoid a naïve identification of one's own confessional position with that of Scripture.³² This is exactly what Bockmuehl endeavors to do, for instance, in his detailed study *Law and Spirit*. In the first volume Bockmuehl analyzes the ethics of the confessional writings of the Reformation; he thus chooses those writings that he regards as being generally recognized by most churches of the Reformation tradition. However, due to illness, he was unfortunately unable to carry out his plan to devote a second volume to the "study of the origins of Protestant ethics in the literature of Martin Luther" and a third to the "outlining of the reception of this heritage in the nineteenth and twentieth century."³³

We now take a closer look at those issues that Bockmuehl advocated strongly and those that he felt urged to engage with critically when turning to the Reformers. This analysis will be limited to an examination of the influence of Luther and Calvin on Bockmuehl, taking into account his own interpretation of the Reformers' theology. It is not our concern in this part of our study to deal with the various confessional theologies within the Reformed and Lutheran traditions that have been generated throughout the last five centuries.

---

30. Cf. *GG*, 517–19.

31. Cf. Bockmuehl, "Great Commandment," 13, 22–23; Bockmuehl, "The Ten Commandments," 29, 32, 37.

32. Cf. *GG*, 530. Similarly, Barth did not shrink from critically evaluating Reformation theology as he states himself: "I have been led to a *critical* (in a better sense of the word) discussion of church tradition, and as well of the Reformers, and especially of Calvin" (Barth, *How I changed*, 43).

33. *GG*, 26.

Part One—Bockmuehl's Theological Work

Creation Ethics

The first thing to note is that Bockmuehl attaches the greatest significance to the Reformers' emphasis on creation ethics, including the creation and preservation ordinances. In this context, Bockmuehl acknowledges that the Reformers brought about a necessary and invaluable change in ethics.[34] Contrary to the conviction of the medieval church that Christian perfection and true Christianity can only be found in monasticism, hence, in the separation of the sacred and the profane, Bockmuehl asserts that "[t]he Reformation refuses to set the sacred apart; it moves into the profane world, declaring all of it sacred, because of its quality of being God's creation."[35] This sanctification of the profane had, in Bockmuehl's view, far-reaching consequences for the understanding of ethics.

First of all, it brought the cultural mandate back into focus along with the "tasks of stewardship in creation"[36]—e.g., preserving the life of one's neighbor and of community. According to Bockmuehl, this, in turn, reveals the central role that the neighbor plays in Reformation ethics, thereby conforming with biblical ethics.[37] The second consequence of the sanctification of the profane was, what Bockmuehl calls, an "ethics for the layperson" ("*Laisierung* der Ethik")[38] due to the Reformers' dismissal of the medieval belief of an elite-ethics for the few. Hence, not only the monk but even the lay person in the profane world was expected to, and was deemed to be capable of, living a Christian lifestyle and could thus be called a saint. They were, however, expected to fulfill their duties according to their civil vocation or "station in life".[39] This brings us to the third consequence: the unequaled honoring of the civil vocation or station in life by the Reformers. It was their conviction that true Christian service did not consist of withdrawing from secular stations in life and vocations but rather of serving God precisely in the different stations in life such as in the family, e.g., as a parent, in the society, and in the state.[40] Despite

---

34. Cf. *GG*, 209–10, 214.

35. Bockmuehl, "Secularism and Theology," 50; cf. Bockmuehl, "Recovering Vocation," 88–90; Bockmuehl, "Secularization and Secularism," 55.

36. Bockmuehl, "Recovering Vocation," 95. Bockmuehl greatly appreciated the Reformers' unique recapturing of "the biblical domestic ethos in its time" (*GG*, 527).

37. Cf. *CW*, 25; *GG*, 81, 93.

38. *GG*, 210.

39. Bockmuehl, "Recovering Vocation," 91; cf. ibid., 90; *GG*, 210; Althaus, *Ethics*, 38–39.

40. Bockmuehl, "Recovering Vocation," 90–91; Althaus, *Ethics*, 38–41. We are

Theological and Spiritual Influences on Bockmuehl

the fact that, as we shall see later, Bockmuehl criticizes "a narrowness of the term of (civil) vocation"[41] and the exclusiveness of the civil vocation as the only principle for differentiation and individualization of ethics, he approves of the Reformers' recovery of the civil vocation for ethics.[42]

The Significance of the Law

Besides the fact, as we have just seen, that "Luther's ethics is an ethics of station and vocation,"[43] Bockmuehl also mentions the great significance of the law, particularly the Decalogue, for Reformation ethics: "That Christian ethics has its foundation in the Ten Commandments is in my opinion set forth convincingly by Luther. One will certainly complete one's study of the first chapter of the Large Catechism with the utmost respect, indeed, with admiration, satisfaction, acclaim, and gratitude."[44] According to Bockmuehl, the Reformers not only recovered the Decalogue for ethics in a comprehensive way, writing numerous expositions of it, but also defended the validity and importance of the law for the believer.[45]

In this context, Bockmuehl points to Calvin's *Institutes* that distinguishes between three main functions of the law: first, the accusing function (*usus elenchticus legis*), i.e., exposing sin ("mirror"), secondly, the civil function (*usus politicus*), i.e., preserving civic peace ("halter"/"bridle") and, thirdly, the function for the regenerated (*usus legis in renatis*), i.e., instructing the Christian about good works ("rule").[46] Particularly with view to antinomians, Calvin emphasized strongly that Christ, despite the fact that he abolished the curse of the law, did not remove or change the content of the law. Instead, through regeneration, the believer is freed to

---

aware that there are differences between Luther's and Calvin's concept of vocation. However, since the main thrust of their concepts is very similar, as Bockmuehl points out, a more detailed analysis is not necessary for our purposes. Cf. *GG*, 211–13, 335–38.

41. *GG*, 233.

42. Cf. *GG*, 211–12, 214, 217.

43. Althaus, *Ethics*, 41.

44. *GG*, 111; cf. ibid., 119; Bockmuehl, "Gebote, Zehn," 188.

45. Cf. *GG*, 323; *CW*, 16. Bockmuehl contends that despite the fact that the Decalogue did already gain some importance from the thirteenth century onward, it was due to the Reformation that the Decalogue was recovered again. Cf. *GG*, 210.

46. Calvin, *Institutes* 2.7.7, 10/11, 13; cf. 2.7.6–17; *GG*, 323–24; Leith, *John Calvin's Doctrine*, 49–50.

obey the law willingly and is provided with the necessary ability to keep it. Hence, Calvin viewed the third use of the law to be the main one.[47]

Regarding Luther's understanding of the third use of the law, the later Bockmuehl asserts that, though Luther did not use the same terminology as Calvin, the subject matter itself can be found in his works.[48] This was and still is a contested issue among Lutheran scholars. However, according to Engelbrecht, the scholarly consensus throughout the second half of the twentieth century has been that Luther did not teach the third use of the law.[49] Bockmuehl himself, in his early article "Revolution of Ethics" (1971), argues that "Luther himself had never spoken of any such 'third use' of the Law. It was the Holy Spirit who was the teacher and would tell the believers all the time what to do in the actual application of the commandments."[50] Later, however, Bockmuehl takes it for granted that the subject matter of the "third use" can already be found in Luther. For instance, he points out that for Luther, according to his *Thesis concerning Faith and Law* (1535), only those who are perfectly filled with the Holy Spirit will be able to discern everything correctly and thus be able to create new Decalogues.[51] Yet, because every Christian remains constantly *simul justus et peccator* and cannot therefore claim not to err, contrary to the apostles, it is better to adhere to the commandments.[52] Bockmuehl concludes that, for Luther, the law continues to play a role in the life of the Christian.[53] That this role was not only negative, i.e., exposing sin, but also positive, i.e., leading the believer, can best be seen, according to Bockmuehl, in the following quotation in Luther's commentary on Galatians written in 1519: "[T]he Commandments are necessary, not in order that we may be justified by doing the works they enjoin, but in order that as

---

47. Cf. Calvin, *Institutes* 2.7.12; *GG*, 323–24; Leith, *John Calvin's Doctrine*, 48–49.

48. Cf. Bockmuehl, "Protestant Ethics," 105; *GG*, 55.

49. Cf. Engelbrecht, *Friends*, xiii–xiv; *GG*, 455–8; Bockmuehl, "Der Streit," 96, 100–101.

50. Bockmuehl, "Revolution," 57.

51. Cf. Bockmuehl, "Der Streit," 100–101; Bockmuehl, "Ten Commandments," 135–36; *GG*, 317.

52. Cf. Luther, "Theses concerning Faith and Law," 112–13; Bockmuehl, "Der Streit," 100; *CW*, 135–36.

53. It is worth quoting Bernhard Lohse who holds a similar view to Bockmuehl's with regard to Luther's understanding of the law: "Luther actually assumed a persistence of the law into eternity . . . The law is and remains God's Word" (Lohse, *Martin Luther's Theology*, 275).

Theological and Spiritual Influences on Bockmuehl

persons who are already righteous we may know how our spirit should crucify the flesh and direct us in the affairs of this life."[54]

Hence, when arguing against antinomistic tendencies in contemporary Christian ethics, it should not be surprising to discover that Bockmuehl refers regularly to the Reformers in order to strengthen his argument regarding the continuing validity of the law for the believer.[55]

Such observations indicate clearly that, "[a]s one who belonged to both the Reformed and Lutheran traditions, Bockmuehl inherited Calvin's teaching of 'the third use of the law,'"[56] as Arthur D. Thomas asserts. Thus, the great value that Bockmuehl attached to the Ten Commandments for Christian ethics, apparent when looking at his lecture notes published in the book *The Christian Way of Living: An Ethics of the Ten Commandments*, can be traced back to the influence of the Reformers. This is confirmed by the fact that Luther and Calvin are the two theologians he most frequently refers to.[57] Furthermore, according to Neuer, it is especially Bockmuehl's seminal work *Law and Spirit* that best reflects Bockmuehl's conviction that "the return to the Reformation ethics of the Decalogue would demonstrate an essential and inevitable step toward the renewal of Protestant theology for which he was striving."[58]

While Bockmuehl's criticism of the Reformers' ethics will be examined in more depth at the beginning of Part Two, it is worth mentioning the greatest charge he brings against the Reformers, namely, the charge to have reduced Christian ethics merely to vocation and the Decalogue. Instead, as Bockmuehl points out, Christian ethics should also comprise specific Christian actions such as love toward God, spirituality, church-building activities—including evangelism, teaching, and service (*diakonia*)—and "differential ethics," in particular the guidance of the Holy Spirit.[59]

---

54. Luther, "Galatians—1519," 232. Bockmuehl cites this quotation in *GG* 55. Cf. *CW*, 22; *GG*, 317.

55. Cf. Bockmuehl, "Ten Commandments," 131, 133, 135–36; Bockmuehl, "Der Streit," 100; Bockmuehl, "Zur Frage nach der Maßgeblichkeit," 45; *SU*, 24–29; Bockmuehl, "Problem der Ethik," 77–78. Bockmuehl even points out that "[d]uring the last decade of his life, Luther himself battled with all his might against those theologians who denied the need for holiness, whom he called 'the antinomians'" (Bockmuehl, "Keeping His Commandments," 95).

56. Thomas, "Spirituality of Klaus Bockmuehl: Part Two," 30.

57. Cf. *CW*, 137–38.

58. Neuer, "Weite," 3.

59. Cf. *GG*, 514; see also 25, 217, 287, 513; *CM*, 115–16; Bockmuehl, "Recovering Vocation," 83–87.

PART ONE—Bockmuehl's Theological Work

Love for God

Regarding the issue *love for God*, we discover that Bockmuehl identifies love for God with love for one's neighbor in one of his earliest publications, his doctoral thesis. In the second edition twenty years later, however, he describes this identification, which in his view stemmed from Luther, as a gross error and a distortion of the Christian message.[60] Bockmuehl expounds Luther's position in more detail in his book *Law and Spirit*, drawing attention to the fact that Luther and Melanchthon mainly focused on loving one's neighbor while neglecting direct love for God. This he considers to be a reaction "to the medieval linking of God's love with the doctrine of justification. As the Reformation lets go of one it also loses the other."[61] Despite the fact that Luther rightly rejected the medieval doctrine of justification, Bockmuehl believes that Luther's negligence of love for God as the central theme of theology and ethics was an invalid overreaction.[62]

Significantly, it is where Bockmuehl judges Luther to have been overcautious of avoiding the medieval position, and thereby misinterpreting Scripture, that he feels unable to follow him.

As far as the Reformed tradition is concerned, the assessment turns out to be quite the opposite. Bockmuehl, in fact, praises the Reformed tradition for their recovery of the central position of the double commandment of love for Christian ethics. He even declares that "love for God, namely, as the intention to direct one's whole life toward the honor of God, becomes virtually the characteristic feature of the Reformed lifestyle."[63] Accordingly, Bockmuehl holds Calvin in high esteem for re-gaining a horizon, a goal for Christian ethics—to exalt God's glory.[64] Thus, there can be no doubt in this respect as to the great influence of the Reformed tradition on Bockmuehl.

---

60. Cf. "Nachwort," *LuG*, 288–89.
61. *GG*, 275; cf. Bockmuehl, "Aktualität," 304–5.
62. Cf. *GG*, 84, 109; Bockmuehl, "Great Commandment," 11, 17; *GiE*, 162.
63. *GG*, 353, cf. ibid., 319, 357–60.
64. Cf. *GG*, 360–61. Bockmuehl clearly sympathizes with Calvin's "horizon of eternity," thus emphasizing the eschatological character of ethics. Circular letter written by Bockmuehl June 29, 1985, 3; *LbG*, 34.

Guidance by the Spirit

When looking at his work, it is apparent that Bockmuehl consistently engages with the Reformers regarding this topic.[65] His evaluation is two-fold: on the one hand, he criticizes the Reformers severely; he accuses them of silencing the Spirit in the field of ethics by proclaiming that the Spirit only speaks and guides through Scripture. Bockmuehl judges this to be an over-reaction to their adversaries, the Anabaptists, many of whom claimed to have received direct inspiration from God, valuing this higher than Scripture.[66] On the other hand, however, Bockmuehl acknowledges the fact that Luther as well as Calvin, though only occasionally, show awareness of the juxtaposition of Spirit and Scripture rather than the superiority of Scripture over Spirit.[67]

Regarding Calvin's emphasis on the Spirit's role of motivating and empowering the believer for doing good works, we should note Bockmuehl's twofold evaluation: on the one hand, he criticizes Calvin for overemphasizing the Spirit's task to motivate and thereby neglecting the Spirit's task to teach and inform. Yet, on the other hand, Bockmuehl praises Calvin highly: "No one should underestimate the beneficial effect that his doctrine of the power of the Spirit, at the very least, has had on the motivation of Christian action,"[68] particularly since Lutheran ethics failed to emphasize this appropriately.[69]

In a later chapter, we shall explore the Reformers' concept of guidance and Bockmuehl's criticism of the Reformers regarding this issue in more depth, since it is the Reformers themselves and not only Protestant Orthodoxy that Bockmuehl accuses of neglecting the role of the Holy Spirit for Christian ethics.

Conclusion

Despite Bockmuehl's evident criticism of several aspects of the Reformers' theology, his admiration for and indebtedness to them have been made apparent by his lengthy engagement and constant interaction with their

---

65. Cf. Hofmann, "Revolutionär," 28; *LG*, 121–33; Bockmuehl, "Law and the Spirit," 47; Bockmuehl, "Protestant Ethics," 107, 113–15.
66. Cf. Bockmuehl, "Protestant Ethics," 106–8; *GG*, 244–47.
67. Cf. Bockmuehl, "Protestant Ethics," 113–14.
68. *GG*, 436; cf. ibid., 381; Bockmuehl, "Perimeters," 17.
69. *GG*, 439–40.

theology. Moreover, the many parallels drawn between the Reformers' and Bockmuehl's concept of ethics indicate a more than slight influence.[70] Hence, Neuer correctly describes Bockmuehl's theology as characterized by a "critical linkage to the Reformation theology."[71] When looking individually at Luther's and Calvin's influence upon Bockmuehl, we may conclude that besides Bockmuehl's "great admiration for Luther" there is a "stronger identification with Calvin"[72] apparent in his works.

German Pietism

The first decisive influence upon Bockmuehl's spiritual life and theology was his encounter with German Pietism, first through his grandmother and then at the age of 16 through Wilhelm Busch. Since the latter played an important role concerning Bockmuehl's conversion and since "[t]he Pietist vision he gained from Busch remained with him the rest of his life,"[73] we shall now take a closer look at Busch's life and work.

Excursus: Wilhelm Busch (1897–1966)

Wilhelm Busch was born in Elberfeld in 1897. His father, Dr. Wilhelm Busch, was a pastor and evangelist. His mother had several relatives well known in the pietistic movement in Württemberg.[74] In spite of his Christian upbringing, Wilhelm Busch was not converted until he was a frontline soldier during the First World War.[75]

During his theological studies in Tübingen, Busch was influenced mainly by Adolf Schlatter and Karl Heim. From the former, he acquired

---

70. It should also be noted that Bockmuehl strongly advocates the Reformers' concept of the Two Kingdoms/Governments. Cf. Bockmuehl, "Secularization," 56–57; *CW*, 89–90; Bockmuehl, "Kirche," 134–35. When looking at the book *Living by the Gospel*, the affinity with the Reformers is striking. Not only does Bockmuehl start his book with a chapter on forgiveness as the first gift of the gospel, he also cites the Reformers frequently, particularly in his chapter on prayer. Significant was for him Luther's interpretation of the second commandment as an order to pray. Cf. *LbG*, 64–76. Possibly with a view to this book, Packer draws attention to Bockmuehl's "Reformation faith, focused on forgiveness" ("Legacy," 9).

71. Neuer, "Bockmühl, Klaus," 287.

72. Thomas, "Spirituality of Klaus Bockmuehl: Part One," 7.

73. Ibid., 4.

74. Cf. Parzany, *Im Einsatz für Jesus*, 82, 112.

75. Cf. W. Busch, *Jesus unser Schicksal*, 30, 51–52.

Theological and Spiritual Influences on Bockmuehl

the skill of thorough exegesis; from the latter, he acquired the skill of systematic and philosophical reflection.[76] This theological foundation was indispensable for his later ministry as a pastor and evangelist; so, too, were his studies of the Pietist fathers. The lives of such men were to act as role models for him.[77]

In 1930, Busch became youth pastor in Essen and influenced many young men through his spiritually awakening preaching. His sermons were simple, direct and humorous and he was able to reach educated as well as uneducated young men. One of his most salient skills was storytelling. Every Sunday, he would narrate a biblical story in such a way that the young men listened attentively to his words. At the same time, he trained youth leaders in this skill and gave them the opportunity of exercising it.[78] Moreover, he organized social events such as soccer, hiking, games, retreats etc. and was concerned about the social needs of the people. For instance, he helped the unemployed to find jobs and even founded the "University of the Unemployed" in 1931. Soon about five hundred young men were attending this adult college.[79] During the Second World War, Busch belonged to the "Confessing Church" (*Bekennende Kirche*) that uncovered and countered the distortion of the Gospel by the "German Christians" (*Deutsche Christen*). He was arrested several times because of his uncompromising preaching and Christian commitment.[80] The Nazi Regime also restricted his work among young men. However, as soon as the war was over, his youth work started again. At the time when Bockmuehl joined Busch's youth work, about eight hundred young men attended the regular meetings.[81] Despite these large numbers, Bockmuehl developed a personal friendship with Busch that lasted until Busch's death in 1966. During one visit in 1963, while talking about the current decay in Christian ethics, Busch encouraged Bockmuehl to stand firm and defend the validity of the commandments of God. Bockmuehl appreciated Busch's interest in his situation, his theological comments, and his prayer support.[82]

76. Cf. Parzany, *Im Einsatz für Jesus*, 14–15.
77. Cf. ibid., 267.
78. Cf. ibid., 105–16, 109.
79. Cf. W. Busch, *Man muß doch darüber sprechen*, 27–28; Parzany, *Im Einsatz für Jesus*, 58–60.
80. Cf. W. Busch, *Variationen*, 56–64; Parzany, *Im Einsatz für Jesus*, 201.
81. Cf. Thomas, "Spirituality of Klaus Bockmuehl: Part One," 3; Hofmann, "Revolutionär," 18.
82. Cf. Hofmann, "Revolutionär," 20; letters from Bockmuehl to Wilhelm Busch April 13, and May 30, 1966.

PART ONE—Bockmuehl's Theological Work

When turning to Busch's influence on Bockmuehl, there is little doubt that Bockmuehl's emphasis on a personal conversion as becoming a new spiritual person in Christ with practical implications and his devotion to evangelism, world-mission, and social concerns had its roots in his early encounter with Busch. Indeed, we shall see in a later chapter how important these issues were for Bockmuehl's understanding of Christian ethics. Other concerns that were implanted in those years when attending Busch's meetings were his love of the Bible with its central message—Jesus Christ crucified and resurrected—and with its guiding principles for daily life as well as the practice of a "quiet time" early in the morning. Moreover, it is very likely that his lifelong interest in Pietists such as Philipp Jakob Spener, August Hermann Francke, and Nikolaus Graf von Zinzendorf was awakened during this early period since Busch portrayed them as spiritual men who had fought for the Gospel despite resistance from the government or church officials and who took an interest in political and social matters.[83] Such observations confirm that "Bockmuehl was a child of Pietism. But the Pietism that he encountered as a young man in the Weigle-House in Essen when he joined Wilhelm Busch had a wide horizon. He not only had an eye on the path of Christianity for them, but also on the current social developments and the Christian shared responsibility."[84]

Just how much Busch's wide horizon influenced Bockmuehl can be seen by the fact that Bockmuehl, like Busch, had an eye for current developments in society, the church, and theology, including such issues as secularism, the new morality, Marxism, and atheism in church and theology.

Throughout his whole life Bockmuehl never denied his proximity to Pietism. As a matter of fact, he considered himself to be more closely related to Pietism than to Evangelicalism since, for Bockmuehl, "'evangelical' is the description of an alliance, whereas 'Pietism' is a program."[85] However, it is important to note that Bockmuehl, when writing about Pietism as a program, referred to the classical German Lutheran Pietism mainly represented by Spener, Francke, and Zinzendorf, not necessarily to the contemporary form of Pietism. Thus, when writing about Pietism, his

---

83. Cf. Hofmann, "Revolutionär," 18–19; Parzany, *Im Einsatz für Jesus*, 266; Parzany, "Pietismus und soziale Verantwortung," 1.

84. Burkhardt, "Handeln aus dem Hören," 28.

85. Bockmuehl, "Kopfloser Pietismus," 61; cf. Thomas, "Spirituality of Klaus Bockmuehl: Part One," 3–4.

Theological and Spiritual Influences on Bockmuehl

intention was neither to express his loyalty to a contemporary denomination nor to defend it against all other denominations. Rather, he expressed his indebtedness to the heritage of classical Pietism with its "program for renewal of Church *and* theology,"[86] a theme which was close to his heart.[87] Particularly in view of the diverging tendencies and polarization among the evangelical theologians, Bockmuehl was convinced that a rediscovery of spiritual roots could help to gain orientation and trigger a moral and spiritual renewal, just like the Pietistic movement had once done.[88] Accordingly, he brought into focus the importance of the Pietistic issues for his contemporary churches by publishing, for instance, *The Topical Relevance of Pietism (Die Aktualität des Pietismus)*;[89] here he did not spare the contemporary Pietists and Evangelicals (self-)critical questions concerning spiritual and theological deficiencies. With regard to the various charges brought against Pietism by various theologians—including himself—Bockmuehl responded that, rather than rejecting Pietism for its deficiencies, Pietism should be called upon to recover its original principles. This means, of course, that, for Bockmuehl, the charges brought against contemporary Pietism were at least partially legitimate, since it had moved away from its origin and had to be reminded of it. However, at the same time he defended the program of classical Pietism by demonstrating that it was in accordance with Scripture and often even with the Reformers.[90] Hence, Bockmuehl's deep appreciation of classical Pietism did not merely stem from his experience of the youth work of Busch but, to a greater degree, from his own in-depth assessment of Pietism as bringing biblical

---

86. *LbG*, 118, cf. Bockmuehl, "Leben aus dem Evangelium," 75; Bockmuehl, "Aktualität," 295. Spener, for instance, laid down his program in the well-known treatise published to mark the beginning of Pietism in 1675: *Pia Desideria or Heartfelt Desire for a God-pleasing Reform of the true Evangelical Church*.

87. Cf. Bockmuehl, "Aktualität," 333. In fact, Pietists "hoped to complete the Reformation, which, they felt, the sixteenth century reformers had only begun" (Stoeffler, *German Pietism*, x).

88. According to Erb, it is universally acknowledged nowadays that "Pietism was the most important development in Protestant spirituality" ("Foreword," xiii). Stoeffler confirms this in the following vivid way: "It would be difficult to deny the fact, however, that it was the Pietists who blew the roof off the tight little structures of orthodoxy and ecclesiasticism and afforded Protestantism its first broad look upon the spiritual needs of the world at large" (Stoeffler, *Rise*, 19).

89. It should be noted that he was the only one out of the ranks of the Pietistis who published a book for the 350th anniversary of Philipp Jacob Spener, thus revealing Bockmuehl's great admiration for this Pietistic theologian. Cf. Haizmann, "Ethik," 94.

90. Cf. Bockmuehl, "Kopfloser Pietismus," 62; Bockmuehl, "Aktualität," 306, 311.

issues back into focus.⁹¹ His criterion for evaluating different traditions, including his own, was, in essence, *sola scriptura*.⁹² Significantly, the Pietists emphasized this reformatory criterion to such an extent that they were accused of being Biblicists. Despite Bockmuehl's awareness of the fact that the creeds and the history of doctrine function as correctives, since it is impossible to read Scripture without any preconditions, he maintains that we constantly have the task of re-examining our own theology and traditions on the basis of Scripture, just as the Pietists did. It is, therefore, not surprising that he concludes: "In this respect the pietistic heritage is of immeasurable topical relevance."⁹³

However, the emphasis on Scripture did not hinder classical Pietists, and similarly Bockmuehl, from drawing on various different traditions such as the Reformers, Calvin in particular, or medieval spirituality, including mysticism and spiritualism; the latter were disdained by "Protestant scholasticism then dominating orthodox Lutheranism."⁹⁴ The Pietists, nevertheless, maintained a critical attitude toward their own traditions, criticizing the same—and thereby also many orthodox Lutheran theologians of their day—if they were seen to be disagreeing with Scripture.⁹⁵ How much Bockmuehl's way of dealing with the various traditions that had influenced him reflects this pietistic approach can be seen in the following statement: "[W]e advocate a Protestant self-confidence in the sense of reflective knowledge of one's own position—in light of the higher standard of Scripture."⁹⁶ In fact, the best example for a critical evaluation of his own traditions is certainly his profound book *Law and Spirit*.⁹⁷ What is most striking is the fact that Bockmuehl explicitly mentions the

---

91. Cf. Haizmann, "Klaus Bockmühl," 2, 7.
92. Cf. Bockmuehl, "After Lausanne," 68.
93. Bockmuehl, "Aktualität," 302.
94. Hoffman, "Pietism," 355. M. Schmidt, *Wiedergeburt*, 193; Rüttgardt, "Speners Wiedergeburtslehre," 9–11. Stoeffler points out that Francke as well as Spener were "closer to the Reformed Tradition than to Luther." Stoeffler, *German Pietism*, 18; cf. Stoeffler, *Rise*, 231–32. As we have seen, this is also true for Bockmuehl. Regarding the reference to medieval spirituality, in particular the appreciation of the mystical writings of John Tauler and the devotional book *The Imitation of Christ*, compare Spener, *Pia Desidera*, 110–11, and Spener, "Hindrances," 69, with *LG*, 115–16. Cf. Stoeffler, "Pietism," 324; M. Schmidt, "Spener und Luther," 111–13.
95. Cf. Stoeffler, *Rise*, 239.
96. *GG*, 530.
97. Cf. Haizmann, "Klaus Bockmühl," 3.

Theological and Spiritual Influences on Bockmuehl

confrontational element of Pietism; indeed, he regards "Pietism as one of the first critics of the Protestant milieu."[98]

We will now turn to the main issues of Pietism as highlighted by Bockmuehl himself: "Part of the main themes of Pietism were conversion and personal faith of the individual, seeking after sanctification, zeal for mission and evangelization, interest in education as well as commitment to service."[99] Indeed, as an examination of Bockmuehl's writings will show, he was clearly influenced by classical Pietism regarding his understanding of these issues. Let us take a closer look at the Pietist's understanding of conversion and regeneration, sanctification, mission, and social action as well as the topic of guidance by the Spirit, which is an important topic for our study, and at Bockmuehl's appropriation of these topics.[100]

Conversion and Regeneration

Whereas the Reformers regard justification to be the center of theology, classical Pietism places a major emphasis on regeneration, yet without suppressing the reformatory doctrine of justification; this can be seen in the following statement by Spener:[101] "The subject matter regarding Christianity that is needful is certainly the one of regeneration, in which our conversion, justification, and the beginning of our sanctification culminate and which is also the foundation for all other sanctification or the source from which all that is good . . . in our whole life has to necessarily flow. Hence, who among us understands the same, certainly understands correctly the whole of Christianity."[102]

Spener, and similarly Francke, thus brought into focus the neglected issue of regeneration; they viewed it as the main source out of which the

98. *GG*, 507; cf. 511; Haizmann, "Ethik," 94; Stoeffler, *Rise*, 22–23.

99. Bockmuehl, "Aktualität," 297.

100. Since the issue of education is not of great relevance for our present study, an investigation of Bockmuehl's appropriation of pietistic ideas regarding education would not serve our ends. For Bockmuehl's evaluation of Pietism with regard to education, see Bockmuehl, "Aktualität," 319; cf. Stoeffler, *German Pietism*, 23–31.

101. Cf. M. Schmidt, *Wiedergeburt*, 193; Wallmann, *Philipp Jakob Spener*, 264; Stoeffler, *German Pietism*, 16.

102. Spener, *Schriften*, 1 (first sermon; translation from Old German); cf. Tappert, "Introduction," 27; Yeide, *Studies*, 25. It should be noted that Spener, in contrast to other Pietists, held on to the traditional doctrine of baptismal regeneration. However, he believed that regeneration, when lost through unbelief, can be regained. In fact, he also called this second regeneration conversion. Cf. Spener, *Pia Desideria*, 63; Stoeffler, *Rise*, 242; Brown, *Understanding Pietism*, 48–49; Burkhardt, *Christ werden*, 67.

Part One—Bockmuehl's Theological Work

Christian life flows. In fact, they defined regeneration, and likewise conversion, as being a concrete, individual experience of change brought about not by human endeavor but solely by the triune God himself; yet, this did not happen without the subjective appropriation of the Gospel consisting of repentance, i.e., confession of sin, followed by forgiveness of sin, i.e., accepting God's mercy and grace. The old person is put to death, whereas the new person now lives in a close relationship with God equipped with the gift of the Holy Spirit and bringing about good fruit.[103]

When turning to Bockmuehl's concept of conversion and regeneration, it should not surprise us to discover that his writings clearly reflect the emphasis laid on conversion and regeneration so distinctive of Pietism. Particularly with regard to the ongoing process of secularization that evoked the Marxist quest for the new human being, Bockmuehl reminds evangelical Christians in his book *The Challenge of Marxism* of the importance of regeneration: "The message we must declare is the message of human regeneration . . . We must certainly not give up our message and goal of regeneration which is our best heritage. It must be the message of regeneration not only of the soul or of our moods, but of an inclusive rebirth, a regeneration of 'gross weight.' The conversion of Zacchaeus must be our guideline, showing how true conversion changes the whole person."[104]

Bockmuehl's purpose in this passage is to remind the Evangelicals among his readers of their pietistic legacy, particularly of their doctrine of regeneration and conversion, since the new human being demanded by Marxism to renew society can only come into being through regeneration.[105] Thus, he defines conversion "as a moral change with practical consequences"[106] brought about by an experience of repentance, confession of sin and acceptance of God's grace.[107] His conviction is therefore that Christian ethics has to start with the regeneration/conversion of the individual since without it the foundation for a transformed life cannot be laid.[108]

103. Cf. Francke, "Autobiography," 106; Erb, "Introduction," 6. Contrary to the traditional interpretation of Francke's understanding of conversion as an experience of a penitential struggle, Stoeffler argues that Francke's "real interest was in the indiviudal's new relation to God which must lead to a progressive amendment of life." Stoeffler, *German Pietism*, 8, and cf. pp. 14–15; Beyreuther, "Vorwort," 11–12.

104. *CM*, 166.

105. Cf. Bockmuehl, "Zur Frage nach der Maßgeblichkeit," 46.

106. Bockmuehl, "Perimeters," 6.

107. Cf. *CM*, 158–59.

108. Cf. Bockmuehl, "Zur Frage nach der Maßgeblichkeit," 46.

Theological and Spiritual Influences on Bockmuehl

The importance of this conviction can be seen in the way he defends it in various ways. First, he regards the greatest mistake of the "new morality," championed by Joseph Fletcher and John A. T. Robinson, to have been that they concealed the possibility of transformation, and he criticizes them accordingly.[109] Secondly, Bockmuehl rejects the doctrine of universalism, which he considers to be advocated by the majority of theologians. Contrary to this position, he highlights the necessity of an individual, concrete experience of conversion that includes the dying of the old person as well as a conscious "change of leadership."[110] In this context, he explicitly draws on Pietism for support, revealing his indebtedness to the latter.[111]

To sum up, then, our conclusion thus far is that Bockmuehl's understanding of regeneration as the source and indispensable prerequisite of a spiritually and morally changed life is shaped by classical Pietism.[112]

Sanctification

As mentioned above, Pietism expects that regeneration manifests itself in a visible transformation in the individual's moral and spiritual life, thus leading to a sanctified life. In reaction to the orthodox emphasis on pure doctrine, which was, according to Stoeffler, as "dry-as-dust,"[113] Spener contends in his famous treatise *Pia Desideria*: "*[I]t is by no means enough to have knowledge of the Christian faith, for Christianity consists rather of practice.*"[114] Hence, the Christian is not just freed from sin but called to live a life in accordance with God's will, which includes social action, as we will see later. This emphasis on *praxis pietatis*, i.e., on *sanctification* as a logical outflow of regeneration, is characteristic of Pietism.[115] In contrast to orthodox theologians, Spener "believed uncompromisingly that Christ came not only to justify men but to sanctify them as well. Sanctification, he held, is not merely a test of true faith, it is a divine intention and hence

---

109. Cf. *GiE*, 190–91. Cf. Fletcher, *Situation Ethics*; J. A. T. Robinson, *Christian Freedom*.

110. Bockmuehl, "Evangelium," 126.

111. Cf. ibid., 126–27.

112. It should not surprise us that Burkhardt, who acknowledges to have been greatly influenced by Bockmuehl, wrote a book on *The Biblical Doctrine of Regeneration* in which he argues for the rediscovery of the centrality of regeneration as Spener had done. Cf. *The Biblical Doctrine of Regeneration*, 7.

113. Stoeffler, *Rise*, 11.

114. Spener, *Pia Desideria*, 95.

115. Cf. Stoeffler, *Rise*, 5, 9.

PART ONE—Bockmuehl's Theological Work

a valid religious end."[116] Similarly, Stoeffler writes with regard to Francke that "one cannot be sure whether he puts more emphasis on the new birth or on the kind of daily life in which it must result. His preaching constantly revolves around both of these foci, since he was sure that one invariably involves the other."[117]

There are clear echoes of the pietistic concept of sanctification as the true purpose of salvation in Bockmuehl's own writings, as can be seen by the following quote: "Although 'rebirth' is presently much talked of in some quarters of contemporary Christianity, it is disappointing to see how rarely this theme is accompanied by a vigorous quest for sanctification, or renewal of life-style."[118]

Due to the fact that a sanctified life comprehends piety as much as moral integrity, Stoeffler highlights "the profound ethical sensitivity of Pietism."[119] It is interesting to observe Bockmuehl's conviction in this context. He argues "that the gospel always aims at an ethically significant realization in the life of the person."[120] Thus, when defending the visible ethical realization of sanctification against theologians such as Rudolf Bultmann and Barth, he clearly reflects the concern of the pietistic tradition.[121] This is, furthermore, confirmed by the discovery that the title of his book, *Atheism in Christendom*,[122] does not merely allude to Ernst Bloch's book of a similar name but is also reminiscent of Spener's charge of practical atheism brought against the Christians at his time.[123] In fact, as mentioned above, Bockmuehl follows Spener in fighting against those who overemphasize justification at the expense of the visible reality of a sanctified life. Moreover, Stoeffler's judgment that "Pietists hoped to reform society through the efforts of renewed individuals, thus stemming

---

116. Ibid., 241.

117. Stoeffler, *German Pietism*, 18.

118. Bockmuehl, "Sanctification and Christian Mission," 63; cf. Bockmuehl, "Aktualität," 311; Bockmuehl, *Evangelicals*, 32–34.

119. Stoeffler, *Rise*, 20; cf. Stoeffler, *German Pietism*, 21.

120. Bockmuehl, *Evangelicals*, 32.

121. Cf. Bockmuehl, "Aktualität," 309–10. This is confirmed by Stoeffler, who writes that "the religious life . . . is marked by social sensitivity and ethical concern." Stoeffler, *German Pietism*, ix.

122. German original title: *Atheismus in der Christenheit*. English title of the book translated by Geoffrey W. Bromiley in 1988: *The Unreal God of Modern Theology*.

123. Spener, *Theologische Bedencken*, 452; cf. Haizmann, "Klaus Bockmühl," 3; Bloch, *Atheismus im Christentum*. Bockmuehl explicitly uses the term "practical atheism" in *LbG*, 49; cf. Bockmuehl, "Der Säkularismus und die Folgen," 165.

Theological and Spiritual Influences on Bockmuehl

the moral decay that, in their judgement, afflicted both the churches and the body politic,"[124] also applies to Spener as well as Bockmuehl. For instance, Bockmuehl stresses the possibility of a regenerate person bringing about "[s]ocial change, reconciliation and welfare."[125]

However, this emphasis on the ethical qualities of sanctification does not blind him to the danger of legalism, as we shall see later.[126] Rather, he brings the work and power of the Holy Spirit as the enabler of sanctification into focus. In so doing he follows Spener's contention: "It is the same Holy Spirit who is bestowed on us by God who once effected all things in the early Christians, and he is neither less able nor less active today to accomplish the work of sanctification in us. If this does not happen, the sole reason must be that we do not allow, but rather hinder, the Holy Spirit's work."[127]

Similarly, Bockmuehl agrees with Spener that works of supererogation are not contrary to the Gospel, since it is the Holy Spirit who brings them forth in the reborn person. In addition, Spener's contention that faith expressing itself through love exceeds the demands of the law is clearly echoed in Bockmuehl's own writings.[128] In *Spirit and Law*, Bockmuehl, for instance, maintains that we do not only need the commandment of God but also the instructions of Jesus as well as the concrete command of the Holy Spirit.[129] As we shall see at the beginning of Part Two, Bockmuehl arrives at his position by rejecting the belief of the Reformers that the law, mainly the Decalogue, is already sufficient for Christian ethics. In fact, Spener himself had already in his time drawn attention to the narrowing of the ethics of the Reformers and, in contrast to them, had reinforced the significance of the double commandment of love for Christian ethics.[130] To what extent Bockmuehl agrees with him can be seen in the following statement: "Christian ethics must transcend the limited ethics of the Decalogue, which is often negatively formulated in the case of the tradition, in order to become an ethic of love, which internalizes the double com-

---

124. Stoeffler, "Pietism," 324. See also Yeide, *Studies*, 26.

125. *CM*, 166; cf. Brown, *Pietism*, 148.

126. Cf. Bockmuehl, "Aktualität," 312.

127. Spener, *Pia Desideria*, 85; cf. Brown, *Pietism*, 91; Spener, *Schriften*, 20; Frische, *Theologie unter der Herrschaft Gottes*, 39.

128. Cf. Haizmann, "Ethik," 97; Bockmuehl, "Aktualität," 323; Bockmuehl, "Sanctification and Christian Mission," 54; Haizmann, *Erbauung*, 129.

129. Cf. *GG*, 119, 303–9.

130. Haizmann, *Erbauung*, 129.

mandment of love to God and to one's neighbor."[131] Moreover, Spener, and in his wake Bockmuehl, emphasize the priority of *love for God*, thereby rejecting any kind of identification of both, yet without neglecting love for one's neighbor.[132] Thus, it is not at all surprising that Albrecht Haizmann, in his article "An ethic of love?" explicates the striking similarity between Spener's and Bockmuehl's "ethic of love." The following characterization of Spener's ethics by Haizmann reflects the concerns that are also found in Bockmuehl's ethics: "It is an ethic of service, it is an 'ethic of commission,' which instructs us in world preservation and in the shaping of the world, as well as in spirituality, in Christian service, as well as in mission and church development. An ethic with this broad horizon is only possible where the first *and* the second table of the Decalogue are asserted, where love of God and love of one's neighbor are adhered to."[133]

Hence, the judgment that Bockmuehl pronounces against Protestant ethics regarding the neglect of spirituality, love for God, and church-building activities, as a consequence of reducing Christian ethics to the interpretation of the law, does not apply to Pietism.[134] On the contrary, all of these issues can already be found in the writings of Spener, as Haizmann correctly demonstrates, if not in Pietism in general. This is due to the fact that Spener, as well as Bockmuehl, regards Christian service as characteristic of Christian ethics.[135] Having drawn these parallels, we now need to explore this ethics of Christian service by investigating the Pietist's concept of mission and Christian service as well as Bockmuehl's own concept.

Mission and Christian Service/Diakonia

It is generally acknowledged that "[a]mong the most profound changes which Pietism wrought within Protestantism was its bequest to the latter of a new vision of a world in need of the Gospel of Christ—hence

131. *GG*, 514.
132. Cf. Haizmann, "Ethik," 95–96; *GG*, 516.
133. Haizmann, "Ethik," 97–98.
134. Compare *GG*, 311, with Bockmuehl, "Aktualität," 313, 332–33, and *LbG*, 50. Cf. Haizmann, "Ethik," 97–98.
135. In his exposition of Spener's concern for the renewal of theology, Frische holds the view that Spener would have agreed with Bockmuehl's statement that "the characteristic feature of Christian ethics, service, is also mandatory for theology." Bockmuehl, "Der Dienst der Theologie," 78; Frische, *Theologie unter der Herrschaft Gottes*, 40.

Theological and Spiritual Influences on Bockmuehl

the tremendous impulse it gave to the expansion of the Protestant missionary enterprise."[136] Contrary to the orthodox belief that the task of the Great Commission had already been fulfilled by the Apostles, early Pietism insisted on the necessity of proclaiming the Gospel to the whole world in obedience to God's commandment. Their missionary zeal was, furthermore, fuelled by their own experience of a new birth, their conviction that every person is in need of an individual conversion in order to be saved, and the hope and expectancy of a spiritual and moral reformation in the future.[137] Due to their emphasis on mission, they not only founded an institute for the evangelization of Jews in Halle, but they also set up mission organizations such as the Danish-Halle mission and Moravian mission, which sent missionaries, including lay personnel, overseas. Names particularly associated with overseas mission were Francke and Zinzendorf.[138] Yet, this emphasis on evangelization did not result in the negligence of Christian service. On the contrary, it was a matter of course for them to extensively promote the *Innere Mission*, i.e., social activities, by establishing schools, orphanages and, within the Moravian movement, even "an outstanding social system."[139] Hence, there is little doubt that "[t]he beginnings of the social outreach of the Church are in no small part the result of the Pietistic impact."[140] We may conclude, then, that it was characteristic of early Pietism to hold together evangelism on the one hand and social activity on the other.[141] Unfortunately, this holistic view of mission was increasingly lost within Protestantism over the course of time due to the distinction between the secular and religious realms brought about by the Enlightenment. In reaction to Rationalism, Pietism was more

---

136. Stoeffler, "Preface," x; cf. Hoffman, "Pietism," 355–56; Taber, *The World Is Too Much with Us*, 59; Bosch, *Transforming Mission*, 255.

137. Cf. Stoeffler, *Rise*, 19; Bosch, *Transforming Mission*, 252–53. That the Pietists aimed at renewing the whole world is confirmed by Stoeffler who writes about August Hermann Francke: "Lives changed, a church renewed, a nation reformed, a world evangelized—these were the great objectives in the realization of which he meant to employ his energies" (Stoeffler, *German Pietism*, 7).

138. Cf. Hoffman, "Pietism," 355–56; Bosch, *Transforming Mission*, 255.

139. Zimmerling, "Maßstäbe für das Wirtschaftsleben bei Zinzendorf," 120. Cf. Bosch, *Transforming Mission*, 254; Brown, *Pietism*, 131.

140. Stoeffler, *Rise*, 4.

141. According to Bosch, one of the first missionaries of the Danish-Halle mission, "Ziegenbalg[,] declared that the *Dienst der Seelen* ('service of the souls') and the *Dienst des Leibes* ('service of the body') were interdependent and that no ministry to souls could remain without an 'exterior' side." Bosch, *Transforming Mission*, 254; cf. Gensichen, "'Dienst der Seelen' und 'Dienst des Leibes,'" 163, 168; cf. Bauch, *Lehre*, 49–50.

PART ONE—Bockmuehl's Theological Work

or less forced to withdraw to the religious, spiritual realm. Consequently, mission was often reduced to evangelism. However, as Bockmuehl points out, at the beginning of the nineteenth century a number of Pietists started again to invest their time and money in improving the living conditions of the poor and sick because they were not only concerned about the spiritual needs of the people but also about their social needs.[142]

According to Bockmuehl, it was Pietism that showed awareness of the negligence of world mission. This negligence was a consequence of the Reformers' over-emphasis on the civil vocations, i.e., vocations and professions pertaining to the cultivating and sustaining of life. Hence, "[f]oreign mission is particularly, even though not exclusively, characteristic of Pietism."[143]

For Bockmuehl, the Great Commission together with Christian service are part and parcel of Christian ethics, as we will see later. With regard to wide parts of contemporary Pietism, Bockmuehl stresses again and again the importance of "proclamation and service."[144] Not only does he bring into focus the tendency of some circles to neglect social engagement, he also draws attention to the "missional weakness in the Federal Republic"[145] of Germany in comparison to other countries. Particularly in his book *The Importance of Pietism for Today*[146] published in 1985 he reminds the contemporary Pietists and Evangelicals of their great heritage and challenges them to learn from their predecessors.[147] Given this, there is every reason to believe that Bockmuehl's understanding of and emphasis on mission and Christian service is, to a great extent, shaped by classical Pietism.[148]

---

142. Cf. Bosch, *Transforming Mission*, 276; Bockmuehl, "Aktualität," 324–26.

143. Bockmuehl, "Aktualität," 313–14; cf. Bockmuehl, "Recovering Vocation," 84, 92.

144. Bockmuehl, "Der sendende Herr," 190; cf. *WM*, 165.

145. Bockmuehl, "Aktualität," 313.

146. German original title: *Die Aktualität des Pietismus*. The book is a collection of articles by Bockmuehl that had been published in 1983 and 1984 in the Christian magazine *idea-spektrum*. References are to the reprint in *DH*.

147. Bockmuehl refers particularly to Spener, the "father of Pietism" (*DH*, 328). In the context of mission he mentions August Hermann Francke and Christian Friedrich Spittler (*DH*, 313).

148. Bockmuehl, "Aktualität," 313, 323–29; cf. *GG*, 507; *LbG*, 98.

Guidance by the Spirit

Since Bockmuehl devotes his last book, *Listening to the God who Speaks*, to the portrayal of his understanding of guidance, this seems a good place to begin our search for pietistic influences on Bockmuehl with regard to this topic. Although Bockmuehl's only explicit reference to a Pietist in this book is to the biblical scholar Johann Albrecht Bengel, Arthur D. Thomas correctly remarks that we can "discern a spirituality nurtured by the devotional practices of the Pietists."[149]

When turning our attention to Bockmuehl's other works, especially his book *Law and Spirit*, we discover that Bockmuehl draws on several Pietists for support when presenting his understanding of direct guidance by the Spirit. He does this in contrast to the concept of the Protestant milieu that, according to Bockmuehl, reduces guidance to divine providence.[150] After analyzing hymns by Pietists such as Nikolaus L. von Zinzendorf and Paul Gerhardt, he concludes that they had a balanced view of guidance.[151] In fact, they not only believed that the Holy Spirit guides through particular circumstances and the commandment of God, but also "through actual instruction, through 'council' or through the inspiration of love and the Spirit of God respectively."[152] Hence, it should not come as a surprise that Bockmuehl praises those Pietists particularly for their juxtaposition of inspiration and Scripture as means of the Spirit's guidance.[153] It is notable that his concept of the inner testimony of the Holy Spirit alongside Scripture, yet not contrary to Scripture, can also be found in Spener's and Francke's writings, as some scholars suggest.[154] Spener, for instance,

---

149. Thomas, "Spirituality of Klaus Bockmuehl: Part One," 4. Concerning the use of Scripture for prayer and meditation, Thomas observes similarities between Francke's concept outlined in his "Short Course of Instructions on How Holy Scripture Ought to Be Read For One's True Edification" and Bockmuehl's in his book *LG*. This assumption is supported by the fact that Bockmuehl was responsible for the publication of Francke's Treatise in *Crux*. Cf. Thomas, "Spirituality of Klaus Bockmuehl: Part One," 4–5.

150. Cf. *GG*, 411, 473–82; *SU*, 33.

151. Cf. *GG*, 473, 481–82. Bockmuehl's analysis, at least of Zinzendorf, is supported by the following statement by Bosch: "Typical of Zinzendorf's thinking was the idea of improvising, of remaining open to the guidance of the Spirit and being willing to try something novel or to move on to new challenges" (Bosch, *Transforming Mission*, 254).

152. *GG*, 480.

153. Cf. *GG*, 480, 487; *LbG*, 50, 54.

154. According to Brown, "it is apparent that both Spener and Francke allowed the possibility of direct special revelations apart from the Bible. From the perspective

maintained that God at times gives an inner impulse and command to do good.[155]

Hence, we agree with Haizmann that we can find "in Spener exactly what Klaus Bockmuehl was missing in the ethics of the confessional writings: a pneumatologically formulated situation ethics."[156] We can, therefore, reasonably assume that Bockmuehl found a positive affirmation of his concept of guidance in Spener. We conclude with a quotation from a former colleague of Bockmuehl at Regent College, James I. Packer, who rightly believes that Bockmuehl "was a pietist in the noble sense in which Spener, Francke, Whitefield and Wesley, Edwards and Brainerd, were pietists: That is to say, he was as far as possible from complacency, obscurantism, sectarianism, and sloth, and he was moved by his personal knowledge of God's grace and forgiveness to all kinds of compassionate efforts for others' benefit."[157]

Different Twentieth Century Theologians

In this chapter we shall look more closely at the influence of great twentieth-century theologians such as Adolf Schlatter, Emil Brunner, and Karl Barth on Bockmuehl. Although Bockmuehl engages with many different theologians, we will have to confine ourselves to those whose influence upon Bockmuehl appears to have been most significant in shaping his understanding of ethics and pneumatology. Particularly interesting is the fact that Bockmuehl, when giving an account of his holidays in 1982, mentions that he had read the autobiography of Schlatter as well as parts of Barth's *Church Dogmatics*.[158]

---

of the Pietist, however, all such revelations were required to conform to Scripture. The Bible must at all times remain the norm in interpreting the content . . . Instead of allowing mystical experiences to undermine the authority of the canon as their opponents feared, the Pietists looked upon Biblical study as a real source of experience. They were convinced that the application of the Biblical test to all revelations guarded sufficiently against undesirable subjective tendencies" (Brown, *Pietism*, 71; cf. 70, 106; M. Schmidt, "Spener und Luther," 123).

155. Cf. Rüttgardt, *Heiliges Leben*, 86–87.

156. Haizmann, "Ethik," 99; cf. Rüttgardt, *Heiliges Leben*, 95–96.

157. Packer, "Introduction," viii; cf. Swarat, "Gesetz und Geist," 39.

158. Cf. Bockmuehl, "Quiet Holidays," n.p. For our purposes here we are most interested in these three theologians as their influence on Bockmuehl seems to be the greatest in comparison with other biblical theologians. However, we should at least mention Niels H. Søe on whom Bockmuehl draws in some of his writings and whose ethics Bockmuehl praises as being prudent and widespread (cf. *GG*, 296, 508;

Adolf Schlatter

When we turn to Schlatter, we find that Bockmuehl introduces him, first of all, as being "the great exegete of the first half of the twentieth century"[159] and, secondly, as being an "excellent systematic theologian"[160] whose theology still has relevance in the present. In fact, besides promoting the reprint of some of Schlatter's works, he published a book on Schlatter and encouraged other theologians to study him in depth.[161] In the introduction to his book *The Topical Relevance of the Theology of Adolf Schlatter (Die Aktualität der Theologie Adolf Schlatters)* Bockmuehl summarizes concisely the reason for dealing with Schlatter: "Whoever finds himself in need of a general revision of the modern Protestant worldview, discovers in Schlatter an alternative, the examination of which yields a rich reward."[162]

However, we must acknowledge that, as Dintaman points out, "the theological work and influence of Adolf Schaltter is one of the great enigmas of twentieth-century theology. Here is a man who is regarded by many as one of the most original and significant theologians of his time, and yet

---

Bockmuehl, "Revolution," 59; Bockmuehl, "Zur Frage nach der Maßgeblichkeit," 30). When turning to Jürgen Moltmann, whom Bockmuehl served as a teaching assistant for three years, we might assume that, though Bockmuehl disagreed with Moltmann on a variety of issues, he shaped Bockmuehl's understanding of social ethics in some way or other, though he was not the only influential source. As mentioned above, Bockmuehl was confronted with social issues from an early stage due to the post-war situation. However, similar to Moltmann, Bockmuehl held the view that Christians should engage in social-political matters and he did not hesitate to challenge the contemporary pietistic movement regarding this topic. (Cf. Bockmuehl, "Aktualität," 327–32). It is also worth noting that Moltmann, as well as Bockmuehl, concerned himself with Marxism and with the reality and the implications of the Christian belief. Cf. Bockmuehl, "Kommunismus," 561.

159. *CM*, 30. Later, in the same book, he also refers to Schlatter as being "one of the two or three most eminent theologians of our century" (ibid., 71). See also Bockmuehl, "Situation Ethics," 49; *UG*, 146.

160. Bockmuehl, "Vorwort des Herausgebers," 2.

161. In the series "Theologie und Dienst," of which Bockmuehl was an editor besides others, there are several reprints of Schlatter's works; cf. Schlatter, *Atheistische Methoden in der Theologie*; Schlatter, *Die Gabe des Christus: Eine Auslegung der Bergpredigt*. Very revealing is the foreword of the reprint of Schlatter's book on service [*Dienst*], in which Neuer writes: "We owe thanks to the ethicist Klaus Bockmühl, who died in 1989, for initiating the reprint of the work, which he highly valued but which had been out of print for a long time" (Neuer, "Einführung," 7).

162. Bockmuehl, "Vorwort des Herausgebers," 3–4.

PART ONE—Bockmuehl's Theological Work

his voluminous writings were never interpreted into English."[163] Fortunately, in the past few years, several theologians have begun to discover the potential in Schlatter's works and have taken an interest in making them accessible to the English-speaking world.[164] Nevertheless, before displaying the parallels and similarities between Schlatter's and Bockmuehl's theology, a brief portrayal of Schlatter's life and work might help access Schlatter's unique theology. To this we now turn.

Excursus: Adolf Schlatter

Adolf Schlatter was born in St. Gallen/Switzerland in 1852 as the seventh child of Hektor Stephan and Wilhelmine Schlatter.[165] He grew up in a Christian family in which he saw love lived out in daily life. As a result, he believed, first, in the importance of the Bible for faith as well as for life and logical thinking, secondly, in the priority of the actual *faith* of the believer over the *content* of faith (which lead to an ecumenical openness), and finally, in the positive combination of creation and salvation.[166]

In 1871, he began to study theology, philosophy, history, and Arabic, first in Basel, then later in Tübingen, where Johann Tobias Beck's biblical theology made a great impact on him. Due to the fact that he passed his theological exams with distinction in 1875, he was offered a scholarship to proceed with a doctoral thesis. However, as he was determined to become a pastor, he served different churches in Switzerland for five years. During this time, he was engaged in a study of the writings of Franz von Baader, a Catholic philosopher and lay-theologian. In 1878, he married Susanna, née Schoop, and they had two sons and three daughters.

Due to the fact that pietistic circles in Bern appealed to him to become a professor at the mainly liberal university in Bern, he left his pastoral work and wrote a "doctoral dissertation (*Habilitation*)"[167] in June 1880, followed by a grueling exam procedure in December; in his case, this consisted of eight essays and oral examinations in five of the main subjects. In Janu-

---

163. Dintaman, *Creative Grace*, xi. Theologians who appreciate Schlatter's works are, for example, Bultmann, Käsemann, Fuchs, Barth, Stuhlmacher (ibid.).

164. Cf. Yarbrough, "Translator's Preface," 9, 11; Gasque, "The Promise of Adolf Schlatter," 21. For further bibliographical information concerning English translations or English books on Schlatter, see Neuer, "Einführung," 6.

165. Cf. Neuer, *Adolf Schlatter. A Biography*, 23–24.

166. Cf. Neuer, "Schlatter, Adolf," 135.

167. Neuer, *Adolf Schlatter. A Biography*, 71.

Theological and Spiritual Influences on Bockmuehl

ary 1881, he received permission to teach.[168] Six years later, he accepted an invitation to lecture in New Testament at Greifswald University and was blessed by the fruitful personal friendship with Hermann Cremer, a Lutheran biblical theologian, despite their different denominational backgrounds. Both tried to establish a biblical reformatory theology as an alternative to the prevailing "school" founded by Ritschl. Unfortunately, this inspiring and delightful time at Greifswald came to a close after five years when Schlatter felt compelled to follow the call of the university of Berlin to become a professor of systematic theology. Particularly interesting is the fact that this call from the *Emperor Wilhelm II* can be traced back to positive church circles in Berlin feeling the need for someone to represent the viewpoint of the church as an alternative to Adolf von Harnack who held a critical position with regard to the Apostles' creed. Unexpectedly, Harnack welcomed Schlatter right from the beginning, and they were on good terms throughout his time there.[169] Five years later Schlatter accepted the offer of becoming a professor for New Testament at Tübingen University, though he also lectured in systematic theology. It was in Tübingen that he "exerted an intellectual and spiritual influence that can barely be gauged. Students streamed to Tübingen from both Germany and elsewhere to hear him, so that at times his lectures were attended by more than six hundred. For many these lectures became a fascinating experience."[170]

Besides lecturing, he gave talks at different conferences, preached regularly, and had daily consultation hours for the students, which included a pastoral dimension.[171] It is therefore astounding that in spite of all these activities he was still able to write an extensive number of books and articles, particularly during his time in Tübingen (about 400 published works) and after retiring from his lecturing post at the age of 78. As his main focus was on the exegesis of the New Testament, he first published a ten-volume commentary covering the whole New Testament designed for lay church workers. Unfortunately, these works often brought him the reputation of being merely a naïve, conservative theologian who wrote for the pietistic milieu.[172] That this is not the case can be seen by the fact that

168. Cf. ibid., 71–76. Neuer, *Adolf Schlatter. Ein Leben*, 147, 149, 151, 155.

169. Cf. Neuer, *Schlatter. Ein Leben*, 292–95, 305. How much Schlatter valued the friendship and exchange with Cremer can be seen by the fact that he declined offers from the universities of Heidelberg (1890), Bonn (1890), and Marburg (1892). Cf. Neuer, *Schlatter. Ein Leben*, 289–91.

170. Neuer, *Adolf Schlatter. A Biography*, 130.

171. Cf. ibid., 137–41; Neuer, "Schlatter, Adolf," 137.

172. Cf. Dintaman, *Creative Grace*, xiii, 17.

PART ONE—Bockmuehl's Theological Work

he also published nine voluminous scientific New Testament commentaries in which he included many references to Palestinian and Hellenistic Judaism. Furthermore, that he engaged with philosophical and theological topics in depth, composing, for instance, a *Metaphysics* and a voluminous *Dogmatics* and *Ethics*, establishes him as a theologian who has to be taken seriously.[173]

At the age of 85, after having completed a large devotional book on *Do we know Jesus?*, Schlatter's fruitful productivity was impeded by health problems.[174] His life ended "quietly and peacefully"[175] in May 1938.

Having outlined Schlatter's life and work, we now turn to his influence upon Bockmuehl. As already noted above, Bockmuehl regarded Schlatter as an outstanding exegete. He particularly commended the commentaries on *Matthew, Romans,* and the *Epistles to the Corinthians* to his students, as they "are especially of lasting value."[176] It is therefore hardly surprising to discover that Bockmuehl referred to these three commentaries several times to substantiate his own view. Yet, more important for our concern is the fact that Bockmuehl considered Schlatter to be "absolutely essential for systematics."[177] One outstanding feature of Schlatter's systematic theology is his originality, as he did not let his theology be confined by "the dogmatic decisions of the Reformation nor by those of post-Enlightenment Neo-Protestantism";[178] instead, he only felt bound by the standards of Scripture. Beyond this, according to Bockmuehl, Schlatter's dogmatics "offers us the rare picture of a non-Kantian theology; it is as if for a brief moment we were given a glimpse of the other side of the moon."[179] Indeed, contrary to most contemporary dogmatics, Schlatter did not hesitate to expound a *theology of perception,*[180] as he held the firm conviction that "Christian

---

173. Cf. Neuer, "Schlatter, Adolf," 138–40. Schlatter, *Metaphysik. Eine Skizze*; Schlatter, *Das christliche Dogma*; Schlatter, *Die christliche Ethik*.

174. This book by Schlatter was first published as *Kennen wir Jesus?* in 1937.

175. Neuer, *Adolf Schlatter. A Biography*, 153.

176. Bockmuehl, "Introduction," 55, cf. *VG*, 70.

177. Bockmuehl, "Introduction," 55.

178. Bockmuehl, "Wahrnehmung," 96.

179. Ibid. Schlatter's *Metaphysik* is decisive as philosophical background for his Dogmatics since it is there that he develops his understanding of reality. Neuer, "Schlatter, Adolf," 140.

180. In *Briefe über das Christliche Dogma*, Schlatter uses different terms for his

Theological and Spiritual Influences on Bockmuehl

theology is not based on postulates of faith that cannot be verified but on *facts* that can be rationally apprehended and that constitute the Christian faith."[181]

Hence, God's reality in this world is perceivable when observing nature, mankind, and history, since God revealed himself in creation, and in the life and work of Jesus Christ.[182] Consequently, according to Schlatter, history and the work of the Spirit are indissolubly united as Bockmuehl points out in his article on "the perception of history in the Dogmatics of Adolf Schlatter."[183] Important for Schlatter's concept is, nevertheless, that Scripture operates as a corrective to theological cognition. Thus, a theology based on perception and experience is not contradictory to the authority of Scripture, since the latter is the only source for the self-revelation of God in Christ.

When turning to Bockmuehl's works, there is little doubt that he not only approved of Schlatter's concept of perception but, moreover, tried to apply it accordingly. In his book *The Challenge of Marxism* he explicitly refers to Schlatter as the one who "always reminded scholars of the need for perception before thinking or theorizing"[184] in order to back up his own approach. Furthermore, it is highly revealing that in the final key chapter of *The Unreal God* Bockmuehl argues for the perceptibility of God's Work in this world, after bringing to light Bultmann's and Barth's tendency to exclude God from the realm of reality in earlier chapters.[185] Not surprisingly, he refers to Schlatter as his main advocate when asserting that God's work is manifest in this world. And, contrary to Bultmann and Barth, who "regarded history, experience, and practice—in short, all the evidence of God's work—as almost theologically illegitimate,"[186] Bockmuehl agrees with Schlatter on the perceptibility of God's work in each of these domains.[187]

---

theology such as "observing theology" and "empirical theology" (77). Yet, considering the term "perception," he writes: "I, for my part, describe the formula 'perception' as being applicable for my method and goal; it characterizes what I have in mind" (76). Cf. Neuer, "Schlatter, Adolf," 139.

181. Neuer, *Zusammenhang*, 44; cf. Schlatter, *Ethik*, 41–44; Bockmuehl, "Wahrnehmung," 106–7.

182. Cf. Neuer, *Dogmatik*, 45.

183. Cf. Bockmuehl, "Wahrnehmung," 105–6, 109, 112.

184. *CM*, 71.

185. Cf. *UG*, 144–62.

186. *UG*, 110.

187. Cf. Bockmuehl, "Wahrnehmung," 96–112, concerning history; *UG*, 146

PART ONE—Bockmuehl's Theological Work

It is particularly interesting for our purposes to take a closer look at the implications of this concept for pneumatology and ethics. According to Schlatter, "[t]he Spirit, who is in himself invisible, is made visible by his operations."[188] Neuer suggests that "[t]he conviction that the work of the Spirit is visible and perceptible is for Schlatter's dogmatic-ethical thinking of great importance. According to Schlatter, a pneumatology that denies the perceptibility of the Holy Spirit in humans or forbids the wish to perceive the work of the Spirit in one's personal life falls short of the standard of the New Testament."[189]

We can, therefore, conclude that in Schlatter's view ethics and pneumatology are inseparable since the Holy Spirit works in the life of the individual believer in a perceivable way. Thus, the work of the Holy Spirit is indispensable for Christian ethics—so much so that without the pre-condition of the Holy Spirit, Schlatter's concept of a distinct *Christian* ethics is inconceivable. Neuer points out that "[t]he Christian character of ethics depends, according to Schlatter, on the fact that it is *pneumatic ethics*, i.e., that it gives comprehensive instructions how walking in the Spirit is accomplished in concrete terms. Schlatter took remarkable pains to take into account the pneumatic character of the Christian ethos."[190] While Schlatter himself does not use the term "pneumatic ethics," there can be no doubt that the term is entirely appropriate as a summary of his ethical concept, as the following quotation by Schlatter shows: "Christian ethics can be summarized in the sentence: 'Walk by the Spirit,' Gal 5:16."[191] Although Schlatter acknowledges the law's lasting validity, he demonstrates that a pneumatic ethic cannot be limited to the law.[192]

Before portraying Schlatter's pneumatic ethics in more detail, we shall compare what we have established thus far with Bockmuehl's concept

---

concerning experience; Schlatter, *Ethik*, 43, 376n1, and Bockmuehl, "Leiblichkeit," 45, concerning practice.

188. Schlatter, *Paulus der Bote Jesu*, 338; English translation by Bockmuehl in *UG*, 146.

189. Neuer, *Dogmatik*, 207; cf. Schlatter, "Noch ein Wort," 109.

190. Neuer, *Dogmatik*, 212; cf. ibid., 211.

191. Schlatter, *Ethik*, 22. Neuer describes Schlatter's ethics in general as a redemption ethic since it presupposes the redemptive work of Jesus. Yet, "[i]ts distinctive quality as salvation ethics reveals itself in the fact that as *pneumatic* ethics it presupposes the Holy Spirit . . . , as *faith* ethics the Christian faith . . . , as *ethica regenitorum* the new existence of human beings reconciled with God . . . and as *christocentric ethics* fellowship with Jesus Christ as Lord and redeemer of the believer" (Neuer, *Dogmatik*, 241). For our purposes here we are most interested in Schlatter's pneumatic ethics.

192. Cf. Schlatter, *Ethik*, 25, 37; Neuer, "Schöpfung und Gesetz," 129.

Theological and Spiritual Influences on Bockmuehl

of ethics. Neuer, for instance, draws attention to the fact that "Schlatter's twofold adherence—on the one hand, to the continuing validity of the law, and, on the other hand, to the christocentric-pneumatic character of the Christian ethos that transcends any ethics of law—finds an impressive confirmation in the seminal work *Law and Spirit* by Klaus Bockmuehl."[193] Particularly interesting is the fact that Bockmuehl insists on the necessity of an "ethic of the Spirit"[194] since, for him, the main reason for the insufficiency of mainstream Protestant ethics is a deficient pneumatology in Protestantism. Thus, he aims at a "re-gaining of the pneumatic dimension of New Testament ethics (love for God, guidance of the Spirit, works beyond the duty of the law etc.)."[195] It is striking how much Bockmuehl owes to Schlatter with regard to the rediscovery of the pneumatic dimension, including love toward God, guidance by the Spirit, and works of supererogation, since Schlatter brought precisely these themes back into focus.[196] Similarly, Bockmuehl follows Schlatter in tracing back the weakness of Reformation ethics not just to Lutheran Orthodoxy but also to Luther's own theology. Not many people before Schlatter dared to criticize Luther so openly. It is therefore worthwhile to take a closer look at Schlatter's criticism, particularly since Bockmuehl strongly supported it:[197] "The following questions gripped me forcibly: why were tensions allowed to develop between faith directed toward God and love directed toward God? Was Luther's reasoning partly responsible for these tensions? How does the weakness of our church ethics relate to these tensions?"[198]

According to Schlatter, Protestant theology clearly defined what it meant by *believing* in God, whereas their understanding of *loving God* remained rather vague "as if it was more difficult, 'more mystical,' even more unnatural to love God than to believe in him."[199] Not surprisingly, Schlatter himself became aware of the insufficiency of the doctrine of love in Protestant theology when studying the Catholic lay theologian Franz von

---

193. Neuer, "Schöpfung und Gesetz," 130.

194. *GG*, 514; cf. 517.

195. Neuer, "Bockmühl, Klaus," 287. In *GG*, Bockmuehl clearly states that his main concern is to outline the importance of pneumatology for ethics (cf. 22). Thus, he examines the writings of the Reformation theology as to whether or not they embrace a "pneumatological personal and situational ethics" (418). However, in his final chapter, Bockmuehl draws attention to the fact that we have to recover an "ethical pneumatology" (520), a pneumatology that includes ethical topics such as guidance by the Spirit.

196. Cf. *GG*, 291, 300.

197. Cf. Bockmuehl, "Introduction," 60–61; *CM*, 30.

198. Schlatter, *Rückblick*, 90.

199. Schlatter, *Der Dienst*, 68. Cf. *GG*, 507–8.

Baader. Consequently, Schlatter started to inquire into the theological and historical roots of this deficiency in order to regain a biblical theology of love that includes the realm of ethics.[200] Hence, when examining the interrelation between love and service, he came to the following conclusion: "If a clear detailing of the notion of love is missing, then this implies actually that the attention given to the service of God continues to be limited. For love and service belong together. Love equals willingness to serve; with service, love becomes action."[201]

Schlatter arrived at his definition of love as "willingness to serve" by ascertaining that, according to Scripture, "God's love creates our love; his will desires our good will; his work consists in making us effective."[202] Thus, God not only forgives our sins but also equips us with love in order to be able to serve him. Since the relation between faith and service, i.e., good works, is often seen as being an antithesis in the Reformation tradition, we will take a closer look at how Schlatter resolves this tension: "[B]ecause faith is effective and is our attachment to God, because it *is* righteousness, belonging to Christ, and possession of the Holy Spirit, we are not only given the strength but also *the will and the duty* to serve."[203] Hence, it is precisely God's purpose for our life that we might love and serve him. Service, consequently, should not be reduced to keeping the commandments or avoiding evil as these are rather self-centered, negative, and minimal aims for service. Rather, according to Schlatter, the positive aims of service are "the restoration of that which is depraved, the healing of the affliction that we suffer from."[204] Due to the fact that the Reformation tradition neglected these positive aims, Protestant ethics became mainly a passive ethics of duties instead of an ethic of love that holds both aims together—viz., to fulfill what is required but, beyond that, to carry out the impulse of love which includes to strive unselfishly and spontaneously for the best of the other.[205]

Even though Schlatter himself did not specify the latter as works of supererogation, in contrast to Bockmuehl, from the content and from the

200. Cf. Neuer, "Einführung," 8, 12; Neuer, *Dogmatik*, 318; Neuer, "Die ökumenische Bedeutung," 76–77.

201. Schlatter, *Der Dienst*, 68.

202. Schlatter, *Ethik*, 117.

203. Schlatter, "Noch ein Wort," 101. See also Schlatter, *Dogma*, 440, 513.

204. Schlatter, *Der Dienst*, 60; cf. ibid., 66; for Bockmuehl on this issue, see, for example, *Conservation and Lifestyle*, 17.

205. Cf. Schlatter, *Der Dienst*, 74; Schlatter, *Ethik*, 76, 121; Neuer, "Schöpfung und Gesetz," 126. Bockmuehl argues similarly in *GG*, 306–8, 510–11.

Theological and Spiritual Influences on Bockmuehl

references made to Schlatter there can be little doubt that Bockmuehl was strongly influenced by him concerning the positive definition of service of God and the criticism of Reformation ethics. In a review on *Law and Spirit*, Swarat contends: "With this examination B[ockmuehl] is basically implementing a program that Adolf Schlatter outlined in 1897 under the heading of 'The service of the Christian in the older Dogmatics'; that is why Schlatter is quoted several times in a positive way."[206]

If this is the case, Bockmuehl's concern for the rediscovery of the Holy Spirit for Christian ethics owes much to Schlatter's exposition of Christian service. In fact, when expounding the role of the Holy Spirit in the Protestant milieu, Bockmuehl refers again and again to Schlatter, agreeing with him, for instance, that as long as there is an insufficient doctrine of service, the doctrine of the Holy Spirit will inevitably suffer as well.[207] One indication of a deficient doctrine of the Holy Spirit in Protestant ethics was, for Schlatter, the loss of the illuminating work of the Holy Spirit in the believer, including personal guidance in daily life; this can be traced back to the "anxiety the church has always felt regarding pneumatology, so that she preferred to lock away the Spirit in the sacrament and the word of the Apostle when, in fact, the Spirit, as certainly as he is the Spirit, carries out his work in our inner life."[208] Schlatter goes on to argue that, due to this fear, Protestantism reduced the work of the Holy Spirit to the authority of the ordained minister. As a result, it created a passive church that expected God's guidance solely from the pastor.[209] In turn, Schlatter calls for a balanced biblical view that takes into account the individual and specific *guidance of the Holy Spirit* as long as it is in accordance with Scripture; he maintains this argument because he was convinced "that God does not only guide us externally but also internally, he does not only instruct us through offices but also through the Spirit, and he does not subject us to human beings but calls everyone to himself through his truth and grace."[210] If this is true not only for the leaders of the church but for every single believer, there can be no doubt, according to Schlatter, that *mission* is not just a commitment solely entrusted to the office but rather to the whole church. In fact, since every Christian has

---

206. Swarat, "Gesetz," 37.
207. Cf. *GG*, 501; Schlatter, "Zur Förderung christlicher Theologie," 33.
208. Schlatter, "Noch ein Wort," 120.
209. Cf. Schlatter, *Der Dienst*, 14, 33; *GG*, 231, 502; *VG*, 78.
210. Schlatter, *Ethik*, 300; cf. Schlatter, *Der Evangelist Matthäus*, 104; Schlatter, *Erläuterungen zum Neuen Testament*, 138.

Part One—Bockmuehl's Theological Work

received God's love and guidance through the Holy Spirit, "everyone of us [has] the power to approach and help those who are in distress and those who have strayed."[211] With regard to mission, this implies that it is not only through *proclamation* but also through practical service that the Gospel unfolds its full power and attracts people to put their trust in God.[212] Since Bockmuehl's emphasis on this two-fold interpretation of mission can be found in many of his publications, it is particularly revealing to discover the same approach already in Schlatter's ethics. Moreover, given the fact that Bockmuehl appeals to Schlatter for support of his view on mission and ethics, this suggests that Bockmuehl was to a great extent influenced by Schlatter in this regard. Even more interesting is the fact that both draw attention to the fact that mission is part of ethics.[213] Schlatter, for instance, includes such topics as "evangelism a) The task for all . . . b) The tools for work"[214] and in a later chapter, "The other religions a) The responsibility toward mission . . . b) The difficulties that have to be overcome by mission"[215] in his exposition of Christian ethics.

Even though it would be worthwhile to examine further similarities and parallels, such as their common "dedication to biblical renewal of theology and church,"[216] their criticism of dialectic theology concerning its negligence of history, experience, and ethics,[217] and such as their appreciation of nature,[218] this would go beyond the limits of our current study.

Nevertheless, one last parallel should be mentioned as this leads us to another theologian. Schlatter, as well as Bockmuehl, supported Brunner's concept of natural revelation with its emphasis on the perceptibility of God's work in the world. To this theologian we now turn our attention.

---

211. Schlatter, *Ethik*, 203; cf. 200–203, 248; Schlatter, "Die Dienstpflicht des Christen," 124–5; Schlatter, *Der Dienst*, 30–31. Bockmuehl, "Der sendende Herr," 186–87, Bockmuehl refers to Schlatter as his advocate regarding this issue.

212. Cf. Bockmuehl, "Der sendende Herr," 190; Schlatter, *Ethik*, 207.

213. For Bockmuehl's approach, see, for instance, *GG*, 516–17; "Der sendende Herr," 190; *WM*, 164–5.

214. Schlatter, *Ethik*, 200, 204; cf. ibid., 200–209.

215. Schlatter, *Ethik*, 242, 245; cf. ibid., 242–48.

216. Neuer, *Adolf Schlatter. A Biography*, 153; with regard to Bockmuehl, see, for instance, Burkhardt, "Zur Einführung," 5; Frische, "Zur Bockmühl-Werk-Ausgabe," xi.

217. Cf. Neuer, "Schlatter, Adolf," 137; *UG*, 77–88.

218. Cf. Neuer, "Naturtheologie," 243, 247–48; *CaL*, 8, 10.

Emil Brunner

According to Bockmuehl, it was Brunner who played a decisive part in linking the reality of God's work with the doctrine of the Holy Spirit: "The question he raised has often enough been viewed with suspicion in the history of the official German Protestant theology. It concerns the perceptibility of the works of God in a fundamental way regardless of the dictates of the theological transcendentalists. That he, furthermore, linked it to the doctrine of the work of the Holy Spirit—which is being similarly suppressed by us—is an extraordinary achievement of Emil Brunner."[219]

What is interesting to note is that Brunner started to write on the work of the Holy Spirit and its ethical impact after a personal encounter with the Oxford Group movement in 1932.[220] Since Bockmuehl's understanding of the Holy Spirit, particularly regarding the guidance of the Holy Spirit and ethics, is to a great extent shaped by the Oxford Group movement, it is more likely that the similarities between both can be traced back to their common appreciation of this movement rather than to Brunner's direct influence on Bockmuehl. Thus, we shall look at the Oxford Group and its influence on Bockmuehl in a later chapter. Furthermore, even though Bockmuehl refers to Brunner approvingly concerning the perceptibility of God's work and linking it with the doctrine of the Holy Spirit, he distances himself clearly from Brunner with regard to other issues such as the role of the law for Christians.[221] We may conclude that Schlatter's influence on Bockmuehl appears to have been in shaping his understanding of ethics and the Holy Spirit, besides other areas, whereas Brunner seems to have confirmed Bockmuehl's conviction of the need to rediscover the Holy Spirit for Christian ethics including the experiencing of the works of the Holy Spirit.

---

219. Cf. *GiE*, 12. For Schlatter, see Neuer, "Schlatter, Adolf," 137. For Brunner, see Brunner, *Vom Werk des Heiligen Geistes*, 53; Brunner, *Die Kirchen*, 39, 51–52.

220. Cf. *VG*, 149; Brunner, "Meine Begegnung mit der Oxforder Gruppenbewegung," 268, 270, 273, 277, 281.

221. Cf. *GG*, 524, 526. However, Bockmuehl agrees with Søe that Brunner, despite his tendencies to minimise the role of the law, "never turns out a *Situationsethiker.*" Søe, "The Personal Ethics of Emil Brunner," 255. Cf. *GiE*, 116. Brunner himself acknowledges that "when we ask about the relation of these Commandments to the one Divine Commandment, we see that they are authentic 'expositions' of the One Commandment... 'The Commandments' are the God-given examples of what His will and His love mean in the concrete situations of life" (Brunner, *The Divine Imperative*, 135).

Part One—Bockmuehl's Theological Work

Karl Barth

When turning to Barth's theological influence on Bockmuehl, we are left with the impression that it is of an ambiguous nature. On the one hand, Bockmuehl admired Barth throughout his entire life, calling him "the greatest theologian of the century";[222] yet, on the other hand, he did not shrink from criticizing him frequently in his publications. In his lecture on the *Introduction to the Theology of the (Nineteenth and) Twentieth Century*, Bockmuehl explains this two-fold reaction himself: "My seminars have on occasion been called the 'Karl Barth Appreciation Society.' Others have quoted me as saying, 'All theology is but a footnote to Karl Barth.' But it is not true. I am a lapsed Barthian. I try to 'Test everything. Hold on to the good' . . . and try to become no earthly man's uncritical disciple. The first thing is that a clear acknowledgement of the different phases needs to be made."[223]

Before turning to Bockmuehl's distinction between these different phases in Barth's understanding of the reality of God, let us examine the reasons for Bockmuehl's extensive engagement with Barth's theology. First of all, this engagement was very likely due to the fact that he had visited Barth's seminars and lectures while studying at Basel University and had become acquainted with him. Secondly, since Barth had already gained a high theological reputation during his lifetime and was generally regarded as one of the most influential theologians of the twentieth century, it became a necessity to interact with him.[224] Thirdly, Barth was one of the few theologians who dared to stand up to liberalism. According to Bockmuehl, "Barth's life was a nodal point in the history of theology, a moment of special illumination, so that the cause of theology caught the attention of a larger audience. Seen in perspective, two elements of his theological contribution are particularly noteworthy and of continuing relevance: 1) his passion for the primacy of God, and 2) his struggle in recovering the reality of God."[225] In what follows, we will first take a closer look at these two issues before drawing more parallels.

---

222. Bockmuehl, "Introduction," 100, cf. *VG*, 131.
223. Bockmuehl, "Introduction," 103, cf. *VG*, 134.
224. Cf. Mueller, *Karl Barth*, 143.
225. Bockmuehl, "Karl Barth," 28.

Theological and Spiritual Influences on Bockmuehl

THE PRIMACY AND REALITY OF GOD

Barth's greatest contribution was, according to Bockmuehl, his concern for the *primacy of God in the church and in theology*. Thus, Barth drew attention to the fact that a person's relationship with God is more important than any political, social, or cultural problem. Even in times of political turbulence, Barth contended publicly that the primary task of the church should be to "let God be God,"[226] to listen to the voice of Jesus Christ and preach the Word of God.[227]

Bockmuehl's admiration for Barth's steadfastness is revealed in the following statement: "One of the great services Karl Barth rendered to the church was when he insisted in 1933 on theology's task to keep the God question first, even in view of the demand of 'national resurrection of Germany' for attention and assent."[228] In a personal conversation with Karl Barth in 1963, Bockmuehl told him that he longed for someone who would do the same for the current generation what Barth had done for his generation, particularly during the National-socialist rule. Barth responded by requesting that Bockmuehl do it himself. Even though Bockmuehl felt inadequate for this task, he accepted it as a calling from God.[229] Particularly in 1968, while a student pastor at Heidelberg University, Bockmuehl faced the fact that many of the student leaders in his congregation wanted to set aside the God question during the time of crisis. Yet, Bockmuehl did not give in. As a consequence, "[h]is fearless commitment to the priority of the question about God lost him his student pastorate in Heidelberg in the inferno of the neo-Marxist student revolution."[230]

We should furthermore note that, according to Bockmuehl, Barth's concern for the primacy of God springs directly from the first commandment, which is "particularly relevant in times of worldliness of the people of God."[231] The extent to which Bockmuehl shared Barth's engagement for the primacy of God will become even clearer when we turn to Bockmuehl's main theological concerns in a later chapter.

Barth's influence on Bockmuehl can also be found concerning *the understanding of the reality of God*. However, the influence here is of a

226. Ibid. Cf. *CM*, 66.
227. Cf. Bockmuehl, "Secularism and Theology," 52.
228. Bockmuehl, "God and Other 'Forgotten Factors,'" 48.
229. Cf. letter from Bockmuehl to P. Engelbert Heller and Martin-Eckart Fuchs, March 5, 1965; cf. Hofmann, "Revolutionär," 21.
230. Burkhardt, "Handeln aus dem Hören," 28; cf. *UG*, 134.
231. Bockmuehl, "Karl Barth," 29; cf. Bockmuehl, "Der sendende Herr," 181–83.

Part One—Bockmuehl's Theological Work

rather ambiguous nature since Bockmuehl distinguishes mainly between two phases in Barth's understanding of the reality of God and evaluates them very differently. According to Bockmuehl, the early Barth held the view that God's actions in nature, history, or the Christian life cannot be observed or experienced, whereas later in life Barth made statements about the concrete and perceivable reality of God's actions in this world.[232] In order to ascertain Bockmuehl's evaluation and assessment of the different phases, let us look at his own assertion: "He [Barth] is indeed to be 'loved and honored' for having finally overthrown the idol of 'non-observability' set up by himself and others. Not often in our own or other theological generations have we been taught the reality of God's work as clearly as by him."[233] This clearly reveals Bockmuehl's positive view of the second phase regarding Barth's understanding of the reality of God.[234] According to Bockmuehl, Barth himself acknowledged a change in his theology in the 1956 lecture "The Humanity of God."[235] Comparing his earlier theology with a half-moon, he admits that the emphasis on the deity of God was only "partially right"[236] and has to be complemented by the humanity of God, which is most visible in Jesus Christ. His intention behind emphasizing the humanity of God can best be seen in the following statement: "Who God is and what He is in His deity He proves and reveals not in a vacuum as a divine being-for-Himself, but precisely and authentically in the fact that He exists, speaks, and acts as the *partner* of man, though of course as the absolutely superior partner."[237]

Thus, the emphasis in Barth's theology shifts from the "otherness" of God to the "togetherness"[238] of God and man. Furthermore, this implies that God's actions in our world are perceivable since, as Barth puts it, "[w]e believe the Church . . . as the place where God's glory wills to dwell

232. Cf. Bockmuehl, "Wende, 280–90. Bockmuehl, furthermore, draws attention to the fact that traces of Barth's later understanding of the reality of God can already partly be found in his pre-dialectical writings. Cf. *UG*, 102–3; Bockmuehl, *Evangelicals*, 47.

233. *UG*, 107–8.

234. Bockmuehl, "Wende im Spätwerk Karl Barths," 280; cf. Bockmuehl, "Nachwort zur 3. Auflage," in *Atheismus in der Christenheit*, 160–61.

235. Cf. Barth, *The Humanity of God*, 33–42. Bockmuehl also finds this changed understanding in the later parts of *Church Dogmatics* 4/2 and in 4/3 (cf. "Karl Barth," 31). Concerning the change in Barth's theology, see, e.g., E. Busch, *Karl Barth. His Life*, 423–4; Mueller, *Karl Barth*, 142.

236. Barth, *Humanity*, 38–39.

237. Ibid., 42.

238. Ibid.; cf. *UG*, 88.

Theological and Spiritual Influences on Bockmuehl

upon earth, that is, where humanity—the humanity of God—wills to assume tangible form in time and here upon earth."[239]

It is interesting that Bockmuehl concludes his article on "[t]he turning point in Karl Barth's late work" by suggesting that Barth, after his turning point, came closer to the pietistic[240] and Catholic understanding of the concrete reality of justification and sanctification. Moreover, "[t]he new reality in Karl Barth's late work will finally help in addressing the modern person more effectively who asks after practice and facts and does not want to know anything about a merely imagined change."[241]

To sum up, then, our conclusion thus far is that Bockmuehl thoroughly approves of Barth's late understanding of God's reality and praises him for applying Scripture as a corrective. Yet, when dealing with the first phase, Bockmuehl criticizes Barth rather severely, as can be seen when looking at the title of the chapter on Barth in *The Unreal God*: "A Deterioration of the Doctrine of God: Barth and the Unreality of God in the World."[242] According to Bockmuehl, Barth's emphasis on the non-observability of God's actions prepared the way for atheism as well as secularism in theology and church.[243] We shall look more closely at this criticism in Part Two when outlining Bockmuehl's portrayal and evaluation of the theology of the unreality of God.

Concept of Vocation

As well as these two elements, Bockmuehl agrees strongly with Barth's recovery of *vocation*: "Among Karl Barth's many innovative approaches to theology is his rediscovery of an essential aspect of the biblical doctrine of salvation. Barth pointed out that God's saving work for us consists of not

---

239. Barth, *Humanity*, 63; cf. Bockmuehl, "Spätwerk Karl Barths," 282.

240. Bockmuehl, "Karl Barth," 32. When looking at Barth's writings, it is obvious that in his early years he criticizes pietism rather severely whereas in his later years he not only admits that he understands the concerns of the pietists better but also attempts to take them into consideration. Cf. Barth, *Church Dogmatics* 4/2:x; Barth, "Concluding Unscientific Postcript," 262; E. Busch, *Karl Barth und die Pietisten*, 291–303 (esp. 300); Knobloch, "Karl Barth und 'unsere Gemeinschaftsleute,'" 399–401.

241. "Spätwerk Karl Barths," 290. The new understanding of reality can, according to Bockmuehl, also be found in Barth, *Church Dogmatics* 4/3.2:481–680 (§ 71), particularly 660 (cf. *LbG*, 14, 19) and in Barth's last letters; cf. Bockmuehl, "The Latter Letters of Barth," 37.

242. *UG*, 77.

243. *UG*, 99.

PART ONE—Bockmuehl's Theological Work

only justification and sanctification, as the traditional formula has it, but justification, sanctification, and *vocation*."[244]

Contrary to Luther, who gave *civil* vocation great weight, Barth emphasized the primacy of a specific *Christian* vocation. Yet, what vocation does the Christian have for his or her life? In view of the Great Commission, every Christian is called to be a witness for Christ and thus to participate in Christ's prophetic ministry. Moreover, that Barth saw vocation as being part of salvation and applying to every single Christian was, according to Bockmuehl, "a revolutionary development."[245] When examining Bockmuehl's writings, it is obvious that he both appreciates Barth's concept of vocation and criticizes the Reformers' concept of civil vocation.[246] In fact, he praises the extensive chapter on vocation as being "one of the finest sections in *Church Dogmatics*."[247] It should not be surprising to discover that Barth wrote this chapter late in life, even though his rediscovery of the Christian vocation can already be found in earlier parts of his *Church Dogmatics*, particularly in the context of the ethics of creation.[248]

Barth's concept of vocation has similarities with Bockmuehl's "specifically Christian level of vocation," which belongs to salvation ethics and includes the "call to witness," as well as with the "spiritual calling of the individual," which includes concrete guidance by the Spirit. According to Bockmuehl, there can be times when the "call to the Kingdom"[249] might imply a call to leave one's profession, one's station in life, i.e., one's civil vocation. Barth, similarly, suggests that "the situation into which man is summoned by the command of God, as opposed to that in which he already finds himself on the basis of the divine creation and providence, may

---

244. *LbG*, 21–22.

245. Bockmuehl, "Introduction," 92; cf. *VG*, 120. For Barth, see, for instance, *Church Dogmatics* 4/3.2:481. In his chapter, "The Christian as Witness," Barth clearly states with view to Christians that "[t]he essence of their vocation is that God makes them His witnesses" (ibid., 554, 575).

246. Cf. Bockmuehl, "Recovering Vocation," 96–97; *GG*, 117; Bockmuehl, "Mit Christus dienen," 13; Bockmuehl, "Aktualität," 316, 322; *UG*, 114; Bockmuehl, "Der sendende Herr," 189.

247. *UG*, 103. Cf. Barth, *Church Dogmatics* 4/3.2:481–680 (§ 71). Bockmuehl's praise is to a great extent due to the fact that in this later section in the *Church Dogmatics* "the world of man becomes again the locus of the Christian life" (*UG*, 103). Barth, in fact, states that "the vocation of man should not be divested of its concrete historicity nor transcendentalised." Barth, *Church Dogmatics*, 4/3.2:498.

248. Cf. Bockmuehl, "Recovering Vocation," 97; Barth, *Church Dogmatics* 3/4:595–647 (§ 56.2).

249. Bockmuehl, "Recovering Vocation," 96–97; cf. *CW*, 26–27.

Theological and Spiritual Influences on Bockmuehl

be astonishingly reversed in substance."[250] However, Barth, in contrast to Bockmuehl, maintains that even this Christian vocation "is proper to all men inasmuch as all are destined to be recipients of the divine calling and hearers of the divine command,"[251] whereas Bockmuehl sees this vocation as a "special call to Christians." Instead, he views the "cultural mandate" to sustain life as a vocation within creation ethics that applies to all of humanity.[252] We shall explore Bockmuehl's concept of vocation in more depth when looking at Bockmuehl's main theological concerns.[253]

ETHICS

With regard to ethics, we find that Barth's influence on Bockmuehl was of an ambiguous nature. On the one hand, Bockmuehl criticizes particularly the early Barth for "indifference to ethics" due to "his doctrine of the transcendence of God."[254] However, he does acknowledge that Barth, due to his reading of Scripture and not because it follows from his presuppositions, nevertheless encourages human action and political activism.[255] We shall examine Bockmuehl's critique of Barth's ethics, particularly the ethical implications of Barth's understanding of the (un-)reality of God, in more depth in Part Two, chapter 3.[256]

With regard to the question of the *proprium* (distinctiveness) of Christian ethics, Bockmuehl commends the late Barth for starting to write "an ethic of the 'order of reconciliation' for Christians to supplement the creation ethic which applies to all people."[257] Since the concept of a specific Christian ethic has been, and still is, in contention, there can be no doubt that Bockmuehl highly appreciates Barth's endeavor and, in fact, considers it to be a "bold step."[258] Moreover, he believes that if Barth had completed his exposition of his ethics of reconciliation he might have taken the Great Commission into account. Bockmuehl himself, as we shall see later, points

250. Barth, *Church Dogmatics*, 3/4:596; cf. 595.
251. Barth, *Church Dogmatics*, 3/4:599.
252. Bockmuehl, "Recovering Vocation," 97, 96; cf. *CW*, 26–27.
253. Cf. chapter 2, pages 102–4.
254. *UG*, 88.
255. Cf. *UG*, 89–80.
256. Cf. pages 124–27.
257. *CM*, 111–12; cf. *GG*, 85. Bockmuehl is here referring to the unfinished *Church Dogmatics 4/4: The Doctrine of Reconciliation: The Foundation of the Christian Life (Baptism)*.
258. *CM*, 111.

PART ONE—Bockmuehl's Theological Work

out the necessity of salvation or redemption ethics, alongside creation ethics, which includes the Great Commission.[259]

Similarly, when evaluating *situation ethics*, Bockmuehl refers more than once to Barth as his advocate in order to strengthen his argument that "[w]hat matters in a given situation is not in the first place what circumstances may demand, but what is acceptable to God and fulfills His purposes."[260] This leads us on to the issue of discerning God's will in a particular situation and the role of the Ten Commandments in this process. Contrary to many theologians, Barth, and in his wake Bockmuehl, maintain that the Ten Commandments are valid for all Christians and serve as a framework when making decisions.[261] However, for discerning the concrete will of God in a particular situation it is necessary to strive for the individual, specific commandment (*mandatum concretissimum*)[262] within this framework.

We conclude this section on situation ethics with a citation by Bockmuehl, in which his immense appreciation for Barth's endeavor to hold together the individual, specific command of God, on the one hand, and the Decalogue, on the other hand, is evident: "Hardly any other theologian has carried out such theological pioneering work in order to create a *theocentric situation ethic* as did Karl Barth with his broad presentation of the (temporal) 'definiteness of the divine decision'; at the same time, Barth has adhered to the Decalogue as the framework of legislation for the people of God."[263]

A central topic of Bockmuehl's ethics, particularly his redemption ethics, is the topic of *love for God*. With regard to this topic, Bockmuehl draws attention to the fact that Barth corrects his concept of love for God toward the end of his life due to his thorough study of Scripture. Only then does Barth acknowledge that it is possible to argue in favor of a direct love for God and love for Christ.[264] This is particularly interesting with regard

---

259. Cf. *CW*, 26–27. Gunton, "Salvation," 154–55.

260. Bockmuehl, "Revolution," 67; cf. *GiE*, 150, 152; Bockmuehl, "Über die Geltung," 59.

261. Cf. Bockmuehl, "Ten Commandments," 129–30.

262. *GG*, 117; cf. 247, 267; Barth, *Church Dogmatics* 2/2:662, 669. In *Church Dogmatics* 3/4, Barth speaks about the "differentiating will of God in His word and command as given to man, i.e., to this man" (598). This is similar to Bockmuehl's "differential ethics," though Bockmuehl specifies that the "differential" principle is given with the guidance by the Holy Spirit (Bockmuehl, "Protestant Ethics," 102; *GG* 514).

263. Bockmuehl, "Der Streit," 98; cf. Barth *Church Dogmatics* 2/2:744, § 39.2.

264. Cf. Bockmuehl, "Great Commandment," 11; *CW*, 38.

Theological and Spiritual Influences on Bockmuehl

to Bockmuehl's own development since, initially, he himself denies the possibility of direct love for God and identifies love for God with love for one's neighbor in his doctoral thesis. In the second edition, however, he changes his view and even criticizes his earlier statement as being a distortion of the Christian message.[265]

RELATIONSHIP BETWEEN CREATION
AND REDEMPTION

With regard to the relationship between creation and redemption there is little doubt that Bockmuehl was influenced by Barth since he adopted Barth's contention that creation is the external basis of the covenant, whereas the covenant is the inner basis of creation.[266] Bockmuehl, for instance, states in his doctoral thesis: "Thus it is creation which externally, *materialiter*, makes the covenant possible, and yet it is created towards this covenant, destined towards it, and has achieved its purpose in it. Creation receives its authorization out of the covenant as well as it experiences its relativization through it."[267] Upon this foundation, Bockmuehl develops the concept that just as creation is integrated into the covenant, human embodiment is integrated into the kingdom of God; the latter becomes the horizon of purpose for human action.[268] We shall be exploring this topic further when outlining Bockmuehl's main theological concerns, first and foremost, the primacy of the reality of God and his kingdom.

CONCLUSION

In summary, Bockmuehl's constant interaction with Barth's theology leads him to reject vigorously certain aspects of Barth's theology while approving strongly of others; these latter aspects are found mainly in Barth's later writings. Bockmuehl particularly commends Barth for his willingness to apply Scripture as a corrective to his own theological thoughts: "He is one of those great theologians who, when necessary, are willing to criticize

---

265. Cf. *LuG*, 268, 289.

266. Cf. *LuG*, 284; Bockmuehl, "Leiblichkeit," 42; For Barth's view, see Barth, *Church Dogmatics* 3/1:42–329 (§ 41), particularly 94, 96–97. Loos points to Bockmuehl's dependency on Barth in this regard (cf. "Human Embodiment," 94, 134).

267. *LuG*, 284. English translation in Loos, "Human Embodiment," 94.

268. Cf. Bockmuehl, "Leiblichkeit," 42–47.

their earlier productions."²⁶⁹ Not surprisingly, Bockmuehl himself demonstrates this willingness to let Scripture correct certain aspects of his theology and ethics. Particularly toward the end of his life, he, for instance, spoke out against the dangers of Christian activism by pointing to John 15:15.²⁷⁰

Similarly, Bockmuehl appreciates that Barth, unlike many other German theologians, does not shrink back from criticizing the theology of the Reformers due to his conviction of Scripture as a corrective, and he follows in Barth's footsteps.²⁷¹

Hofmann sums up well Bockmuehl's engagement with Barth when he states that Barth's *Church Dogmatics* can be compared to a mountain range with "peaks and a central massif but also dark ravines and dangerous slopes. Through lifelong appreciation of his theological teacher, Klaus Bockmuehl learned to distinguish and to describe this diversity."²⁷²

Roman-Catholic Theologians/Saints

Bockmuehl not only benefitted from the ethical and spiritual insights of the Church Fathers and the great saints of the medieval period, as we have already seen above, but also from those of Roman Catholic theologians and saints. Neuer puts it well when he points out that Bockmuehl tried to overcome narrow-mindedness "with scrutinizing openness to the spiritual traditions of other denominations."²⁷³

With regard to *spirituality*, and in particular *love for God*, Bockmuehl admits that "it is an open secret that concerning love of God the Protestant has to go and search for wisdom either in Roman Catholic spirituality, or perhaps with a few mysterious figures in the history of Protestantism who, however, clearly do not represent its mainstream."²⁷⁴ Bockmuehl himself greatly appreciates the contribution of one Catholic saint called

---

269. *CW*, 38.
270. Cf. Bockmuehl, "Listeners," 4; *GG*, 516.
271. Cf. *GG*, 117; 267; Barth, *How I changed*, 43.
272. Hofmann, "Revolutionär," 21.
273. Neuer, "Bockmühl, Klaus," 287; cf. Neuer, Review of *Gesetz und Geist*, 39.
274. Bockmuehl, "Great Commandment," 10. See also Thomas, "Spirituality of Klaus Bockmuehl: Part Two," 33. Bockmuehl wrote on Feb. 16, 1989 in his "Journals": "[A]fter . . . 500 yrs of negative criticsm of Cath. spirituality we are in for a generation or two of its re-appraisal—in the light of Scripture, to rediscover its—forgotten—Scriptural elements."

Theological and Spiritual Influences on Bockmuehl

Charles de Foucauld to the issues of spirituality and love for God.[275] In his article about the Sahara missionary he, for instance, includes the following quotation by Foucauld on love of God: "The Lord alone deserves to be loved passionately. Blessed ruins (of our life) which throw us earlier and more completely into this truth!"[276] At the same time, Foucauld's life shows clearly, as do his words, that love toward God always includes love toward mankind.[277]

Unlike many Protestant theologians, Bockmuehl advises studying the lives of "great saints of Christendom" in order to gain "encouragement and instruction for our own life of discipleship and sanctification."[278] He particularly commends Charles Foucauld to the readers of *Christianity Today* and refers to him in several of his publications.[279] As "this man is particularly worth listening to,"[280] yet somewhat unknown, we will take a closer look at him now.

Excursus: Charles de Foucauld

Charles-Eugène Vicomte de Foucauld was born in Strasbourg in 1858, he became an orphan four years later and was raised by his grandfather in Nancy. While at school, he lost his faith in God. On completing school, he joined the military academy in Saint-Cyr. Even before becoming a cavalry lieutenant, he started to live an idle, dissipated life, more like a playboy than a lieutenant. In 1881, he was dismissed from the army because of his disagreeable lifestyle and lack of discipline. Even though he spent his time amusing himself, he sensed more and more the meaninglessness and restlessness of his life. When reading about the severe battles of his former regiment against rebellious Arabs in Algeria, he volunteered to join them. The military department hesitated at first but finally agreed to take him in again. After his arrival in Africa, he was sent directly to the front line where his engagement and courage during the battle were a surprise to

---

275. In a letter to the "Sekretariat Charles de Foucauld," Feb. 8, 1966.

276. Cited in "Saint for Our Day," 56. See also the quotations from Charles de Foucauld on "passion" in the book edited by Frische, *Wasser in der Wüste*, 53–57.

277. Cf. Six, *Leben*, 77.

278. Bockmuehl, "Saint for Our day," 55.

279. Cf. Bockmuehl, "Saint for Our Day," 55–56. See also Bockmuehl, "Great Commandment," 13; Bockmuehl, "Mit Christus dienen," 19.

280. Bockmuehl, "Saint for Our Day," 55.

his regiment.²⁸¹ After leaving the army, he made a reputation for himself as a geographer by exploring previously unmapped countries like Morocco (1883/84). Because of the hostility against Western people, he had to disguise himself as a Jew. In 1883, he received the gold medal from the geographic society for his exploration. Yet, in spite of a brilliant career, he was still dissatisfied with life. Challenged by the religious fervor of the Muslims in Africa, he started to search for God. As a result, Foucauld consulted Abbé Huvelin, priest at Saint-Augustin in Paris, in October 1886, who helped him to a personal experience of reconciliation with God. A consequence of his conversion was his willingness to give up everything for God.²⁸² Yet, it was only a few years later that he discovered the specific vocation for his life, which was to imitate Christ by taking "the last place"²⁸³ among humankind; this included voluntary humility and suffering.

After some years of uncertainty as to where and how he would be able to live according to his call, he joined the Trappist Order Notre-Dame des Neiges in January 1890 to live a life of poverty and discipline. When asked why he chose the monastic life, his answer was: out of love.²⁸⁴ After six months, he moved to the even poorer monastery of Notre-Dame du Sacre Coeur in Akbes/Syrien, which meant a total separation from his family. Some time later, he obeyed the instruction given by the superior to study theology in Rome, even though he had applied for permission to leave the Order as he feared losing the "last place" that Jesus had taken. Only after finishing his studies in 1897 did the head of the Order allow Foucauld to follow his plans and move to Nazareth where he spent several years working at a poor monastery as a servant.²⁸⁵ There he tried to live in seclusion for the purpose of deepening his spiritual life without, however, neglecting his social work.²⁸⁶ In his times of prayer and meditation,

281. Cf. Six, *Leben*, 11–19; Carrouges, *Soldier of the Spirit*, 3–20.

282. Cf. Six, *Leben*, 27–36; Voillaume, *Seeds*, 6. In 1901, Foucauld wrote about his conversion and vocation in a letter: "As soon as I believed that there was a God, I understood that I could do nothing else than live for him exclusively: my religious vocation dates from the same hour as my faith" (Foucauld, cited in Carrouges, *Soldier of the Spirit*, 86, cf. 72–88; Six, *Charles de Foucauld*, 56).

283. "Our Lord took the last place to such an extent that no one has been able to take it away from him" (Huvelin, cited in Carrouges, *Soldier of the Spirit*, 87). This remark by Abbé Huvelin aroused Foucauld's passion to imitate Christ in finding the lowest place. Cf. Voillaume, *Seeds*, 7–8, 51.

284. Cf. Carrouges, *Soldier of the Spirit*, 91–98.

285. Cf. Six, *Leben*, 37–40, 55–58; Voillaume, *Seeds*, 10; Frische, "Gott lieben und seinen Willen tun," 130.

286. "As time goes on, he gives more and more time to exercising charity . . . deeply

Theological and Spiritual Influences on Bockmuehl

he regularly received spiritual and practical insights and recorded them. Hence, he often experienced the concrete guidance of the Holy Spirit, and, due to his deep spirituality, he soon attracted many people. After a few secluded years in Nazareth, friends encouraged him to enter into full time spiritual ministry. Foucauld himself recognized at the same time the necessity of caring for the physical as well as the spiritual life of those who live in the greatest affliction and agreed to go back to France in order to be ordained. During his stay in France in 1900/1901, he felt the call to bring the love and the message of Jesus to the non-Christians in the Sahara. Due to his vocation, he moved to Beni-Abbès/Algeria, an oasis with a French garrison near the border with Morocco and left France even without seeing most of his relatives.[287] While staying in a small cloister, he spent much of his time receiving visitors. Many French soldiers and colonial officers consulted him on a variety of matters as well as many Arabs and poor people, who, for instance, received barley and dates from him. As Beni-Abbès was situated near a caravan crossroads, about 60–90 people visited him every day. For Foucauld, it was his greatest wish to be a true brother to all of them whether they were Christians, Muslims, Jews etc. in order to show them God's love. In fact, this was only possible because he spent a lot of time praying, meditating, and asking God for guidance.[288]

It is interesting to note that as soon as he discovered that slavery was still in existence in the Sahara, he felt compelled to fight against it. He not only wrote to the responsible French Officers, but he also interceded for slaves, tried to buy their freedom, and provided a place for them to stay.

In spite of his growing ministry at Beni-Abbes, a friend encouraged him to become a missionary among the Tuareg, a nomadic tribe in the Sahara just recently subjected to the French. This obviously included giving up any kind of private life.[289] After consulting the bishop in Algeria, he accepted the call and moved to Tamanrasset, a small village far away from any kind of western civilization. Even though he was the only European in that area, he was content to live with the Tuareg, trying to become like one of them in order to win them for Christ. One way of achieving this was to open his home to the sick, the poor, the homeless, and the passers-by, and to care for them. Only after building up friendships and gaining their

---

struck as he has been by the idea that love of God and love of one's brothers not only go together but are, in fact, one and the same" (cf. Voillaume, *Seeds*, 65).

287. Cf. Six, *Leben*, 66–67, 73–74.
288. Cf. Frische, "Gott lieben," 132; Six, *Leben*, 76.
289. Cf. Amstutz, *Charles de Foucauld*, 4.

confidence did he start telling them the Gospel. It is, therefore, hardly surprising that even leaders of the Tuareg consulted him. It is, furthermore, remarkable that he not only learnt their language but was the first to translate the Gospel into Tuareg, write a catechism for them, and to compile a complete Tuareg-French and French-Tuareg dictionary. This he mainly did for the purpose of helping succeeding missionaries to learn the language more quickly.[290]

As early as July 1893, Foucauld considered the possibility of founding a new Order, the "Fraternities."[291] During his ministry, he planned and prayed for like-minded brother- and sisterhoods consisting of 3–4 members, either monks, priests, or laymen. According to his plans, the "Little Brothers" and "Little Sisters of Jesus" would in the first place love Jesus with all their strength and help non-believers to get to know the Gospel, not mainly through preaching but through living; this could be regarded as pre-evangelism. Secondly, their place would be among the poorest and neediest, and their work would consist of practical and pastoral ministry. Thirdly, it would be characteristic of them to work for their living, to share everything they have and live in poverty, and, finally, to retreat regularly for prayer and worship.[292] All this clearly shows Foucauld's desire to imitate Christ. He was convinced that, as Christ suffered for us, real love should comprise the willingness to suffer as well.[293] Accordingly, Foucauld's life displayed this to a high degree. Yet, not only did his life show this, so also did his death at the age of 58. He was killed in 1916 by looting Senussis and Tuareg, betrayed by one of his former visitors.[294]

It is of interest that about twenty years after Foucauld's death the "Little Brothers" and "Little Sisters of Jesus" were founded in Algeria, adopting the rules laid down by Foucauld in modified form. Even up to the present day, they live and work among the poor all over the world, mainly in areas where Christianity is not the main religion.[295]

290. Cf. ibid., 8–9, 12–13; Carrouges, *Soldier of the Spirit*, 200–228, 271.

291. Cf. Voillaume, *Seeds*, 11, 93.

292. Cf. Six, *Leben*, 45–46, 51–53; Greshake, "Foucauld," 1372–73; Voillaume, *Seeds*, 22–23. Foucauld insisted that contemplation should be the source for their practical ministry. Characteristic for him was his belief that Jesus could not only be experienced in contemplation but also in fellowship with the poor. Cf. Amstutz, *Charles de Foucauld*, 7.

293. Cf. Six, *Leben*, 37–38.

294. Cf. ibid., 232–33.

295. Cf. Frank, "Jesus Christus, XIII. Religiöse Gemeinschaften," 844–45; Carrouges, *Soldier of the Spirit*, 297–98; Little Sister Magdeleine of Jesus, *He took me by the hand*, 16–18.

Theological and Spiritual Influences on Bockmuehl

In his article on Foucauld, Bockmuehl stresses that Foucauld's conversion was a returning "from secularism to belief," from a materialistic, luxurious lifestyle to "Christian simplicity."[296] Consequently, the Kingdom of God became Foucauld's first priority; this is revealed in a quotation by Foucauld that Bockmuehl refers to at the end of his article: "I am infinitely weak. But however I examine myself, I find no other desire in me than this one: Thy Kingdom Come! Hallowed be Thy Name!"[297] Bockmuehl himself strongly emphasizes the relevance of the Kingdom of God for the Christian. Other similarities between Bockmuehl and Foucauld are the unity of Christian service and pastoral ministry in their teaching and living,[298] the call not to surrender to secularism[299] but rather to devote oneself to a simple lifestyle, the emphasis on prayer, meditation, guidance by the Holy Spirit, and spiritual fervor, the practice of listening to God and taking notes during the quiet time,[300] a compassion for the unredeemed, the willingness to suffer for Christ's sake, and, above all, the desire to love God and live according to his will. The latter is quite obvious when comparing the title of Bockmuehl's memorial volume: "Loving God and Keeping His Commandments" with the title of a short biography of Foucauld: "Loving God and doing his will."[301] Foucauld's biography was written by Reinhold Frische, a member of the Gomaringen Circle (*Gomaringer Kreis*), which Bockmuehl had founded in 1979. Not surprisingly, Frische acknowledges in his article that Bockmuehl was the one who awakened his interest in Foucauld's life and work.[302] Such observations are further indications for the great appreciation Bockmuehl had for Foucauld.

296. Bockmuehl, "Saint for Our day," 55, 58. Bockmuehl points out how valuable Foucauld's writings still are for today since he had been one of the first to have come out of secularism and had known of the priority of God above all else. Cf. Bockmuehl, "Der sendende Herr," 180; cf. also 186. In a later chapter, we shall look more closely at Bockmuehl's evaluation of secularism.

297. Cited after Bockmuehl, "Saint for Our Day," 56.

298. Cf. Bockmuehl, "Serving," 25. Cf. *GG*, 288.

299. Bockmuehl notes that these fraternities "represent a revolution in the history of monasticism by not living holiness in the seclusion of the enclosure but 'in the midst of the world.' There they live as a small group of monks and nuns in a secular environment, in secular employment; yet, they do this for the sanctification of the name of Jesus" (Bockmuehl, *Säkularismus und christlicher Glaube*, 42).

300. Cf. Foucauld, *Wasser aus der Wüste*, 66–69, 72–74.

301. Cf. Frische, "Gott lieben," 122–41.

302. Frische even published meditations written by Foucauld and arranged them topically in the book *Wasser aus der Wüste*.

77

Part One—Bockmuehl's Theological Work

Bockmuehl also refers to Foucauld and to the "Catholic moral theology" concerning the unity of *love and obedience* or, more generally, *Christian service*, by supporting the distinction made by the latter between "affective love" and "effective love."[303] Furthermore, he criticizes Protestantism's neglect of the importance of *the Holy Spirit and love* for salvation, as expressed in Romans 5:5, merely because this verse played a major role in the Catholic doctrine of justification. Bockmuehl suggests that we should try to overcome the confessional one-sidedness and learn from each other.[304] Not surprisingly, therefore, Bockmuehl refers to different Catholic theologians as his advocates when dealing with the "new morality" while admitting that the great mass of contemporary American Catholic moral theologians had left their own background to join the new approach.[305] His affinity with some Catholic moral theologians can be seen by the fact that Theo G. Belmans, a contemporary Dutch Catholic theologian, refers to Bockmuehl several times as his advocate. Belmans mentions Bockmuehl even in his foreword by affirming the truth of Bockmuehl's statement, "atheism in Christendom."[306] Later on he explains this in more detail: "It is finally encouraging that the atheistic implications of situation ethics are directly named by a Protestant moralist."[307]

One of the contemporary Catholic theologians Bockmuehl held in high esteem was Hans Urs von Balthasar, the great Swiss Catholic theologian (1905–1988).[308] He even regarded Balthasar as fighting on the same side as himself, for instance, in the then current debate on "new morality" where Christianity was mainly seen as a special form of humanism.[309] In a 1968 lecture on the tendencies in theology, Bockmuehl, after describing the alarming tendencies in Christian doctrine, ethics, and social ethics, turns to Balthasar: "The well-known Catholic theologian H. U. von

303. Bockmuehl, "Great Commandment," 13.

304. Cf. *GG*, 508–12.

305. Not only does Bockmuehl refer to two American Catholic theologians to support his view but also to an Indian Thomist. Cf. *GiE*, 215.

306. Belmans, *Der objektive Sinn*, 4. Belmans describes the book *God in Exile?* as an "excellent contribution" (21).

307. Belmans, *Der objektive Sinn*, 16; see also 153, 425, 442, 458, 484. It is obvious that Bockmuehl and Belmans have the same assessment of situation ethics.

308. During his pastoral work in Heidelberg, Bockmuehl entered into a correspondence with Balthasar in order to ask for permission to print one of Balthasar's lectures about the basics of the Christian belief. As a result, Bockmuehl published Balthasar's *ABC of Christianity* (*ABC des Christentums*) in 1967 for the Protestant student pastorate in Heidelberg. Cf. letter from Bockmuehl to Balthasar, June 14, 1966.

309. Cf. letter from Bockmuehl to Reinhard (Kuster), June 23, 1965.

Theological and Spiritual Influences on Bockmuehl

Balthasar has in the midst of the conflicts . . . , which is shaking the Catholic church just as it is the Protestant one, precisely outlined the pathway: 'Hence, if we want to avoid the church ultimately losing its depth, the true, unabbreviated church program for today needs to be: The greatest force of light in the world is generated through closely following Christ."'[310]

Besides this *concentration on Christ and his will* in the midst of divergent theological tendencies, it is Balthasar's emphasis of listening to God that impressed Bockmuehl particularly. In fact, Bockmuehl advocates very strongly Balthasar's contention that "[w]ho would speak to the world must first listen to God";[311] this can be seen by the fact that he mentions it in several different articles or books. In Balthasar, he finds a positive affirmation of his conviction that listening to God and action or proclamation are inextricably connected. Just like Jesus, who spent time with his Father in order to know his will, we need to acquire an attitude of listening but also of obeying God's will. Hence, Bockmuehl as well as Balthasar draw attention to the necessity of *"being-led by the Holy Spirit."*[312] It is, furthermore, interesting that both deal explicitly with a concrete, personal calling in the context of *vocation*, even though the overall concept differs noticeably.[313]

Another point of contact is that both try to bring *the double commandment of love* back into focus. They particularly concern themselves with the relation of *love toward God* and love for one's neighbor; they both repudiate the belief that loving one's neighbor is the only means of loving God and, instead, defend the primacy of love toward God.[314]

The Oxford Group and Moral Re-Armament

As early as 1963, Bockmuehl wrote a short book on "Frank Buchman's Message and its Significance for the Protestant Churches" following a visit to a World Conference of Moral Re-Armament in Caux in 1959. Besides

310. Bockmuehl, "Tendenzen der Theologie," 5. Same quote also in letters from Bockmuehl to Marienschwesternschaft, July 2, 1968. Cf. Bockmuehl, "Wie lebt ein Christ, " 6.

311. Cited after Bockmuehl, "Is there a Christian 'Life-Style'?," 49. Nearly identical quotation in Bockmuehl, "How Did Jesus Decide His Actions?," 4; "Leben aus dem Evangelium," 34; cf. *LbG*, 53.

312. Balthasar, *Christian State*, 406.

313. Cf. ibid., 392–95; Bockmuehl, "Recovering Vocation," 96–97.

314. Cf. Balthasar, *Christian State*, 25; Balthasar, *Cordula oder Der Ernstfall*, 96; O'Donnell, *Hans Urs von Balthasar*, 127. For Bockmuehl, see "Great Commandment," 10–11.

PART ONE—Bockmuehl's Theological Work

this book, he seldom mentions MRA explicitly in any of his publications until shortly before his death. It is therefore of great importance that Bockmuehl refers to Frank N. D. Buchman and Peter Howard, the leaders of Moral Re-Armament in the introduction to his last book, *Listening to the God who speaks*, for the purpose of emphasizing his conviction that God still speaks today. As this is a major issue emphasized by Buchman and Howard, there is, indeed, little doubt that Bockmuehl's understanding of God's present guidance is profoundly shaped by them. Hence, Thomas, the first to examine Bockmuehl's spirituality, including the influences upon him, remarks that "his interest in ethics and the Holy Spirit came originally from the Moral Re-Armament leaders."[315] It is therefore necessary to take a closer look at this worldwide spiritual and moral movement and particularly at the life of its founder Frank Buchman.

Excursus: Frank N. D. Buchman

Frank N. D. Buchman, born in Pennsburg, Pennsylvania, on 4 June 1878, grew up in an orthodox Lutheran family. Due to the fact that his ancestors had emigrated from Switzerland to America in the eighteenth century, Frank's family still spoke a German dialect.

After graduating from a Lutheran theological seminary in 1902, Buchman started church work in Overbrook, a suburb of Philadelphia. During a trip across Europe a year later, he was impressed by the fact that the Lutheran Inner Mission had set up Christian Hospices in Switzerland and Germany for young men to stay in; he went on to establish a similar Hospice in Philadelphia, supported by the Mission Board of the Lutheran Church.[316] Unfortunately, disagreements between Buchman and the Mission Board about the Hospice came to a head in 1907 and Buchman had to resign from his job as a housefather. Deeply hurt by this, he was quite resentful toward the members of the Mission Board. As the whole episode had seriously depleted his strength, he was advised to take a break and go abroad.[317] As it happened, this journey completely changed his life.

While walking in the countryside in Keswick one Sunday afternoon, Buchman discovered a small chapel and decided to attend the service led by the evangelist Jessie Penn-Lewis. It was during this service that he fully

---

315. Thomas, "Spirituality of Klaus Bockmuehl: Part One," 7.
316. Cf. Lean, *On the Tail of a Comet*, 18–20.
317. Cf. ibid., 22, 25–28.

Theological and Spiritual Influences on Bockmuehl

grasped the meaning of the cross of Christ for his own life by recognizing the distance between himself and Christ caused by his own sin. He described his experience in the following way: "For the first time I saw myself with all my pride, my selfishness, my failure and my sin. 'I' was the centre of my own life. If I was to be different, then that big 'I' had to be crossed out."[318] As a result of his experience of the cross of Christ,[319] he knew that God wanted him to ask the members of the Mission board for forgiveness. Obediently, he wrote a letter to every single member enclosing the first verse of the famous hymn written by Isaac Watts, as this best summed up the change that had taken place in him:

> When I survey the wondrous Cross
> On which the Prince of Glory died,
> My richest gain I count but loss,
> And pour contempt on all my pride.[320]

When coming back to America, he looked for a job and eventually accepted the post of YMCA Secretary at "Penn State" (Pennsylvania State College) even though this College was infamous for student strikes, high alcohol consumption, brutality etc. Shortly after entering into his new ministry, the attendance at the Bible study classes he was leading increased drastically and Buchman even made contact with some of the leaders of College life. Yet, the longer he worked at the College, the more he observed the lack of permanent change in so far as the conversions did not really have any affect on the atmosphere of the college.[321] Worried by this, he sought advice from Frederick B. Meyer, who wisely pointed out to him that "[y]ou need to make personal, man-to-man interviews central, rather than the organising of meetings."[322] As a result, Buchman subsequently attempted not to think "in terms of numbers, but in terms of people."[323] In addition to that, Meyer even challenged Buchman on his

---

318. Buchman, *Remaking the World*, 187.

319. Buchman emphasized the personal experience of the cross emphatically: "I feel a great many people speak of the Cross, but it does not mean a thing. It isn't real. It is something they hear about or read about, something somebody else has. But an *experience* of the Cross is vital, real and goes straight into your life . . . With an experience of the Cross, you will shrink from nothing. I learned at Keswick that I was as wrong as anybody else; I was most in need of change. I was the one to begin" (cited in Howard, *Frank Buchman's Secret*, 21).

320. Cited in Howard, *Frank Buchman's Secret*, 20.

321. Cf. Lean, *On the Tail of a Comet*, 30–35.

322. Ibid., 35.

323. T. Spoerri, *Dynamic out of Silence*, 30.

PART ONE—Bockmuehl's Theological Work

practice of guidance by asking him: "Do you let the Holy Spirit guide you in all you are doing?"[324] Even though Buchman affirmed that he read his Bible, prayed every morning, and received guidance now and then, Meyer again questioned him as to whether he really gave God enough time to show him what to do. As the answer to this was negative, he decided to lay aside one hour every morning between five and six o'clock in order to listen to God. In these "quiet times," he adopted the habit of writing down whatever instructions he received from God and consistently tried to carry them out.[325] During the following years, Buchman experienced the life-changing conversions of three key people from the College. The impact was such that the whole atmosphere at the College changed considerably. The news about this change spread even beyond Pennsylvania, so that religious leaders from other Colleges started to visit Buchman and even adopted his methods.[326] We may conclude from what we have already noted that Buchman's growing effectiveness can be traced back to his practice of listening to God.

After preparing a large religious campaign in India in 1915, Buchman spent most of the following years traveling around the world doing missionary work, leading "house-parties," and meeting people from various social backgrounds. While on a trip to China (1917–1919), he even had the extraordinary opportunity of speaking, more than once, to Sun Yat-sen, the first President of the Republic of China.[327]

During his time in America, he lectured at Hartford Seminary on personal evangelism and visited various Colleges in order to counsel students. However, in 1921, he resigned from his teaching job in order to be free for another work he felt called by God to do, i.e., spiritually training people of all social classes and challenging them to dedicate their lives fully to God, and allow themselves to be guided by God.[328] He was convinced that, as a result, they would experience transformation in the lives of people as well as in social matters. His main aspiration was, in fact, to start a movement that would change the world.[329]

---

324. Lean, *On the Tail of a Comet*, 35.

325. Cf. T. Spoerri, *Dynamic out of Silence*, 30–31.

326. Cf. Ekman, *Experiment*, 30–31; Lean, *On the Tail of a Comet*, 39; T. Spoerri, *Dynamic out of Silence*, 31–32.

327. Cf. T. Spoerri, *Dynamic out of Silence*, 47–49.

328. Cf. Lean, *On the Tail of a Comet*, 84–96.

329. Cf. ibid., 93.

Theological and Spiritual Influences on Bockmuehl

One means of achieving this was, for Buchman, by starting house-parties in various countries. As the largest took place in Oxford,[330] and as many young men from Oxford accompanied Buchman on his worldwide journeys, the movement became known as the "Oxford Group."[331] In 1938, Buchman changed the name to "Moral Re-Armament," since he felt the need for a "moral and spiritual re-armament"[332] throughout the world as a Christian alternative to the military re-armament taking place at that time. It was obvious to him that the world had to change; this, however, would only happen if individuals changed first.[333] Consequently, Buchman proposed three interdependent steps to personal change:[334] 1) The application of the *four absolute moral standards* to personal and social life: "Absolute honesty, absolute purity, absolute unselfishness, absolute love."[335] 2) *Listening to God in a quiet time*, including confession of sin, radical dedication to God's will, and forgiveness.[336] 3) Gathering a *group of young people*.[337]

The fact that Swiss supporters of MRA purchased the former Caux Palace Hotel in 1946 had lasting implications as this hotel became the international headquarters of the movement. It was here that reconciliation took place between the different nations, particularly between Germany and its former enemies. In fact, Buchman was personally in touch with various statesmen such as Robert Schuman, when he was the French Foreign Minister, and Konrad Adenauer, Chancellor of the Federal Republic

---

330. Every summer between 1930 and 1937 thousands of people attended these house-parties. Characteristic of the house-parties were the personal testimonies of young believers in which they shared how they had been changed by God. Cf. Lean, *On the Tail of a Comet*, 159; T. Spoerri, *Dynamic out of Silence*, 80–81.

331. Wordwide journeys: 1924 England, Romania, Turkey, Israel, India (where Buchman met Gandhi several times), Pakistan, Australia. Cf. T. Spoerri, *Dynamic out of Silence*, 71, 75; Lean, *On the Tail of a Comet*, 120–21. During a trip to South Africa in 1928, the young men were called the "Oxford Group." Cf. Lean, *On the Tail of a Comet*, 138; The Oxford Group, *The Oxford Group*, 11–14; Howard, *The World Rebuilt*, 125.

332. Lean, *On the Tail of a Comet*, 262.

333. Buchman was of the opinion "that when man listens, God speaks; when man obeys, God acts; when men change, nations change" (Buchman, *Remaking the World*, 46).

334. Cf. for the three steps: Goessel, *Die Moralische Aufrüstung*, 19–21.

335. Buchman, *Remaking the World*, 40.

336. Buchman believed that everybody could experience God's guidance. Cf. Buchman, *Remaking the World*, 29.

337. Buchman actually felt directed by God to gather a group around him as he knew that a "solo effect is a false principle." Cited in Ekman, *Experiment*, 55. The group provided spiritual support for the individual. Cf. Russel, *For Sinners Only*, 240.

PART ONE—Bockmuehl's Theological Work

of Germany.[338] Particularly interesting is the fact that Buchman had a lasting impact on some of the statesmen he met; this can be seen in the following text written by Adenauer in 1951 and published in the New York Herald-Tribune: "In recent months we have seen the conclusion, after some difficult negotiations, of important international agreements. Here Moral Re-Armament has played an invisible but effective part in bridging differences of opinion between negotiating parties, and has kept before them the object of peaceful agreement in the search for the common good which is the true purpose of human life . . . It is my conviction too that men and nations cannot outwardly enjoy stable relationships until they have been inwardly prepared for them. In this respect, Moral Re-Armament has rendered great and lasting service."[339]

It is remarkable how the reconciliatory work of MRA expanded over the years mainly due to conferences held at new MRA assembly centers throughout the world, including the Far East, India, South America, and Africa.[340]

In August 1961, while staying in a hotel in Freudenstadt in order to rest from his work at Caux, Buchman died. This was rather unexpected, even though he had been paralyzed for some time and had been continually losing strength. Strikingly, Freudenstadt had been the place where, back in 1938, he had felt the urgency for a "moral and spiritual re-armament for all nations."[341]

After Buchman's death, Peter Howard (1902–1965), a brilliant journalist, sportsman, author, and playwright, took over the responsibility of leadership. He had joined MRA in 1940 after changing from an agnostic to a Christian. This took place after Garth Lean, one of Buchman's co-workers and his biographer, had challenged him to take time to listen to God. Peter Howard had soon become one of the decisive men in the movement through his engagement, creativity, and journalistic ability. He wrote about fourteen plays, many of which were performed all over the world, causing in-depth changes in human relationships. This was due to the fact

---

338. Schuman even wrote a Preface when Buchman's book *Remaking the World* was published in French ("Préface," vii–viii). See also Ekman, *Experiment*, 73–74; Reimer, "Moralische Aufrüstung," 542; Howard, *The World Rebuilt*, 121–22.

339. Cited in Lean, *On the Tail of a Comet*, 382. See also Howard, *Frank Buchman's Secret*, 65.

340. Cf. Ekman, *Experiment*, 76–78; P. Spoerri, "Moralische Aufrüstung," 452. For Buchman's reconciliatory impact on Africa, see Howard, *Frank Buchman's Secret*, 56–59.

341. Lean, *On the Tail of a Comet*, 528.

Theological and Spiritual Influences on Bockmuehl

that they all dealt with acute, present-day issues and conveyed Christian content without using traditional Christian language. Unfortunately, Peter Howard outlived Buchman by only four years and died in 1965 in Lima/Peru on one of his journeys.[342]

Immediately after Howard's death, Bockmuehl wrote a letter to some of his friends expressing his great appreciation for Howard's work: "Through Peter Howard's death, God has started to speak to us in a powerful way. I can truthfully say that, through his plays, his friendship, and his battle, he, more than any other person, has shown me the magnitude, reality, and vitality of the kingdom of God in our times. Now is the moment where we should pray for a portion of the Spirit who was in him and take on the responsibility for the work that he did . . . He himself has outlined the goal given to us in a lasting formulation: 'to strive to shape humanity according to the image of Christ.'"[343]

In order to fully understand what influence Moral Re-Armament and its leaders had on Bockmuehl, we need to briefly outline the main characteristics of this movement. These include the practice of listening to God in a quiet time, radically observing ethical standards, and regularly meeting as a group. Moreover, its *message* was that God can completely change the individual and therefore also the world. Sin was seen as separating men from God and neighbor. It had to be confessed so that the way to God and one's neighbor was free again. Furthermore, the group's *method* was to share the life-changing experience in public such as through house-parties or the media but, most importantly, in personal meetings. Quite different from the church convention at the time, the language used was not of a traditional religious style. The same was true for new songs, musicals, plays, and films that were produced or performed. Emphasis was

342. Cf. Gordon, *Peter Howard*, 141–57, 270–72, 394–97. Bockmuehl refers to Peter Howard in "How Did Jesus Decide His Actions?," 2, and closes his book *The Unreal God* with a quotation by Howard (162). In "Was heißt Glaube?," 68 Bockmuehl quotes Howard who describes the church as having a revolutionary, reforming commission which should, when performed, have a perceivable impact on society. In *LG*, Bockmuehl draws attention to the fact that the source of creativity by Howard can be traced back to the inspiration of the Holy Spirit. He also endorses Howard's description of the practice of listening to God. Cf. *LG*, 7.

343. Letter written by Bockmuehl to P. Engelbert Heller and Martin-Eckart Fuchs, March 5, 1965. In another letter to Jörg Gutzwiler and Alfred Kunz, March 1, 1965, he notes he would have liked to go to England for Peter Howard's funeral but was prevented by business commitments.

PART ONE—Bockmuehl's Theological Work

also laid on promoting the new believers so that they themselves would become moral and spiritual leaders for others. Most distinctive was the universal vision that the movement had; this was to revive the whole world by having impact on all spheres of life, i.e., moral, social, political, and spiritual.[344]

However, in Christian circles, there were differences of opinion about Frank Buchman and the "Oxford Group"/MRA. Many criticized the emphasis on *moral* re-armament instead of *spiritual* re-armament. Consequently, they feared that the new MRA program would affect the original spiritual concern of the movement. Other contested issues concerned the importance of the cross of Christ for Buchman and the group, particularly when dealing with other religions.[345] Were they not in danger of overemphasizing their own personal spiritual experience instead of Christ's work for humankind?[346]

While it would be interesting to engage with these issues at length, we must confine ourselves to analyzing Bockmuehl's own evaluation of Buchman and MRA after attending a World Conference of MRA at Caux and reading several books written by Frank Buchman and Peter Howard. Particularly interesting is the fact that Bockmuehl not only wrote an article shortly after Buchman's death in which he pays tribute to him,[347] but he also published a short book in which he deals with some of the contested issues mentioned above.[348] In this book, he not only tries to prove that the criticism was unfounded by referring to Buchman's speeches, but he also points out at length the significance of Buchman's message for the contemporary church. This message includes the four absolute moral standards,[349] the change through an experience of the cross of Christ,[350] guidance by

344. Cf. T. Spoerri, *Dynamic out of Silence*, 91–94, 104.

345. The "Marburg Circle" was one of those movements originally initiated by MRA in Germany that distanced itself later from it because of the ambiguous relationship to other religions. Cf. Reimer, "Moralische Aufrüstung, " 542–43.

346. Cf. Brunner, "Begegnung," 270. Brunner describes in this article his initial reservation about the methods of MRA but also his appreciation of it after attending a house-party in Zürich. See also Goessel, *Die Moralische Aufrüstung*, 37.

347. Bockmuehl, "Zum Tode Frank Buchmans, " 389–91.

348. Bockmuehl, *Frank Buchmans Botschaft und ihre Bedeutung für die protestantischen Kirchen* (English unpublished translation: "Frank Buchman's Message and its Significance for the Protestant Churches").

349. "A person is confronted with absolute moral standards and experiences a general re-evaluation of life" (*CM*, 159).

350. The importance of Christ can best be seen in the following saying of Buchman: "Sin is the disease. Jesus Christ is the cure" (Buchman, *Remaking the World*,

Theological and Spiritual Influences on Bockmuehl

the Holy Spirit, the call to win people (the Great Commission), and the expansion of the kingdom of God. In the last chapter, Bockmuehl quotes Buchman's summary of his message: "You must have that emphasis on morals plus the saving power of Jesus Christ. Then you experience the dynamic which is almost forgotten—the Holy Spirit, that gives the guided answer . . . That's the programme for the Church today."[351]

According to Bockmuehl, this program was exactly what the contemporary church needed to hear. What is of interest for us is that his approval of Buchman's message did not change over the years; this can be seen by the fact that, some twenty years later, Bockmuehl wrote to Garth Lean, the biographer of Frank Buchman: "The genius of Moral Re-Armament . . . is to bring the central spiritual substance of Christianity (which often it demonstrates in a fresher and more powerful way than do the Churches) in a secular and accessible form. Hence the emphasis on absolute moral standards. But the direction of the Holy Spirit is just as essential . . . The genius . . . is in the balance of the two."[352]

The latter statement clearly shows Bockmuehl's indebtedness to Buchman and MRA concerning *ethics and the Holy Spirit*.[353] Especially regarding the issue of *guidance by the Holy Spirit* through *listening to God*, Bockmuehl was personally as well as theologically influenced by Buchman and Howard. He, for instance, strongly advocated Buchman's conviction "that when man listens, God speaks."[354] In an address delivered at a Moral Re-Armament Conference in Caux in 1973, Bockmuehl drew attention to the fact that Frank Buchman rendered an invaluable service for today's church by not only reminding the latter that guidance by God can be a daily reality and that it is possible to know God's will but also by training the church accordingly.[355]

142; cf. Bockmuehl, "Frank Buchman's Message," 9). It is worth mentioning again that Buchman, like Bockmuehl, had a significant experience of the cross of Christ that changed his life completely.

351. Buchman, *Remaking the World*, 144; cf. Bockmuehl, "Frank Buchman's Message," 47.

352. Bockmuehl to Garth Lean, cited in Lean, *On the Tail of a Comet*, 513–14.

353. This also includes the importance of the Great Commission, "to reach the millions of the world"; Buchman, *Remaking the World*, 54; cf. Bockmuehl, "Frank Buchman's Message," 48. It was essential for Buchman to think not only of the rearmament of the church but also of the whole world. Bockmuehl affirmed this in his article "Three Horizons for Theology," 9.

354. Buchman, *Remaking the World*, 46. For Bockmuehl's references to this quote, see *LG*, 8; Bockmuehl, "Zum Tode Frank Buchmans," 390; Bockmuehl, "Zur Hermeneutik Martin Luthers," 279.

355. Bockmuehl, "Wie treffe ich eine Entscheidung?," 4.

Furthermore, they not only practiced listening to God and living a God-controlled life themselves but also challenged others to do the same. And they knew that God had commissioned them to give their lives for this great task even though they felt inadequate. The same was true for Bockmuehl who himself felt God's calling to work for the *moral re-armament* of the Christian world: "What we need today is a shift on a major scale toward the will of God in Christendom, in theology, and the church. That is Moral Re-Armament for Christendom. At the same time, I realized that God has called and commissioned me to take up this goal as the leitmotif of my life . . . That God calls me to take on this huge task and to lead the way toward this goal seems unreal to me. It is nevertheless true. And who would not be called?"[356]

Hence, Bockmuehl, as Buchman before him, invested his energy, time, and knowledge in encouraging Christians to dedicate their lives totally to God's will. This lifestyle can be summed up by one of Buchman's statements that Bockmuehl refers to in several of his articles or books: "I live for one thing only: to make Jesus Christ regnant in the life of every person I meet."[357]

Conclusion

When faced with the question of assessing which influences shaped Bockmuehl's theology the most, it seems to be the general consensus that Bockmuehl was most closely affiliated with Pietism, in spite of his critical attitude toward contemporary Pietism.[358] It is certainly not irrelevant that the earliest spiritual and theological influence Bockmuehl experienced can be traced back to Wilhelm Busch who played an important role in German Pietism. However, as Neuer points out, even though Bockmuehl is rightly considered to be a *"friend of pietism* (or of the evangelical movement)," it is remarkable "that Bockmuehl, according to my knowledge, never called himself a 'Pietist,' let alone an 'Evangelical'. Despite all his

---

356. Letter written by Bockmuehl to P. Engelbert Heller and Martin-Eckart Fuchs, March 5, 1965.

357. Bockmuehl, "Frank Buchman's Message," 40; Bockmuehl, "How Did Jesus," 2; German citation in *WM*, 37. Bockmuehl also refers to Howard who said that our passion should be to help people experience God. Cf. Bockmuehl, "Der einzelne und die Gemeinschaft," 61.

358. Cf. Thomas, "Spirituality of Klaus Bockmuehl: Part One," 2; Neuer, "Theologie," 28; Neuer, "Weite," 1–2; Packer, "Introduction," viii; Frische, "Zur Bockmuehl-Werk-Ausgabe," x.

Theological and Spiritual Influences on Bockmuehl

appreciation of Pietism, a certain distance could always be felt . . . Bockmuehl was conscious of the fact that the message of the Holy Scripture extends far beyond what is thought of and lived out in Pietism—or in any other movement devoted to piety."[359]

Although Bockmuehl's earliest spiritual influence can be traced back to Pietism, his theological studies enabled him to discern "restricted views of and dangers to Pietism."[360] Furthermore, "the unreality of the theological discussion and the spiritual paralysis in the Christian churches"[361] kindled in him a passion for the reality of God and for God's will.

When turning to the issue of guidance by the Spirit, which was crucial for Bockmuehl's Christian ethics, Thomas concludes that, "[w]ith a discerning spirit, Bockmuehl benefited from the inspiration he had received from the Pietist, Moral Re-Armament, and Medieval theologians when it came to developing a rationale for listening to God . . . These three sources of his piety marked his lectures, sermons, books, discussion groups, and counselling sessions."[362]

359. Neuer, "Weite," 1.
360. Ibid., 2.
361. Hofmann, "Revolutionär," 19.
362. Thomas, "Spirituality of Klaus Bockmuehl: Part One," 9.

2

Bockmuehl's Main Theological Concerns

THUS FAR IN OUR examination of various influences that shaped Bockmuehl's theology, some of Bockmuehl's main theological concerns have certainly become apparent by way of repetition. Our aim in this section, however, is to outline Bockmuehl's main theological concerns in the different areas of systematic theology.

The focal points of Bockmuehl's theology are the passion for the reality of God and his kingdom, for God's will, i.e., keeping his commandments and loving God, and for the recovery of the Holy Spirit. Since everything is inter-related, it is difficult to give a brief systematic overview of Bockmuehl's theology, particularly as many themes will be examined later in depth. However, the following sketch of Bockmuehl's theology will provide a framework for an examination of Bockmuehl's understanding of pneumatic Christian ethics.

Due to the limits of our study, we will outline only Bockmuehl's main theological concerns, leaving aside his exposition of ideologies like Marxism, humanism, and secularism, as well as ethical issues such as homosexuality and abortion, property and possessions, environmental and economical ethics. It should, furthermore, be noted that Bockmuehl's aim is first and foremost to strengthen the church as well as theology with regard to real trials and thus to be a "provider" for Christians, particularly those engaging in theology, since he is convinced that "theology can make or break a nation."[1] Since he considers Scripture as the Word of God to be

---

1. Bockmuehl, "Forgotten Factors," 49; cf. Bockmuehl, "Theology as Servant," 45–46. It comes as no surprise, then, to find that Bockmuehl particularly cared for students who were struggling with their faith due to liberal theology. Cf. Packer, "Introduction," viii.

the foundation for and corrective of theology, he attempts to base his own theology on biblical grounds. Furthermore, he also feels the responsibility to raise his voice against those theologies and movements that he assesses as posing a threat to the biblical understanding of the reality of God and of ethics.

Passion for the Reality of God and His Kingdom

The Primacy of the Reality of God and His Kingdom

Since Bockmuehl sees the autonomy and lordship of humankind to be at the root of secularism, he does not grow weary of reminding theology of its main task: "to make God again the subject and object of theology."[2] Following Barth, he defends this claim passionately against those who suggest that theology should take its starting point from the world, from anthropology, from "the self-understanding of modern man,"[3] as Bultmann does, or from religious experience.[4] He asserts that theology ceases to make an essential contribution if it identifies speaking about humanity with speaking about God, since it then ceases to acknowledge God as its supreme authority and center and the Word of God as its foundation.[5] According to Bockmuehl, there can never be such a time, even in the midst of the greatest crises, when the primacy of God in theology can be discarded in order to focus on seemingly more relevant topics.[6]

Whatever topic Bockmuehl was evaluating, be it ethical, social, ecological etc., he sooner or later raised the "God question," the main theme of theology and the church, since this question served him as his paramount criterion.[7] Bockmuehl's main concern was, consequently, the call to "let God be God,"[8] i.e., to acknowledge the sovereignty and lord- or kingship

---

2. Bockmuehl, "Pre-Suppositions," 358.

3. *UG*, 17.

4. Cf. Bockmuehl, "Pre-Suppositions," 351; Bockmuehl, "Kirche," 144; Bockmuehl, "Secularism," 50–51; Bockmuehl, "Der sendende Herr," 182; *CM*, 64–67.

5. Cf. Bockmuehl, "Der sendende Herr," 183.

6. Cf. Bockmuehl, "Vorbereitungen für Nairobi," 177; Bockmuehl, "Secularism," 51f.

7. Cf. Bockmuehl, "Kirche" (social ethics), 143–45; *CaL*, 21–22 (ecology); Bockmuehl, "Secularism," 51–52; *GG*, 23.

8. *CM*, 66.

PART ONE—Bockmuehl's Theological Work

of God in theology and in the church.[9] Accordingly, the commitment to the expansion of the lordship and honor of God among humankind runs like a red thread throughout his whole theology since he considers it to be "the pivotal point of Christian theology and must take precedence over all other concerns."[10]

However, Bockmuehl does not understand the kingdom of God as other-worldly, transcendent, removed from our reality, as Barth does, or completely immanent, this-worldly, as Bultmann does. Quite to the contrary, for Bockmuehl, everything hinges on the reality of God and the growing realization of his kingdom, not only in the Christian but also through him in our outer perceivable, experiential reality.[11] In this context, Bockmuehl introduces the distinction between perceptibility and provability; he concludes that in spite of the non-provability of God's work and his kingdom, it is none the less perceivable, since God is a living, active God.[12] Bockmuehl defends this view vehemently against Bultmann's and Barth's concepts of the reality of God and his kingdom.

When dealing with the kingdom of God, the question arises as to the relationship between the kingdom of God and the world. Since Bockmuehl considers the church, which is the community of the believers, to be the place where the lordship of God is recognized, and considers its members to be "bridgeheads of the kingdom of God on earth,"[13] we will take a closer look at the relationship between church and world and then at the relationship between church and state. This will lead us finally to an analysis of the relationship between creation and redemption.

When examining Bockmuehl's concept of the *relationship between church and world*, we discover mostly a total dualism and separation between both.[14] The background of this dualism is Bockmuehl's description of the *fallen world* as the place where human beings strive for autonomy

9. Cf. *GG*, 23; *CM*, 67; *GiE*, 192.

10. Bockmuehl, "Karl Barth," 30; cf. *CM*, 33; Bockmuehl, "Humanism," 208; Bockmuehl, "Der sendende Herr," 185; *GG*, 269–70; Burkhardt, "Handeln aus dem Hören," 28.

11. Cf. *UG*, 3; *GG*, 23; Bockmuehl, "Der sendende Herr," 185; Bockmuehl, "European Evangelicals," 61.

12. Cf. *CM*, 20, 33; Bockmuehl, "Humanism," 208; *UG*, 102, 151.

13. Bockmuehl, "Scheidung," 15. It should, however, be mentioned that Bockmuehl does not merely equate the kingdom of God with the church. Instead, he points out, "that the church is not itself the kingdom of God but its servant" (Bockmuehl, "Eine Geschichte der Lehre von der Kirche," 26).

14. Cf. *WM*, 77; Bockmuehl, "Der sendende Herr," 184.

Bockmuehl's Main Theological Concerns

and for self-realization. This, according to Bockmuehl, leads not only to a non-Christian, non-moral world, but also to a non-human world, in which hatred replaces love and upon which God has already passed judgment. Therefore, there can be no fellowship of the church with the world, only complete withdrawal and separation as implied in the terms saints and *ekklesia*—viz., the Christians are called out of this world. They are strangers, aliens, who do not belong to this world since their true citizenship is in heaven. In the community of Jesus Christ, there is a different lordship and a different Spirit than in the world (Eph. 2:1-5). The laws enforced in the church and in the world are incompatible. Bockmuehl, furthermore, compares the contrast between church and world with the contrast between the old life according to the flesh and the new life according to the Spirit, which is made possible through the cross of Christ.[15] He believes that the new life, the new creation, is not merely an improvement of the old but a completely and utterly new creation since the old life has to be put to death through participation in Christ's death. New and old life, church and world, are completely irreconcilable.[16]

Furthermore, Bockmuehl is convinced that "the dualism of church and world is not to be resolved before Christ's second coming, the two are thoroughly distinct bodies."[17] Bockmuehl defends this view against those theologians who encourage total assimilation into the world in order to serve it. Moreover, as Bockmuehl points out, in such a case, theology and the church neglect the "inner turmoil of creation, which has turned away from God,"[18] and are therefore in danger of losing their identity in Christ and ending in syncretism.[19]

Hence, only when the church separates itself from the world and consolidates itself can it turn toward the world. Even though the church is not of this world, it is nevertheless called into the world to proclaim the Gospel of Christ in order to save some. Bockmuehl, in fact, uses the illustration of a doctor who diagnoses his patient as critically ill and yet devotes himself to the patient to heal him. He also points to God's way of dealing with the world—while he completely and utterly distances himself from evil, he turns toward the world to save it.[20] "Hence, the attentiveness

---

15. Cf. "Scheidung," 13-19.
16. Cf. Bockmuehl, "Der sendende Herr," 194-95.
17. Bockmuehl, "Presuppositions," 356.
18. Bockmuehl, "Der sendende Herr," 184.
19. Cf. *WM*, 14-15.
20. Cf. Bockmuehl, "Der sendende Herr," 184; Bockmuehl, "Scheidung," 26; Bockmuehl, "Überlegungen," 120.

PART ONE—Bockmuehl's Theological Work

of the church toward the world is an attentiveness which passes through deliberate contradictions."[21] As well as the interpretation of the world as fallen, unjust, and selfish, which is in complete contrast to the loving, just God, and from which the church has to separate itself, Bockmuehl is, nevertheless, aware that some authors of the New Testament also use the term "world" at times to refer to the *creation of God* and to the object of his love.[22] Consequently, the church not only has the task of proclaiming the Gospel but also the responsibility for being the steward of creation and fulfilling the cultural commission by taking care of and tending it like a gardener.[23] Bockmuehl, accordingly, challenges those churches that remain in a state of withdrawal to engage in their God-given task in the world.

Regarding the *relationship between church and state*, Bockmuehl suggests a combination of a revised version of Luther's doctrine of the Two Kingdoms and the Anabaptist concept.[24] Following Luther, he distinguishes between church and state, maintaining that even though God is lord of both realms, he rules them in different ways. Whereas Christ rules in the church according to the Gospel, i.e., by means of forgiveness, God rules in the world by means of the state, to whom he has given the task of containing evil, preserving, and sustaining life, and of promoting good by using the law and force.[25] Consequently, when dealing with secularism, Bockmuehl, on the one hand, points out that "[e]verywhere—theology must insist that God's claim to kingship over the world is a public claim, addressing the whole of society. God does not claim to be the Lord of the Church only."[26] The state is not autonomous but is rather under God's authority; and his commandments, particularly the second table of the Ten Commandments, are "the grammar of creation"[27] that limit the authority of the state. On the other hand, however, Bockmuehl rejects Barth's doctrine of the lordship of *Christ* in church and state and argues that "the border-

21. Bockmuehl, "Scheidung," 26.

22. Cf. Bockmuehl, "Is Christianity a Counterculture?," 52; Bockmuehl, "The Christian as Lawyer," 10; Bockmuehl, "Überlegungen," 120.

23. Cf. "Überlegungen," 122.

24. Cf. Bockmuehl, "Secularization," 56–57; *CW*, 89–92; letter from Beyerhaus to Bockmuehl, March 10, 1970. In the next chapter, we will deal with Bockmuehl's criticism of Luther's doctrine of the Two Kingdoms.

25. Cf. Bockmuehl, "Kirche," 136; *CW*, 89.

26. Bockmuehl, "Secularism and Theology," 51.

27. Bockmuehl, "Is Christianity a Counterculture?," 52. Cf. Bockmuehl, "Kirche," 135; Bockmuehl, "Der Streit," 104; *CW*, 88–92.

line between church and world is ignored, and we make demands on the world for which it does not have the necessary presuppositions."[28] Instead, Bockmuehl insists on distinguishing between *creation and redemption ordinances* and, accordingly, between creation ethics, which he regards as binding for all humans, and redemption ethics. The latter he views as only being in force in the church, since the redemption ordinances can only be presupposed in the church.[29] That redemption ethics not only differs from creation ethics with view to the question of motivation but also regarding its content Bockmuehl derives from the Anabaptist tradition with its strong emphasis on the ethical material of the New Testament, for instance, the Sermon on the Mount.[30] We will analyze this in more depth in the second half of Part Two.

It is particularly interesting that Bockmuehl also portrays the proper relationship between creation and redemption as one of integration/surpassing (*Aufhebung*)[31] in the sense of creation being integrated into and surpassed by redemption or the covenant, as Barth describes it, "since creation 'in itself' is disintegrated."[32] Only in the realm of the lordship of God does creation find its purpose and aim. Moreover, as Bockmuehl concludes, "[i]n this area can be located the immeasurable surpassing of the creation of God which in itself is already glorious."[33] He was convinced that this concept of the "dialectic of integration and surpassing" ("Dialektik der Aufhebung")[34] safeguards sufficiently against the negligence either of creation, which he found in many contemporary evangelical or pietistic concepts, or of redemption.[35] However, this integration of creation into the kingdom of God as its purpose does not imply that creation has already been fully restored. Rather, the "kingdom is still in process of realization.

28. Bockmuehl, "The Socialist Ideal," 56; cf. *WM*, 149.

29. Cf. *WM*, 149; Bockmuehl, "The Christian as Lawyer," 33; Bockmuehl, "Kirche," 132.

30. Cf. Bockmuehl, "Kirche," 135–37.

31. It is interesting to discover that already Barth, as well as Hegel and his pupil Marx, used this term. Due to the different connotations the term carries, it can be translated in various ways such as negation or abolition, preservation or transcendence. Cf. Lyon, "The Challenge of Marxism," 117; Störig, *Kleine Weltgeschichte* 460–1; Tsanoff, *The Great Philosophers*, 448. Bockmuehl, however, uses it interchangeably with the (German and English) term "I/integration" when referring to the relationship between creation and the lordship of God. Cf. "Leiblichkeit," 46.

32. Bockmuehl, "Leiblichkeit," 46; cf. *CW*, 83.

33. Bockmuehl, "Leiblichkeit," 43.

34. *LuG*, 285.

35. Cf. *GG*, 210; Bockmuehl, "Is Christianity a Counterculture?," 52.

PART ONE—Bockmuehl's Theological Work

That is to say, it is still controversial in the world."[36] This also implies that the reality of God and his kingdom depends on interpretation and as such remains contested until Christ's second coming and the final judgment. Bockmuehl tries to hold together present and future eschatology by, on the one hand, defending the contention that God's kingdom is, indeed, real and perceivable in our objective world and, on the other hand, stressing that it is God who will bring about his kingdom. With this conviction he rejects any notion of a merely immanent eschatology.[37]

The Reality of God and the "New Man"

Bockmuehl repeatedly engages with the Marxist quest for the "new man"[38] by evaluating it in the light of the Christian view. He is convinced, for instance, that the change of human nature cannot be achieved at all through humankind itself, not even through any change of structures as the Marxists believe. According to Bockmuehl, their error in this regard was to belittle the reality of the corrupted and fallen human nature with its inclination to self-glorification. In order to change the world and humanity, education as a means is therefore doomed to fail in the long run. Bockmuehl believes that only God can bring about the radical, concrete, real change that the Marxists are searching for.[39] Thus, the question regarding God's reality is directly related to the question of the new human being. Because God is real and active in this world, as Bockmuehl pleads for throughout his whole life, "the new birth was not and is not simply a change in status before God but an alteration in one's entire earthly being. In addition, what has just been said about the reality of the new birth must also be said about the concreteness of the ongoing process of sanctification."[40]

Likewise, justification and rebirth not only include forgiveness of sins but also the creation of the "new man," which means that "the past is gone; a new set of values and a new strength is in effect"[41]—namely, the Holy Spirit. When turning to the human response to God's regenerating work, to conversion, Bockmuehl again draws attention to the reality of the

36. Bockmuehl, "Humanism and the Kingdom of God," 208; cf. *CaL*, 17.
37. Bockmuehl, "Pre-Suppositions," 352–55.
38. Bockmuehl, "The Marxist New Man," 53–54.
39. Cf. *CaL*, 21–22; *CM*, 144, 161; Bockmuehl, "Perimeters," 17.
40. *CM*, 32.
41. Bockmuehl, "Perimeters," 10; cf. Bockmuehl, "Scheidung," 16–17.

Bockmuehl's Main Theological Concerns

Christian conversion in the New Testament, since the latter is described as being of a practical, ethical, and existential nature. First and foremost, conversion is portrayed as a radical and concrete change of lordship—no longer living for oneself and one's desires but for God and his will.[42] According to Bockmuehl, the old self with its ego-centricity has to die; in this way, there is a participation in Christ's innocent death on the cross, which takes place in repentance and confession. The willingness to be self-critical, uncovering one's own opposition to God and his will, and the acceptance of Christ's work of redemption is a pre-condition before God raises the new self with its exo-centricity.[43] This new human being enters into a personal relationship with Christ, living wholly committed to God and fellow-humans in love and thus furthering his kingdom. Consequently, Bockmuehl claims that the realization of the kingdom of God depends on and comes about through individuals who let God be their lord and who obey his will.[44] Similarly, he defines *faith* as change of lordship, gaining a new aim, i.e., living for and in expectancy of the realization of God's lordship, which includes obeying God's will and loving him. Bockmuehl, consequently, highlights strongly that faith according to Scripture encompasses "not only our thinking and our affirmation, but also our obedience and our action."[45] The new human being is thus a human being changed in every aspect of their life. After looking at the initial stage of the Christian life, let us now turn to the implications this change has for the individual and for society and thus to the manifestations of God's reality.

The Reality of God and Its Manifestations in This World

Closely linked to the question of God's reality is, for Bockmuehl, the question of the perceptibility of God's works in this world. When turning to Bockmuehl's examination of Feuerbach's and Marx's critique of religion, we discover that he evaluates it in a self-critical manner. His conclusion is that if theological concepts are not able to offer some kind of manifestation of God's work in this world they are under suspicion of the unreality

---

42. Cf. Bockmuehl, "Perimeters," 9–14; Bockmuehl, "Humanism," 209; Bockmuehl, "Pre-Suppositions," 355.

43. Cf. Bockmuehl, "Leiblichkeit," 37–40; Bockmuehl, "Pre-Suppositions," 355.

44. Cf. Bockmuehl, "Perimeters," 11–12; Bockmuehl, "Der sendende Herr," 195–6.

45. Bockmuehl, "Wahrnehmung," 342. Cf. Bockmuehl, "Glaube," 62, 71–72; *CM*, 28, 165.

of God and thus no different from practical atheism. Bockmuehl bases this accusation on his conviction that, according to Scripture, God manifests himself in a perceivable way and has done so first and foremost in "the life, death and resurrection of Jesus of Nazareth."[46] Hence, he points out that in contrast to the Greeks, the Christians consider *history* to be the realm in which God has revealed himself visibly; this culminated in the resurrection of Jesus Christ. This event Bockmuehl describes as "the key to the whole reality and perceptibility of salvation history."[47] It is of utmost importance for Bockmuehl that God's act of salvation took place in history and therefore in our objective reality since Christ's death on the cross was not merely cognitive but implied actual pain and suffering. If this had not been the case, God's redemption would not have been able to deal with our sin in a real manner since the nature of the latter is of actual reality. It is interesting to note that Bockmuehl finds traces of this view of the reality of sin in the early Marx, particularly in "his assessment of the fundamental discrepancy in man between Is and Ought"[48] and in his understanding of self-alienation. At the same time, however, Bockmuehl points out that Christianity's evaluation of humanity's self-centeredness and wrongdoing but also of its ability to change and forgive is more realistic.[49]

If "Christ became history so that all history might be salvation history,"[50] as Bockmuehl contends, what implications does this have for human history? Would it be valid to conclude that all of human history, including all religious experiences, can be seen as God's revelation in time and space? Bockmuehl rejects this as syncretism and accuses all those holding this position of disregarding the authority of Scripture.[51] Though revelation does take place in history, it cannot be inferred that therefore all history can be regarded as revelation, as theologians such as Friedrich Gogarten suggest.[52] Nevertheless, Bockmuehl maintains that "[i]t is the task and the glory of theology to point to the traces of God in history and to help people find the right path. Traces of God are to be found

---

46. *UG*, 161; cf. 155; *GG*, 265, Bockmuehl, "Wahrnehmung," 340.

47. *UG*, 155.

48. Bockmuehl, "Perimeters," 15.

49. Cf. ibid., 7–8, 15, 17; *CM*, 32.

50. *UG*, 158.

51. Cf. *UG*, 158; Bockmuehl, "Nairobi," 176; Bockmuehl, "Pre-Suppositions," 353.

52. Other theologians that Bockmuehl mentions are the ecumenical theologians J. C. Hoekendijk, M. M. Thomas and those advocating a "theology of culture and mediation." *WM*, 77; cf. 74–75; Bockmuehl, "Pre-Suppositions," 353–54.

Bockmuehl's Main Theological Concerns

everywhere in the history of the disciples of Christ."[53] This implies, for Bockmuehl, that God is not only perceivable in this world through his works but can also be directly experienced. Bockmuehl thus values *experience* as legitimate, indispensable evidence for the work of God in this world as long as it is in accordance with Scripture. He even speaks about "doctrine and experience complement[ing] each other."[54]

Besides history and experience, Bockmuehl holds the conviction that God's manifestations are also perceivable in *practice*, i.e., in human actions, due to the fact that one of God's means of working in this world is through human beings.[55] Bockmuehl, therefore, considers ethics as the field in which God's reality is made manifest.[56] The reality of God cannot be established ontologically or epistemologically but ethically. In this respect, Bockmuehl agrees with Marxism that the value and aim of a theory lies ultimately not in its theoretical outworking but in its effect on the practical life of humans, i.e., if it is able to change the world visibly, starting with the individual.[57] Bockmuehl, accordingly, asserts that "[t]he saving work of God purposes to achieve, even in man, a perceptible practical alteration: that is, an alteration of his practice. For man's action is perceptible."[58] We may conclude that, for Bockmuehl, only an ethic that pre-supposes the reality of God's lordship and expects his action in human beings, changing not just their mind or will but particularly their practice, reaches the standards of Christian ethics and affects our reality.[59]

What consequence does this view of God's reality manifest in human practice have for man's *corporeality*? Bockmuehl demonstrates that the latter "and not just his self-understanding is the field of God's action and hence the realm to which Christian dogmatics and Christian ethics refer . . . *The bodily reality of man and the bodily reality of world history are the theaters of God's glory*."[60] Hence, whoever rejects corporeality as God's field of action underestimates the reality of creation and of the incarnation of Christ in this corporeal world. Particularly the incarnation, in Bockmuehl's view, confirms corporeality in its dignity, though only if the

---

53. *UG*, 161. Cf. Bockmuehl, "Wahrnehmung," 354.
54. Bockmuehl, "Nairobi," 175. Cf. Bockmuehl, "Wahrnehmung," 346; *UG*, 142.
55. Cf. *UG*, 110.
56. *GiE*, 11.
57. *CM*, 27; *UG*, 154.
58. *UG*, 147.
59. Cf. *GiE*, 12, 191; *GG*, 24; *UG*, 160.
60. *UG*, 51–52.

PART ONE—Bockmuehl's Theological Work

body is used to further God's kingdom.[61] The consequence is, according to Bockmuehl, that salvation history occurs not only in world history but, more precisely, in human corporeality without which history could not even take place.[62]

For Bockmuehl, the *social* consequences of regeneration are closely related to the ethical manifestations of God's work in this world. If the new birth cannot be reduced to a mere inner religious experience, but rather manifests itself in a renewed moral life, as we have outlined above, this would inevitably cause "a transformation of people including their interpersonal relationships and their relationship to material things."[63] In this context, Bockmuehl points particularly to Jesus' encounter with Zacchaeus and the social implications it provoked such as his radically changed attitude to other people and to material possessions, particularly money. The "new man" is consequently not only restored in his relationship to God but also to his neighbor, and he thus becomes a facilitator of "real humanism"[64] that heals humanity as described and demonstrated by Jesus.[65] This real humanism, this orientation toward others, was fully realized only in Jesus, the true human. The purpose and destiny for humanity is, therefore, to be transformed into the likeness of Christ, which can be described as a process of humanization and is identical with sanctification. The pre-supposition of this process, as Bockmuehl emphasizes, is the lordship and the reality of God in the life of the individual. Hence, it is not surprising that Bockmuehl views sanctification and true humanity as being the reverse of secularism with its emphasis on self-orientation instead of orientation toward God and one's neighbor: "Sanctification does not mean perfection but listening to God, simply to take 'steps toward the center' before taking steps toward people. Sanctifying means: to be disengaged and to stay away from the zeitgeist, from serving oneself, from materialism. Sanctification means: to place oneself at the disposal of God; sanctification therefore is the opposite term to the term secularization."[66]

61. Cf. *LuG*, 274; Bockmuehl, "Leiblichkeit," 42–45.

62. Bockmuehl, "Leiblichkeit," 37, 43–44.

63. Bockmuehl, "Theorie," 120; cf. *WM*, 190. According to Bockmuehl, the negligence of the social implications of many theologians can be traced back to a merely inward interpretation of rebirth. Cf. "Der sendende Herr," 196.

64. Bockmuehl, "Real Humanism," 5–8; *CM*, 31; *UG*, 63–64;

65. Cf. *CM*, 31–32; Bockmuehl, "Theorie," 119–21; Bockmuehl, "Perimeters," 12–13, Bockmuehl, "Humanität," 83–84.

66. Bockmuehl, "Evangelium," 136; cf. Bockmuehl, " . . . to live soberly," 5; "Humanism," 209, 224.

Bockmuehl's Main Theological Concerns

It comes as no surprise then to discover that Bockmuehl engages himself with the analysis of secularism, pointing out the destructive consequences for humanity and pleading urgently for an acknowledgement of God's lordship in one's life. Bockmuehl is convinced that only in that way the process of secularization can be reversed.[67]

The Reality of God and the Holy Spirit

For Bockmuehl, the reality of God's works on earth is directly linked to the work of the Holy Spirit. In fact, he is adamant that theology without a concrete pneumatology can have nothing to say about the reality of God since it neglects the "Realizer" of God's work: "The power of God comes into the world with the Holy Spirit . . . *The Spirit leaps the barrier between the other world and this world.* Through the Spirit, through God's indwelling in man, the reality of God is at home on earth. The Spirit is the great Realizer; he realizes the counsels of God."[68]

Without the work of the Holy Spirit, the transformation of the individual and, as a result, the change of society is not possible. After all, it is the Spirit living in the new human being who not only changes the mind but who effects the externally visible good works and fruit, as well as the *charismata*. Thus, Bockmuehl points out the significance of the Holy Spirit for bridging "the nasty gap between theory and practice,"[69] between dogmatics and ethics, by motivating and empowering people who are open for his guidance to act according to God's will.[70] It is the Spirit himself who realizes the kingdom of God through the transformation of the believer into the likeness of Christ. Though the internal work of the Spirit in the believer is and remains hidden, yet its effects are made visible through the believer's glorification of God with his body. Consequently, as Bockmuehl argues, God's reality is mediated in this world by the Holy Spirit who uses human corporeality as an instrument to bring about God's kingdom in time and space.[71]

---

67. Cf. Bockmuehl, "Christianity Has a Moral Backbone," 55.
68. *UG*, 159; cf. Bockmuehl, "Der sendende Herr," 197.
69. Bockmuehl, "Theorie," 122.
70. Cf. *UG*, 146–47; Bockmuehl, "Problem der Ethik," 82–84; Bockmuehl, "Theorie," 122.
71. *LG*, 149; *GG*, 95; Bockmuehl, "Humanism," 221; Bockmuehl, "Der sendende Herr," 197; Bockmuehl, "Leiblichkeit," 44–45.

PART ONE—Bockmuehl's Theological Work

Passion for God's Will: Loving God and Keeping His Commandments

In Bockmuehl's view, theology's commitment lies in its basis and its goal: that is, in the promise and the program: "your will be done, on earth as it is in heaven" (Matt 6:10). If it is true to its essence, Christian theology will serve the hope of a large-scale swing back to the will of God—in theology, church, and culture.[72]

This renewed commitment to the will of God was Bockmuehl's primary concern throughout his whole life. He was convinced that a return to God and his will, i.e., the furtherance of the kingdom of God, is the only remedy for the social problems of humanity since it is God's power that brings about restoration and justice.[73]

But what is the content of the will of God? When looking at Bockmuehl's definition, the content can be summarized as "loving God and keeping his commandments"; this is the title of the memorial volume for Bockmuehl.[74] This leads us to Bockmuehl's concept of ethics, which, if divided into the main building-blocks, is constituted of love, law, and, the frequently forgotten factor, Spirit. Characteristics particular to Bockmuehl's ethics are "[e]thical standards, both personal and socio-political, on the one hand, and spiritual life on the other,"[75] which Bockmuehl sees as originating from love for God.

Having outlined the main principles of Bockmuehl's ethics, we must now go into more depth, first, by portraying Bockmuehl's ethics as a whole with law and Spirit as the double principle, then, by explicating his understanding of loving God as the aim of ethics and taking into account the role of the Spirit.

God's Will: Law and Spirit

It is interesting to note that Bockmuehl divides Christian ethics into three different parts comparing them to different layers of a wedding cake.

72. *UG*, 4; cf. letter from Bockmuehl to Fuchs et al., March 29, 1968.

73. Cf. *CM*, 45; *GiE*, 188–89; Bockmuehl, "Keeping His Commandments," 98; M. Bockmuehl and Burkhardt, "Preface," 7; letter from Bockmuehl to P. Engelbert Heller and Martin-Eckart Fuchs, March 5, 1965.

74. Bockmuehl and Burkhardt, *Gott lieben und seine Gebote halten—Loving God and Keeping His Commandments*; cf. *UG*, 7, *GG*, 514–15.

75. Packer, "Introduction," 4:viii.

Bockmuehl's Main Theological Concerns

First, humankind is called to take up its stewardship regarding the creation and its cultural mandate assigned to him by God, which includes "preservation of life and community,"[76] but also includes sustenance of the environment. Instructions for these duties, which are dealt with in social and ecological ethics, are partly given in the Golden Rule, the Ten Commandments, and the double commandment of love as a summary of the latter. In fact, these tasks of *creation ethics* are not just limited to the Christian, since they do not presuppose conversion, but are given to humankind as a whole.

Secondly, the Christian is called to a life of holiness. This includes loving God and taking time for communion with him (spirituality) as well as loving one another, even one's enemies, and fulfilling the Great Commission with the final goal to "present everyone fully mature in Christ" (Col 1:28).[77] Christian mission encompasses, for Bockmuehl, church-building activities, evangelism, teaching, and Christian service (*diakonia*).[78] However, while the task related to creation ethics is about sustaining life, redemption ethics, as Bockmuehl names this second, specifically Christian vocation, is about saving and healing life.[79]

A third vocation for the Christian is to listen to the instructions the Holy Spirit gives to the "individual person at a certain time in a certain place."[80] The guidance of the Holy Spirit can include a call to cross-cultural mission, a clear command to share the Gospel with someone, an instruction to give up one's own right for certain things such as property, a home, a call to live in a community etc. Since the Holy Spirit functions like a "differential" principle, i.e., the Holy Spirit applies the general will of God to the individual in his or her specific situation, Bockmuehl calls this third vocation, in distinction to the other two, "differential ethics" ("Differentialethik").[81]

Characteristic of Bockmuehl is that he neither advocates only a creation ethic nor only a kingdom ethic but, rather, insists on holding them together. The foundation, like the first layer of a wedding cake, is given with creation ethics; upon this the kingdom ethics is built, not in the sense of reaching a higher stage where one can leave behind the foundation, but

---

76. *CW*, 26.
77. Cf. *CW*, 26; *UG*, 158.
78. Cf. *GG*, 514; Bockmuehl, "Der sendende Herr," 188–90, 198.
79. Cf. *CW* 26–7; *SU*, 37–40.
80. *CW*, 25.
81. *GG*, 514.

as affirming the foundation and at the same time surpassing it (cf. Matt 5:20). Bockmuehl makes it very clear that redemption ethics and differential ethics, which he conceives of as the *proprium* of Christian ethics, fall into the broader framework of creation ethics. Hence, the specific Christian vocation remains in the framework of the Decalogue. Likewise, the guidance of the Holy Spirit does not contradict either the teaching of Jesus or the law. Rather, as Bockmuehl asserts, "as they follow the leading of the Spirit, believers see the eternally just requirements of the law fulfilled in their lives."[82] In fact, Bockmuehl considers Spirit and law to be the main building-blocks, the double-principle, of a Christian ethic. One without the other either leads to antinomianism or legalism. Whereas the law maintains its role as norm for the will of God as a guard-rail for our lives, the Holy Spirit has the function of motivating and guiding the believer.[83]

Another decisive mark of Bockmuehl's ethics is its trinitarian structure in so far that "the Father corresponds to creational ethics, the Son to redemption ethics, and the Holy Spirit to the ethics of individual guidance."[84] We will look more closely at this structure in a later chapter.

God's Will: Love and Spirit

One of Bockmuehl's major concerns is to recover the double commandment of love as the summary of God's will for Christian ethics. While the commandment to love one's neighbor as oneself has been emphasized by theologians throughout the centuries, the commandment to love God has, in Bockmuehl's opinion, often been neglected; this was particularly true in Lutheranism. Since he considers love of God to be the positive fulfillment of the first commandment as well as the synopsis of the Decalogue, he consequently endeavors to regain "love for God as a sphere of activity for Christian ethics."[85] In order to fully comprehend Bockmuehl's concept of ethics we have to take a closer look at his interpretation of loving God.

Although, for Bockmuehl, love of God as used in Scripture comprises emotions such as joy, enthusiasm, and passion, thereby loving God with our soul, he highlights particularly that we are also called to love God with our heart. This he understands to refer to a total dedication of our will as the center of our lives to God. Accordingly, Bockmuehl concludes that love

82. Bockmuehl, "Sanctification and Christian Mission," 60.
83. Cf. ibid., 59; *GG*, 517, 526; *SU*, 28–29; Bockmuehl, "Ten Commandments," 134.
84. *CW*, 27.
85. *GG*, 515; cf. 275; *CW*, 31–32, 37, 48.

encompasses voluntary, active *obedience* since "[l]ove of God is shorthand for doing his will and keeping his commandments."[86] Moreover, Bockmuehl points out that love, while remaining within the framework of the law, surpasses it by, for instance, "doing something beautiful for God,"[87] such as the works of supererogation. Hence, though the commandments are like a practical commentary of love, love is at the same time the aim of the commandments.[88]

When we turn to the question of where the strength arises to love God with our whole heart, soul, and mind, as the double commandment of love requests of us, we find that Bockmuehl answers in a twofold manner: first, love for God is an immediate response to God's saving love for us revealed to us, above all, in the experience of forgiveness and thus originates from gratitude.[89] Secondly, although the double commandment of love is a *commandment* to love God, Bockmuehl points out that it is also a *promise* that God himself fulfills by pouring out his love into the heart of the believer through the Holy Spirit (cf. Rom 5:5). For Bockmuehl, this connection between love and Spirit is of paramount importance. In fact, he argues that one's pneumatology also determines one's knowledge about the love of God.[90] The task of the believer is therefore to pray for the fruit and gift of the Spirit, i.e., for love, but likewise to listen to the Spirit's guidance for the concrete application of how to love God. In fact, Bockmuehl considers *prayer* itself to be the application of love for God in so far as it is the expression of friendship with God and union with Christ. He does not understand prayer as a monologue but rather as a constant "confidential conversation with God,"[91] a sharing of one's whole life with him, including listening to his promises and plans, and thus participating in his concerns for this world. It is, furthermore, out of this communion with Christ that obedience as well as creativity flow, and it is also in those quiet times that God's love and his forgiveness are received.[92] This enables the believer to serve God and love his neighbor, and, in so doing, to further the kingdom of God. Bockmuehl is convinced that without the practice of

86. *CW*, 45; cf. 43, 47; Bockmuehl, "Great Commandment," 13.

87. *CW*, 44.

88. Cf. *GG*, 515; Bockmuehl, "Great Commandment," 25; Bockmuehl, "Sanctification and Christian Mission," 60; Bockmuehl, "Protestant Ethics," 112.

89. *UG*, 162; Bockmuehl, "Great Commandment," 16; *LbG*, 12; *CW*, 44.

90. *GG*, 516; cf. *CW*, 42; Bockmuehl, "Great Commandment," 17.

91. *LbG*, 61; cf. 60–62; *LG*, 146–49; *CW*, 41, 45f; Bockmuehl, "Säkularismus," 186.

92. Cf. Bockmuehl, "Toward a Spirituality," 42; *LbG*, 62; Thomas, "Spirituality of Klaus Bockmuehl: Part Two," 33.

biblical spirituality, above all, love for God, the foundation for Christian service is missing in theology and church. Hence, theology needs to move from a "theo-logy" to a "theo-philia"[93] as Bockmuehl remarks in a letter to friends.

Conclusion

After having outlined Bockmuehl's concern for the reality of God as well as for the love of God, one may ask what the relation between these main concerns is. The following quotation of Bockmuehl indicates a very close inter-relation: "This is where everything depends on recognizing the right to God's love, even the priority of God's love—just as the wording of the double commandment of love implies. For this is where a primary source of the reality of God in ethics can be found. The loss of love for God and the corresponding chapter of Christian life . . . is the beginning of the 'unrealization' of God and the beginning of atheism in ethics."[94]

Indeed, since love of God as well as the reality of God is only and truly realized by the Holy Spirit, as mentioned earlier, Bockmuehl's main concern is to rediscover the role of the Spirit for Christian ethics as we shall see in the following chapters.

---

93. Circular letter written by Bockmuehl on Dec. 12, 1977, 3.
94. *GiE*, 162.

Part Two

The Holy Spirit and Christian Ethics in the Theology of Klaus Bockmuehl

IN THE COURSE OF this part we shall discover what Bockmuehl's answers are to such relevant questions as the following: Is the law, and in particular the Decalogue, still valid for Christians or do Christians now only live by the Spirit? Does something like a natural law, a universally binding moral law exist? Does a Christian ethic differ from a non-Christian one? And if so, what would be distinctive about a Christian ethic? Should a Christian focus mainly on looking after the environment and on practicing social responsibility or on preaching the Gospel and on mission? How can inner transformation happen that leads to a changed life? Are love for God, spirituality, mission, and guidance by the Spirit topics that should be dealt with in a Christian ethic? And, above all, what role does the Holy Spirit play within Christian ethics?

However, before outlining Bockmuehl's answers to these questions, we shall first examine three different ethical concepts that Bockmuehl considered to have been responsible for a severe lack of a proper doctrine of the Holy Spirit within Christian ethics at his time.

3

The Neglect of the Holy Spirit in the History of Christian Ethics and Bockmuehl's Response

THE NEGLECT OF THE Holy Spirit in the history of Christian ethics has to be seen in the wider context of "a tragic history in the church concerning the Holy Spirit."[1] Bockmuehl contends that it was as early as the second and third century, when the church had to react to movements that overemphasized the Holy Spirit, such as Montanism, that the proper balance between the Spirit and authority was lost: "In the traditional Catholic doctrine of the church, everything seems to be organized and codified. The spontaneity of the work of the Holy Spirit has merged into human administration, in order to restrain it . . . The teaching office is now the substitute for the teaching role of the Holy Spirit."[2]

Expositions of the Holy Spirit were, according to Bockmuehl, limited to the doctrine of the person of the Holy Spirit in the context of the Trinity leaving aside the specific work of the Holy Spirit.[3] This, in turn, had the consequence that many concepts of Christian ethics throughout subsequent centuries suffered from a severe lack of a doctrine of the work of the Holy Spirit; this was true particularly of his informative function. In this chapter, we will mainly focus on those concepts that Bockmuehl regards to be very influential and to be responsible for the pneumatological weakness in theology, particularly in ethics, during his lifetime.

Bockmuehl himself deems the Holy Spirit to have a seminal and crucial role to play in the field of Christian ethics. In Bockmuehl's

1. Bockmuehl, "Introduction," 114.
2. Bockmuehl, *Kirche*, 52.
3. Cf. Bockmuehl, "Introduction," 114.

PART TWO—The Holy Spirit and Christian Ethics in the Theology

understanding, the work of the Holy Spirit in Christian ethics is, as mentioned above, directly related to the reality of God in ethics since it is the Holy Spirit who realizes God's works in a perceivable manner in time and space.[4] In addition, however, the Holy Spirit is also relevant for issues that Bockmuehl considers to be the *proprium* of Christian ethics such as love for God, spirituality, church-building activities, which consist of mission and Christian *diakonia*, and the concrete guidance of the Holy Spirit.[5] An ethic that does not give due attention to these issues, among others, is, as we will discover shortly, regarded by Bockmuehl to have neglected the Holy Spirit. It should also be noted that Bockmuehl, when evaluating the different ethical concepts, particularly focuses on the question regarding "the relationship of the invariable norms to the variable situation or, in the most general sense, on the question of the means of differentiation of ethical principles."[6]

Reformation Ethics

Before taking a closer look at how the Holy Spirit is neglected in Reformation ethics, we must first investigate the Reformation concept of the relationship between Scripture and the Holy Spirit since, according to Bockmuehl, this concept had major implications for Reformation ethics.[7]

Word and Spirit

When examining the early works of Luther, Bockmuehl discovers recurrent references to the Holy Spirit.[8] Particularly in Luther's lectures on the Psalms, delivered from 1513–1516, "the themes of divine guidance and listening to the God who speaks stand out in a number of places."[9] Yet, he

   4. Cf. *GiE*, 12.
   5. Cf. *GG*, 514; Bockmuehl, "Protestant Ethics," 102–3.
   6. *GG*, 13. Cf. LeRoy Long Jr., *A Survey of Christian Ethics*, 40.
   7. Cf. *GG*, 516–21.
   8. Cf. *GG*, 246–47.
   9. *LG*, 122. In 1977, Bockmuehl wrote to his friend Horst-Klaus Hofmann, with whom he had discussed Luther's concept of guidance by the Spirit: "In 1516 in his lecture on Psalms, Luther was still able to speak of guidance, of an 'intus duci' (= to be guided inwardly) as a matter of course. Even in the battle against monasticism he still spares the great saints severe criticism and speaks of them and of their experience of guidance in a surprisingly positive way. But that seems to be something that only

110

The Neglect of the Holy Spirit in the History of Christian Ethics

finds evidence that Luther does not conceive of God's guidance as happening immediately but rather interprets it as receiving an external word such as that of Scripture or, alternatively, as a result of his monastic conditioning, the counsel of a superior. Indeed, according to Bockmuehl, the early Luther still holds to the Roman Catholic authority and hierarchy with its strong sense of submission and obedience to the superiors since he believes that God speaks through their directions. Beyond that, he even considers the proper interpretation of Scripture to be restricted to the leaders. Hence, before the Reformation, Luther binds the Spirit to Scripture and human counsel, even agreeing with the then current Catholic tradition that the unity of the church is rightly preserved through hierarchy.[10]

However, as Bockmuehl points out, when Luther has to defend his interpretation of Scripture against the Roman Catholic authorities, he changes his view radically, "at least during the decisive moments of the Reformation." This "illustrates the tensions with which the Reformers struggled in the debate over personal inspiration."[11]

According to Bockmuehl, it was not long after the beginning of the Reformation that Luther feels forced to emphasize the precedence of the external means, such as the written or proclaimed word and the sacraments, over the inward speaking of the Holy Spirit; this is due to the controversy with the Prophets of Zwickau and other Anabaptists in 1522. As a consequence, Luther seems to dispute on the whole any kind of guidance not mediated by external means.[12] Only a few times does Bockmuehl detect in the writings of Luther scattered allusions to the concept of Spirit *with* the Word, despite his general emphasis on Spirit *through* the Word, i.e., the superiority of the Word over the Spirit.[13] For instance, in a treatise on prayer written in 1534, Luther describes the experience of having thoughts during a prayer time that clearly originate from the Holy Spirit. He goes on to encourage the Christian to jot down the words imparted

---

occurs in the past" (cited in Hofmann, "Revolutionär," 28).

10. Cf. *LG*, 123-24; Bockmuehl, "Hermeneutik," 271. This interpretation of Luther—his openness to the Spirit's guidance in his early years, yet also the dependence on the word—can also be found in Lohse, *Martin Luther's Theology*, 237.

11. *LG*, 124.

12. Cf. *LG*, 126-27; *GG*, 246-47; Althaus, *The Theology of Martin Luther*, 36-37. Lohse concludes similarly: "To Luther's way of thinking, there is a further, important consequence: there is no special guidance of the Spirit in the life of the Christian. Exception is made only in the case of prayer" (*Luther's Theology*, 238). Cf. Plathow, "Der Geist hilft unserer Schwachheit," 158, 161; Schmidt, *Gesammelte Aufsätze*, 122-24; Spiegel-Schmidt, *Kirche ohne Geist?*, 20; Lage, *Martin Luther's Christology*, 142-43.

13. Cf. *GG*, 244-45; *LbG*, 51.

PART TWO—The Holy Spirit and Christian Ethics in the Theology

by the Holy Spirit since these words are more precious than any human prayer.[14] Similarly, Luther contends in the Smalcald Articles a few years later "that God gives no one his Spirit or grace except through or with the external Word which comes before."[15] Though his main emphasis is certainly on the Spirit coming *through* the Word, Bockmuehl draws particular attention to the fact that Luther—at least in this particular passage—does not exclude the possibility of the Spirit's coming *with* the Word.[16] This statement by Luther is, however, when compared to the whole of his writings rather exceptional.

When turning to Calvin and the Reformed Confessions, Bockmuehl also charges them with not having arrived at the proper balance between the Word and the Spirit. This might seem surprising at first sight since Calvin is often entitled "the theologian of the Holy Spirit."[17] This is, indeed, acknowledged by Bockmuehl, as can be seen in the following statement: "There is no doubt that in the theology of Calvin the notion of the Holy Spirit and his teaching and leading is truly present, if not even omnipresent."[18] Nevertheless, he accuses Calvin of having reduced prophecy to the interpretation of Scripture and, likewise, the guidance of the Holy Spirit, or the "inner testimony of the Holy Spirit," to comprehending, confirming, and remembering the proclaimed word of God.[19] Instead, as Bockmuehl points out, Calvin should have allowed the Spirit to reveal new information as well as illuminating Scripture, thus not chaining the Spirit to the word but allowing the Spirit to speak *together with* the word instead of merely *through* the word.[20] That Calvin was at least aware

---

14. Luther writes: "If such an abundance of good thoughts comes to us we ought to disregard the other petitions, make room for such thoughts, listen in silence, and under no circumstances obstruct them. The Holy Spirit himself preaches here, and one word of his sermon is far better than a thousand of our prayers" (Luther, "A Simple Way To Pray," 198). Cf. *SU*, 33–34; Bockmuehl, "Der neue Mensch und die ideologischen Systeme," 6; *LbG*, 51–52. See also Lehmann, *Luther and Prayer*, 93; cf. 92–94.

15. Luther, "The Smalcald Articles," 312 (III, art. 8); cf. Bockmuehl, "Protestant Ethics," 114.

16. Cf. *GG*, 244; Bockmuehl, "Protestant Ethics," 114.

17. Bockmuehl, "Protestant Ethics," 107.

18. *GG*, 372; cf. 440.

19. *GG*, 374; cf. 376–77, 419–20, 437; Bockmuehl, "Protestant Ethics," 107–8; *LG*, 129–30; Calvin, *Institutes*, 1.7.4; 3.1.4; 3.2.15; 3.2.33–36; Barth, *The Theology of John Calvin*, 167; Krusche, *Das Wirken des Heiligen Geistes*, 214–16, 288–94.

20. That the Spirit took second place behind Scripture had, according to Bockmuehl, also implications for Calvin's doctrine of the Trinity in that the latter comes close to a binity. Cf. *GG*, 434.

of that concept can, according to Bockmuehl, be seen in his sermons on Job in which Calvin remarks on the consensus between Spirit and Word, thus viewing them as two separate voices that, nevertheless, witness to the same truth. It is rather unfortunate, in Bockmuehl's opinion, that Calvin does not develop this concept further.[21]

A direct consequence of binding the work of the Holy Spirit to Scripture, as Bockmuehl concludes, is that guidance by the Holy Spirit is experienced mainly through the interpretation of Scripture.[22] Calvin even regards the preacher or teacher of the Gospel to be the representative of Christ. He develops this view particularly in reaction to the Spiritualists and Anabaptists who strove to abolish the teaching office altogether. Bockmuehl, however, indicates that Calvin's over-emphasis on the ministry of the skilled teacher led to "a spiritual disempowerment of the church,"[23] which clearly runs counter to the New Testament concept of the priesthood of all believers and thus neglects the promise of the gift of the Holy Spirit for every Christian.[24] Furthermore, in Bockmuehl's opinion, this over-emphasis also accounts for the "one-man show" that was apparent in Protestantism.[25]

Bockmuehl's criticism of the Reformation concept of Word and Spirit is best summarized in the following text: "The loss of knowledge about acts and utterances of the Spirit is a tragedy that presumably occurred at the time of the Reformation when Protestant theology, in defense against the unbridled excesses of the enthusiasts, minimized the voice of the Spirit to mean no more than the printed word of Holy Scripture. That laid inspiration to the chain, and today that still is the hedge that confronts Protestant theology: 'God speaks only through Scripture.'"[26]

Having outlined the Reformers' understanding of the relationship between the Word and the Spirit, we now turn to their concept of ethics, giving particular attention to the consequences of the neglect of the Spirit in ethics as Bockmuehl explicates. Since the two main building-blocks of

21. Cf. *GG*, 438–39; Bockmuehl, "Protestant Ethics," 114.
22. *GG*, 405.
23. *GG*, 409.
24. Cf. Bockmuehl, *Kirche*, 52; Bockmuehl, "Protestant Ethics," 111; *GG*, 400–410. It should be mentioned that Bockmuehl was aware of the importance of the inner witness of the Holy Spirit for the individual in Calvin's theology. Nevertheless, Bockmuehl concludes that, since Calvin more or less equated prophecy with the interpretation of Scripture, the proper balance of Spirit and Word was lost. Cf. *GG*, 410.
25. Cf. Bockmuehl, "Introduction," 61; *GG*, 502.
26. Bockmuehl, "Frank Buchman's Message," 36–37.

PART TWO—The Holy Spirit and Christian Ethics in the Theology

Reformation ethics are, according to Bockmuehl, "law" and "vocation," as outlined in an earlier chapter, we shall now investigate Bockmuehl's evaluation, first, of the Reformers' conviction of the sufficiency of the law and, secondly, of the Reformers' understanding of vocation as the individual differential principle of ethics.

The Sufficiency of the Law as General Differential Principle

As mentioned above, the law and particularly the Decalogue play a significant role in Reformation ethics.[27] In fact, the Reformers regard the Decalogue as comprising the whole of Christian ethics.[28] Luther, for instance, declares the Ten Commandments to be "the true fountain from which all good works must spring . . . Apart from these Ten Commandments no deed, no conduct can be good or pleasing to God, no matter how precious it may be in the eyes of the world."[29] According to Bockmuehl, this is due to a variety of reasons. First, that the Reformers stress the sufficiency of the Decalogue for every Christian has to be understood as a reaction against the medieval distinction between an ethic of the Decalogue for the uneducated people and an ethic of the evangelical counsels of the New Testament for those in the ecclesiastical office; the latter were regarded as being of greater importance than the former. The intention of the Reformers is thus to abolish any kind of two-tier ethics by bringing the Decalogue back into focus.[30] Secondly, the concept of the sufficiency of the Decalogue cannot be understood apart from the method of *synecdoche* that Luther as well as Calvin apply in their exposition of the Decalogue. This method of reflecting upon the positive corollary to the negative commandment enables the Reformers to extrapolate a complete ethical system from the Decalogue, which partly includes New Testament material.[31]

While Bockmuehl applies the method of *synecdoche* in his explication of the Decalogue, thereby acknowledging its value, he simultaneously raises strong objections against the Reformers *vis-à-vis* their conviction of the sufficiency of the Decalogue for the entirety of Christian ethics. It

---

27. Cf. chapter 1, pages 33–35.
28. Cf. *GG*, 31, 113; *CW*, 16–17.
29. Luther, "The Large Catechism," 407; cf. *CW*, 16.
30. Cf. *CW*, 16; Bockmuehl, "Recovering Vocation," 89–90.
31. Cf. Bockmuehl, "Protestant Ethics," 106; *CW*, 20–21.

The Neglect of the Holy Spirit in the History of Christian Ethics

is this conviction, in Bockmuehl's opinion, that eventuated in a neglect of the Spirit for Christian ethics as well as in a reduction of Christian ethics.[32] We shall examine this in more depth now.

First, Bockmuehl accuses the Reformers of over-emphasizing creation ethics to the detriment of redemption ethics and points out that their exposition of the Decalogue by way of *synecdoche* did not comprise all significant ethical parts of the New Testament. According to Bockmuehl, the Reformers neglect all those actions specific to Christian ethics such as spirituality, with its emphasis on love toward God, but also mission, particularly church-building activities, and works of supererogation.[33] Hence, whereas medieval theology regards the contemplative life (*in sinu*), particularly the monastic vows, to be of more importance than the tasks of mission (*in agro*) and the work of sustenance, and civil vocation (*in mola*), the Reformers, though trying to recover all three areas for every Christian, stress particularly the latter one. Given that Bockmuehl considers spirituality (*in sinu*) and mission (*in agro*) to be the work of the Holy Spirit, as we shall explore in more depth in a later chapter, it comes as no surprise then to discover that he charges the Reformers with neglecting the work of the Spirit in their concept of ethics.[34]

Secondly, while Bockmuehl approves of the Reformers' recovery of the Decalogue as fundamental for Christian ethics, he at the same time asserts that "without a flexible epistemological principle regarding the positive fulfillment of the commandments in the specific situation . . . ethics degenerates into casuistry and legalism."[35] Bockmuehl traces this legalistic character of Reformation ethics back to the neglect of the Holy Spirit as a differential principle for Christian ethics alongside the law and, in particular, the Decalogue.[36]

Thirdly, due to the rejection of individual, situational guidance by the Holy Spirit, Reformation ethics was, in Bockmuehl's opinion, mostly concerned with not breaking the law. This led not only to an ethic of

---

32. Cf. *GG*, 113–14. Other factors for criticizing the method of *synecdoche* are, for Bockmuehl, the overemphasis upon a skilled teacher trained in this method as well as the danger of arbitrariness in applying this method. Cf. Bockmuehl, "Protestant Ethics," 106; *GG*, 329.

33. Cf. *GG*, 117, 286–87, 291, 311; Bockmuehl, "Protestant Ethics," 111–12.

34. Cf. *GG*, 289, 310–11, 340; Bockmuehl, "Horizons," 15. For the reaction of Luther against medieval theology, see his explication of Genesis 18:15 in "Lectures on Genesis," 217.

35. *GG*, 117.

36. Cf. *SU*, 31–32; *GG*, 117, 246, 454.

avoidance, particularly due to the negative form of the Decalogue, but also to an ethic of permission, inasmuch as everything is seen as permissible as long as it does not contravene the law. In contrast, Bockmuehl is in favor of an ethic of restoration and commission that takes into account the individual guidance of the Holy Spirit. Though he does also affirm the validity of the Decalogue as the foundation of Christian ethics.[37]

Vocation as Individual Differential Principle

As seen above, the law functions as a general differential principle in Reformation ethics applying to every Christian under any given circumstance. In order to know the will of God for the individual, i.e., his or her individual tasks and duties, the Reformers refer to the specific orders or estates in life such as household, state, and church, which brought with them specific requirements. In this context, Bockmuehl points out that the Reformers identify one's divine vocation or calling with the civil vocation and order one happens to be born into.[38] Though Bockmuehl agrees with the Reformers on the significance of civil vocation for Christian ethics, he severely criticizes their failure to distinguish appropriately between a creational vocation, particularly a civil vocation (*Beruf*), and a special vocation (*Berufung*) for Christians. Bockmuehl, for instance, draws attention to the fact that Paul regards his civil vocation, tent-making, as a voluntary and secondary task compared to his vocation to preach the Gospel. He concludes that "[a] concept of vocation that is reduced to civil duties pertaining to one's station in life is in biblical terms a stunted and therefore deficient concept of vocation."[39]

Consequently, Bockmuehl accuses the Reformers of omitting the special vocation for the Christian, which, on the one hand, involves tasks related to the Great Commission given to all Christians and, on the other hand, includes the *charismata* and particular guidance given specifically to each individual Christian by the Holy Spirit. For Bockmuehl, this accounts for the absence of mission practice in Protestantism for two

---

37. *GG*, 119; cf. 118–19; *SU*, 30; Bockmuehl, "Revolution," 67.

38. Cf. *GG*, 99, 345; cf. *CM*, 115; Luther, "Lectures on Genesis," 217; Luther, "Confession Concerning Christ's Supper," 364–65; Luther, "On the Councils and the Church," 177. Luther, "Appeal for Prayer Against the Turks," 236; Lage, *Luther's Christology*, 120–21. Of interest is the fact that Paul Althaus gives a very similar description of Luther's concept of vocation as Bockmuehl does. Cf. Althaus, *Ethics*, 36, 40.

39. *GG*, 306; cf. 279.

The Neglect of the Holy Spirit in the History of Christian Ethics

centuries as well as the secularization of the *charismata*, i.e., the application of the spiritual gifts to the context of the family and the society and the reduction of the spiritual gifts to natural dispositions.[40] Suffice to say that the latter is, for Bockmuehl, a further indication of the Reformers' underestimation of the Spirit's role for Christian ethics.

When turning to the Reformers' claim that vocation is the only differential principle individualizing God's will even for the Christian, Bockmuehl identifies several weaknesses stemming from this claim. In the first place, Bockmuehl charges Luther particularly with allowing his ethics to be determined by a patriarchal structure not found in the New Testament; for Luther, the three different orders are based on three different "fatherly" ministries as can be seen in his explication of the fourth commandment in the Large Catechism.[41] Bockmuehl indicates that, whereas medieval theology substitutes divine guidance with the counsel of the superior, the Reformation substitutes it with the counsel of the father.[42] Secondly, due to the fact that for the Reformers one's vocation is determined by one's birth and circumstances, Bockmuehl concludes that "we are faced with a mute concept of vocation, with the God of Providence. God speaks to the individual only indirectly, through circumstances."[43] In fact, as Bockmuehl maintains, the Reformers request the Christians to submit passively to their fate instead of actively obeying God's guidance.[44] Thirdly, with regard to Reformation ethics, Bockmuehl identifies "natural human reason" as the decisive factor used for interpreting God's will with regard to the particular vocation.[45] Similarly, in situations where God's will is not determined by either one's vocation or the law, Bockmuehl claims that, according to the Reformers, it is our reason that plays the greatest part in the decision-making process. Bockmuehl's evaluation of the role of reason in ethics can be seen in the following text: "As a rule, regarding civil voca-

---

40. Cf. Bockmuehl, "Recovering Vocation," 84-87, 91; *GG*, 109, 232, 279, 306; *LbG*, 98.

41. Luther, in fact, states: "Thus we have three kinds of fathers presented in this commandment: fathers by blood, fathers of a household and fathers of the nation" (Luther, "The Large Catechism," 387; cf. 384-87). Bockmuehl traces patriarchy back to Jesus Sirach and concludes that Reformation ethics "remains on the level of canonical and apocryphal Old Testament material." *GG*, 107; cf. 105-7.

42. Cf. Bockmuehl, *Kirche*, 40-41; *GG*, 409; "Recovering Vocation," 92. The early Bockmuehl accused Protestant Orthodoxy, rather than the Reformers themselves, of the above-mentioned substitution. Cf. Bockmuehl, "Revolution," 57.

43. Bockmuehl, "Recovering Vocation," 91-92.

44. Cf. *GG*, 286, 434.

45. *GG*, 237; cf. 496.

tion, it might be the case that reason is sufficient for the accomplishment of the task . . . But when a second field of action is added, namely, mission in a broad sense . . . then we *need* a corresponding second epistemological principle that determines action: guidance by the Spirit."[46]

Not surprisingly, therefore, Bockmuehl holds the Reformers responsible for neglecting the guidance of the Holy Spirit as the appropriate principle for the discernment of God's will by favoring, instead, reason, law, and civil vocation.

Conclusion

What is clear from the above survey is that Bockmuehl identifies the main pneumatic weakness in Reformation ethics itself as the failure of allowing God to both speak to and guide the Christian in a direct way through the Holy Spirit. This eventuated in the fact that "traditional Protestant ethics was reduced to the Decalogue plus a few exhortations regarding varying roles in society taken from the New Testament. The actual situation remained empty of concrete instructions for action."[47] This silence regarding the discernment of God's will in a particular situation had, according to Bockmuehl, far-reaching implications for later developments in Christian ethics, as our discussion about the "new morality" will show.[48]

A further indication of the neglect of the Holy Spirit in Reformation ethics was, in Bockmuehl's opinion, the omission of the *proprium* of Christian ethics, including redemption ethics, which is intricately linked to the work of the Holy Spirit. This omission led to a serious reduction of Christian ethics, as Bockmuehl asserts frequently. He attempts to rectify this through his own concept of Christian ethics, which we shall explore in a later chapter.

The Theology of the Unreality of God

We have already seen that the passion for the reality of God and his kingdom was one of Bockmuehl's main theological concerns. In this context, we discovered that Bockmuehl considers the work of the Holy Spirit to be

---

46. *GG*, 247; Bockmuehl, "Situation Ethics," 47.

47. *CM*, 116.

48. Cf. Bockmuehl, "Zur Frage nach der Maßgeblichkeit," 48; Bockmuehl, "Ten Commandments," 134.

The Neglect of the Holy Spirit in the History of Christian Ethics

so intricately linked to the reality of God that one stands or falls with the other. Hence, any theology falling under Bockmuehl's verdict of advocating the unreality of God in this world is, inevitably, charged with neglecting the work of the Holy Spirit.

The two main theologians charged by Bockmuehl to have promoted a theology of the unreality of God are Bultmann and the early Barth. Accordingly, in the following chapter, we will present Bockmuehl's evaluation of Bultmann's and Barth's theologies of the unreality of God by focusing first of all on the (un-)reality of God in history, secondly, on the (im-)possibility of ethics, and lastly, on the tendency to atheism in ethics.

However, before we embark upon a study of these issues, let us briefly consider Feuerbach's and Marx's critiques of religion in so far as they have bearing on Bockmuehl's criticism of the theology of Barth and Bultmann. Bockmuehl, for instance, explicitly draws attention to the fact that "[i]t is always the danger of the *déformation professionelle* of theology to get stuck in the construction of mere edifices of thought. Therefore we must always keep an open eye on the Marxist critique of religion."[49]

Does God manifest himself in this world in a way that is "real," i.e., perceivable and experiential? In Bockmuehl's view, the answer to this question is the decisive component for the evaluation of different theologies. All those who answer in the negative are an easy target for Feuerbachian and Marxist critiques of religion. If God does not act in this world in a perceivable, real manner, how can we as Christians be sure that we have not created our own image of God, a mere theory, as Feuerbach accuses us of doing?[50] Bockmuehl continues to ask how we can be sure that religion, including the Christian God, is not "the opium of the people,"[51] as Marx claims that it is, since it might delude people by diverting their attention from the present unjust situation of life to a fantasy of the perfect state in the after-life. Bockmuehl notes that what is, instead, needed in Marx's opinion is practical change in the world, not merely theoretical interpretations of the world by philosophies and religions. Hence, as Bockmuehl

---

49. Bockmuehl, "Karl Barth," 31. In the epilogue to the second edition of his doctoral thesis on Feuerbach's and Marx's critique of religion and anthropology in their early writings, Bockmuehl points to "[t]he—critical—importance of the Feuerbach-Marxist method for theology" (*LuG*, 287).

50. Cf. *UG*, 39–40, 63, 72, 91–92; *CM*, 68–69; *WM*, 78; *VG*, 174; "Marxist Critique," 23–24.

51. Marx, *Critique*, 131; cf. *CM*, 57.

points out, Marx only accepted practical, sociological, economic, and political change as a clear indication for the truth.⁵²

As we shall see in this chapter, Bockmuehl deems that Bultmann's and Barth's theologies, particularly their ethical concepts, fall prey to this criticism.

The Unreality of God in History

According to Bockmuehl, Bultmann's as well as Barth's point of departure is Immanuel Kant's cleavage of reality into "this side," i.e., the sense world such as nature and history in which the laws of causality and analogy apply, and "the beyond," i.e., God who cannot be proved or disproved by logical reasoning and about whom nothing definite can be known. Due to the impenetrable wall between the two realities, "[n]o intervention of the beyond into this world, such as God's revelation of himself in history, can take place."⁵³ That Bultmann as well as Barth accept these presuppositions of Enlightenment in order to escape criticism can, first of all, be seen in the fact that both tend to discount human history as the realm in which God's works might be visibly manifested. Instead, they play an "arbitrary trick," as Bockmuehl calls it, by differentiating between *Historie*, i.e., historical events in time and space, and *Geschichte*, i.e., historic events, attributing theological significance only to the latter.⁵⁴ Though Barth and Bultmann define *Geschichte* in different ways, as we shall see later, they both, according to Bockmuehl, insist on the non-observable character of historic events, even if they are the works of God. Hence, as Bockmuehl concludes with view to Barth's and Bultmann's concept of the two-fold reality: "The world, society, the outward actions necessary for human beings, all objective reality then remains empty of God and of God's work in and through humanity."⁵⁵

Thus far we have outlined the parallels in Barth's and Bultmann's concept of reality that Bockmuehl traces back to the same starting point, namely, the sharp distinction between this side of the world and the beyond, ruling out any visible intervention of the beyond into our sense world. When turning to the question of how it is possible to accept these

---

52. Cf. *CM*, 55–59.
53. *UG*, 10; cf. *VG*, 103; Kant, *Critique of Pure Reason*, 359–60, 370–72.
54. Cf. *UG*, 93, 85; Bockmuehl, "Marxist Critique," 23; Bockmuehl, "Wahrnehmung," 93; *CM*, 68; *VG*, 170.
55. *CM*, 33; cf. *UG*, 86.

The Neglect of the Holy Spirit in the History of Christian Ethics

presuppositions and yet, at the same time, to preserve the essential message of Scripture, it is necessary to look at Bultmann's and Barth's answers separately.

According to Bockmuehl, *Bultmann's* solution consists of his renowned program of demythologization which enables him to re-interpret in an existential way all those biblical stories that he regards as myths.[56] For Bultmann, the characteristic of myth is that "the beyond" is portrayed as intervening into the sense world with its objectives of time and space, thus giving "to the transcendent reality an immanent, this-worldly objectivity."[57] However, the true intention of the myths found in Scripture is to express existential, anthropological truths.[58] The significance of the proclamation of the kerygma of the New Testament lies in its triggering of a change in the perception of one's own existence, as Bultmann points out. Faith is thus identical with gaining a new self-understanding, for instance, the understanding of one's self as participating in the crucifixion and resurrection of Christ.[59] Bultmann, in fact, claims that it is irrelevant whether God's saving work took place in *Historie*, manifesting itself in past historical events such as cross and resurrection. What is existentially significant is merely that God, by way of proclamation, acts in *Geschichte*, in the (what Bultmann considers to be) real, time-less, ever present history, in which human beings stand; this is not to be confused with human, factual history.[60] Hence, Bockmuehl concludes that since no tangible change occurs in reality, i.e., in this world of time and space, faith, as portrayed by Bultmann, is merely the subjective, contemplative re-interpretation of reality, the interpretation of natural events as God's works, despite all appearances to the contrary.[61] Not surprisingly, Bockmuehl considers

---

56. Bultmann, for instance, asserts that "if a man will speak of God, he must evidently *speak of himself*" (Bultmann, "What does it Mean to Speak of God?," 55). Similarly, he contends: "I *am* trying to substitute anthropology for theology, for I am interpreting theological affirmations as assertions about human life" (Bultmann, "A Reply to the Theses of J. Schniewind," 107; cf. *VG*, 173).

57. Bultmann, *Jesus Christ*, 19.

58. Cf. Bultmann, "New Testament and Mythology," 1972, 10–11, 15–16; *VG*, 171; *UG*, 13.

59. Cf. *UG*, 15, 51; "Marxist Critique," 23; Bultmann, "New Testament and Mythology," 41–43; Bultmann, *Jesus Christ*, 76; Bultmann, "The Case for Demythologizing," 192.

60. Cf. *UG*, 55; Bultmann, *Jesus Christ*, 61–62.

61. Cf. Bultmann, "The Case for Demythologizing," 192. Bultmann regards "[t]he old quest for visible security, the hankering after tangible realities, and the clinging to transitory objects" ("New Testament and Mythology," 19) as nothing less than sin.

Part Two—The Holy Spirit and Christian Ethics in the Theology

Bultmann's concept of faith and reality to fall prey to Feuerbach's accusation brought against the Christians of perceiving things that are not really there.[62] Not only is the reality of the *Geschichte*, so relevant for Bultmann's theology, highly questionable in Bockmuehl's view, since it is completely removed from our perceivable, objective history, but also the reality of God is called into question through the emphasis on the invisibility and non-demonstrability of God's works in this world.[63] Bultmann even goes so far as to assert the autonomy of this world and its profane character, thereby, according to Bockmuehl, eradicating the lordship of God over this world.[64] Before we explore the consequences this has for Bultmann's concept of ethics, let us look more closely at Bockmuehl's analysis of Barth's understanding of the reality of God in history.

Unlike Bultmann, who by way of existential and anthropological interpretation of the biblical message internalizes and subjectivizes the object of faith, the dialectical *Barth*,[65] as Bockmuehl points out, transcendentalizes and objectivizes the matter of theology.[66] In fact, Barth's presupposition of "what Kierkegaard called the 'infinite qualitative distinction' between time and eternity,"[67] the *diastasis* between God and human beings, leads him to the conviction that the works of the transcendent God are not visible in our world of time and space.[68] Consequently, as Bockmuehl summarizes, Barth believes that "[f]aith can claim no historical or psychological reality, for it is 'the inexpressible reality' of God. The observable reality of human life in time and 'the inexpressible reality' of God are

---

62. Cf. *VG*, 175; *UG*, 57–61, 66.

63. Cf. *UG*, 74. See also Webster, "The Legacy of Barth and Bultmann," 10; Cullmann, *Salvation in History*, 12, 320–21.

64. Cf. *UG*, 65; Bockmuehl, "Secularism," 44, 50.

65. If not stated otherwise, any mention of Barth in this chapter refers to the early, dialectical Barth. It is notable that Bockmuehl distinguishes between three main periods evident for him in Barth's theological writings: (1) During the dialectical period the main emphasis lay on the *diastasis* between God and man; (2) The principle of *analogy* dominated the main part of the *Church Dogmatics* (3) After 1955/56 Barth combined the principle of analogy with that of condescension, thus, highlighting the humanity of God. This implied a return to the reality of God in this world. *VG*, 126–27, 130–31; *UG*, 91–92, 103.

66. Cf. *VG*, 123; *UG*, 78; Bockmuehl, "Secularism," 45.

67. Barth, in the preface to the second edition of *Epistle to the Romans*, 10; cf. ibid., 57; *VG*, 94.

68. Cf. Barth, *Epistle to the Romans*, 38. Wingren consequently concludes: "God is and remains in heaven. How he can work on earth is a problem for Barth" (*Theology in Conflict*, 33).

The Neglect of the Holy Spirit in the History of Christian Ethics

set in antithesis."[69] Due to this ontological cleavage between God and human beings, Barth, not unlike Bultmann, sets living by faith in antithesis to living by sight, claiming that the true reality of God and human beings, including salvation history (*Geschichte*), is—and in fact has to be—completely invisible and transcendent to the human eye.[70] Faith, as Bockmuehl concludes, is therefore for Barth identical with gaining a different perspective on God and oneself.[71] Since the only alteration in the Christian seems to take place in the mind, Bockmuehl accuses Barth of "an intellectualism of faith,"[72] which he views as an indicator of the unreality of God and his works.[73] When turning to Barth's interpretation of the kingdom of God, we discover that he describes it as radically transcendent, other-worldly, invisible, which therefore—not nevertheless—has to be believed: "[T]he Kingdom of God has not 'broken forth' upon the earth, not even the tiniest fragment of it; and yet, it has been *proclaimed*: it has not come, not even in its most sublime form; and yet, it is *nigh at hand*. The Kingdom of God remains a matter of faith, and most of all is the revelation of it in Christ Jesus a matter of faith."[74]

The emphasis on the completely transcendent character of the kingdom of God, that can neither be perceived nor experienced, confirms, for Bockmuehl, the unreality of God's works and thus of God himself in Barth's theology.[75]

According to Bockmuehl, the unreal character of Barth's theology remains even after his attempt to substitute the principle of *diastasis* with that of "analogy of faith" (*analogia fidei*) in his *Church Dogmatics*.[76] This

---

69. *UG*, 80; cf. Bockmuehl, "Problem der Ethik," 70; Barth, *Epistle to the Romans*, 98.

70. *UG*, 79, 93; *VG*, 103, 171; Bockmuehl, "Wahrnehmung," 93; Bockmuehl, "Marxist Critique," 23; *LuG*, 286–87. Barth, for instance, highlights that if "the mercy of God is thought of as an element in history or as a factor in human spiritual experience, its untruth is emphasized." Barth, *Epistle to the Romans*, 102; cf. ibid., 39, 151; Willis, *The Ethics of Karl Barth*, 430.

71. For Barth, faith is "awe in the presence of the divine incognito" (Barth, *Epistle to the Romans*, 39). As mentioned in an earlier chapter, Bockmuehl deems the late Barth to have changed with regard to his understanding of the reality of God in history. Cf. Bockmuehl, "Marxist Critique," 23.

72. Bockmuehl, "Karl Barth," 30.

73. Bockmuehl adopted this criticism from Wingren. Cf. *UG*, 96; Wingren, *Theology*, 37, 42–43. For a different view on Barth, see Hart, "Revelation," 54.

74. Barth, *Epistle to the Romans*, 102.

75. Cf. *UG*, 80, 95; *CM*, 33.

76. *UG*, 91–92. For Barth's use of *analogia fidei*, see Palakeel, *The Use of Analogy*, 60–66.

means that Barth now endeavors to bridge the gap between this world and the beyond by applying "the principle of analogy from the above downward"[77] between Christ as the starting point and the human being as "that which is being analogized."[78] Even though he does not insist on the radical difference between God and human beings anymore as he used to do, the distinction between heaven and earth nevertheless remains. In fact, Bockmuehl is of the opinion that the platonic, idealistic character of Barth's theology is even more noticeable, since the reality of human beings is reduced to that of a copy of the original as a result of putting all the emphasis on the reality of Christ.[79]

What implications does this theology of the unreality of God, as Bockmuehl terms it, have for Bultmann's and Barth's understanding of ethics? It is to this that we must turn in order to comprehend Bockmuehl's at times rather severe criticism of Bultmann's and Barth's concept of reality.

The Implications for Ethics

In accordance with their insistence on the invisibility of God's works in this world, Bultmann and Barth hold that justification and sanctification are non-observable and do not result in a real, concrete change, as Bockmuehl points out. Whereas in Barth's theology, as Bockmuehl contends, "[t]he question of man's *justification* has been replaced by the question of man's *knowledge* of God,"[80] Bultmann substitutes it with man's knowledge about himself in relation to God, i.e., with gaining a new self-understanding.[81] This, furthermore, implies that for Bultmann and Barth the only change justification brings about is the alteration of God's judgment on the human person. Accordingly, even after conversion and regeneration Christians remain sinners in the same way as before, albeit viewing themselves as having been justified by God.[82] Due to their belief that everything

---

77. *UG*, 92.

78. Bockmuehl, "Introduction," 92.

79. Bockmuehl, "Introduction," 92–93; *VG*, 120–21; *UG*, 91–92; *LuG*, 286–87. With regard to Barth, see Lee, *God Suffers For Us*, 97.

80. *UG*, 96.

81. Cf. Bultmann, *The Gospel of John*, 54. Bultmann asserts with regard to the believer: "Outwardly everything remains as before, but inwardly his relation to the world has been radically changed" (Bultmann, "New Testament and Mythology," 20).

82. Cf. Bockmuehl, "Aktualität," 309; "Perimeters," 8–9; Bockmuehl, "Werk des Hl Geistes," 2–3. See also Barth, *Epistle to the Romans*, 317; Henning, *Die evangelische Lehre*, 52.

The Neglect of the Holy Spirit in the History of Christian Ethics

is utterly dependent upon the grace of God, any desire for a concrete, visible change is, in fact, regarded by Bultmann and Barth as a symptom of the human endeavor for self-justification and, therefore, sin.[83] What consequences does this have for Bultmann's and Barth's concept of ethics?

When turning to *Bultmann*, we discover that he denies the necessity and possibility of any Christian ethic.[84] First of all, like justification, sanctification has to be believed as the work of God in spite of all appearances to the contrary since, for Bultmann, the renewal of the believer is strictly a matter of change in his or her self-understanding.[85] While Bockmuehl approves of Bultmann's contention that the Gospel results in a new self-understanding, he censures the latter for rejecting the concrete character of sanctification. This can be traced back to Bultmann's re-interpretation of the salvation events, particularly the resurrection, as Bockmuehl states: "For those who regard the resurrection as only the interpretation of the significance of the earthly life of Jesus, rising again with Christ likewise logically implies no real change in life but only a change in the way of looking at life, a new way of interpreting the fact that in reality everything remains unchanged. The resurrection of Christ and the renewal of the Christian correspond to one another. As the body of Jesus remained in the tomb, so the ethical and existential quality of human life must stay the same."[86]

Bockmuehl also draws attention to the fact that Bultmann denies the possibility of a specific Christian ethic when asserting that "[i]t is faith which makes the world profane and restores to it its proper autonomy as the field of man's labours."[87] Bockmuehl points out that any striving for a sanctified life, any search for specific Christian norms, is regarded by Bultmann as being contrary to the true message of the Gospel.[88] In

---

83. Cf. Bockmuehl, "Problem der Ethik," 73–74; *VG*, 96. See also Hauerwas, *Character*, 131.

84. Cf. *UG*, 65–67; Hauerwas, *Character*, 131.

85. This can best be seen in the following contention by Bultmann: "[M]y new self-understanding, by its very nature must be renewed day by day, so that I understand the imperative self which is included in it" (Bultmann, *Jesus Christ*, 75–76; cf. Bultmann, "Bultmann Replies," 211).

86. *UG*, 50. Cf. 47–48.

87. Bultmann, "Bultmann Replies," 211. Cf. Bultmann, *Jesus Christ*, 85; "Problem der Ethik," 70. According to Bockmuehl, it is precisely the autonomy of the world and the profane character of the world that should be deemed by faith as being untrue vis-à-vis the reality of the lordship of God in this world. Cf. *UG*, 66.

88. Cf. *VG*, 175–76; *UG*, 64–65. It is worth pointing out the similarities between Bockmuehl's and Hauerwas's criticism of Bultmann. Cf. Hauerwas, *Character*, 132, 167.

PART TWO—The Holy Spirit and Christian Ethics in the Theology

Bultmann's opinion, the autonomous believer has to make decisions in each moment according to the situation, without being bound by any laws. Suffice to say that Bockmuehl disagrees strongly with Bultmann by holding that the Christian belief should not only shape one's own personality but also society as a whole, including such areas as economy and politics. Otherwise, as in the case of Bultmann, ethics takes on an individualistic and ego-centric character and results in the loss of sociality.[89]

When considering *Barth's* understanding of ethics, Bockmuehl states that, although Barth outlines a Christian ethic, it is merely theoretical, since the Christian message only initiates a new outlook, not a new practice.[90] In fact, Bockmuehl is of the opinion that the dialectical Barth considers the task of the commandments to be that of condemning human sinfulness and of exposing human being's nothingness. Hence, Bockmuehl believes that ethical change seems to be impossible for Barth.[91] The "middle Barth," however, as Bockmuehl points out, revised his view, claiming that the whole of humankind is already justified with Christ, participating in the cross and resurrection. For Bockmuehl, this implies that Barth, in fact, denies the necessity of a concrete, practical change.[92] Furthermore, with regard to sanctification, Bockmuehl concludes that, for Barth, "Christ alone is seen as sanctifying Himself, but doing it also for us; and we are invited to contemplate His vicarious sanctification. For us, sanctification then is only a poetic event: literally 'theory', not practice."[93] Bockmuehl also points out that Barth, nevertheless, argues that we have to believe in the reality of sanctification despite the fact that our experiences do not confirm this divine reality. He, however, criticizes Barth's concept of divine reality and argues that by putting all emphasis on the non-observable reality the divine reality "achieves only the quasi-reality of 'as though'"[94] in this world. By ascribing true reality only to the beyond, e.g., to the true, essential person hid in Christ, the earthly reality, e.g., the

---

89. Cf. *UG*, 53–54, 65–67, 74–75; *VG*, 164–65. See also Wingren, *Theology*, 147.

90. Cf. Bockmuehl, "Problem der Ethik," 73; Bockmuehl, "Perimeters," 8. See also Hauerwas, *Character*, 136.

91. Cf. Bockmuehl, "Problem der Ethik," 71; Barth, *Epistle to the Romans*, 294.

92. Cf. Bockmuehl, "Perimeters," 8. Bockmuehl calls attention to the fact that only the late Barth acknowledged that conversion has concrete character.

93. Bockmuehl, "Sanctification and Christian Mission," 56. Cf. Bockmuehl, "Aktualität," 310; Bockmuehl, "Wende," 283–84. For Barth, see *Church Dogmatics* 4/2:511–16; and Willis, *The Ethics of Karl Barth*, 256.

94. *UG*, 83. *VG*, 122; Bockmuehl, "Revolution," 60. For Barth, see *Church Dogmatics* 2/2:777; *Epistle to the Romans*, 195.

concrete human being, seems to have vanished into unreality.[95] Moreover, because of Barth's claim that God's works are not visible in our concrete reality, Bockmuehl charges him with indifference toward ethics—at least according to his dogmatic presuppositions: "[T]here is a danger that obedience will disappear in faith, the grace of sanctification in the grace of justification, and the law in the gospel."[96] Yet, at the same time, Bockmuehl draws attention to the fact that, despite Barth's dogmatic presupposition of laying all emphasis on God's work so that even faith is stripped of any practical character, he, nevertheless, encourages political involvement. This, in Bockmuehl's opinion, is due to Barth's endeavor to take Scripture seriously, not because it follows logically from his presuppositions. Bockmuehl, therefore, concludes that "a paradox remains, generated by the broken link between dogmatics and ethics. Human action appears to be accidental, not following logically from his dogmatics both in terms of its motivation and in relation to the content of actual decision."[97]

Conclusion

Having outlined Bockmuehl's evaluation of Bultmann's and Barth's theology of the unreality of God as well as the ethical implications, let us conclude with Bockmuehl's criticism of the neglect of the Holy Spirit in Bultmann's and Barth's ethics.

Bultmann's endeavor to demythologize the biblical text led to his understanding that theological statements convey existential, anthropological truths. Consequently, when talking about the Spirit in Paul, instead of referring to the latter as the one bringing about concrete, perceivable change in the life of the believer, Bultmann re-interprets the Spirit as "the possibility of a new life which is opened up by faith."[98] In Bockmuehl's assessment, Bultmann substitutes the *reality* of the Holy Spirit with the *possibility* of a new quality of life (the latter being a quality of human life)

---

95. *UG*, 82, 94–95. *VG*, 121. Barth, in fact, says explicitly: "I, the temporal and corporeal man of this world, am not the new man" (Barth, *Epistle to the Romans*, 312; cf. 195, 197, 296, 314–15). Interesting to note is that Henning arrives at the same conclusion as Bockmuehl does. Cf. Henning, *Die evangelische Lehre*, 54.

96. *UG*, 86; cf. Henning, *Die evangelische Lehre*, 66, 290. Willis similarly asks with regard to Barth's understanding of Christian action "whether . . . the requisite obedience imposed on man as an actualization of his freedom could ever be forthcoming in such a way as to gain direct embodiment in his action" (*The Ethics of Karl Barth*, 271–72).

97. *UG*, 90; cf. *CM*, 34.

98. Bultmann, "New Testament and Mythology," 22.

PART TWO—The Holy Spirit and Christian Ethics in the Theology

thus not only deobjectifying the Spirit but also shifting the focus from the work of God to the work of the human person.[99] Regarding the Pauline distinction between indicative and imperative, Bockmuehl points out that Bultmann's existential interpretation, with its merging of the theological and anthropological assertions, results in the fact that "[t]he imperative which in Paul *followed* the indicative of the gospel now has to carry both contents including what was previously portrayed as the miraculous act of the Spirit of God."[100] Hence, since Bockmuehl considers all statements made by Bultmann about the work of the Spirit to be reduced to those about the work of human beings and thus resulting in the absence of God in the observable reality of this world, Bockmuehl charges Bultmann with having paved the way for atheism in Christian ethics.[101]

Similar to Bultmann, *Barth* claims that the work of the Spirit, including its effects, is a matter of faith not of sight. Yet, contrary to Bultmann, Barth insists on the complete otherness of the Spirit. Whereas Bultmann reduces the Spirit to the possibility of new life thus to a human form of existence, Barth declares that "the Spirit is the frontier and meaning and reality of human life: as affirmation, the Spirit is the new, transfigured reality which lies beyond this frontier."[102] Hence, Bockmuehl draws attention to the fact that in Barth the statements about the concrete human person, e.g., about the new life of the believer, are at risk of being swallowed up by the statements about God, e.g., the Holy Spirit, the transcendent reality.[103] Hence, as seen above, any attempt to shape this world seems to Bockmuehl to be rather arbitrary and contingent in Barth, thus resulting in the disintegration of theory and practice. Bockmuehl agrees with Machovec that this can lead to all those interested in getting involved in practical life dismissing the reality of the transcendent as not having any direct significance for the concrete life here and now and, as a consequence, turning to secularism for help. Not surprisingly, Bockmuehl holds not only Bultmann but also the early Barth (because of his theoretical theology and thus partial atheism) responsible for opening the door to atheism in Christian ethics.[104]

99. Cf. *VG*, 173; *UG*, 26–30.

100. *UG*, 27; cf. 28–29.

101. Cf. *UG*, 29, 73–75; Bockmuehl, "Tendenzen der Theologie," 1–2.

102. Barth, *Epistle to the Romans*, 272; cf. 273, 275.

103. Cf. *UG*, 85. See also Henning, *Die evangelische Lehre*, 97, 290; Schaeder, *Das Geistproblem der Theologie*, 42, 125.

104. Cf. *UG*, 98–99, 127, 131, 142; *CM*, 34; *GiE*, 193; Bockmuehl, "Tendenzen der Theologie," 2.

The Neglect of the Holy Spirit in the History of Christian Ethics

To what extent Bockmuehl considers the Holy Spirit to be given too little weight in Barth's early theology is apparent by the following citation in which Bockmuehl praises the late Barth for recovering the Holy Spirit:

> Barth late in life tried to provide a synthesis between his earlier objectivism and Bultmann's subjectivity. He finds the synthesis in a doctrine of the Holy Spirit. The Holy Spirit is that principle which subjectifies the objective. The Holy Spirit is the realizer of the gospel. The Holy Spirit brings the majestic God, the transcendent God, into my heart. The Holy Spirit is that principle which brings objectivity into subjectivity. Theology is not only about God (as he had said in the 1920s), neither is it only about man (as Bultmann said). But theology is about the communion of God and man in Christ and through the Holy Spirit.[105]

Furthermore, Bockmuehl is convinced that it is only through the retrieval of the work of the Holy Spirit that the wide gap between theory and practice, evident in Bultmann's and Barth's ethics, can be bridged. It is the Holy Spirit who not only inspires believers to do good but also empowers them so that they are able to accomplish good works in a this-worldly, perceivable reality, thus bringing about concrete moral and social change.[106]

New Morality

Before turning to Bockmuehl's evaluation of the new morality, let us briefly consider the theological conditions that account for the emergence of the new morality. First and foremost, Bockmuehl views the "new morality" of Fletcher and Robinson as a rebellious reaction to the "old morality" represented by Protestant ethics and Roman Catholic moral theology. According to Bockmuehl, the "old morality" was justly criticized for not taking into account the individual situation regarding ethical decisions but, instead, putting emphasis mainly on the law.[107] Another valid point of criticism that the new morality raised against the old morality was the

---

105. Bockmuehl, "Introduction," 97. It is interesting to note in passing that Gunton also charges Barth with neglecting the Holy Spirit; this though with view to people's appropriation of salvation. Cf. Gunton, "Salvation," 152–53.

106. Cf. Bockmuehl, "Problem der Ethik," 82. See also Parsons, "Man Encountered by the Command of God," 62.

107. Cf. Bockmuehl, *Sexualethik*, 14; cf. 11–12; *GG*, 16–17, 526; *CW*, 135; Bockmuehl, "Tendenzen der Theologie," 2; Bockmuehl, "Revolution," 65.

PART TWO—The Holy Spirit and Christian Ethics in the Theology

latter's insistence on mediated guidance.[108] Bockmuehl, furthermore, shares the concern of the new morality to clear a third path in-between antinomianism and legalism. He, however, disagrees fundamentally with the alternative concept of the "new morality," the so-called situationism.[109] Secondly, when turning to those theologians who in some way or other opened the door for situationism, it may come as a surprise to discover that Bockmuehl also mentions Barth and Bultmann, among others.[110] With regard to Bultmann, Bockmuehl asserts that "the 'new morality' in Christendom is a direct *consequence* of the lack of content in Bultmann's ethics and is motivated expressly by his demythologization program."[111] In fact, as stated earlier, Bockmuehl notes that Bultmann himself advocated a situation ethics in as much as he denied that any external authority, such as norms, can be universally valid and in as much as he stressed the autonomy of the moral agent.[112]

As for Barth's responsibility with regard to the emergence of the new morality, Bockmuehl more than once refers to a conversation he had held with Barth in 1963 in which Barth had asked himself: "I often think the problem of John Robinson is more a problem of Karl Barth. What have I done wrong that this is now possible again—the force and breadth of this reaction?"[113] According to Bockmuehl, the main weakness in the early Barth that prepared the way for situationism was his over-emphasis on the transcendent character of the reality of God that resulted in the de-realization and abstractionism of Christian ethics and thus in its diminished significance for social or existential life.[114] Due to its unreal ethical character, Bockmuehl believes that this kind of a theology inevitably leads

---

108. Cf. Bockmuehl, "Revolution," 57–59; *GG*, 17.

109. Cf. *GiE*, 215; Bockmuehl, "Ten Commandments," 134–35. See also Fletcher, *Situation Ethics*, 18–31.

110. Other theologians are, for instance, Brunner and Tillich. With regard to Brunner, Bockmuehl emphasizes that Fletcher partly distorts Brunner's theology in order to serve his own purpose but that the early, dialectical Brunner does play a role in opening the way for situation ethics. Cf. *VG*, 146; "Revolution," 62; *GiE*, 115–17. MacIntyre similarly holds the view that Barth and Bultmann, among other theologians, played a part in preparing the way for situation ethics. Cf. MacIntyre, "God and the Theologians," 217–19.

111. *UG*, 131.

112. Cf. *GiE*, 117–22. Cf. Fairweather and McDonald, *Quest*, 252.

113. *UG*, 77; cf. 78; *VG*, 99. Bockmuehl, letter to Karl Barth, Oct. 26, 1963.

114. Cf. *UG*, 116–17; Bockmuehl, "Revolution," 59–60.

The Neglect of the Holy Spirit in the History of Christian Ethics

to situation ethics: "*a proclamation of the world without God followed the proclamation of God without the world.*"[115]

Let us now turn to Bockmuehl's evaluation of the main issues of situation ethics as outlined by Joseph Fletcher who was one of the main representatives of the new morality. Reference to John A. T. Robinson's ethics is made in those instances where the latter differs notably from Fletcher.

Situation

"[W]hat is sometimes good may at other times be evil, and what is sometimes wrong may sometimes be right when it serves a good enough end—*depending on the situation.*"[116] This citation by Fletcher, the last phrase appearing again and again in his writings, discloses for Bockmuehl the outstanding importance of the term "situation" for the new morality. Not only does Fletcher (and Robinson) hold that in the final moment one is to look only to the situation for direction in the process of decision-making, but they also insist on the autonomy of moral agents and the subjectivity of their decision due to the uniqueness of the situation. Bockmuehl, however, when examining the meaning of the term "situation," judges it to be void of any content; he perceives that aims, motivations, and the results of a decision lie, strictly speaking, either before or after a situation. He also draws attention to the constraining nature of the new morality in that it does not pay any attention to the possibility of a change of situational circumstances.[117] Not surprisingly, Bockmuehl criticizes Fletcher for not taking into account the specifically Christian perspective of every situation, i.e., "the *presence of God in Christ*"[118] mediated through the Holy Spirit. Bockmuehl is convinced that on account of Christ's death and resurrection, we are not bound merely to the rationally perceivable circumstances of a particular situation in our decision-making; rather, they can be handed over to the one who is the Lord of each situation.[119] He, therefore, accuses

---

115. *UG*, 116–17. For a lengthy delineation by Bockmuehl of Barth's theology as a preparation for the new morality, see "Revolution," 59–62. It is worth mentioning that Hauerwas, like Bockmuehl, is of the opinion that Barth's and Bultmann's ethics played a part in opening the door for the new morality. Cf. Hauerwas, *Character*, 177. See also Biggar, "Barth's trinitarian ethic," 221.

116. Fletcher, *Situation Ethics*, 123.

117. Cf. Bockmuehl, "Revolution," 63–64.

118. *GiE*, 141.

119. Cf. *GiE*, 144, 152. See also Oyen, "'New Morality' und christliche Ethik," 153–4.

Fletcher of not giving sufficient weight to the power of the resurrection of Christ and of neglecting "the fundamental *openness* of every situation."[120]

With regard to Fletcher's concept of situation, Bockmuehl finds clear indications of atheistic tendencies due to the fact that Fletcher does not regard the divine presence and the transcendent nature of a situation as relevant for the process of decision-making. Thus, in Bockmuehl's opinion, the new morality neglects the Holy Spirit as the one mediating the presence of God and giving guidance to the individual believer.[121]

Love—the Only Norm

Regarding Fletcher's concept of the relationship between love and law, the following phrase captures his main thesis in a nutshell: "Love replaces law."[122] Fletcher even refuses to acknowledge the continuing validity of the law as giving ultimate direction and, instead, holds that the situationist lets "ethical maxims of his community and its heritage"[123] advise and illuminate him in the decision-making process. The only binding principle in his view is the commandment to love one's neighbor, to which every other commandment has to be subjected, and which, if necessary, can be set aside for love's sake. Hence, Fletcher is convinced that law and *love* have to be separated since there is generally a tension between the two that can only be resolved by following the principle of love, even if that implies breaking the law.[124] He is, nevertheless, unwilling to predefine love, certainly not by pointing to the law and, instead, characterizes it as being "*goodwill at work in partnership with reason*" and that "[i]t seeks the neighbor's best interest with a careful eye to all the factors in the situation."[125] Yet, what this implies in a concrete situation must be decided by the individuals themselves and by no one else. However, when examining the diverse examples Fletcher uses to define love, Bockmuehl directs attention to the fact that Fletcher, though not explicitly giving an account of any criteria, applies two very different, sometimes even opposing, criteria in order to judge the correctness of a decision.

---

120. *GiE*, 181.
121. *GG*, 23.
122. Fletcher, *Situation Ethics*, 69.
123. Ibid., 26.
124. Cf. ibid., 69–71; Robinson, *Christian Freedom*, 19–21; *GiE*, 55–57.
125. Fletcher, *Situation Ethics*, 69, cf. 27.

The Neglect of the Holy Spirit in the History of Christian Ethics

First, as Bockmuehl highlights, Fletcher evaluates decisions employing a seemingly objective utilitarian principle. Fletcher, for instance, asserts that he cannot perceive a difference between general utility spoken about by philosophers and love as used by theologians: "Let's say plainly that *agapé* is utility; love is well-being."[126] And, since Fletcher defines general utility as "seeking the greatest amount of the 'good' possible for the greatest number of neighbors possible,"[127] he, accordingly, emphasizes the importance of the doctrine of personalism. For him, love is people- and not thing-oriented, since "the *summum bonum* or first-order value, is human welfare and happiness (but not, necessarily, pleasure)."[128] However, what this *summum bonum* requires in a certain situation is contingent solely on the actual situation, as Fletcher emphasizes. He consequently claims that every action can only be assessed *vis-à-vis* its contribution to love, thus rendering the value of means and ends relative to its agapeic purpose. For him it is the end or the outcome of an action, rather than the means, that decides whether or not an action was right, i.e., furthering love, or not. In fact, Fletcher is of the opinion that only the end justifies the means as long as the latter is more or less appropriate. Bockmuehl, however, calls attention to the fact that Fletcher's examples reveal the arbitrariness of his understanding of the appropriateness of means.[129]

The second criterion, besides the first seemingly objective one that Bockmuehl finds in Fletcher's ethics, is that of "a subjective ethic of basic convictions."[130] Since Fletcher views every norm as relative with the exception of the love commandment, which he, however, refuses to define content-wise, Bockmuehl prognosticates that this kind of situation ethics will sooner or later lead to antinomianism and even ethical anarchism.[131] Furthermore, if, as Fletcher believes, "[e]very man must decide for himself according to his own estimate of conditions and consequences; and no one can decide for him or impugn the decision to which he comes,"[132] Bockmuehl is convinced that this will terminate in a breakdown of the whole legal system.[133]

---

126. Fletcher, "What's in a Rule?," 332; cf. *GiE*, 73.
127. Fletcher, "What's in a Rule?," 332; cf. *GiE*, 70.
128. Fletcher, *Moral Responsibility*, 33; cf. *GiE*, 66–67.
129. Cf. Fletcher, *Situation Ethics*, 120–22; cf. *GiE*, 74–75.
130. *GiE*, 157.
131. Cf. *GiE*, 138.
132. Fletcher, *Situation Ethics*, 37.
133. Cf. *GiE*, 138.

Part Two—The Holy Spirit and Christian Ethics in the Theology

When assessing Fletcher's concept of love, Bockmuehl also raises the suspicion that the main point of contact between the biblical concept of love and Fletcher's own concept is merely the term itself rather than the content.[134] He traces this back to Fletcher's neglect of several crucial biblical characteristics of love.

First, Bockmuehl accuses Fletcher of discounting *love for God* by equating it with, and thus reducing it to, loving one's neighbor, thereby not giving the first half of the double commandment of love its proper attention. Secondly, "[t]he so-called 'new morality' of the sixties maneuvered itself into an antithesis of law and love which certainly does not represent the spirit and substance or the wording of the New Testament."[135] Thirdly, Bockmuehl is convinced that Fletcher's utilitarian principle can not be brought into accordance with Jesus' demand to provide even for "one of the least" (Matt 25:40), regardless of any success or profit. This leads us to the fourth observation Bockmuehl makes, which is that Fletcher omits the notion of *mercy*, the willingness to give to the undeserving, by over-identifying love with justice. It comes as no surprise, then, to discover that Bockmuehl criticizes Fletcher as having eliminated from love any theological meaning.[136]

When examining the role the Holy Spirit plays in Fletcher's situation ethics, Bockmuehl calls attention to the fact that Fletcher uses the term Holy Spirit "as a theological pseudonym for love."[137] In fact, when examining Fletcher's references to the Holy Spirit, we discover that he views the Holy Spirit as the source of every expression of love shown by Christians or non-Christians alike since "[l]ove is not the work of the Holy Spirit, it *is* the Holy Spirit—working in us."[138]

Bockmuehl concludes that Fletcher not only abandons any norm as a valid guide to making moral decisions but also empties love, as the only criterion, of any theological content. Furthermore, in accordance with his equation of the Holy Spirit with love, Fletcher discards any notion of the guidance of the Holy Spirit. As a consequence, Fletcher, as Bockmuehl judges, is not able to guard his concept of situation ethics sufficiently

---

134. Cf. *GiE*, 159.
135. *CW*, 134. Cf. Bockmuehl, "Revolution," 65.
136. Cf. *GiE*, 159–64. See also Oyen, "Verantwortung und Norm," 160–61, 164.
137. *GiE*, 99.
138. Fletcher, *Situation Ethics*, 51.

The Neglect of the Holy Spirit in the History of Christian Ethics

against the charge of antinomianism and practical atheism—contrary to Fletcher's own claims.[139]

Reason

What is ultimately involved *vis-à-vis* the process of decision-making for the situationists? Fletcher summarizes his approach as follows: "*[O]nly love and reason really count when the chips are down!*"[140] Although the new morality accepts love as the only criterion for discerning what is right or wrong in a situation, it gives reason a prominent place "as the instrument of moral judgment."[141] Bockmuehl argues that it is only because of the intellectual faculty that Fletcher is able to insist on the moral autonomy of the human person. Bockmuehl, in fact, believes reason to be "the secret queen of this ethics"[142] and to replace the role of the Holy Spirit in ethics. He finds this confirmed by Fletcher's identification of conscience with reason since Fletcher insists that conscience is not an inbuilt faculty or an external power but the rational, non-emotional weighing up of facts.[143] At the same time, Fletcher rejects any notion of inspiration or intuition, and thus any guidance by the Spirit for decision-making, since he considers these to open the door for antinomianism by excluding the necessity to employ reason. A matter of concern for Fletcher is, therefore, Robinson's reference to an innate moral compass that aids love in making the correct decisions in any situation.[144] Though Bockmuehl approves of Robinson's allusion as pointing in the right direction, he, nevertheless, criticizes him for not developing this concept further by taking into account the guidance of the Holy Spirit.[145]

Bockmuehl is convinced that *reason*, or prudence, alone is not sufficient to adequately evaluate any given situation in a theological manner.

---

139. Cf. *GiE*, 115. In his reaction to Robinson's book *Honest to God*, MacIntyre similarly makes it clear that he regards Robinson to be an atheist. Cf. MacIntyre, "God and the Theologians," 215–17.

140. Fletcher, *Situation Ethics*, 31.

141. Ibid., 26; cf. Fletcher, "Rule," 346.

142. *GiE*, 144.

143. Cf. Fletcher, "Rule," 340–41.

144. Cf. Fletcher, "Rule," 341; Fletcher, "Situation Ethics," 23–24; Robinson, *Honest to God*, 115.

145. Cf. *CM*, 116; *GiE*, 42–43; Bockmuehl, "Zur Frage nach der Maßgeblichkeit," 47.

PART TWO—The Holy Spirit and Christian Ethics in the Theology

With view to Fletcher's over-emphasis on reason, Bockmuehl, therefore, concludes: "This reason is arrogant enough to ignore intuition and supra-rational guidance, and afterwards, it is subdued and distraught."[146]

Instead, Bockmuehl points out that since Christians are expected to act in extraordinary, particular, at times even irrational, ways,[147] they are consequently in need of more than merely rational judgment purely based on the circumstances.[148] Therefore, the mind needs to be taken captive in obedience to Christ (cf. 2 Cor 10:5) in order to be renewed and in order to be able to listen to God. Only then, according to Bockmuehl, is knowledge of God's will in a particular situation possible (cf. Rom 12:2). This knowledge of God's will that surpasses our natural rational capacities is only given to us by the Holy Spirit (cf. Col 1:9) and enables us to live a fruitful life worthy of the Lord. Bockmuehl concludes that without this knowledge "it has to be considered that the situation will be missed and that one will not see the intended good things come to pass."[149]

From all this it will already be apparent that Bockmuehl charges the new morality with having grossly neglected the role of the Holy Spirit in ethics by substituting the guidance of the Holy Spirit with reason while, at the same time, equating the Spirit with love. Furthermore, rather than acknowledging the sovereignty and authority of God over human beings, Fletcher, as Bockmuehl believes, insists on the autonomy, and therefore the lordship, of each human being over their own lives.[150] Bockmuehl accuses the new morality of offering an anthropological, secular, atheistic ethics instead of outlining a biblically based alternative to the old morality, which includes the guidance of the Holy Spirit.[151]

---

146. *GiE*, 148.

147. Bockmuehl particularly refers in this context to "the second mile" of Matthew 5:41 and the "more" (*"perisson,"* GG 302) of Matthew 5:47. Cf *GG*, 301–2; *GiE*, 146.

148. Cf. *GiE*, 48.

149. *GiE*, 150.

150. Cf. *GiE*, 192–93.

151. Cf. *GiE*, 204, 211. One of the few ethicists who gives particular emphasis to the importance of the Holy Spirit for ethics is Barnette, who points out: "There is more—the function of the Holy Spirit in moral decisions, a sadly neglected factor by almost all Christian ethicists. Yet the fruit of the Spirit is presented in ethical terms: love, joy, peace, patience, kindness, goodness, faithfulness, gentleness, self-control (Gal. 5:22–23) . . . Without the energizing and enabling power of the Spirit the Christian ethic is impossible. For it is the Spirit who ultimately informs the Christian in concrete moral decisions and guides him 'into all the truth' (John 16:13)" (Barnette, "The New Ethics," 140).

4

Bockmuehl's Understanding of Christian Ethics

Creation Ethics/General Christian Ethics

The Cultural Mandate

THE KEY COMMISSION BELONGING to the realm of creation ethics is, for Bockmuehl, the cultural mandate given in Genesis 1:27–28 and Genesis 2:15, which includes the procreation commission as well as the commission to stewardship over the creatures and the earth. Since the overall intention of this mandate is the preservation of creation, Bockmuehl regards the commission to be a call to collaborate in God's own work of preservation and sustenance.[1] Not surprisingly, therefore, Bockmuehl describes creation ethics as being an "ethics of preservation."[2] In terms of human responsibility, this entails the task of "stewardship: a dialectic or combination of rule and service . . . to the end of preservation."[3] Aware of the

1. Cf. Bockmuehl, "Recovering Vocation," 83; *LbG*, 79–80; Bockmuehl, "Perimeters," 13; Bockmuehl, "Is Christianity a Counterculture?," 52. At times Bockmuehl calls the cultural mandate "culture commission" (cf. "The Christian as Lawyer," 34).

2. *CW*, 26. "Ethic" and "ethics" seem at times to be used interchangeably. It is interesting to note that the German word "Ethik" can be used as a translation for both words as can be seen in Bockmuehl's works.

3. *LbG*, 80. According to Richard Bauckham, the interpretation of Genesis 1:26–28 as the call to stewardship "remains the most popular image, at least in evangelical contributions" ("Stewardship," 102). He, however, draws attention to the danger inherent in the concept of stewardship of over-emphasizing the vertical relationship between

danger of the abuse of power for subjugating the earth and the creatures, Bockmuehl advocates a responsible use of human power under God's sovereign reign. Since human beings were made in the image of God, they have been entrusted with the task of being God's stewards over a world that belongs to God. Hence, as Bockmuehl spells out, even though people have the God-given *right* to rule over animals and the earth due to their supreme position, they are at the same time assigned the life-long *duty* of preserving and caring for God's creation, including human life.[4]

Bockmuehl repeatedly emphasizes in this context that the concern for the preservation of creation can be found not only in the Old Testament or in the apocryphal wisdom writings, which particularly influenced Reformation ethics, but also in the New Testament.[5] Not only does Christ in some of his parables commission his disciples to be faithful and responsible stewards over property that has been entrusted to them (Matt 25:14–30; 21:33–43), but he also reminds them persistently of their task to preserve and sustain the life of their fellow humans.[6] That this task plays a crucial role in Christian ethics can, according to Bockmuehl, be deduced from the parable of the Good Samaritan, in which loving one's neighbor was identified with preserving life, as well as from Christ's juxtaposition of doing good and saving life in Mark 3:4.[7] Furthermore, Bockmuehl draws attention to the fact that, by being called to sustain creation, the Christian is called to participate in God's own work of preservation and provision.[8]

With view to the practical application of the task of preservation, Bockmuehl regards the six works of mercy (Matt 25:31–46) to be of paramount importance.[9] Consequently, Bockmuehl challenges Christians to take seriously the call to preserve life by providing poor people with material resources and by caring for people in need, such as the disadvantaged,

---

human beings and the rest of creation over against the horizontal relationship and, thus, to underestimate the value of the non-human creation in and of itself regardless of their service for humankind (cf. ibid., 103–5).

4. Cf. *CaL*, 5–7; Bockmuehl, "Überlegungen," 121, 125. With view to the OT, Bockmuehl refers to Leviticus 25:35 and several times to the person of Joseph as an example of a good steward who saved the lives of many. Cf. Bockmuehl, "Horizons," 7; Bockmuehl, "Lean Years," 68; Bockmuehl, "Destroyer," 50.

5. Cf. *GG*, 513–14; Bockmuehl, "Recovering Vocation," 83–84; *LbG*, 80.

6. Cf. *CaL*, 12; Bockmuehl, "Überlegungen," 125–26.

7. Cf. *LbG*, 87; Bockmuehl, "Lean Years," 68; Bockmuehl, "The Christian as Lawyer," 34; *CW*, 26; Bockmuehl, "The Ten Commandments," 43.

8. Cf. Bockmuehl, "The Christian as Lawyer," 34; Bockmuehl, "Überlegungen," 125; Bockmuehl, "Destroyer," 50.

9. Cf. *CW*, 26; Bockmuehl, "Kirche," 136; Bockmuehl, "Der Streit," 103; *GiE*, 197.

Bockmuehl's Understanding of Christian Ethics

the unemployed etc.[10] This necessarily requires the willingness to employ one's property as provision for other people. Bockmuehl, in fact, believes that the biblical understanding of individual property differs considerably from that of the Roman law since the former ties obligations to the ownership of property: "From the commission of creation to preserve life follows . . . by necessity the social responsibility regarding possessions."[11]

In addition, Bockmuehl agrees with the Church Fathers as well as with Thomas Aquinas and the Reformers that any surplus of material goods is owed to the sustenance of the poor.[12] However, when examining the decisive factor for distinguishing between necessary and surplus possessions, Bockmuehl distances himself from the principle of "proportionality of property and consumption which corresponds to one's social station in life"[13] that the Reformers, following Thomas Aquinas, applied. He points out that the social order that relied on stations or vocations had been dissolved through capitalism. Instead, he suggests the criterion of a "simple lifestyle," namely, "a lifestyle of personal moderation, economy, frugality, and a regular reduction of pretension and consumption,"[14] guided by the cultural commission of preservation, on the one hand, and by the Great commission, on the other.[15] In this context, Bockmuehl points out that considering Christ's comment regarding the leftovers after feeding the five thousand, "[l]et nothing be wasted,"[16] the attitude of social responsibility applies not only to private property but also to nature and its resources in general. Hence, there can be no Christian justification for the exploitation of nature and the pollution of the environment. Instead, Bockmuehl is convinced that Christians should work toward the conservation of the environment by exercising their task of stewardship wisely.[17]

Despite critical remarks regarding the "traditional ethic of the social classes,"[18] Bockmuehl, nevertheless, as mentioned in an earlier chapter,

---

10. Cf. *LbG*, 88–89; Bockmuehl, "Überlegungen," 128–29. It is interesting to note that Bockmuehl lists the unborn among those people that need the attention and support of the Christian. Cf. *LbG*, 89.

11. Bockmuehl, "Kirche," 138; Bockmuehl, "Überlegungen," 123–24.

12. Cf. Bockmuehl, "Überlegungen," 114–17, 124; *CaL*, 13–14; Bockmuehl, "Wealth," 48.

13. Bockmuehl, "Überlegungen," 115.

14. *LbG*, 81; cf. *CaL*, 12.

15. Cf. Bockmuehl, "Überlegungen," 119.

16. John 6:12; cf. *LbG*, 81–82.

17. Cf. *CaL*, 16.

18. Cf. Bockmuehl, "Überlegungen," 118.

PART TWO—The Holy Spirit and Christian Ethics in the Theology

praises the Reformers for affirming the possibility of serving God in one's civil vocation. Bockmuehl even claims that "[a]s individuals, all humans have vocations within the mandate to cultivate and sustain creation, such as the vocation of farmer, housewife, teacher, blacksmith, doctor, and all the other 'civil vocations' that keep life together."[19] The civil vocations, therefore, provide specifications for the individual *vis-à-vis* the universal character of the cultural mandate.[20]

The Laws of Creation

THE LAWS OF CREATION AND THE DECALOGUE

Besides the cultural mandate, it is the Decalogue that, in Bockmuehl's opinion, plays a pivotal role in creation ethics.[21] This is due to the fact that Bockmuehl considers the Decalogue, particularly the second table with its regulations regarding inter-personal relationships, to be the most lucid expression of the "laws of creation."[22] Following Irenaeus and the Reformers as well as the famous German theologian and martyr Dietrich Bonhoeffer, Bockmuehl asserts repeatedly: "The Ten Commandments commend themselves to every person as an appropriate formulation of natural law."[23] In fact, to illustrate the interconnectedness of the Decalogue with creation, Bockmuehl calls the Decalogue, in accordance with Gustaf Wingren, the "moral 'grammar' of creation"[24] and compares it to the law of gravity. Furthermore, he considers the Ten Commandments, together with the cultural commission, to constitute the creation ordinances.[25] For Bockmuehl, it is beyond doubt that "the Ten Commandments recommend themselves to every man and nation as an admirable definition of

---

19. Bockmuehl, "Recovering Vocation," 84.
20. Cf. ibid., 83.
21. Cf. Bockmuehl, "Kirche," 135; *CW*, 4.
22. Cf. *CaL*, 20; *GG*, 513; Bockmuehl, "Humanität," 92; Bockmuehl, "Natural Law," 59.
23. Bockmuehl, "Humanität," 91. Cf. *CW*, 4, 12, 18; Bockmuehl, "Ten Commandments," 130. For Irenaeus, see Lawson, *The Biblical Theology of Saint Irenaeus*, 234. For Luther, see Luther, "Against the Heavenly Prophets," 97–98; Luther, "How Christians Should Regard Moses" 172–73; Althaus, *Ethics*, 27–28. For Bonhoeffer, see Bonhoeffer, *Ethics*, 274–80, 293. Cf. Bockmuehl, "Der Streit," 101; Bockmuehl, "Kirche," 135.
24. Bockmuehl, "Kirche," 135; *VG*, 239.
25. Cf. Bockmuehl, "Der Streit," 104; *CW*, 23, 25; Bockmuehl, "Horizon," 8.

Bockmuehl's Understanding of Christian Ethics

the good and just";[26] this is based on the fact that the content of the Decalogue comes close to various moral instructions of different religions or nations such as, for instance, the Hellenistic concept of natural law.[27] This is evident particularly in the case of the golden rule, i.e., the principle of reciprocity, which Bockmuehl, in consonance with Luther, holds to be the summary of the Decalogue since its negative form is widely acknowledged as one of the basic moral standards.[28] Bockmuehl traces this back to the fact that, as Paul had written in Rom 2:14-15, even non-Christians knew about God's commandments in their consciences.[29] Because of the universal and eternal character of the Decalogue, Bockmuehl is convinced that it should be (or remain) integrated into the constitutional law and not be restricted to its proclamation in the church.[30]

The most important argument for the continuing significance of the Decalogue is, however, for Bockmuehl, that Christ himself confirmed the authority of the Decalogue by viewing it as an apt interpretation of the double commandment of love and by mentioning explicitly its lasting validity. Thus, Bockmuehl disagrees fundamentally with those theologians who refer to Jesus' healing ministry on a Sabbath as proof of the abrogation of the Ten Commandments as a binding norm for humanity and for the Christian.[31]

The Natural Moral Law

After having outlined Bockmuehl's view of the Decalogue as having outstanding significance in creation ethics as a result of its consonance with the natural moral law, let us briefly examine the background of Bockmuehl's insistence on the eternal validity not only of the Decalogue but also of the natural moral law itself. Not only did Bockmuehl feel urged to engage himself with this topic *vis-à-vis* the denial of the existence of

---

26. Bockmuehl, "The Ten Commandments," 43; cf. 126.

27. Cf. Bockmuehl, "Recovering Vocation," 83; Bockmuehl, "Der Streit," 102; *LG*, 18; *CW*, 12; Bockmuehl, "Humanität," 90-91.

28. Cf. Bockmuehl, "Humanität," 87; Bockmuehl, "Ten Commandments," 133; *CW*, 11; *GG*, 309. For Luther, see Luther, "Admonition to Peace," 27; Althaus, *Ethics*, 33.

29. Cf. *LG*, 18; Bockmuehl, "Ten Commandments," 131; *CW*, 12; *CaL*, 19-20. For Luther, see Luther, "Against the Heavenly Prophets," 97; Althaus, *Ethics*, 25.

30. Cf. Bockmuehl, "The Christian as Lawyer," 34; Bockmuehl, "Humanität," 91-92; Bockmuehl, "Zur Frage nach der Maßgeblichkeit," 45; *CW*, 4.

31. Cf. Bockmuehl, "The Ten Commandments," 43; *CW*, 23.

PART TWO—The Holy Spirit and Christian Ethics in the Theology

a universally and eternally valid natural law by various philosophers as well as theologians, but he was also concerned about the ongoing political discussion, for instance in Germany, of whether or not to include basic moral laws ("moral order"[32]) in the constitutional law. Concerning the philosophical tradition in the modern era, Bockmuehl judges that it was, above all, Immanuel Kant who had brought about a major shift in Protestant theology.[33] According to Bockmuehl, Kant "tried to substitute the ethical external directedness with an internal directedness"[34] by abolishing the necessity of any externally binding laws and, instead, by calling attention to the personal awareness of one's duty as summarized in the categorical imperative. Hence, he laid emphasis on the principles of autonomy and self-responsibility of the individual as foundational for his ethics. Bockmuehl draws attention to the fact that these Kantian principles found their way into several Protestant ethics such as those of Schleiermacher, Herrmann, and Tillich.[35] Most of them, in fact, believed that by advocating an autonomous ethics they adhered to Luther and the Protestant cause.[36] Bockmuehl is aware that the main authority with regard to Luther, Karl Holl, seems to confirm this argument when he interprets Luther's statement about Christians creating new Decalogues to imply that laws are generally not necessary any more for moral actions.[37] Bockmuehl, however, rejects this view by arguing that Luther's statement is directly addressed to Christians and thus not applicable in the debate about basic moral laws in society, and that the wider context of Luther's statement demonstrates sufficiently the continuing importance of the law even for Christians.[38] These antinomian tendencies apparent in numerous Protestant ethics through their aversion to the continuing authority of any form of law promoted, directly or indirectly, the "demand for an 'autonomy' of the state,"[39] as Bockmuehl claims. Indeed, Bockmuehl strongly repudiates the idea that the church should not get involved in the debate about basic

---

32. Bockmuehl, "Humanität," 99. Cf. "Der Streit," 99.

33. Cf. *GG*, 493, 522.

34. *GG*, 522; cf. Bockmuehl, "Der Streit," 93–94.

35. Cf. *GG*, 522–24; Bockmuehl, "Der Streit," 93, 96; Schleiermacher, *Der christliche Glaube*, § 27, 1. Schleiermacher, *Lectures on Philosophical Ethics*; Herrmann, *Ethik*; Tillich, *Systematic Theology* (esp. 232); Tillich, *Writings in the Social Philosophy and Ethics*.

36. Cf. *GG*, 522–4; Bockmuehl, "Der Streit," 93–96; *VG*, 164–65, 176.

37. Cf. Bockmuehl, "Der Streit," 96, 100–101.

38. Cf. ibid., 97–98; Bockmuehl, "Ten Commandments," 135–36; *GG*, 524–25.

39. Bockmuehl, "Humanität," 94.

Bockmuehl's Understanding of Christian Ethics

moral laws with regard to the shaping of the constitutional law since he considers the general moral law to be applicable to all of humankind.[40]

Bockmuehl consistently suggests that it is mainly "the task of the state to give expression to the divine order of preservation through law and measures."[41] Hence, the dismissal of the natural moral law will, according to Bockmuehl, result in the discharging of "the idea of a common moral ground without which any culture will soon fall into disintegration and destruction."[42] Another theologian who, in Bockmuehl's opinion, evoked an estrangement from the idea of a universally recognizable natural moral law is Barth, though Bockmuehl still praises him for paying special attention to the Decalogue.[43] He also reproaches Barth for discarding the validity of any kind of natural law and for insisting that Christian ethics, and thus any law, has its foundation entirely in God's revelation in Christ.[44] Bockmuehl is, furthermore, concerned that, "[w]hile Lutherans and Anglicans seek to consolidate this lesson anew, Protestant and Roman-Catholic theologians influenced by Karl Barth pursue . . . the complete abandonment or at least the formalization and dissolving of the natural law."[45]

Not surprisingly, Bockmuehl criticizes those theologians in the wake of Barth who endeavor to apply the ethos of Christ to the constitutional law, thus resulting in over-involvement in society. And he criticizes those who deny the possibility of the church contributing to societal morality, since this leads to withdrawal.[46] Regarding the former tendency, he accuses Barth and his followers of failing to distinguish appropriately between the responsibilities of church and state as outlined in Scripture (Rom 13) and between Christians and non-Christians as a result of their inclination toward universalism.[47]

---

40. Cf. Bockmuehl, "Der Streit," 99.

41. Bockmuehl, "Kirche," 136.

42. Bockmuehl, "Natural Law," 59. See also Bockmuehl, "Humanität," 103.

43. For positive comments on Barth, see Bockmuehl, "The Ten Commandments," 43; Bockmuehl, "Der Streit," 98.

44. Cf. Barth, *Church Dogmatics* 2/2:557; Bockmuehl, "Natural Law," 59; Bockmuehl, "The Christian as Lawyer," 11; Bockmuehl, "Revolution," 61; Burkhardt, "Einführung des Herausgebers," in *Christliche Lebensführung*, xvii.

45. *GiE*, 170.

46. Cf. Bockmuehl, "Humanität," 93; Bockmuehl, "The Christian as Lawyer," 10–11, 33–34; Bockmuehl, "Natural Law," 59.

47. Cf. Bockmuehl, "The Christian as Lawyer," 33.

Part Two—The Holy Spirit and Christian Ethics in the Theology

Which theologians does Bockmuehl refer to in order to substantiate his conviction of the importance of upholding the idea of natural law in Christian ethics? First and foremost, Bockmuehl draws on the Reformers for support and demonstrates time and again his adherence to them on this issue. Worth mentioning in this context is also Brunner, though Bockmuehl's assessment of him concerning his concept of the law is only partially positive.[48] Bockmuehl approves of Brunner's recovery of the natural law, particularly with view to social ethics, and states that Brunner "is, besides Adolf Schlatter, the only Protestant theologian who even takes note of this traditional and reformatory way of social ethics."[49] Conversely, Bockmuehl objects to Brunner's disregard of the Decalogue in his individual ethics as well as to his outright aversion against the third use of the law (*tertius usus legis*).[50] Other theologians Bockmuehl fundamentally agrees with are Schlatter,[51] on account of his affirmation of natural theology and natural law, Knud E. Løgstrup,[52] and Wingren[53] who stress that a basic moral compulsion to care for the life of one's fellow human being is intrinsic to humanity. Bockmuehl asserts that Wingren "did much to ensure that this perspective remains on the agenda in the midst of the hidden or open, partial or total antinomianism of theology of our time."[54] Moreover, Bockmuehl specifically commends Wingren's endeavor to recover a theology of creation as well as a creation ethic.[55]

The Function of the Law in Creation Ethics

When examining the function of the law in creation ethics, we discover that Bockmuehl links the principle function of the law directly to the cultural mandate by arguing that the Decalogue and its various expositions provide general specifications of the cultural mandate. Thus, as

---

48. Cf. *VG*, 146–47.

49. *VG*, 147; cf. Bockmuehl, "Natural Law," 59; *GiE*, 117.

50. Cf. *GG*, 524; *VG*, 146. Bockmuehl, for instance, points out that Brunner does not once mention the Ten Commandments in his book on ethics entitled *The Divine Imperative*. Cf. *VG*, 146.

51. Cf. *VG*, 73–74; Schlatter, *Ethik*, 107–8.

52. Cf. Bockmuehl, "Natural Law," 60; *VG*, 240; Bockmuehl, "Kirche," 135.

53. Cf. *VG*, 235–39.

54. *GiE*, 170.

55. *VG*, 239.

Bockmuehl's Understanding of Christian Ethics

Bockmuehl emphasizes, both were given for one aim: the preservation of life.[56] As well as this overall function of the law in creation ethics, Bockmuehl also mentions different aspects of the "law of life,"[57] as he once calls the Ten Commandments. First, Bockmuehl repeatedly emphasizes the importance of the laws of creation for the protection and promotion of one's own life as well as that of one's neighbor.[58] Indeed, these are important even for the survival and welfare of a community, culture, or society, which depends on the keeping of the Decalogue. As Bockmuehl claims: "'To save a crumbling civilization' means nothing else than to go back to the Ten Commandments and especially the First, and to teach nations respectively."[59] Bockmuehl, therefore, confirms explicitly the civil use of the law in creation ethics by regarding the law to be the "guiding principle of public life,"[60] thus providing a basis for the constitutional law and for social ethics. Its main function is to constrain and hinder evil in public life, which can, according to Bockmuehl, be inferred from the negative way the Decalogue is worded.[61]

In this context it should be pointed out that Bockmuehl seems somewhat unclear as to which ethical material creation ethics exactly comprises. In one passage Bockmuehl mentions specifically the negative form of the Decalogue and the golden rule as belonging to creation ethics.[62] Yet, at other times, Bockmuehl includes the *synecdochic* interpretation of the Decalogue as well as the positive form of the golden rule.[63] Similarly, Bockmuehl notes regarding the laws of creation that "[t]hey are intended to guide the individual's walk in righteousness and are summed up in the commandment to love one's neighbour."[64] This suggests that Bockmuehl not only regards the law as functioning as a fence, as in the civil use of the law, but he also considers the law to operate as a rule in creation ethics as in the third use of the law.[65] Beyond this, Bockmuehl also includes the ac-

---

56. Cf. Bockmuehl, "Recovering Vocation," 83; *CaL*, 19.
57. Bockmuehl, "Ten Commandments," 133.
58. Cf. *GiE*, 166, 179, 196; Bockmuehl, "Ten Commandments," 133; *LG*, 16, 18.
59. Bockmuehl, "Horizons," 10; cf. 8; Bockmuehl, "Der Streit," 101, 105; *LG*, 17–18.
60. Bockmuehl, "Zur Frage nach der Maßgeblichkeit," 45.
61. Cf. *CW*, 22–23, 26; Bockmuehl, "Der Streit," 101.
62. Cf. *GG*, 309.
63. Cf. *CW*, 25; *GG*, 513–14; Burkhardt, "Einführung des Herausgebers," *Christliche Lebensführung*, xv.
64. Bockmuehl, "Recovering Vocation," 83; cf. 96.
65. Cf. *CW*, 21–22; Bockmuehl, "Destroyer," 50.

cusing function of the law in creation ethics, as the following text suggests: "Christians must grasp the task of conveying to humanity a sense of God's righteousness. If we were to drop this as being none of our business we would soon find out that we have also done away with the prerequisite for the message central to Christianity, namely, the forgiveness of sins. Where there is no accusation, proclamation of acquittal becomes obsolete."[66]

Creation Ethics as the Basis of Christian Ethics

Since Bockmuehl's understanding of the relation between creation ethics and specific Christian ethics will be discussed at greater length in a future chapter, we will only briefly mention two observations at this point. The first is Bockmuehl's emphasis on the *universality* of creation ethics in comparison to the specific Christian ethics, which is only applicable for Christians. Bockmuehl is convinced that creation ethics offers a common ground for Christians and non-Christians alike with regard to "social, medical and legal ethics"[67] since it is not distinctly Christian. The second observation is that Bockmuehl considers creation ethics to be the indispensable *basis* of Christian ethics upon which the specific Christian redemption and differential ethics are built.[68]

Of interest, furthermore, is that Bockmuehl has to defend his view regarding creation ethics as the basis of Christian ethics against several different fronts. First, he criticizes the Evangelicals, particularly the Pietists of his day, for neglecting creation ethics, and thus also social ethics, by focusing nearly solely on redemption ethics. This is evident in the following assertion by Bockmuehl: "But maybe today's Pietism has to learn once again that the preservation of the bodily life of the needy is, according to the quoted word of Jesus, not a task of secondary importance that one leaves to others because oneself has more noble things to do. We have to relearn that we are commissioned to embrace not just the order of salvation but also the order of preservation with regard to theory and practice, doctrine and life."[69]

---

66. Bockmuehl, "Natural Law," 59; cf. Bockmuehl, "Keeping His Commandments," 92–93.

67. *CW*, 26. Cf. Burkhardt, "Einführung des Herausgebers," *Christliche Lebensführung*, xvii.

68. Cf. *LbG*, 80; *CW*, 26; Bockmuehl, "Überlegungen," 110; Bockmuehl, "Josef," 5.

69. Bockmuehl, "Problem einer evangelikalen Sozialethik," 203; cf. Bockmuehl, "Pre-Suppositions," 356; Bockmuehl, "Horizons," 9; *VG*, 101.

Bockmuehl's Understanding of Christian Ethics

Secondly, by emphasizing creation ethics with its focal factors of cultural mandate and the laws of creation as the basis of Christian ethics, Bockmuehl distances himself from theologians associated with the new morality that regard the law as outdated as well as from Barthians who deny the existence of any natural, generally accepted law. Yet, thirdly, Bockmuehl also reproaches those theologians, for instance, the Reformers, who hardly take into account a specific Christian ethic but, instead, remain on the basic level of creation ethics.[70] Regarding the content of creation ethics, however, Bockmuehl mentions explicitly the close proximity to Reformation ethics.[71] This is reflected in the fact that Bockmuehl does not outline any specific role of the Spirit in creation ethics, in contrast to redemption and differential ethics, but, instead, maintains that "[h]uman reason, or even 'illumined human reason,' as some claim, may indeed be appropriate for decision-making in the realms of creational ethics and civil vocation."[72]

Specific Christian Ethics

Foundation of Specific Christian Ethics

FOUNDATION AND HORIZON OF SPECIFIC CHRISTIAN ETHICS: LORDSHIP OR KINGDOM OF GOD[73]

The reality of the lordship or kingdom of God is not only central to Bockmuehl's theology, as unpacked above, but also for his ethics. Bockmuehl, in fact, understands the lordship or kingdom of God to be the foundation for specific Christian ethics.[74] Not the autonomy of the human person but, instead, the lordship of God enables specific Christian ethics. As we shall see in the next chapter, Bockmuehl is of the opinion that without regeneration or a change of lordship it is impossible to live according to specific Christian ethics.[75]

---

70. Cf. *GG*, 529.
71. Cf. *GG*, 513–14.
72. *LbG*, 54. Cf. *GG*, 514.
73. Cf. Burkhardt, "Einführung des Herausgebers," *Christliche Lebensführung*, xvi.
74. Cf. *GG*, 354; Bockmuehl, "Der sendende Herr," 185; *CM*, 110.
75. Cf. *GiE*, 193; Bockmuehl, "Humanism," 208–9, 223; *CM*, 33; Bockmuehl, "Der sendende Herr," 195; Bockmuehl, "Revolution," 66.

Furthermore, Bockmuehl time and again draws attention to the fact that the honor and lordship of God is the horizon, aim, goal, purpose, or framework of specific Christian ethics.[76] It was of particular importance for him to recover this horizon for Christian ethics after it had been neglected for so long by the so-called "old morality," particularly by the Lutheran Reformation, yet also by theologians of the "new morality."[77] Bockmuehl argues that without a horizon or purpose to live and strive for, life becomes meaningless, and he was, therefore, not surprised that the Marxist-Leninist ideology captured the attention of many, particularly young people, due to its teleological nature.[78] Indeed, Bockmuehl believes that Marxism poses certain challenges to Christians that the latter should investigate in a self-critical way. Bockmuehl, for instance, points out that the Marxist-Leninist ethics as well as the Christian one "both emphasize a central purpose, the need to forsake the past and a functional concept of action."[79] He consequently insists: "We need to grasp and exercise the insight that the Christian's task is not exhausted by living a decent life according to the creational order. We must learn to dedicate our lives to the larger commission of God's kingdom with the same consciousness and purposiveness, circumspection and energy that we have seen in Lenin."[80]

Hence, Bockmuehl, like the Marxist-Leninist ethics, considers Christian ethics to be a functional one, insisting that any choice regarding lifestyle, but also everyday matters, should be made in view of the overall purpose and horizon.[81] However, Bockmuehl is well aware that the purpose propagated by Marxism differs diametrically from the Christian aim: "One cannot go far wrong in assuming that Marxism is a secularized vision of the kingdom of God. It is the kingdom of man."[82] Whereas the Marx-

---

76. Cf. Bockmuehl, "The Christian as Lawyer," 34; *GG*, 267–68; Bockmuehl, "Der sendende Herr," 185.

77. Cf. Bockmuehl, "Humanism," 223; *GG*, 269; Bockmuehl, "Revolution," 63–66; *GiE*, 179–80; *SU*, 35–37. Regarding the old morality, Bockmuehl comments that, though it considered the kingdom of God to be the main horizon in ethics, it considered the kingdom "in a static fashion, eternal, non-historical, not related to the situation." "Revolution," 65.

78. Cf. Bockmuehl, "Recovering Vocation," 81; *GG*, 270; *CM*, 37, 44–45; *GiE*, 182.

79. *CM*, 119; cf. 10–12.

80. *CM*, 112. Cf. *GG*, 18–19, 270; Bockmuehl, "Keeping His Commandments," 96.

81. Cf. *GiE*, 182; Bockmuehl, "Überlegungen," 113; Bockmuehl, "Leiblichkeit," 48; Bockmuehl, "Revolution," 67; *SU*, 36.

82. *CM*, 17. However, though promoting a teleological ethics, Bockmuehl does not embrace the Marxist-Leninist maxim that the *telos* of an action justifies the means. Cf.

Bockmuehl's Understanding of Christian Ethics

ist goal of a communist future on earth does not offer any hope beyond death, Bockmuehl characterizes the Christian alternative, the kingdom of God, as awaiting its perfect completion at the end of times, in eternity.[83] Particularly with a view to the conviction held by many theologians of his time of the irrelevance of eternity for ethics, Bockmuehl stresses that "[t]oday we must recover the eschatological framework of all our activities ... Calvin urged Christians to have a 'concern for eternity,' an awareness that we now live in preparation, as it were, for the glory of the Heavenly Kingdom."[84] Yet, at the same time, Bockmuehl also draws attention to the dynamic realization of the kingdom of God throughout history since the resurrection of Christ; thus, he endeavors to hold together the present and future reality of the kingdom of God.[85] With regard to the present realization of the kingdom of God in this world, Bockmuehl is convinced that it is through the change or, as he sometimes calls it, the revolution in people's lives from autonomy to the lordship of God that the kingdom of God is established.[86] Though Bockmuehl is aware that God himself is ultimately the agent in realizing his kingdom, he, nevertheless, urges every Christian to pursue this aim vigorously and passionately by living a life in obedience to the will of God and by calling others into this life under the rule and will of God.[87] That the kingdom of God comes about where God's will is done on earth as it is in heaven can, according to Bockmuehl, best be observed when looking at Jesus Christ who lived in complete accordance to the will of God. Instead of following his own plans, Jesus first of all listened to the Father's guidance before acting upon it.[88] Consequently, Bockmuehl regards the lordship of God as being realized in people by listening to and acting upon the guidance of the Holy Spirit: "The guidance of the Holy Spirit is the practical unfolding of the kingdom of God, which remains an

---

CM, 122; Bockmuehl, *Der Mensch auf der Suche nach Menschlichkeit*, 16.

83. Cf. *CM*, 43.

84. *LbG*, 34–35. Cf. Bockmuehl, "Under the Perspective," 65; *CM*, 140; Bockmuehl, *Evangelicals*, 42. In this context it is interesting to note Bockmuehl's indirect reproach of Moltmann's eschatology: "Of course, the 'theology of hope' has meant a step forward, but it often seems to be a hope geared to goals of social development, designed to be attained in the near future" ("Under the Perspective," 64).

85. Cf. *CM*, 115; Bockmuehl, "Keeping His Commandments," 97; Bockmuehl, "The Christian as Lawyer," 34; *SU*, 22; Bockmuehl, "Humanism," 208–9.

86. Cf. Bockmuehl, "Revolution," 66; Bockmuehl, "Humanism," 209.

87. Cf. *CW*, 124; *CM*, 111; *GiE*, 188–89; *SU*, 37; Bockmuehl, "Leiblichkeit," 48; Bockmuehl, "Is there a Christian 'Life-style'?," 49.

88. Cf. *CM*, 110, 162; Bockmuehl, "Is there a Christian 'Life-Style'?," 48; Bockmuehl, "How Did Jesus," 3; *GiE*, 190.

abstract concept without it . . . Whoever would speak of the kingdom of God must recapture the doctrine of the Holy Spirit. The Word of the Spirit as the interpretation of the kingdom is central for Christian ethics."[89]

When examining the question of whether the present kingdom of God is an internal, invisible, or external, visible reality, we discover that Bockmuehl seeks to hold both together. Hence, Bockmuehl agrees with the Reformers and contemporary Evangelicals that the kingdom of God is realized in the individual believer by a change of lordship and can, therefore, be seen as an internal, spiritual quality.[90] Furthermore, he is convinced that through the Holy Spirit the Christian brings forth the perceivable, external fruits of sanctification. He maintains that "these fruits of the Kingdom radiate into their human surroundings, spilling over into the world and preserving it as salt preserves food or in the manner of the ten just men for whose sake a city may be saved."[91] For Bockmuehl it is a matter of course that the inward transformation, brought about by the change of lordship, should manifest itself in outward actions; thus he rejects any characterization of the kingdom of God as merely internal.[92] At the same time, however, he distances himself from those theologians who completely externalize the kingdom of God by, for instance, equating it with secular cultural improvements.[93]

Regarding the individual or communitarian understanding of the kingdom of God, Bockmuehl attempts to show that, according to the Bible, the individual is called to participate in the universal kingdom, the goal here being that God's lordship will be enhanced more and more.[94] However, not merely the individual but the church itself as the body of Christ has only one purpose: to live under the horizon of the lordship of God and to serve as a paradigm of the kingdom of God by living in accordance with the standards of the kingdom, pre-eminently love.[95] Bockmuehl is convinced that in those cases in which the church fails to live in obedience to the Lord the kingdom of God is not realized. All this suggests

89. *CM*, 118. Cf. *LG*, 56, 149; Bockmuehl, "Raison," 55; Bockmuehl, "Humanism," 221–22; Houston, "Foreword," *LG*, xi.

90. Cf. *GG*, 263.

91. Bockmuehl, "European Evangelicals," 61–62.

92. Cf. *GG*, 263, 267–68; Bockmuehl, "Humanism," 223 ; Bockmuehl, "European Evangelicals," 61; *CM*, 159.

93. Cf. Bockmuehl, "European Evangelicals," 61; *GG*, 269.

94. Cf. Bockmuehl, "Humanism," 209; Bockmuehl, "Revolution," 69; Bockmuehl, "Humanism," 208, 223.

95. Bockmuehl, *Kirche*, 26, 81.

that Bockmuehl considers the kingdom of God to depend ultimately upon the individual's willingness to live under the kingship of God. Moreover, since for Bockmuehl this is inherently linked to loving one's neighbors, which he interprets as offering friendship and initiating reconciliation by extending God's forgiveness to others, the effects of the divine rule in one's life should, first of all, be visible in the Christian fellowship and then also in the wider community.[96] Nevertheless, Bockmuehl is of the opinion that it is not always necessarily possible to trace back expressions of love directly to the presence of the kingdom of God.

To sum up, then, our conclusion so far is that Bockmuehl regards the kingdom of God to be of paramount importance for Christian ethics as being the overall horizon toward which the whole life of the Christian should be directed. Above all, it is the Holy Spirit who, according to Bockmuehl, brings about the kingdom of God by giving guidance to the believers and by motivating and empowering them to act according to the standards of the kingdom.

Individual Foundation of Specific Christian Ethics: Regeneration and New Creation

When writing about ethics, Bockmuehl regularly raises the question of the individual foundation of specific Christian ethics. In fact, every ethics that claims to be Christian but does not answer this question falls prey to his criticism on account of the fact that, for him, Christian ethics is impossible without the foundation of regeneration and new creation.[97] For how can the fruits of a tree be good unless the tree is made good in the first place? Bockmuehl more than once refers to Christ's statement about the tree bringing forth fruit in order to underline the necessity of the transformation and regeneration in the individual person as a prerequisite for a life in accordance with the will of God.[98] Hence, we need to explore how regeneration and new creation come about and what they, according to Bockmuehl, entail.

Bockmuehl, above all, stresses that "those who want to find out more about the genesis of the new person will hear about the death and

---

96. Cf. Bockmuehl, "Friendship with Jesus," 3-4; *LbG*, 89, 91.

97. Cf. *GiE*, 190-91; Bockmuehl, "Kommunismus," 560.

98. Cf. Bockmuehl, "Socialist Ideal," 56; *CM*, 166-67; *WM*, 164; Bockmuehl, *Evangelicals*, 32-33; Bockmuehl, "Zur Frage nach der Maßgeblichkeit," 46.

resurrection of Jesus Christ and about 'dying and rising with Christ.'"⁹⁹ For the death of the old person and the resurrection of the new creation to take place, there needs to be the willingness for repentance and confession on the part of the human person. For Bockmuehl, this comprises the acknowledgment of one's sin and the acceptance of God's forgiveness as well as the "aversion from evil and the conversion to God's will, in thought and action,"¹⁰⁰ thus resulting in the change of lordship from human autonomy to God's reign.

Bockmuehl, furthermore, clarifies that, whereas conversion refers to the action of the human being responding to God's work, regeneration and renewal refer solely to God's saving and transforming acts. It is God who offers the gift of forgiveness, accomplished through Jesus' death and resurrection, and grants the experience of salvation since only "God's pardon brings the new creation to life."¹⁰¹ In fact, it is paramount, for Bockmuehl, that the new creation is not an improvement or development of the old person but, instead, is created by God *ex nihilo*.¹⁰² A completely new subject takes over in the life of the believer—the indwelling Holy Spirit, the "Christ-in-you."¹⁰³ Bockmuehl, therefore, argues that it is the Holy Spirit who realizes the reign of God in the life of individuals by transforming them through the power of Christ's resurrection into the image of God. Moreover, the Holy Spirit not only sanctifies Christians initially, at conversion, but continues to impart holiness to them, albeit not without the cooperation of the believers.¹⁰⁴ He bestows all those who ask for the gift of the Spirit with new motives, "spontaneity, insight and power to do the good."¹⁰⁵ Hence, Bockmuehl concludes that without the Holy Spirit the problem of the change of motivation necessary to bring about an ethical revolution, as is apparent in Marxism, cannot be solved.¹⁰⁶ It is only because of the Holy Spirit that a radical transformation of the inner being is possible, resulting in a new way of life. For Bockmuehl, any understanding of conversion, regeneration, and new creation that does not encompass

99. Bockmuehl, "Wiedergeburt", 53.

100. Bockmuehl, "Perimeters," 10; cf. *CM*, 158–60; Bockmuehl, "Der sendende Herr," 194–95, 198; Bockmuehl, "Humanism," 209.

101. *CM*, 159. Cf. *LbG*, 8–10, 14.

102. Cf. Bockmuehl, "Der sendende Herr," 194.

103. Cf. Bockmuehl, "Wiedergeburt", 36–38; 40.

104. Cf. Bockmuehl, "Sanctification," 615–16.

105. Bockmuehl, "Humanism," 222; cf. *CM*, 158–59; Bockmuehl, "Der sendende Herr," 197; *GiE*, 191–92; Bockmuehl, "Ostern 1975," 1.

106. Cf. *CM*, 154.

Bockmuehl's Understanding of Christian Ethics

perceivable moral change fails to do justice to the character of realism and concreteness that the New Testament conversion stories display.[107]

To sum up, then, Bockmuehl insists that without the experience of regeneration and new creation realized through the Holy Spirit dwelling in the believer, specific Christian ethics loses its presupposition and foundation.[108]

Redemption Ethics

With redemption ethics, which Bockmuehl also describes as "the ethics of salvation for believers,"[109] we enter into the realm of specific Christian ethics. When examining the content of this ethics, we discover that Bockmuehl regards redemption ethics to encompass the ethical material of the New Testament such as the commandments given by Jesus Christ, for instance, the positive form of the golden rule, the sermon on the Mount, and particularly the Great Commission, as well as the parenetic material of the New Testament, including the household codes. The main features he extracts from this material are love for God, spirituality, and mission, which he considers to be "[t]he Christian's additional tasks in church and mission."[110] Hence, we shall investigate each of these topics in turn.

SPECIFIC CHRISTIAN FORM OF LOVE FOR GOD

That, for Bockmuehl, the commandment to love God is of utmost importance can be seen by the fact that he considers it to be "the principle and the first chapter of Protestant ethics."[111] In fact, he at times even characterizes specific Christian ethics as an ethic of love since he is convinced that human endeavors only derive their value from being undertaken first and foremost out of love for God.[112] He regards, furthermore, love for God to be the fulfillment of the first commandment and the goal of our life.[113] Not

---

107. Cf. Bockmuehl, "Perimeters," 10; Bockmuehl, "Der sendende Herr," 195; Bockmuehl, "Problem einer evangelikalen Sozialethik," 204.

108. Cf. *LbG*, 40; Bockmuehl, "Der sendende Herr," 197; Bockmuehl, "Wiedergeburt," 40.

109. *CW*, 26.

110. Bockmuehl, "Protestant Ethics," 103; cf. *GiE*, 214; *GG*, 514.

111. *GG*, 508–9.

112. Cf. *GG*, 514, 516.

113. Cf. *CW*, 48.

surprisingly, therefore, Bockmuehl attempts to recover love for God as a central theme for theology and deems the promotion of love for God to be an essential criterion for a theology's significance and worth.[114] Similarly, Bockmuehl insists that "[l]ove of God must be the aim of all Christian preaching, mission and counselling."[115]

In order to comprehend the characteristics of love for God as maintained by Bockmuehl, we need to consider his interpretation of the first half of the double commandment of love. Contrary to Luther and many modern Protestant theologians, who hold the assumption that God can only be loved indirectly through loving one's neighbor, Bockmuehl strongly believes that the commandment is calling for direct love for God.[116]

With regard to the qualifications attached to the love for God, namely, loving God with heart, soul, and mind, Bockmuehl proposes that "love is determined, joyful, passionate and circumspect, all at the same time."[117] Moreover, he suggests that the biblical references to the heart comprise a wholehearted commitment of the will to God, whereas the references to the soul point to the emotional quality of love such as joy, passion, and admiration. Bockmuehl also interprets loving God with our mind as referring to a surrendering to God of our reason, i.e., our ability for discernment.[118] Notwithstanding that Bockmuehl, in his article on "The Great Commandment," puts forth a holistic understanding of love as involving mind, will, and feelings, there seems to be a tendency in Bockmuehl's theology to highlight love for God particularly as "something that can and must be willed."[119] Perhaps this can be understood as a reaction to those concepts that, in his view, emphasize love as sentiment. He suggests: "The best model for love of God we have in Jesus as e.g. the Gospel of John depicts him. His is not a sentimental but a determined love, comprising utter trust, unity of mind, obedience, and a commitment to loyalty, come rain or shine."[120]

---

114. Jüngel summarizes one of Bockmuehl's articles accordingly: "Bockmuehl has drawn attention to love of God as the center of all theological deliberation and has warned of the loss of zeal for the honor of God" (Jüngel, "Summary of Klaus Bockmuehl," 112–13).

115. *CW*, 45.

116. Cf. Bockmuehl, "Great Commission," 10–11; *CW*, 37–38; Bockmuehl, "Aktualität," 304–5; *GG*, 275; M. Bockmuehl, "Love God," 39.

117. Bockmuehl, "Great Commandment," 15–16.

118. Cf. "Great Commandment," 13–15; *CW*, 43.

119. *CW*, 43.

120. Bockmuehl, "Three Horizons," 12; cf. *GiE*, 161–62; Bockmuehl, "Erneue-rung," 205; *CW*, 45.

Bockmuehl's Understanding of Christian Ethics

When examining Bockmuehl's understanding of the source and motivation of love for God, two aspects are apparent. First, Bockmuehl views love for God to come about as a response to God's love, which is primarily revealed in his willingness to forgive. In this context Bockmuehl refers to the comment Jesus made at the time when a sinful woman was anointing him: those who have been forgiven much, love much. Bockmuehl concludes therefore that without the experience of forgiveness, the prerequisite for loving God, i.e., gratitude for God's action in one's life, is missing.[121] However, despite it being God's love that generates a loving response in us, Bockmuehl emphasizes the fact that our love for God is, nevertheless, always first and foremost the gift of the Holy Spirit. This second aspect, the Holy Spirit as the source of love for God, has in Bockmuehl's opinion too often been neglected with the consequence that "[w]here this reduction of the doctrine of the Holy Spirit's work exists, it is no wonder that the idea of love for God also falls by the wayside."[122] In fact, as Bockmuehl points out, even Jesus' love for God was due to "the impulse of the Holy Spirit."[123] Consequently, Bockmuehl endeavors to recall attention to the importance of the Holy Spirit as the indispensable power and driving force in a Christian's life by engendering love for God. Not surprisingly, therefore, Bockmuehl encourages his readers not only to pray for love but also for the gift of the Spirit.[124]

Bockmuehl, in fact, deems prayer to be an eminent pathway to an increased love for God. At the same time, he believes that *prayer* is also a key expression and application of love for God. While Bockmuehl's elucidations of prayer will be discussed at greater length in the following section, it is, nevertheless, worthwhile making a few brief comments on this issue here. Bockmuehl, for instance, regards communication, i.e., sharing one's lives with each other, to be an essential characteristic of love. Accordingly, Bockmuehl draws attention to the fact that, since prayer has to be understood as a two-way conversation, it comprises not only talking but also listening.[125] He particularly stresses the latter aspect as being of immense importance since the practice of listening to God is closely related to another application of love of God—that of *obedience*. This he interprets

121. Cf. *UG*, 162; *LbG*, 12; Bockmuehl, "Great Commandment," 16; *CW*, 44.
122. *LbG*, 48.
123. *LbG*, 30.
124. Cf. Bockmuehl, "Three Horizons," 12; *CW*, 42; Bockmuehl, "Great Commandment," 17; *LbG*, 30; *LG*, 148–49; *GG*, 516; "Sanctification and Christian Mission," 60.
125. Cf. *LG*, 146, 148–49; *CW*, 45–46; Bockmuehl, "Säkularismus," 186.

above all as doing God's will. However, the presupposition for obedience to God is, first, the knowledge of his will, which can be gained through considering the commandments in Scripture as well as through listening to the directions given by the Holy Spirit, and, secondly, by an attitude of willingness and readiness to carry out God's commissions. This, however, requires the surrendering of one's own plans in order to live solely for God and his will. Bockmuehl does not hesitate to challenge his readers by raising the following question: "To what extent do we live within earshot of God, standing by for his instructions, making his interests in the world our own?"[126]

To make God's plans and concerns one's own leads, according to Bockmuehl, inevitably to the commission to love one's neighbor as oneself; this is the second half of the double commandment of love. Hence, Bockmuehl identifies the basis for loving and serving one's neighbor as love for God and considers it to be not a substitute but an expression and a fruit of the latter.[127] He finds this connection between love for God and love for one's neighbor displayed clearly in the story of Peter's reinstatement in John 21: "[L]ove for . . . Jesus, love for the crucified and resurrected one is consequently to be regarded as the foundational principle of all Christian ethics. It is the source of energy for Christian service to one's neighbor."[128] Bockmuehl thus claims that the extent of our love for God will have a direct effect on the extent of our obedience.[129]

When considering the relationship between love for God and obedience, it is interesting to note that certain statements by Bockmuehl seem to suggest that he not only regards obedience to be the expression of love for God, thus flowing out of the latter, but more or less its definition. The following text comes close to such an assumption: "Love for God is shorthand for doing his will and keeping his commandments."[130] The question turns, however, on whether obedience itself is a sign pointing to another reality, a deeper source, or whether Bockmuehl equates loving God with

---

126. *CW*, 48; cf. 45; Bockmuehl, "Three Horizons," 11; *LbG*, 76.

127. Cf. *CW*, 45, 48; *GiE*, 162–63; Bockmuehl, "Friendship," 3–4.

128. *GiE*, 163; cf. Bockmuehl, "Erneuerung," 205; Bockmuehl, "Toward a Spirituality," 42; *GG*, 508. It is interesting to note in passing that, for Bockmuehl, "love for God" includes "love for Jesus," the latter being a favorite subject of pietism. However, though Bockmuehl asserts the need for the practised concentration on the love for Jesus, he himself employs more often the expression "love for God" than "love for Jesus." Cf. "Aktualität," 304–5; *GG*, 514–15.

129. Cf. *CW*, 48.

130. *CW*, 45; cf. Loos, "Human Embodiment," 88, 136.

obeying God. Even though Bockmuehl does acknowledge that love encompasses different aspects such as our emotions, his main emphasis time and again is that "loving God, or Jesus, means to obey him."[131]

SPECIFIC CHRISTIAN FORM OF SPIRITUALITY

It was with sorrow that Bockmuehl observed a widespread neglect, even decline of, the specific Christian form of spirituality in Protestant theology and ethics as well as in Protestant, even evangelical, churches. In fact, Bockmuehl accused the Lutheran ethical tradition of a greater inattention to spirituality than the Reformed one due to the silence of the former with regard to the notion of love for God.[132] It is interesting to note that Bockmuehl remarks *vis-à-vis* Calvin's insistence on the possibility of direct love for God: "The consequence of the reintroduction of this topic brings also a new sound of spirituality, an expression of spiritual life, of communion with God."[133]

The main content of a Christian spirituality comprises, for Bockmuehl, our relationship or communion with God.[134] Since one of the main characteristics of this relationship should be love, it goes without saying that the notion of love for God inevitably constitutes a part of spirituality.[135] However, when surveying Bockmuehl's outline of redemption ethics, we discover that he at times juxtaposes love of God, spirituality, and mission, defining spirituality in this context primarily as "the life of prayer."[136] To what an extent spirituality and love for God are intrinsically linked can be seen by the fact that Bockmuehl considers prayer to be an application of love for God. Similarly, Bockmuehl comments that "[p]rayer is the expression of friendship, of keeping company with Christ."[137] And the friendship that Christ offers can be characterized as being immediate, personal, and intimate, full of trust, openness, and trans-

---

131. *CW*, 45; cf 43. Bockmuehl, "Great Commandment," 13; Loos, "Human Embodiment," 137.

132. Cf. Bockmuehl, "Protestant Ethics," 112–13; Bockmuehl, "Toward a Spirituality," 42; *GG*, 311.

133. *GG*, 353.

134. Cf. *GG*, 309–10; Bockmuehl, "Toward a Spirituality," 42.

135. Cf. Bockmuehl, "Great Commandment," 10; Thomas, "Spirituality of Klaus Bockmuehl: Part Two," 33.

136. *GG*, 514; cf. 516.

137. Bockmuehl, "Friendship," 3; cf. *LbG*, 78; *CW*, 41.

parency.[138] Not only are we allowed to talk about everything to Christ, but we have, according to Bockmuehl, the privilege that he "does not keep secrets from his friends,"[139] i.e., that he guides, directs, and commissions us. The main content of the Spirit's counsel is, according to Bockmuehl, the practical application of the double commandment of love for the individual person in a particular situation. The prerequisite for receiving this counsel is listening prayer, which encompasses spending time with God, outward and inward stillness, seeking his presence, being honest before him as well as "actively petitioning God for his specific instruction: What is his plan for this day, and for the current stage of our pilgrimage?"[140] However, it is of paramount importance for Bockmuehl that the inspiration gained in those times of listening to the Counselor needs to be tested against Scripture as its norm: "Scripture must continue at all times—like the bass line in music—to underlie momentary insights."[141] Alongside listening prayer, Bockmuehl, therefore, highlights the necessity of in-depth Bible study and meditation.[142]

Bockmuehl is conscious of the fact that the statement he adopted from the Moral Re-Armament, "when people listen, God speaks,"[143] was rather disputed, particularly by those, in the wake of the Protestant Reformers, who held that God only speaks through Scripture and its exposition.[144] Hence, it was one of Bockmuehl's main objectives throughout his life to rediscover particularly the notion of the Holy Spirit's direct counsel and guidance for the individual believer, which served the purpose of promoting the kingdom of God. Hence, when examining the aim of spirituality, of communion with God expressed through prayer, we may conclude that, for Bockmuehl, this is ultimately the realization and furtherance of the kingdom of God. In fact, Bockmuehl points out that "Scripture proposes a *spirituality of the kingdom*" since he considers spirituality to be "the backbone of service."[145] Bockmuehl believes that without time spent

---

138. Cf. Bockmuehl, "Friendship," 2; Bockmuehl, "Der sendende Herr," 180.

139. Bockmuehl, "Friendship," 3.

140. *LbG*, 61; cf. 50; Bockmuehl, "Toward a Spirituality," 42; Bockmuehl, "Friendship," 3.

141. *LG*, 149.

142. Cf. *LbG*, 50, 77.

143. *LG*, 9; cf. Buchman, *Remaking the World*, 46.

144. Cf. *LG*, 132–33: Bockmuehl, "Frank Buchman's Message," 36–37. Regarding Luther, cf. *LG*, 126–27; regarding Calvin, cf. ibid, 130.

145. Bockmuehl, "Toward a Spirituality," 42; cf. *LG*, 149; Bockmuehl, "Friendship," 4.

Bockmuehl's Understanding of Christian Ethics

in communion with Christ, in listening to the guidance of the Holy Spirit, authentic Christian life, for instance, involvement in mission and in social action, is not viable. For it is only through fellowship with Christ that the Christian receives, on the one hand, the motivation and strength to love God and one's neighbor and, on the other hand, peace, creativity, and insight.[146] Hence, with regard to the relationship between contemplation and action, Bockmuehl holds that Scripture gives "primacy to listening, but not without a subsequent 100 percent commitment to Christian action."[147] This precedence of contemplation is, according to Bockmuehl, best illustrated by the fact that Jesus commends especially Mary's attitude of listening.[148] However, this story, though censuring activism, should not be interpreted, in Bockmuehl's opinion, as encouraging passivism. Rather, as Jesus' own life reveals, his actions derived from his communion with his Father.

Due to Bockmuehl's emphasis on the kingdom of God as the purpose and horizon of the Christian life, it seems that a tendency can be observed, particularly in his earlier writings, to view communion with Christ and listening prayer as a means to an end: the end is the promotion of the kingdom of God which is primarily brought about by mission and social action. This we shall discuss in more depth in a later chapter.

Of further interest in this context is the investigation of the relationship between spirituality and ethics displayed by Bockmuehl. First of all, Bockmuehl draws attention to the fact that spirituality, more precisely, communion with God, "inevitably constitutes part of Christian ethics."[149] He, in fact, differentiates between the ethics of the first table of the Decalogue, which focuses on our relationship to God, and the ethics of the second table, which is concerned "with the earthly behavior of persons."[150] Given that ethics is commonly seen as dealing only with the second table of the Decalogue, Bockmuehl occasionally suggests a close connection between ethics and spirituality, or ascetics as he also calls it, defining the latter in this context as the ethics of the first table of the Decalogue.[151]

---

146. Cf. Bockmuehl, "Protestant Ethics," 113; Bockmuehl, "Toward a Spirituality," 42; *LbG*, 50, 64; Bockmuehl, "Evangelium," 137.

147. Bockmuehl, "Listeners," 5.

148. Cf. ibid.; Bockmuehl, "Toward a Spirituality," 42.

149. Bockmuehl, "Protestant Ethics," 112–13; cf. *LbG*, 65; Bockmuehl, *Grundlagen*, 7.

150. Bockmuehl, "Ethics/Spiritual Life," 237.

151. Cf. ibid.; *GG*, 516; Bockmuehl, "Toward a Spirituality," 42; Bockmuehl, "Protestant Ethics," 103.

Part Two—The Holy Spirit and Christian Ethics in the Theology

More frequently, however, he emphasizes the necessity of reintegrating the ethics of the first table, including spirituality, into an outline of a Christian ethic, as he himself attempts, thereby understanding Christian ethics to mean Christian life in general. Regardless of the different definitions of ethics and spirituality, the following statement by Neuer adequately summarizes Bockmuehl's understanding of the relationship between ethics and spirituality: "[F]or him, the foundation of all ethics continued to be a biblically grounded spirituality with its focal point in an adherence to Christ lived out in a committed way."[152]

Specific Christian Form of Mission

The fact that the topic of the specifically Christian form of mission rarely occurred in Christian ethical literature was, according to Bockmuehl, a grave neglect since he regarded the calling to mission to be the "first and foremost imperative of Christian ethics"[153] and a clear example of a *proprium* of Christian ethics. Since the inclusion of mission in an outline of Christian ethics is rather exceptional, it is worth pointing out, as mentioned above, that Adolf Schlatter in his ethics incorporates such topics as evangelism and mission.[154] In addition, Bockmuehl as well as Schlatter describe Christian ethics not merely as an exposition of the moral life but also of the life and service of the Christian as a whole.[155]

When examining the *aim of mission*, we discover that Bockmuehl's passion for the realization of the lordship of God in this world directly shapes his understanding of the aim of mission. In order that Christ's lordship can be established in this world, Christians should participate in God's act of salvation by helping people come under the lordship of Christ. Bockmuehl insists that this is brought about through conversion and regeneration, which results inevitably in changed lives, namely, in a change of thinking and volition, in changed actions, and thus in changed relationships. Bockmuehl, in fact, describes such changed people as living for Christ, not for themselves, obeying and honoring God so that they grow in maturity and perfection in Christ (cf. Col 1:28, which Bockmuehl regarded as Paul's equivalent to Jesus' Great Commission). This also

---

152. Neuer, "Für eine Theologie aus Liebe zu Gott," 28.

153. *CM*, 112; cf. *GG*, 88; Bockmuehl, "Revolution," 67; Bockmuehl, "Zur Frage nach der Maßgeblichkeit," 48–49.

154. Schlatter, *Ethik*, 200–209; 242–48.

155. Cf. *GG*, 517; Neuer, *Dogmatik*, 253.

Bockmuehl's Understanding of Christian Ethics

comprises for Bockmuehl living according to God's will, as spelt out in the double commandment of love, and getting involved in the realization of Christ's lordship through engaging in mission.[156] Given that the ultimate goal of mission is the furtherance of the reign of Christ, it not only aims at the salvation of people but also at their spiritual maturity and their involvement in the service of God, which includes mission.[157] Bockmuehl, in fact, states that "[t]he disciples' communion with Jesus is not the goal; it is to equip and dispatch them to be 'fishers of men,' to have them teach all nations and turn them into followers too. As soon as we propose to be pious without being on the road to bring other people under the rule of God we are parasites in the kingdom of God."[158]

These strong words by Bockmuehl underline the fact that he deems mission to be a pivotal part of Christian vocation for every believer. In contrast to Luther, who Bockmuehl criticizes for giving *civil* vocation more weight than the specific Christian vocation, Bockmuehl, as Barth before him, points out that in view of the Great Commission every Christian is called to be a witness for Christ and thus to participate in Christ's prophetic ministry.[159] Bockmuehl even goes as far as to say that it is mission that gives the believer meaning and purpose in life: "The Christian, who is the witness to Christ's kingdom, only lives meaningfully when he evangelizes."[160]

When looking at the ecclesiological implications of this, we discover that Bockmuehl considers mission to be "the lifeblood of the Church."[161] Without it, her very existence is in danger since her purpose is to participate in God's own work of bringing about salvation and establishing his kingdom.[162] Bockmuehl finds evidence for this conviction by pointing to Jesus' statement in John 4:34 that doing the will of the Father and finishing his work is his food and provision.[163] Bockmuehl concludes from this that God's commission given to the individual Christian and the church

---

156. Cf. Bockmuehl, "Wie lebt ein Christ," 6.

157. Cf. Bockmuehl, "Recovering Vocation," 85.

158. Bockmuehl, "Frank Buchman's Message," 39–40; cf. *LbG*, 22; "Recovering Vocation," 85. See also Burkhardt, "Mission im Zeichen des Säkularismus," 222.

159. Cf. Bockmuehl, "Introduction," 92; *VG*, 120; Bockmuehl, "Recovering Vocation," 96–97; *GG*, 117; Bockmuehl, "Serving," 14.

160. *WM*, 36; cf. 21, 37.

161. Bockmuehl, "Theology as Servant," 45; cf. *LbG*, 25; *WM* 46.

162. Cf. Bockmuehl, "Recovering Vocation," 85; Bockmuehl, "Der sendende Herr," 179; *GG*, 88; Bockmuehl, "Frank Buchman's Message," 38; *WM*, 21.

163. Cf. *LbG*, 24; Bockmuehl, "Problem der Ethik," 78.

should not be perceived as a duty or burden but as a gift of grace. For it is this commission that not only provides the Christian with meaning and purpose for life, but also "grants personal dignity; it creates personality . . . Under God's commission can come a remarkable awakening of the gifts and talents in us that had previously lain dormant."[164]

Moreover, Bockmuehl points out that believers are not left alone with their commission but, instead, receive the Holy Spirit as "God's missionary gift,"[165] since it is the Spirit himself who is the leader of mission. Of interest to note is the fact that Bockmuehl even describes the Holy Spirit in an early article on Buchman as "the officer-commanding of the missionary enterprise,"[166] thus referring to his role as the instructor and guide of mission. The human precondition for mission is, according to Bockmuehl, therefore, a willingness and readiness to respond to the personal calling, for instance, to full-time mission and situational guidance from the Holy Spirit.[167] For Bockmuehl, another significant task of the Holy Spirit with regard to mission is the endowment of spiritual gifts, the *charismata*, to every believer. In fact, Bockmuehl considers every *charisma* to correspond to a particular task or ministry needed for the edification of the church.[168] The most important ministries are, for Bockmuehl, the so-called church-building activities such as evangelism and "the pastoral, teaching, and serving/diaconal ministries."[169] According to Bockmuehl, many Protestant churches, particularly in Germany, are due to their suspicion of lay participation deficient in carrying out these church-building activities. This he traces back to Luther's secularization of the *charismata*, namely, the application of the spiritual gifts to the context of the family and the society and the reduction of the spiritual gifts to natural dispositions.[170]

Let us now take a closer look at the aforementioned church-building activities, since Bockmuehl devotes considerable time interpreting some of them. The first three church-building activities Bockmuehl occasionally summarizes under the heading of *proclamation*. This Bockmuehl

164. *LbG*, 31.
165. Bockmuehl, "Frank Buchman's Message," 38.
166. Ibid.; cf. *GG*, 95; *WM*, 37–39.
167. Cf. Bockmuehl, "Der sendende Herr," 181, 185–86; Bockmuehl, "Wie lebt ein Christ," 6.
168. Cf. Bockmuehl, "Recovering Vocation," 86–87; *GG*, 514; Bockmuehl, *Kirche*, 37.
169. Bockmuehl, "Protestant Ethics," 102; cf. *GG*, 312, 514.
170. Cf. Bockmuehl, "Recovering Vocation," 84–87, 91, 95; *GG*, 109, 232, 279, 286, 306.

Bockmuehl's Understanding of Christian Ethics

divides into "the *extensive* and *intensive* aspects of proclamation";[171] the extensive aspect comprises evangelism, i.e., bringing to faith, the intensive one comprises teaching and shepherding/counseling, i.e., deepening faith. Whereas Bockmuehl views the evangelists as mainly being outwardly oriented, he considers the teachers and shepherds/counselors to be particularly concerned with the inward upbuilding of the church.[172] When turning to the content of proclamation, Bockmuehl distinguishes between the initial proclamation of the saving works of God and the call to submit to his lordship, and the follow-up instructions of "doctrinal teaching and ethical instruction."[173] Without this intensive teaching, particularly in small groups or, as with shepherding/counseling, often on a one-to-one basis, Bockmuehl believes that the growth of the church will be, and has in the past been, severely hindered.[174] In his lecture on ecclesiology, Bockmuehl particularly identifies one reason for the disregard for teaching in many evangelical churches: "In Evangelicalism, it is somehow in the air that everyone should, in fact, be an evangelist . . . Well, this opinion flatly contradicts the New Testament. It was a real comfort to me when I recognized that God has simply given different people different gifts."[175]

Bockmuehl does acknowledge, however, that theology has time and again not taken up its responsibility for the church: "It is the task of theology not to get drunk with foreign ideas and beat up God's children but to feed and strengthen them. Theology's task is part of shepherding the Church."[176] Thus, not surprisingly, Bockmuehl himself considered his main assignment to be to serve the church and provide nourishment by teaching and writing in the field of theology.[177]

Besides proclamation, Bockmuehl regards *Christian service (diakonia)* to be the second building block of mission.[178] Hence, Bockmuehl agrees explicitly with Stott who uses the term mission not only to refer to evangelism but also in a broader sense as "carrying out the commissions

---

171. *LbG*, 106; cf. 106–9; *WM*, 22, 26; Bockmuehl, "Recovering Vocation," 85; Bockmuehl, *Kirche*, 38–39.

172. Cf. *WM*, 22, *GG*, 516–17.

173. Bockmuehl, *Evangelicals*, 42.

174. Cf. *WM*, 24; Bockmuehl, *Evangelicals*, 42; *LbG*, 109. With regard to Bockmuehl's comments on counselling, see *LbG*, 109; *GG*, 517; *Kirche*, 37.

175. Bockmuehl, *Kirche*, 37.

176. Bockmuehl, "Theology as Servant," 46.

177. Cf. circular letter written by Bockmuehl on Dec. 5, 1988, 2. See also *LbG*, 108; Bockmuehl, *Evangelicals*, 43.

178. Cf. Bockmuehl, "Der sendende Herr," 188, 190.

PART TWO—The Holy Spirit and Christian Ethics in the Theology

of Jesus."[179] Bockmuehl, in fact, compares the church's missionary task to Jesus' own commission given to him by his Father, defining it in reference to Jesus' life as "synthesis of proclamation and social action."[180] Thus, the Christian has the privilege of participating in God's own *diakonia* which consists not only of preservation and sustenance but also of restoration and renewal of different aspects of the human being: According to Bockmuehl, the commission of Christian service confirms, on the one hand, the creational vocation of preservation given to the whole of humankind while, on the other hand, intensifying it by encompassing the calling to restoration, rehabilitation, and renewal.[181] According to Bockmuehl, this preservation and restoration pertains to the whole of one's being. Hence, Christian service cares, first of all, for the *body* by restoring and preserving physical life through giving material aid to the poor, tending the sick etc. The second area of concern for Christian service is the *soul, mind, or spirit*. This implies helping people in need to regain their identity, worth, and meaning in life as well as to heal their relationship with God. Thirdly, Christian service is involved in preserving and restoring *social relationships* since the latter are vital for a healthy human life.[182]

Above all, Bockmuehl regards Christian service to be an expression of the decree to love one's neighbor, while highlighting that the "neighbor" includes more than just the family: "In his teaching Jesus pointed explicitly to the extra-mural *diakonia*, Christians were always to be 'on the way' . . . Christian benevolence spreads beyond the inner circle,"[183] thus overflowing into society.[184] When investigating the source of the inner motivation for and the foundation of Christian service of love, Bockmuehl points first and foremost to the believers' communion with God, to spiritual life. Only by receiving God's love, strength, and inspiration through listening prayer is the Christian enabled to serve continuously, even under severe circumstances. In this context, Bockmuehl particularly emphasizes the empowering, commissioning, and guiding role of the Holy Spirit for

179. Ibid., 188.
180. *WM*, 141.
181. Cf. Bockmuehl, "Serving," 16–17; *CW*, 26; Bockmuehl, "Recovering Vocation," 84–85.
182. Cf. Bockmuehl, "Serving," 11, 17–19; Bockmuehl, "Recovering Vocation," 34–35; Bockmuehl, "Destroyer," 50.
183. Bockmuehl, "Serving," 20–21; cf. 11, 31; Bockmuehl, "Recovering Vocation," 84; *GG*, 311.
184. Cf. Bockmuehl, "Problem einer evangelikalen Sozialethik," 204.

Bockmuehl's Understanding of Christian Ethics

Christian service.[185] Another source for Christian service, though of lesser importance than the first one, is, for Bockmuehl, "the communion with others of like mind"[186] since this can enable teamwork but also provide support for the individual.[187]

With regard to the on-going debate about the biblical understanding of the relationship between proclamation and social action, it is interesting to note that Bockmuehl endeavors to hold both together by placing them under the lordship of God.[188] Hence, he attempts to avoid the tendency he saw among some Evangelicals of over-emphasizing proclamation and with it the winning of souls as the sole aim of mission to the detriment of social action. Instead, he affirms Christian service as "a prominent chapter of Christian ethics."[189] Yet, at the same time, he also warns against the "reduction of the message to a mere 'social gospel,'"[190] by bringing into focus that "[b]iblical truth often consists of two times 100 per cent, a fact that our common or garden logic will not accept and often uses to create division."[191] Thus, convinced that the proclamation of the Gospel accompanied by Christian service leads to faith and love in those people who accept the message and are transformed by it, he is, therefore, encouraging them to engage in proclamation and social action themselves.[192] In this way, economic, social, national, and international change can be brought about. However, when turning to the question of whether every Christian should be equally involved in proclamation and Christian service, Bockmuehl takes into account the diverse *charismata* given to the church and concludes "that in every church there will be some who are called into full-time preaching and others who are called into full-time service to the poor."[193] It is, as Bockmuehl stresses time and again, the guidance of the

---

185. Cf. Bockmuehl, "Serving," 26–28; Bockmuehl, "Toward a Spirituality," 42; Bockmuehl, "Friendship," 3. See particularly *WM*, 38–39, for the fundamental role of the Holy Spirit for mission.

186. Bockmuehl, "Serving," 28.

187. Cf. ibid., 28–29.

188. Cf. Burkhardt, "Mission," 222.

189. Bockmuehl, "Serving," 17; Bockmuehl, "Evangelical Assertions," 45; *WM*, 162.

190. Bockmuehl, "After Lausanne," 67.

191. Ibid., 68.

192. Cf. Bockmuehl, "Der sendende Herr," 190.

193. Bockmuehl, *Kirche*, 37; cf Bockmuehl, "Serving," 21.

PART TWO—The Holy Spirit and Christian Ethics in the Theology

Holy Spirit that plays a crucial role in mission with regard to the personal vocation of the believer.[194]

Bearing in mind the central role Bockmuehl considers the Holy Spirit to play in mission, it is not surprising that he traces the lack of mission, including the church-building activities, in many concepts of Protestant ethics back to an insufficient understanding of the essential functions of the Holy Spirit and of the importance of the lordship of Christ *vis-à-vis* mission.[195] Bockmuehl, therefore, aims at recovering the role of the Holy Spirit for Christian ethics and emphasizes the significance of mission as playing a major part in specific Christian ethics and, more precisely, in redemption ethics.

SPECIFIC CHRISTIAN FORM OF SANCTIFICATION

Although the aforementioned topics love for God, spirituality, and mission belong, for Bockmuehl, to the wider field of sanctification, it is, nevertheless, worthwhile looking into this specific theme in more depth, not least due to the major emphasis Bockmuehl himself puts on it. As shown in the section on the influence of German pietism on Bockmuehl, his concept of sanctification is clearly shaped by his pietistic heritage. He, for instance, defines sanctification as *praxis pietatis*, the actualization of the theoretical beliefs in everyday life, thus accentuating its ethical nature.[196] Furthermore, he not only considers sanctification to be a necessary prerequisite for communion with God, since the unholy cannot enter into God's presence, but he also holds that sanctification, which includes doing good works, is the actual purpose of salvation and thus the "objective of every Christian."[197] Consequently, with regard to the relationship between justification and sanctification, Bockmuehl puts new emphasis on their complementary nature and claims that justification as the life-changing experience of forgiveness of sins forms the foundation for the Christian practice of faith. In fact, he even remarks: "Justification that does not lead to sanctification is a perversion."[198] Hence, Bockmuehl regards

---

194. Bockmuehl, "Recovering Vocation," 96, 98.

195. Cf. *GG*, 517.

196. Cf. Bockmuehl, "Aktualität," 309; Bockmuehl, "Task," 3; Stoeffler, *Rise*, 5, 9.

197. Bockmuehl, "Werk," 11; cf. 1, 11–12; cf. Bockmuehl, "Sanctification," 613, 615; Bockmuehl, "Sanctification and Christian Mission," 60; *CW*, 2.

198. Bockmuehl, "Wiedergeburt," 64; cf. *LbG*, 12–14.

Bockmuehl's Understanding of Christian Ethics

sanctification to be an indication of the genuineness and concreteness of justification and the new birth.[199]

Unlike the dialectical Barth and Bultmann, who declared God's work in this world to be non-observable, Bockmuehl insists on the concrete, visible nature of conversion and regeneration, which he considers to be the starting-point of the observable process of sanctification.[200] More specifically, Bockmuehl distinguishes between sanctification "as a one-time event and as a process, the believers *being* and *becoming* holy;"[201] he identifies regeneration as the saving event when God through the Holy Spirit sanctifies the believer. With regard to the process of sanctification, Bockmuehl differentiates further between God's continuing work of sanctification in the Christian, on the one hand, and "man's action in synergism with God,"[202] on the other. As a consequence, the role of the believer in sanctification has to be seen as being both passive and active at the same time. When providing biblical evidence for his concept of sanctification, Bockmuehl calls for instant attention to the fact that indicative as well as imperative language is used in Scripture with regard to the sanctification of the believer.[203]

Since Bockmuehl explores in some detail the Christian's activity in the process of sanctification, though not independent of the work of the Holy Spirit, let us examine this aspect more closely. First, Bockmuehl describes sanctification negatively as mortification, i.e., putting to death the old Adam, as purification, i.e., the cleansing of the heart, and as avoidance of sin, materialism, and self-service. Hence, Bockmuehl believes that "[s]anctification will find expression in a life of prayer and spiritual warfare and discipline, i.e. in acts of asceticism."[204] Secondly, however, he brings into focus the positive notion of sanctification, namely, dedication to a life for God. This encompasses, for Bockmuehl, "the fulfillment of what righteousness requires through the good works of brotherly and neighborly love"[205] and, especially, human availability for God. Hence, he asserts that holiness does not imply perfection but, instead, "to be at God's disposal;

---

199. Cf. Bockmuehl, "Perimeters," 11.

200. Cf. *UG*, 57–58, 82, 86.

201. Bockmuehl, "Sanctification," 614.

202. Bockmuehl, "Perimeters," 11.

203. Cf. Bockmuehl, "Wiedergeburt," 58; Bockmuehl, "Sanctification," 613–14; *CW*, 47; *VG*, 189.

204. Bockmuehl, "Sanctification," 615; cf. Bockmuehl, "Evangelium," 136.

205. Bockmuehl, "Sanctification and Christian Mission," 60.

it is task-orientated."²⁰⁶ This requires the willingness to direct all one's thoughts and energies toward serving God and accomplishing not one's own but his will as encapsulated in the double commandment of love and specified through the directives given by the Holy Spirit.²⁰⁷ Furthermore, Bockmuehl stresses that the believer is set apart for the service of God and also for the gradual transformation into the likeness of Christ, which he considers to be the fundamental aim of the process of sanctification.²⁰⁸

When examining the means of sanctification, Bockmuehl refers to Word and Spirit, drawing attention to the correlation between them due to their complementary and confirming nature. It is, however, the Holy Spirit who Bockmuehl considers to be the primary agent of sanctification, since he is the one purifying the believers, empowering, and motivating them to lead a new life, offering instructions for a life in holiness, service for God, and mission.²⁰⁹ Not surprisingly, therefore, Bockmuehl compares the Holy Spirit to an artist working continuously at the heart of the believer with the intention of creating the image of Christ.²¹⁰

According to Bockmuehl's assessment, the doctrine of sanctification has been neglected in wide parts of German Protestant theology owing to the lack of attention given to the doctrine of the Holy Spirit. In his view, the Holy Spirit plays a key role in the process of sanctification. Therefore, Bockmuehl is grateful to Brunner for being one of the first German theologians to put new emphasis on the experiential and practical nature of sanctification by bringing into focus the reality of the work of the Holy Spirit in the believer's life.²¹¹

When investigating the relationship between human and divine work *vis-à-vis* sanctification, we discover that Bockmuehl emphasizes the role of the Holy Spirit as the chief agent in the process of sanctification while, at the same time, insisting on the necessity of believers to actively

---

206. Bockmuehl, "Sanctification," 615.

207. Cf. Bockmuehl, "Aktualität," 311; Bockmuehl, "Titus," 5; *CW*, 47; Bockmuehl, "Sanctification and Christian Mission," 63.

208. Cf. Bockmuehl, "Werk," 15; Bockmuehl, "Sanctification," 615-6; Bockmuehl, "Wiedergeburt," 94; *CM*, 138.

209. Cf. Bockmuehl, "Werk," 14, 17-19; "Sanctification," 615-16; "Glaube," 71; *VG*, 190.

210. Cf. "Werk," 16.

211. Cf. *VG*, 150; Bockmuehl, "Aktualität," 310; Bockmuehl, "Macht," 157-58. Another German theologian Bockmuehl considers to have regained the biblical doctrine of sanctification is Dietrich Bonhoeffer. Bockmuehl particularly praises his book *The Cost of Discipleship*. Cf. *VG*, 188-89.

pursue their sanctification.[212] In fact, as Bockmuehl believes, though the gift of the Holy Spirit is given at conversion/rebirth, the presupposition for receiving the power of the Spirit is prayer and obedience on the part of the Christian.[213] We shall look more closely at this relation between divine and human work in a later chapter.

Differential Ethics

Personal and Situational Differentiation

It was Bockmuehl's supreme concern that differential ethics would find its proper place in Christian ethics and that the Holy Spirit would, therefore, be regained for Christian ethics. In Bockmuehl's view, Reformation ethics, with its more or less exclusive emphasis on the law and particularly the Decalogue, civil vocation, and reason as the means of discovering the will of God for one's life, did not allow sufficient room for the individual guidance of the Holy Spirit. Similarly, the new morality, reacting against the somewhat static Reformation ethics, emphasized the extremely flexible principles of love, which, in the eyes of the situationists, was equivalent to utility, and of reason in the decision-making process with the intention of giving adequate weight to the individual situation. Thus, when looking at the relationship between objective norm and subjective situation, Bockmuehl censures Reformation ethics for neglecting the subjective situation, since he believes that "[w]herever we turn we are faced with this problem of 'differential ethics,' with the demand for moral instructions that relates to the respective person and situation."[214] Yet, he at the same time reproaches the new morality for overstressing the situation to the detriment of the objective norm. Instead, Bockmuehl is convinced that only a "Situation Ethics with a Difference,"[215] as he entitled an article, can provide the way out of the dilemma and remain faithful to the biblical data. The solution lies for him in the fact that the Holy Spirit, whom Bockmuehl regards to be the main "differential" principle of Christian ethics, applies the objective commandments to the individual person and to the

---

212. Cf. *VG*, 189; Bockmuehl, "Sanctification," 613–14; *SU*, 36.

213. Cf. Bockmuehl, "Werk," 13–14, 16–18; Bockmuehl, "Glaube," 71; Bockmuehl, "Problem der Ethik," 83–84.

214. Bockmuehl, "Protestant Ethics," 102.

215. Bockmuehl wrote an article in Christianity Today entitled "Law and the Spirit: Situation Ethics with a Difference" (47).

situation by offering guidance to the believer. Only then will the objective commandments as well as the individual person and subjective situation be sufficiently taken into account.[216] In order to buttress this concept, Bockmuehl draws attention to the promise given by Jeremiah and Ezekiel that in the new covenant the commandments "do not need to come to us as stony tables from the outside but live in our hearts. That is precisely the Holy Spirit."[217] Hence, he likens the Spirit's activity to an inward steering of the believer.[218]

Furthermore, Bockmuehl distinguishes between personal differentiation, i.e., the individual Christian calling, and situational differentiation, i.e., actual guidance "in a particular time and place."[219] Personal differentiation comprises for him the *charismata* and the individual spiritual tasks for service. Moreover, any call to renounce one's civil vocation for Christian service, such as fulltime Christian ministry or overseas mission, falls, according to Bockmuehl, into this category, as does the call to celibacy or poverty.[220] However, Bockmuehl makes it very clear that these callings are not given "for merit's sake, but for ministry's sake."[221] Situational differentiation, in contrast, encompasses any divine instructions given by the Holy Spirit for specific times and places. These assignments of the Spirit often lead to spontaneous, voluntary acts of love. Bockmuehl remarks: "There must be room in the Christian life for actions like the anointing of Jesus with the precious ointment by the woman in Bethany . . . Such actions of love, instilled by the Holy Spirit, go beyond the call of duty and commandment."[222] In fact, Bockmuehl regards situational guidance to be the concrete application of the double commandment of love in "the here and now" given by the Holy Spirit.[223] It is of interest to note in this context that Bockmuehl not only links the "present inspiration of the Spirit" with "the prompting of love or the 'mind of Christ' in the believers,"[224] but also seems to employ them interchangeably, thus equating them with guidance

---

216. Cf. Bockmuehl, "Revolution," 65; Bockmuehl, "Protestant Ethics," 102, 113; Bockmuehl, "Recovering Vocation," 86; *LbG*, 52.

217. Bockmuehl, "Zur Frage nach der Maßgeblichkeit," 47l; cf. Jer 31:33; Ezek 36:26–27.

218. Cf. Bockmuehl, "Revolution," 65.

219. *CW*, 27; cf. Bockmuehl, "Raison," 55.

220. Cf. *GG*, 309, 517; *CW*, 27.

221. Bockmuehl, "Recovering Vocation," 96.

222. Ibid.

223. Cf. *LG*, 148.

224. *GG*, 309.

of the Holy Spirit. This could lead to the assumption that for guidance to take place no clear orders need to be given but rather a change of motivation needs to occur. However, this Bockmuehl seems to refute when he notes: "God's guidance always comes by word; he is not silent, not speechless. He guides, not as we might guide a child by the hand or a horse by the reins, but through the instructions he speaks—instructions that we hear and then act upon."[225]

Of interest, furthermore, is Bockmuehl's stress upon the regularity of guidance for every believer because the Holy Spirit "does not abdicate his guiding role or leave his place to be filled by human rules and regulations."[226] Nevertheless, Bockmuehl does point out that in the case of no clear guidance being given, which seems rather the exception, believers should follow their previously given vocations.[227]

That Bockmuehl deems guidance to be of utmost importance for the Christian life is due to his understanding of the enormous benefits of guidance for the individual and for society as a whole. He believes that only those who listen for God's instructions "promote healing instead of creating new problems. They truly become spiritual *resource people*, i.e., constant sources of inspiration instead of a constant source of irritation in their surroundings."[228] Other benefits of acting upon the guidance of the Holy Spirit are, in Bockmuehl's opinion, creativity and spontaneity, unity and true fellowship, wisdom and personal freedom, and, in particular, freedom from prejudices and other people's opinions.[229]

THE PREREQUISITES FOR GUIDANCE

Besides regeneration as the event of the endowment of the Spirit, Bockmuehl regards "[t]he 'art' of listening"[230] to be of paramount importance for the believer in order to experience the guidance of the Spirit.[231] Such was his growing interest in recovering and encouraging this practice that he devoted his last book, which can be understood as his legacy, not to an

---

225. *LG*, 83.
226. *LG*, 83; cf. Bockmuehl, "Frank Buchman's Message," 35–36; *LbG*, 53; *LG*, 25.
227. Cf. Bockmuehl, "Recovering Vocation," 98; *LG*, 83.
228. Bockmuehl, "Listeners," 7.
229. Cf. *CM*, 159, 162; *LbG*, 43, 46, 49; Bockmuehl, "Listeners," 5–6; *LG*, 53, 60, 95, 150, 154–56.
230. *LG*, 154; cf. Bockmuehl, "Listening," 6.
231. Cf. ibid., 5.

abstract theological issue but to the explication of the rather devotional topic "Listening to the God who speaks." Similarly, his final public speech at the Convocation service at Regent College Vancouver was titled "Let us be listeners." In the latter, Bockmuehl professes that "[o]f all priorities in our teaching, the first is that we educate so as to help instill the habit and quality of listening in human hearts."[232] In this context, Bockmuehl refers several times to Solomon's request for a "listening heart," as he translates 1 Kings 3:9, maintaining that the latter is an indispensable faculty for every Christian.[233] Bockmuehl, therefore, maintains that the ability to listen to God is not merely a human endeavor but a gift "which comes by his Holy Spirit through prayer,"[234] particularly listening prayer. Yet, it seems that for Bockmuehl the willingness and openness to listen to as well as obey God's instructions need to be present on the part of the believer in order to experience guidance.[235]

In Jesus Bockmuehl finds the example *par excellence* of listening since "Jesus, in his human nature at least, needed to listen"[236] to his Father in order to receive instructions of what to say and how to act. Likewise, we should be open to the Spirit's guidance instead of following our own thoughts and plans, thus participating in God's work. Bockmuehl particularly mentions in this context the need even for Jesus of further insight concerning an effective way of restoring human relationships: "As he hears, so he judges."[237]

In addition to listening prayer, Bockmuehl states certain other prerequisites for guidance, though not in a comprehensive way, such as repentance, honesty, and humbling oneself before God in order to experience God's forgiveness, which Bockmuehl considers to be "the gateway to guidance."[238] In fact, Bockmuehl points to the necessity of an ethical basis for guidance, which he defines as living according to the double commandment of love, namely, living a holy and obedient life.[239]

---

232. Ibid., 7.
233. Cf. ibid., 6–7; *LbG*, 46; *LG*, 22, 154.
234. *LG*, 154; cf. Bockmuehl, "Listening," 6.
235. Cf. *LbG*, 46; *LG*, 38; circular letter written by Bockmuehl Dec. 1967.
236. *LG*, 58.
237. *CM*, 162–63; cf. *LbG*, 53; Bockmuehl, "Frank Buchman's Message," 34–36.
238. *LG*, 41; cf. *CM*, 159.
239. Cf. *LG*, 48; Bockmuehl, "Frank Buchman's Message," 38.

Bockmuehl's Understanding of Christian Ethics

CRITERIA FOR GUIDANCE

Though Bockmuehl strongly emphasizes the need for guidance, he is well aware of the danger of arbitrariness, caprice, and subjectivism. Therefore, he suggests different criteria as a safeguard for correct listening; the prime criterion being Scripture, particularly the commandments.[240] Secondly, Bockmuehl highlights the importance of the community, namely, the correction, advice, and encouragement given by fellow-believers.[241] Thirdly, Bockmuehl draws attention to the fact that the gift of guidance is granted ultimately for the purpose of realizing and enhancing the kingdom of God. Hence, it is not given for one's own pleasure but for service and witness. Bockmuehl, in fact, characterizes the Holy Spirit as the "giver of love and the leader of Christian mission."[242] Not surprisingly, therefore, Bockmuehl asserts that "[t]he litmus test for God's guidance is the concrete promotion of love of God and love of neighbor."[243]

Law and Spirit—the Double Principle of Christian Ethics

One of Bockmuehl's foremost objectives is to retain the juxtaposition of law and Spirit in his concept of Christian ethics since if either of them are given a place greater than the other, this will lead to a serious distortion of the whole picture. With regard to the law, Bockmuehl underscores the continuous validity of the law, particularly the Decalogue, for the Christian. We, therefore, need to take a closer look at Bockmuehl's understanding of the law in Christian Ethics.

The Law in Christian Ethics

As mentioned earlier in the chapter on the Reformers' influence on Bockmuehl, the latter retains all three functions of the law put forward, for instance, by Calvin and Melanchthon. The *political or civil use of the law*

---

240. Cf. *LG*, 65, 98, 149; Bockmuehl, "Frank Buchman's Message," 37.

241. Cf. *LG*, 150; Bockmuehl, "Recovering Vocation," 97; Bockmuehl, "Frank Buchman's Message," 37.

242. Bockmuehl, "Recovering Vocation," 98; cf. 97; Bockmuehl, "Frank Buchman's Message," 38; *LbG*, 52; Bockmuehl, "Raison," 55.

243. *LG*, 150.

PART TWO—The Holy Spirit and Christian Ethics in the Theology

(*politicus usus legis*), as shown in great length in the context of creation ethics, serves, according to Bockmuehl, the purpose of the preservation of life and community. Bockmuehl particularly regards the cultural mandate to be the main commission of creation ethics. This function also includes the "application of the Ten Commandments . . . to society,"[244] which for Bockmuehl is a protecting and preserving function preventing and containing evil by setting out "the 'user's manual' for creation."[245] For a biblical basis of this function Bockmuehl refers, among other biblical references, to 1 Timothy 1:9, 10.[246]

Besides this first function, Bockmuehl also advocates the pedagogical use of the law (*elenchticus or praecipuus usus legis*), which exposes sin in order to create awareness for the need of forgiveness through repentance, thus paving the way for the gospel of the justification of sinners.[247] Hence, though the task of the law is an accusing one, the aim is ultimately to bring healing. Bockmuehl, therefore, charges all those (Christian) ethics that propagate the abrogation of the law with rejecting the heart of the Gospel itself. He regards these ethics, among them the "new morality," as destroying the way to forgiveness and thereby the doctrine of justification.[248]

When turning to the *third use of the law* (*tertius usus legis*), the subject matter presents itself as somewhat more complex, as already explicated in the chapter on the Reformers' influence on Bockmuehl. This is due to the fact that an inconsistency or development on Bockmuehl's part can be observed. Generally he believes that the law, though losing its validity as a path for salvation, continues to be valid for the Christian as a rule or catechism since it outlines what is good and evil. Bockmuehl at times employs Althaus' distinction between law and commandment, claiming that "for those who believe in Christ and call upon his name, law is turned into commandment. That is to say, Christ has taken away the curse from the law and borne it himself, so that now only the blessing remains on the keeping of the commandments."[249] Furthermore, Bockmuehl holds that in order to advance in a life of sanctification, to which every Christian is

---

244. Bockmuehl, "Der Streit," 101.

245. Bockmuehl, "Keeping His Commandments," 93; cf. *GiE*, 179.

246. *CW*, 11.

247. Cf. *GiE*, 175–79; *SU*, 27; Bockmuehl, "Keeping His Commandments," 92–93. Bockmuehl considered Matthew 15:19 to point to the accusing function of the law. Cf. *CW*, 11; Bockmuehl, "Keeping His Commandments," 89.

248. Cf. *GiE*, 177–78; Bockmuehl, "Frank Buchman's Message," 23–24.

249. Bockmuehl, "Keeping His Commandments," 93; cf. *GiE*, 174. For Althaus's distinction between law and commandment, see Althaus, *Gebot und Gesetz*, 23–24.

Bockmuehl's Understanding of Christian Ethics

called, the commandments together with the Holy Spirit are indispensable as indicators for good deeds that ensue faith.[250]

However, it should be mentioned that Bockmuehl in his fairly early article "Revolution of Ethics," in fact, criticizes the third use of the law. He argues that this function has led to the chaining of the Holy Spirit to the law since it does not take into consideration the guidance and application of the Holy Spirit. Later though Bockmuehl modifies his earlier position by identifying casuistry, not the law itself, as the actual problem. In his book *Law and Spirit*, he contends: "We cannot relinquish the 'third use' of the law, or the commandments as instructions for the life of the believers, or, indeed, the 'reclamation of the law for Protestant ethics.' However, the additional attempt at casuistry, which tries to prescribe the correct behaviour for all possible future situations by *synecdochic* interpretation of the Decalogue, is unnecessary. By making all relevant activities obligatory, this interpretation excludes both the individual guidance by the Spirit and any voluntary activity."[251]

Furthermore, it is of interest to note that Bockmuehl distinguishes in his book *Law and Spirit*, first, between the law, namely, the Decalogue, linking the latter to creation ethics, secondly, between the New Testament parenesis, including Christ's commandments, linking it to redemption ethics, and, thirdly, between the guidance of the Holy Spirit, linking it to differential ethics. In addition, he proposes that an ethic should encompass law as well as Spirit, creation ordinances as well as redemption ordinances, thereby pointing to the double principle of Christian ethics—law and Spirit.[252]

The Importance of the Holy Spirit for Christian Ethics

Many contemporary theologians such as Wolfhart Pannenberg and Jürgen Moltmann lay great emphasis on the role of the Holy Spirit in creation as the "source of all life"[253] or as the "Spirit of life,"[254] defining him as the one through whom God is present in creation and through whom he sustains creation. However, Bockmuehl does not explicitly refer to the Holy Spirit

250. Cf. "Keeping His Commandments," 94–95; *GG*, 514.
251. *GG*, 223.
252. *GG*, 514.
253. Pannenberg, *Glaubensbekenntnis*, 141.
254. See the title of the book by Moltmann, *The Spirit of Life: A Universal Affirmation*.

with regard to creation but, instead, mainly to God the Father as the creator and giver of the law.[255] In fact, in creation or general ethics, the Holy Spirit does not seem to play any role whatsoever. When considering the Holy Spirit's involvement in specific Christian ethics, the matter changes significantly. For, as outlined above in the chapter on the foundation of Christian ethics, Bockmuehl emphasizes the indispensability of the Holy Spirit for regenerating and transforming believers. It is only the Holy Spirit dwelling in believers who grants new motives and new strength to act according to God's will, thus realizing the lordship of God in believers and sanctifying them.[256]

Moreover, in reclaiming the role of the Holy Spirit for specific Christian ethics, Bockmuehl implements certain issues that, according to him, have been neglected in the past. Above all, Bockmuehl insists on the importance of recovering the doctrine of the personal and situational guidance by the Spirit for Christian ethics, as shown in the chapter on differential ethics, maintaining that "[t]he Holy Spirit is the teacher who *speaks*, *rebukes*, *reminds*, and *guides*. In Christian circles, he is far too often represented as the enabler, and thus is reduced to a mute 'force' or impersonal agent."[257] Other issues connected with the work of the Holy Spirit in ethics are, for Bockmuehl, the distinctly Christian actions outlined above, such as love for God, spirituality, and mission, including church-building activities and the *charismata*. Furthermore, Bockmuehl argues that by retrieving the Holy Spirit for Christian ethics the works of supererogation regain their appropriate place since they are an expression of the specific Christian form of love for God and one's neighbor.

The Relation of the Holy Spirit to the Law in Christian Ethics

Despite his positive view of the law, Bockmuehl, nevertheless, strongly refutes the conviction that Christian ethics can more or less be completely extrapolated from the Decalogue when interpreted by way of *synecdoche*, i.e., reflecting upon the positive corollary to the negative commandment. As mentioned earlier, Bockmuehl believes that this view was, for instance,

---

255. Cf. Pannenberg, *Glaubensbekenntnis*, 148–49; *GG*, 514.

256. Cf. *LbG*, 40, 48; Bockmuehl, "Sanctification," 615–16; Bockmuehl, "Der sendende Herr," 197; *UG*, 159.

257. *LG*, 64.

Bockmuehl's Understanding of Christian Ethics

held by the Reformers, yet in their wake also by other theologians.[258] Such a stance, according to Bockmuehl, eventuated in the neglect of the Spirit for Christian ethics as well as in the reduction of Christian ethics itself.[259] Instead of arguing for the sufficiency of the law for Christian ethics, Bockmuehl is of the opinion that the Reformers should have taken into account the guidance of the Holy Spirit, namely, the possibility of the believer undertaking something for God that cannot be directly deduced from the law as long as the actions remain within the framework of the Decalogue. It comes as no surprise, therefore, that Bockmuehl employs the metaphor of a road-barrier to illuminate the function of the law for the Christian. While safeguarding the believer against slipping off the road, the law is not identical with the objective of the journey, which is love.[260] In fact, Bockmuehl believes that love surpasses the law at the same time as it fulfills it: "*First*, love unfolds into the commandments . . . *Second*, conversely, all commandments aim at love as their perfection."[261] Furthermore, as Bockmuehl states, the law in and of itself cannot provide the motivation and the strength for the believer to act lovingly. It is the Holy Spirit who enables, strengthens, empowers, and transforms individuals, so that they can keep the double commandment of love. By doing so, the Christian experiences freedom, since, as Bockmuehl points out, "[t]he indwelling of the Holy Spirit is the prerequisite to Christian freedom because, according to Romans 8:4, the Holy Spirit himself will look after the fulfillment of the legitimate demands of God's law."[262]

Moreover, the law, due to its general character, does not take into consideration the individual person and particular situation. Consequently, as already outlined in the chapter on "differential ethics," Bockmuehl stresses that it is the Holy Spirit who specifies and particularizes the commandments for the believer in a concrete situation by offering individual guidance in the here and now.[263] Yet, the Holy Spirit also inspires spontaneous works of love that surpass the law without violating it. These works are not a priori aimed at fulfilling the law or duty since, as Bockmuehl adds, love

---

258. Cf. *CW*, 20–21.
259. Cf. *GG*, 113–14.
260. Cf. *GiE*, 172; *SU*, 29.
261. Bockmuehl, "Great Commandment," 25; cf. Bockmuehl, "Ten Commandments," 134–35; *GiE*, 179; *CW*, 10, 23.
262. *LbG*, 43; cf. *GG*, 526.
263. Cf. *GG*, 525–26.

focuses on people and not on the law.²⁶⁴ Therefore, "[l]ove is the gift and fruit of the Holy Spirit."²⁶⁵

Bockmuehl argues that any Christian ethic in which the inspiration and instruction of the Holy Spirit is overshadowed by the law tends inevitably toward legalism or to the other extreme of abandoning the law altogether, thus resulting in antinomianism. Bockmuehl, therefore, emphasizes: "It is an ethics with two taproots: Scripture and Spirit . . . The Decalogue must be defended against lawlessness, both in society and as a theological principle; and yet the Decalogue must not be made as stony and cold as the rock it was carved in, but must remain supple so that it can be extended both to the New Testament material and to the individual instruction of the Holy Spirit. Christian ethics must hold a third position between lawlessness and legalism."²⁶⁶

Yet, Bockmuehl also believes that the double principle of law and Spirit not only offers an alternative to either legalism or antinomianism but also provides a solution for the tension between objectivism and subjectivism, tradition and innovation, duty and inclination, responsibility and independence, bond and freedom.²⁶⁷ Hence, Bockmuehl concludes: "*Law and Spirit*—that is the shortest formula for a truly Christian ethic."²⁶⁸

The Relation between Creation, Redemption, and Differential Ethics

The Relation between General Creation Ethics and Specific Christian Ethics

Bockmuehl's distinction between general creation ethics and specific Christian ethics, describing the latter also as ethics of the Spirit, ethics of love, or kingdom ethics, is a decisive feature of his ethics.²⁶⁹ According to Burkhardt, this distinction is rather exceptional when compared to other Christian ethics: "Usually ethics is either designed as general or as Christian ethics. A programmatic distinction between both of these as two areas

---

264. *GG*, 307.
265. Bockmuehl, "Sanctification and Christian Mission," 60.
266. *CW*, 27.
267. Cf. *GG*, 520; Swarat, "Gesetz," 35.
268. *SU*, 32.
269. Cf. *GG*, 514.

of an ethical concept can, according to my knowledge, hardly be found anywhere. And Klaus Bockmuehl has hardly ever formulated this concept in such a programmatic way in his publications. But this distinction is found in substance at every turn, e.g., in the juxtaposition of the cultural mandate and preaching mandate of proclamation, of social responsibility and mission, or of law and Spirit."[270]

It was, for Bockmuehl, of paramount importance to take into account the universal nature of Christian ethics, yet without overlooking the distinctly Christian character in addition to the general creation ethics. This juxtaposition of general and specific Christian ethics can also, to some extent, be observed in Schlatter, as mentioned earlier.[271]

With view to the relation between creation ethics and redemption ethics, Bockmuehl argues, as pointed out earlier, that the foundation of Christian ethics is given with creation ethics, upon which redemption ethics is built, not in the sense of reaching a higher stage where one can leave behind the foundation, but as affirming the foundation and yet, at the same time, surpassing it (cf. Matt 5:20). In this way he believes that he can safeguard against the negligence of creation, which in the past often resulted in the disregard for social (including political, economic, and environmental) ethics or the negligence of redemption.[272] The ethical consequences of the latter were, on the one hand, the dismissal of regeneration as the prerequisite for Christian ethics and, on the other hand, the eclipse of any *proprium* of Christian ethics.

ETHICS OF PRESERVATION—ETHICS OF RESTORATION

According to Bockmuehl, one of the fundamental differences between general creation ethics and specific Christian ethics is that, while the main focus of general creation ethics is the *preservation* of life, specific Christian ethics is also concerned with *restoration* of life, including "saving life."[273] Yet, how can, according to Bockmuehl, life be saved, healed, and restored? First and foremost, it comes about by laboring for the regeneration of human beings, i.e., for "the formation of mankind after the image of Christ."[274] This is the goal of the Great Commission, which, as mentioned

270. Burkhardt, "Einführung des Herausgebers," *Christliche Lebensführung*, xv.
271. Cf. Neuer, *Dogmatik*, 304.
272. Cf. *GG*, 210; Bockmuehl, "Is Christianity a Counterculture?," 52.
273. *CW*, 26; cf. Bockmuehl, "Serving," 16.
274. Bockmuehl, "Revolution," 67.

earlier, Bockmuehl considers to be the key imperative of Christian ethics. Hence, every Christian is not only called to participate in God's work of sustenance and preservation, as are all human beings, but, additionally, in God's work of restoration and redemption.[275]

However, though the chief emphasis of specific Christian ethics lies with the commission to make disciples, Bockmuehl, nevertheless, considers actions going beyond duty or the Decalogue, while still remaining in the realm of creation (such as the "second mile" or the Good Samaritan), to be part of the *proprium* of Christian ethics.[276] This we shall investigate in more depth on pages 180–83. when looking at Bockmuehl's quest for the *proprium* of Christian ethics. Similarly, he regards Christian service (*diakonia*) to be "not exclusively, but predominantly—an extension, an enhancement of God's general creation decree."[277]

Closely connected to the distinction between general creation ethics, or ethics of preservation, and specific Christian ethics, or ethics of restoration, is Bockmuehl's characterization of the former as an ethic of avoidance and of the latter as an ethic of involvement. For Bockmuehl, a Christian should not merely be concerned about preserving the good by avoiding the bad but should, moreover, be involved in actively promoting the good and providing for others spiritually as well as materially.[278] Whereas one of the main features in general creation ethics is, according to Bockmuehl, the keeping of the law, he emphasizes that specific Christian ethics, though acknowledging the continuing validity of the Decalogue and remaining in it as its framework, surpasses the latter by aiming at love as its final goal. Hence, for Bockmuehl, the counterpart of the *law* in specific Christian ethics is the *Holy Spirit* who equips and instructs the Christian to live a life in love.[279]

The Quest for the Proprium of Christian Ethics

Is there a *proprium* (distinctiveness) of Christian ethics? If so, what is it? Bockmuehl endeavored to recover a biblically-based answer to these questions that were greatly disputed among Protestant theologians during his

---

275. Cf. *GG*, 88.
276. Cf. *GG*, 300–302, 306, 309, 515; *CW*, 26.
277. Bockmuehl, "Serving," 16.
278. Cf. *CW*, 21; Bockmuehl, "Die Geburt des Neuen Menschen," 13; *CM*, 139; Bockmuehl, "Revolution," 66–67; Bockmuehl, "Lean Years," 68.
279. Cf. *GG*, 514.

Bockmuehl's Understanding of Christian Ethics

life-time and continue to be a bone of contention today. In fact, Bockmuehl, on the one hand, distances himself from those theologians in the wake of Barth and the dialectical theology that consider all of ethics to be specifically Christian while, on the other hand, disagreeing with all those who advocate the autonomy of ethics, thereby denying any *proprium* of Christian ethics.[280] Instead, as shown at the beginning of this chapter, Bockmuehl distinguishes between a general and a specific Christian ethic. Topics Bockmuehl regards as characteristically, though not necessarily as uniquely, Christian, and which have been neglected, are love of God, spirituality, mission, works of supererogation, and guidance by the Spirit.[281] Since all of these subject matters have been discussed in length in a previous chapter with the exception of the works of supererogation, we shall take a brief look at Bockmuehl's concept of the latter. He defines all those works as works of supererogation that go beyond what the Decalogue, including its *synecdochic* interpretation, commands and what the duties of the particular civil vocation require.[282] With view to specific Christian actions, Bockmuehl emphasizes that "Jesus described the Christian activity very clearly as a 'perisson' (Mt 5:47)—[defining it as] 'the more', the specific, an activity that exceeds the usual one of reciprocal service."[283] The most important characteristic of the works of supererogation is that its main object is the person and not the law. Nevertheless, it will be apparent a posteriori that love did fulfill and surpass the law.[284] When looking at the origin of the works of supererogation, Bockmuehl points to "an encounter with Jesus" and sees them as a "direct consequence of an experience of salvation."[285] Hence, the works of supererogation are not works that are "allowed" as opposed to "commanded," but are rather works that have "love, the Christ-in-us, the Holy Spirit"[286] as their subject.

In his major work *Law and Spirit* Bockmuehl classifies the works of supererogation into four different categories. The *first* category comprises all those works belonging to the realm of creation that Christians are specifically commissioned to do, such as going the second mile (Matt 5:41) or following the paradigm of the Good Samaritan (Luke 10:25–37).

280. Cf. *GG*, 21, 249; cf. Burkhardt, *Einführung in die Ethik*, 108.
281. Cf. *GG*, 251.
282. Cf. *GG*, 302.
283. *GiE*, 184.
284. Cf. *GG*, 307.
285. *GG*, 308.
286. *GG*, 308.

Part Two—The Holy Spirit and Christian Ethics in the Theology

Works that are characterized by voluntary giving out of love beyond what is commanded even of the Christian belong, according to Bockmuehl, to the *second* category. The most salient scriptural illustrations for this kind of works of supererogation are the widow's offering (Luke 21:2–4) and Zacchaeus' generous donation to the poor and to those he had cheated (Luke 19:1–10) as well as the effusive anointing of Jesus in Bethany (Matt 26:6–13). With regard to the woman anointing Jesus, Bockmuehl, following Calvin, believes that "the crucial point is: What she does cannot be explained by pointing to the law or to duty according to one's station in life but, instead, by pointing to the guidance of the Spirit and to love."[287] The *third* category encompasses specific Christian actions related to the realm of salvation ordinances. His exposition suggests that Bockmuehl considers the church-building activities to belong to this category as well as all those works that exceed the duty of the Christian to carry out the Great Commission.[288] For the latter, Bockmuehl, for instance, refers to Paul's renunciation of the right to receive payment from the churches for his ministry (1 Cor 9:1–15). When turning to the *fourth* category, which consists of individual tasks also related to the realm of salvation ordinances, we discover that Bockmuehl differentiates further between "the individual 'must'"[289] of personal vocation, for instance, as an apostle, and the instruction given by the Holy Spirit for specific situations. The works of this final category can be classified as belonging to differential ethics.[290]

It is interesting to note in passing that in order to substantiate his concept, Bockmuehl refers not only to passages that explicitly point to the Holy Spirit as the one urging the believer to undertake specific actions but also to those that speak of love or the word of God as inspiring and compelling the believer.[291]

Though Bockmuehl particularly links the Holy Spirit to differential ethics, emphasizing time and again the crucial role he plays in this context, he is, nevertheless, convinced that "that there is an actual relationship between [the Holy Spirit] and the special activity of the Christian as well as the *proprium* of Christian ethics. If the latter remains in the shadows or

---

287. *GG*, 303.
288. Cf. *GG*, 304–6.
289. *GG*, 305.
290. Cf. *GG*, 309.
291. Cf. *GG*, 305, 307.

Bockmuehl's Understanding of Christian Ethics

is only discussed reluctantly, then this must have a negative impact on the portrayal of the work and the guidance of the Holy Spirit."[292]

The Three-fold Structure of Bockmuehl's Christian Ethics

A decisive feature of Bockmuehl's ethics is its trinitarian structure since, in his opinion, "the Father corresponds to creational ethics, the Son to redemption ethics, and the Holy Spirit to the ethics of individual guidance."[293] According to Bockmuehl, it is particularly the Father as the creator who gives the cultural commission and the law, the son who gives the Great Commission, and the Holy Spirit who gives concrete, individual guidance.[294] It is interesting to note in this context that Bockmuehl calls specific Christian ethics, which encompasses redemption ethics as well as differential ethics, not only kingdom ethics, thereby relating it to the lordship of Christ, but also ethics of the Spirit. Bockmuehl particularly argues that even those areas related to redemption ethics are not possible without the work of the Holy Spirit. Hence, it seems to be clear that the assigning of the three persons of the Trinity to the different levels of ethics are intended as a structural device rather than to be interpreted in the way of a trinitarian ethics *per se*. Bockmuehl himself refers to his ethics, for instance, as "trinitarian in shape,"[295] though he also maintains that his ethics can, indeed, be seen "as an application of the doctrine of the Trinity to ethics."[296] This, however, raises the question if it is possible to separate the roles of each person of the Trinity or if this may come too close to either tritheism (at worse) or social trinitarianism (at best). Since Bockmuehl does not elaborate on this issue, we shall not go into more depth.

Bockmuehl, furthermore, adopts Troeltsch's distinction between three different kinds of ethics that he labels as "church," "sect," and "mystic" type, relating them, first of all, to the Roman-Catholic, Lutheran, and Reformed church, secondly, to the Anabaptist movement, and thirdly, to the Mystics and Spiritualists.[297] Whereas the first type focuses particularly on the Decalogue and the duties attached to one's station, the second type emphasizes the New Testament parenesis, and the third type highlights

292. *GG*, 95.
293. *CW*, 27.
294. Bockmuehl, "Horizons," 15; cf. *GG*, 119.
295. *CW*, 27.
296. *GG*, 309.
297. Cf. *GG*, 529.

PART TWO—The Holy Spirit and Christian Ethics in the Theology

"life in the Spirit and its realization through the individual."[298] Since each type only represents one aspect of Christian ethics, Bockmuehl pleads for a synthesis of the different ethical concepts of the aforementioned church traditions. He is convinced that "[s]uch a synthesis would lead not only to a reconciliation among different denominations, but also to regaining an integrated view of biblical teaching."[299]

When comparing the three levels of Christian ethics that Bockmuehl proposes, it is noticeable that there is an advance in the specification and individuation of God's will. This movement can be ascribed to the intensified work of the Holy Spirit in the different levels of Christian ethics, which, according to Bockmuehl, finds its culmination in the personal and situational guidance of the Holy Spirit. Bockmuehl claims that it is particularly through the Spirit's guidance of the individual believer that the kingdom of God is realized on earth in a concrete way.[300]

---

298. *GG*, 529; cf. *GG*, 25.
299. Bockmuehl, "Protestant Ethics," 115; cf. 103.
300. Cf. Loos, "Human Embodiment," 117–18; *UG*, 159.

Part Three

A Critical Appraisal of and
a Response to Bockmuehl's Concept
of the Spirit's Role in Christian Ethics

IN THIS CONCLUDING PART, we will, first of all, focus on critically appraising Bockmuehl's concept of the Holy Spirit and Christian ethics. After an initial positive appraisal of Bockmuehl's concept of Christian ethics we attempt to answer questions such as the following: Is Bockmuehl's double principle of Christian ethics—law and Spirit—in connection with his concept of the guidance by the Spirit truly the answer to all our ethical questions and dilemmas? Is it more important to pursue the knowledge of God's will, as Bockmuehl at times suggests, or the knowledge of God's nature?

Secondly, as a response to Bockmuehl, we attempt to build upon Bockmuehl's insights with regard to the Holy Spirit and Christian ethics particularly toward the end of his life and to weave them together with a relational concept of the Holy Spirit and Christian ethics. For instance, we suggest that it is the chief role of the Holy Spirit as the loving presence of God to draw the believer into an intimate love-relationship with God the Father and the Son. Yet, how can we experience this intimate love-relationship in such a way that it is truly transforming? Why does being a Christian and knowing about God's love not always "automatically translate into a changed life"?[1] What obstacles might hinder us in living and growing in loving relationship with God, self, others, and creation?

---

1. Chan, *Spiritual Theology*, 79–80.

Part Three—A Critical Appraisal

These are some of the questions that we shall explore and answer in the final chapters of this study.

5

A Critical Appraisal of Bockmuehl's Concept of the Holy Spirit and Christian Ethics

Bockmuehl's Concept of Christian Ethics— An Appraisal

BOCKMUEHL'S ATTEMPT TO RECOVER a meaningful place for the Holy Spirit within Christian ethics can hardly be overestimated, particularly when considering that "little has been done to enunciate the content of an ethics of the Holy Spirit."[1] While listing several Christian ethics focusing on either creation orders or Christology, Hynson, for instance, does not mention any ethics with a special emphasis on the Holy Spirit. Instead, he concludes that "it is striking to recognize the absence of the Holy Spirit in the formation of Christian ethical analysis."[2] It is interesting to note that he himself asserts that "it is the Holy Spirit who guides in knowing and who enables doing,"[3] thus mentioning the two most important functions of the Holy Spirit in Christian ethics according to Bockmuehl. That these functions have been largely ignored and, consequently, have to be regained for Christian ethics was not Bockmuehl's opinion alone. Barnette, a theologian to whom Bockmuehl himself refers to as one of the few to have done justice to the Spirit's activity in ethics, states: "There is more—the function

1. Hynson, "Christian Ethics," 25; cf. Burrell, "11. The Spirit and the Christian Life," 304; Adeney, *Strange Virtue*, 40.

2. Hynson, "Christian Ethics," 26. Cf. Holotik, *Die pneumatologische Note*, 71, 97; Barnette, *Introducing Christian Ethics*, 87.

3. Hynson, "Christian Ethics," 25.

187

PART THREE—A Critical Appraisal

of the Holy Spirit in moral decisions, a sadly neglected factor by almost all Christian ethicists. Yet the fruit of the Spirit is presented in ethical terms: love, joy, peace, patience, kindness, goodness, faithfulness, self-control (Gal. 5:22–23) . . . Without the energizing and enabling power of the Holy Spirit, the Christian ethic is impossible. For it is the Spirit who ultimately informs the Christian in concrete moral decisions and guides him 'into all the truth' (John 16:13)."[4]

With his interest in the concreteness and visibility of the fruits of the Spirit, Bockmuehl takes up the legacies of Emil Brunner and Gerhard Ebeling who, with a view to the ethics of dialectical theologians such as Barth and Bultmann, had an obvious sense of concern with regard to the biblical data on the work of the Spirit.[5] That Bockmuehl draws attention to the Spirit's involvement in bringing about regeneration and new creation resulting in visible, concrete, ethical change and transformation is, indeed, praiseworthy. He rightly emphasizes the Spirit's work as providing the prerequisite for special Christian ethics. Furthermore, that Bockmuehl called attention to the fact that "[t]he solution to the problem of a Christian, namely, a *theo*logical, theocratic situation and individual ethics can be found in the doctrine of the guidance and work of the Holy Spirit,"[6] should not be underestimated.

Furthermore, Bockmuehl's lengthy and skillful critique of Protestant ethics with its neglect of the work of the Holy Spirit and, in its wake, of such issues as spirituality, love for God, church-building activities, works of supererogation, and guidance of the Spirit, can be seen as crucial in paving the way for an awareness of the need to recover the Holy Spirit for Christian ethics. His endeavor to reclaim these important issues for a specific Christian ethic, and with it an ethic of the Spirit and of love, is highly commendable.

Moreover, Bockmuehl suggests that his three-fold ethics could play a crucial role in reconciling ethical traditions of Reformation, Anabaptist, and mystical backgrounds since he is convinced that each of the layers of his ethics corresponds to one of the traditions. In addition, he had a clear ecumenical concern and was willing to learn from Catholic theologians.[7] It is worth repeating in this context that, according to Neuer, "a few years ago none other than the former *Cardinal Ratzinger* and the present Pope

---

4. Barnette, *The New Theology and Morality*, 48–49.
5. Cf. Brunner, *Werk*, 53; Ebeling, "Beunruhigung," 354–68.
6. *GiE*, 215.
7. Cf. Neuer, "Weite," 4–5.

A Critical Appraisal

Benedict XVI acknowledged Klaus Bockmuehl, who is often ignored within Protestant theology, to be a 'spiritual well digger.'[8] Bockmuehl's interest in Catholic moral theology might be rather surprising for a theologian of his background, yet it is a correlative of his ability to highlight and expose theological deficiencies and blind spots found within his own tradition. Particularly his analysis and evaluation of the heritage of Protestant ethics is invaluable due to its precise and challenging nature. Not only does he delineate the cause for the "one-man-show" in many Protestant churches, he also reproaches particularly the neo-pietists for neglecting creation ethics. Furthermore, he challenges them to take a greater interest in social, political, economic, and ecological ethics and even wrote a book on environmental ethics.[9] In fact, Neuer remarks with regard to Bockmuehl's ecological concern: "Already in 1975 (hence, five years before the foundation of the Green party!) he was one of the first Protestant theologians in Germany to comment in a competent and ground-breaking way on the ecological crisis and to call for a return to the biblical understanding of creation."[10]

Law and Spirit—Double Principle of Christian Ethics?

After this positive appraisal of Bockmuehl's overall concept of Christian ethics, we now turn to a more in-depth assessment and critical evaluation of some of the key features of Bockmuehl's ethics, beginning with law and Spirit—his double principle of Christian ethics. Many ethical concepts are in danger of promoting either a rather legalistic approach to ethics by building chiefly upon rules and regulations such as the Decalogue and/or New Testament parenesis, or an antinomian approach to ethics by stressing the freedom of the Spirit as freedom from any kind of law or commandment. Other forms of antinomianism can also be found in an over-emphasis of the individual conscience or of reason. Bockmuehl's concept of the double principle of law and Spirit attempts to safeguard both against antinomian tendencies by stressing the continuing validity of the law and against legalistic tendencies by emphasizing the activity of the

---

8. Ibid., 5.
9. Cf. Bockmuehl, *CaL*.
10. Neuer, "Weite," 6.

PART THREE—A Critical Appraisal

Spirit, particularly guidance by the Spirit.[11] However, without wanting to minimize Bockmuehl's invaluable endeavor to recover the Holy Spirit for Christian ethics, we will argue that his ethics comes close to a pneumatic duty-based ethics that shows legalistic, heteronomous tendencies.

First of all, we need to turn to Bockmuehl's juxtaposition of law and Spirit as seemingly equal partners as the following text suggests: "Law and Spirit operate not only in tandem, in one line, behind each other, the Spirit merely as the power of the law, but as a duo, or even better, like two witnesses, who give corresponding evidence . . . The Holy Spirit is not only assigned to the motivating function but also to an informative function."[12] Here, Bockmuehl shows that any attempt at attributing the Holy Spirit an equal place beside the law was already a break from the traditional Protestant heritage of the "old morality," especially if it also sought to recover the concept of guidance by the Spirit as an aspect of Christian ethics. Janz, however, raises the following questions concerning Bockmuehl's concept of guidance by the Spirit: "But is that really all that can, in ethical terms, be said about the promise and work of the Holy Spirit? Does his work remain restricted to the quasi *hermeneutical* function of the 'guidance by the Spirit'? Is he merely the signpost (in the sense of a pneumatic duty-based ethic)?"[13]

Although Bockmuehl does mention other functions of the Spirit alongside guidance, Janz's criticism that Bockmuehl's ethics comes close to a pneumatic duty-based ethic is justified since Bockmuehl defines guidance by the Spirit as receiving concrete instructions from God, thus remaining within the framework of the objective commandment. And Bockmuehl considers guidance by the Spirit to be the main component in solving the tension between the objective commandment, the individual person, and the subjective situation. In contrast, Janz suggests that "the work of the Holy Spirit [determines] ever anew our behavior both regarding the objective side of the commandment (guidance by the Spirit) and the subjective side of the person."[14] Therefore, rather than overemphasiz-

---

11. Since the main emphasis of our study is the Spirit's role in Bockmuehl's ethics, we will not discuss Bockmuehl's endorsement of the *tertius usus legis* in any length, though we are aware that the issue has been, and continues to be, contested among theologians.

12. *GG*, 519.

13. Janz, "Zwischen Norm und Situation," 15.

14. Ibid. In contrast to Janz, Honecker comments in his review article on ethical discussions in the eighties regarding Bockmuehl's book *Gesetz und Geist (Law and Spirit)*: "Spirituality (guidance by the Spirit) is certainly important for ethics; it is,

A Critical Appraisal

ing the informative function of the Holy Spirit, as Bockmuehl does, we need to focus, first and foremost, on the relational function of the Holy Spirit. Dubay, for instance, points out:

> One of the most valuable contributions offered by St. John of the Cross to this question of listening to God's voice can be missed even in a careful study of his work. It is that the most important element in most divine communications is not the clear idea, the detailed course of action to be followed. It is the love-penetrated touch of the divine in dark faith, a touch that itself communicates humility, love, prayer, strength, peace, joy. The most valuable gift God can share with anyone is himself. And he is no thing, no idea, no pattern of action. The Love who is God is poured out into our hearts by the Holy Spirit who is given to us (Rom 5:5).[15]

This participation in God who is love, brought about by the Holy Spirit, lies at the heart of Christian ethics and is its ultimate goal. Hence, as Harrington suggests, "if we truly love we will be obeying the commandments; but if we seek to observe the law and are without love, then we have missed the point. It is in this sense that we are to understand also the famous saying of St. Augustine: 'Love, and do what you will.'"[16] Therefore, it is necessary to go one step further than Bockmuehl does and give the Holy Spirit primacy over the law, not in the sense of promoting an antinomian approach to ethics that abrogates the law but rather in the sense of promoting an ethic of love, encompassing creation ethics as well as specific Christian ethics, that transcends the law.[17] Only thus can the danger of a pneumatic duty-based ethic be avoided.

The impression might have arisen in the last paragraph that Bockmuehl does not give relationship and communion with God a central place in his ethics. In fact, when speaking about the *proprium* of Christian ethics, he even includes spirituality as part of Christian ethics and emphasizes the importance of it. It is, therefore, not a matter of neglect but a matter of priority. In contrast to Bockmuehl, Dubay, for instance, maintains

---

however, not the universal cure in the midst of the 'crisis of morality'" (Honecker, "Zur ethischen Diskussion," 71). Instead of the guidance of the Spirit, he points to the "inviolability of one's conscience" (ibid., 70).

15. Dubay, *Authenticity*, 114.
16. Harrington, *What is Morality?*, 88.
17. Cf. David Brown, *Choices*, 39–40; Moule, "Obligation in the Ethic of Paul," 394, 404.

that "*Christian morality is primarily vertical, secondarily horizontal*"[18] and concludes that "this makes moral theology a part of spiritual theology."[19] Hence, the primacy, even in Christian ethics, lies in our relationship with God. Bockmuehl himself recovers this notion toward the end of his life when he writes in his journal that "[s]pirituality is the crown of theology."[20]

The Spirit's Role in General Creation and Specific Christian Ethics

When turning to the question of the Spirit's role in general creation ethics, we have already noted in chapter 4. that Bockmuehl does not mention the Spirit in this context. Instead, he links the activity of the Holy Spirit to the realm of specific Christian ethics. With regard to the relationship between general creation and specific Christian ethics, Bockmuehl maintains, as aforementioned: "Both areas together form . . . an ethics of law and Spirit, an ethics both of the ordinances of creation as well as of redemption."[21] That Bockmuehl attempts to hold these two ordinances together is, indeed, commendable. However, two aspects require further investigation. One aspect is the relationship between creation and redemption, and the other aspect is the linking of the law to creation ethics and the Spirit to specific Christian ethics. First, it is interesting to note that regarding the relation of creation and redemption Bockmuehl favors Barth's concept to that of Schlatter. Whereas Barth and in his wake Bockmuehl describe the relationship between creation and redemption as one of integration (*Aufhebung*), Schlatter contends that "grace is not nature's servant but also not its enemy but its consummator."[22] As Loos points out, the danger with the concept of integration is the fact that it could suggest the connotation of subordination of creation to redemption, thus placing the emphasis on discontinuity.[23] In fact, the following critique by Gunton could have been leveled at Bockmuehl instead of Barth: "And yet, there is, as there was in Origen, a tendency to treat the created order instrumentally, as a means to an end in which it shares, indeed, but not as fully as it should. The

---

18. Dubay, *Authenticity*, 241.
19. Ibid.
20. Bockmuehl, "Journals," Feb. 10, 1989.
21. *GG*, 514.
22. Schlatter, "Natur, Sünde, und Gnade," 63; cf. Neuer, "Ökologische Ethik," 253.
23. Loos, "Human Embodiment," 134.

A Critical Appraisal

weakness of Barth's theology of creation is . . . in his repetition, albeit in improved form, of the Western tendency so to subordinate creation to redemption that the status of the material world as a whole is endangered."[24]

That Bockmuehl falls prey to this tendency of subordination can be seen by the fact that he considers the Kingdom of God to be the sole horizon, purpose, and aim of Christian ethics. As a consequence, Bockmuehl promotes functionalism in ethics. He understands this to mean that "everything needs to be related to the one purpose, i.e., for Christians, the great commission of the formation of mankind after the image of Christ. If a man wants to be available for that work he must make himself free from other occupations . . . 'Functionalism' in ethics means relating everything you do, how you eat, what you dress for, your speech and appearance etc., to your purpose."[25]

Before turning to Bockmuehl's concept of functionalism, we shall suggest a more balanced view of creation and redemption. Instead of using the concept of the integration of creation into redemption, it is necessary to recover a concept of completion or perfection, resembling the one by Schlatter, which suggests the affirmation and appreciation of creation, despite its fallenness, thus highlighting the continuity between creation and redemption.[26] Similarly, Pinnock contends that "[r]edemption does not leave the world behind but lifts creation to a higher level. The Spirit has been implementing God's purposes for creation from day one and is committed to seeing to it that they issue in restoration."[27] Only this would safeguard against the danger of instrumentalizing creation and would open up the horizon of the Kingdom of God beyond the aspect of doing his will. Instead of sanctification being "task-orientated,"[28] as Bockmuehl believed, we agree with Gunton that "[t]he content of sanctification is a freedom to be what one is created to be, a child of God living confidently and unafraid in the creator's world, even when surrounded and threatened by death."[29] The emphasis here is on the relational aspect of sanctification, which is closely linked to the relational function of the Holy Spirit. The Holy Spirit helps us to live according to our creatureliness in loving relationship with

24. Gunton, *The Triune Creator*, 165. For this reference I am indebted to Loos, "Human Embodiment," 134.

25. Bockmuehl, "Revolution," 69. Bockmuehl, however, did warn later in life against treating God's creation, the earth, with contempt. Cf. *GG*, 210.

26. Cf. Loos, "Human Embodiment," 30.

27. Pinnock, *Flame*, 54.

28. Bockmuehl, "Sanctification," 615.

29. Gunton, *The Christian Faith*, 150–51.

Part Three—A Critical Appraisal

God, ourselves, and others. Pinnock highlights that it is, indeed, "[t]he love of God [that] grounds creation. His purpose for it has always been union and communion. God loved the world before it fell into sin. His initial relationship with it was not a legal but a loving one."[30] For Pinnock, this is intimately linked with the Spirit's presence in creation. If the latter is not recognized, then God's loving work even outside of the church might be disregarded and the unity of God the Redeemer and God the Creator overlooked. Pinnock rightly points out that "[i]t is not as if creation before the Fall was graceless. Spirit is moving the entire process toward participation in the love of God, and the whole creation is caught up in it."[31]

In addition, this also challenges Bockmuehl's concept of the double principle of law as belonging to creation ethics and Spirit as belonging to specific Christian ethics. According to Bockmuehl, human reason is sufficient for "decision-making in the realms of creational ethics and civil vocation." It is only in the realm of redemption ethics that Bockmuehl regards the Holy Spirit as the "divine Counselor" to be absolutely essential.[32] Instead, we need to recover the relational work of the Spirit not only for specific Christian ethics but also for creation ethics.

Functionalism in Bockmuehl's Ethics

Bockmuehl's definition of "new creation" as "effective faith, observance of the commandments, fulfillment of the righteousness required by the law by walking in the Spirit"[33] reveals a tendency to over-emphasize the fulfillment of the law and concrete, visible change as the consequence of regeneration and as the aim of Christian ethics instead of prioritizing the love relationship with God within the parameters of grace and forgiveness. It is not a matter of the absence of these topics in Bockmuehl's ethics, far from it, but rather a matter of definition and precedence. Loos, for instance, points out that "Bockmühl tends to understand the loving relationship between man and God basically in terms of doing good works which function to promote the concerns of the other. Yet, a relationship, love itself, cannot be viewed only in these categories. There is a deeper value to it."[34]

30. Pinnock, *Flame*, 45.
31. Ibid., 51–52; cf. 54.
32. *LbG*, 54.
33. Bockmuehl, "Wiedergeburt," 64.
34. Loos, "Human Embodiment," 141.

A Critical Appraisal

He correctly concludes that "[i]t is mainly the aspect of relationality that is not fully developed in Bockmühl's approach,"[35] as can, for instance, be seen by Bockmuehl's assertion "that human beings must first be asked 'what they are for' and not 'what they are', just as the knowledge of the will of God is more important than the knowledge of his nature and at least precedes it."[36] This implies that, for Bockmuehl, obeying God's will is more important than knowing God's nature, which is love (1 John 4:16). Loos calls attention to the fact that in Bockmuehl's theology "[m]an's love for God is in danger of being solely understood as man's performance for God."[37] This reveals the tendency toward Christian activism and functionalism in Bockmuehl's ethics, particularly in his earlier works, as he himself admits in his final speech: "Now, in the past, if someone had called me a workaholic, I would secretly have responded: 'Of course, what else?' A workaholic in the Kingdom of God, that was a title of honour!"[38] How fundamental this concept of functionality is for Bockmuehl's ethics can be seen in the following quotation: "This is the basic principle of Christian ethics: We are no longer living for ourselves, but for God's purposes, the instructions of headquarters. Functionalism in ethics simply means that anything that supports the furtherance of God's rule in men is good. Anything that opposes God's rule in men is bad. The relation of decision-making to the circumstances of the situation must then take second place to relating one's decision to the need and service of the Kingdom."[39]

Bockmuehl even compares the Christian to an obedient and disciplined soldier or servant who has surrendered his own wishes in order to live under "the dictatorship of the Holy Spirit."[40] This clearly reveals that Bockmuehl understands the guidance of the Spirit in functional, instrumental terms. Moreover, Bockmuehl is also in danger of functionalizing communion with God, since he sees its purpose as lying in its effects, namely, in loving one's neighbor, in ethical change. The following statement by Bockmuehl makes this very clear: "The disciples' communion with Jesus is not the goal; it is to equip and dispatch them to be 'fishers of men', to have them teach all nations and turn them into followers too. As

---

35. Ibid.
36. Bockmuehl, "Leiblichkeit," 41.
37. Loos, "Human Embodiment," 137.
38. Bockmuehl, "Listeners," 4.
39. Bockmuehl, "Revolution," 67.
40. Bockmuehl, "Frank Buchman's Message," 47.

soon as we propose to be pious without being on the road to bring other people under the rule of God we are parasites in the kingdom of God."[41]

That Bockmuehl emphasized so strongly the functional character of Christian ethics has to be firstly understood against the backdrop of Marxism. Bockmuehl himself insisted that "[t]he Christian ethics of revolution can learn from the cadres of Leninism as regard their strictly functional and purpose-bent ethics."[42] Although it is very laudable that Bockmuehl engaged with Marxism at great length and took their quest for the "new man" very seriously, it is regrettable that, instead of criticizing its concept of functionality, he, in fact, adopted it. The following quote shows to what an extent Bockmuehl was influenced by Marxist functionalism: "We need to grasp and exercise the insight that the Christian's task is not exhausted by living a decent life according to the creational order. We must learn to dedicate our lives to the larger commission of God's kingdom with the same consciousness and purposiveness, circumspection and energy that we have seen in Lenin."[43]

Hence, Bockmuehl links the Marxist emphasis on purposiveness with the emphasis on Christian ministry, especially the task of mission as the overall horizon for the Christian's life found in certain pietistic and evangelical circles. He even claims that "[t]he command of mission, that is the formation of mankind after the image of Christ, here becomes Imperative Number One."[44]

Secondly, Bockmuehl was very much impressed by Moral Re-Armament's aim of moral renewal, not only among Christians but nationwide, serving as a driving-force for the whole of life. Particularly their practice of a daily quiet time as the place where one experiences the direct, active guidance of the Spirit, receiving concrete instructions and inspirations for the day, had enormous influence on Bockmuehl's ethics.[45] Bockmuehl implemented Buchman's statement "that when man listens, God speaks"[46] into the very fabric of his ethics. God's "speaking" was, however, always understood to encompass specific commands and instructions for the purpose of moral change in individual lives as well as in the whole world.

41. Ibid., 39–40; cf. *Gospel*, 22, 97.
42. Bockmuehl, "Revolution," 67.
43. *CM*, 112; cf. *GG*, 18–19, 270; Bockmuehl, "Keeping His Commandments," 96.
44. Bockmuehl, "Revolution," 67.
45. Cf. Bockmuehl, "Frank Buchman's Message," 47.
46. Buchman, *Remaking the World*, 46. For Bockmuehl's references to this quote, see *LG*, 8; "Zum Tode Frank Buchmans," 390; "Zur Hermeneutik Martin Luthers," 279.

A Critical Appraisal

Thirdly, his functionalism also has its roots in his understanding of creation being integrated into redemption, as we have mentioned above. The danger perceivable in Bockmuehl's concept of functionalism is that he emphasizes too much the aspect of performance, of "doing," in order to promote the kingdom of God to the detriment of the relationship with God, of "being" in God's loving presence, as the ultimate aim of ethics. The following comments by Vorländer could have been written with view to Bockmuehl's ethics at the height of emphasizing functionalism[47] and are therefore quoted in length:

> Why does Jesus, who spoke words about bearing one's cross, in fact, gives . . . a much more pleasant, liberated, and 'life-filled' impression than we do, who want to follow his calling into full surrender, radical discipleship (how we like to use this word!), and active obedience of faith?! The problem for this might be that we *reduce* faith totally one-sidedly to the involvement in God's work—and thereby instrumentalize the whole of life, i.e., understand it only as a means to an end: Our body, our life is nothing else than the external prerequisite for our Christian engagement, and Christian engagement gives inner meaning to our earthly existence. Even prayer, silence, fellowship, and the celebration of church services are functional: they serve to make us fit, able and ready for ministry.[48]

In his final speech delivered about a month before Bockmuehl died, a significant change of perspective on Bockmuehl's part with regard to his concept of functionalism is evident, though indications can already be found in earlier writings:[49] "I saw my Christian and human dignity, my self-confidence, and reason for self-respect in being a 'worker' in God's vineyard. But Jesus said: 'No longer do I call you servants' (John 15:15). The sum-total of Christianity, love of Christ, following the Master, is not primarily a labour relationship . . . We need not fear: love for Christ will in itself produce all necessary motivation and identification with his

---

47. Particularly his article "Revolution of Ethics and Ethics of Revolution," published in 1971, emphasizes functionalism to a very great extent.

48. Vorländer, *Der Heilige Geist*, 18–19.

49. For instance, in his discussion on euthanasia in *CW*, Bockmuehl comments with view to handicapped children that "[s]uch children restore to us the true nature of love: They are loved, not for their usefulness, but for their own sake, and that is how all love should be" (142). In *GG*, he criticizes ethical activism and points to the fact that Jesus gave the listening Mary precedence over the active Martha (cf. 516; Bockmuehl, "Listeners," 4).

goals and his work . . . Let us be aware of the seductive glory of Christian workaholism."[50]

This shift in perception from viewing communion with God, to some degree, in functional terms to an appreciation of it as valuable in and of itself might have been caused by the experience of his own limitations regarding actions due to his illness as well as by his deep friendship with James Houston enjoyed through the last years of his life.[51] The latter, Professor of Spiritual theology at Regent College, rightly believes that "[a]s we enjoy the presence of God the Holy Spirit, we learn to see him more for the relationship we have with him than for any particular phenomena he brings,"[52] including active guidance. Nevertheless, Bockmuehl even in his last speech maintains that "[w]e must make ourselves receptive for his instruction."[53] Hence, although he gives communion with God primacy over service for God, he continues to emphasize the need for direct, active guidance in order to know God's will. However, doing God's will does not merely imply doing the right action at any time of the day but has actually to do with living in and out of God's love. Hence, the main focus when spending time with God is not necessarily on receiving concrete instructions, but rather on being in God's loving presence.[54] We conclude with a quote from Dubay who summarizes this poignantly: "The deepest value in a divine communication does not lie in clear concepts or blueprints for future action. It lies in a deeper drinking of the divine, a drinking that is general, dark, nonconceptual, love-immersed."[55]

Guidance of the Spirit and the Role of Reason

Since Bockmuehl's concept of guidance by the Spirit lies at the heart of his ethics, it is worth evaluating it in more depth, particularly with regard to the role of reason. As seen above, Bockmuehl's concept of guidance by the Spirit has to be understood as a response to Reformation ethics

50. Bockmuehl, "Listeners," 4.
51. Cf. Loos, "Human Embodiment," 144.
52. Houston, *Transforming Friendship*, 121.
53. Bockmuehl, "Listeners," 5.
54. Dubay, for instance, remarks that, "[w]hat God usually does speak to the ordinary person is inner transformation. He speaks goodness in a general manner" (*Authenticity*, 70).
55. Ibid., 117.

A Critical Appraisal

with its disregard for any direct guidance and its over-emphasis of "God's providential guidance."[56] Furthermore, Bockmuehl reacted against the old morality's and the new morality's emphasis on reason as a major factor in any decision-making process, accusing them of substituting the Spirit in ethics with reason. In fact, while rightly attempting to recover the Spirit's role for the decision-making process, Bockmuehl seems to come close to a dualism between reason and Spirit. He, for instance, notes that "[j]ust as, according to church doctrine, the Holy Spirit rather than reason must be the interpreter of Scripture . . . so also the decision should lie with the Holy Spirit and not with reason as to how the commandment of God is to be understood and fulfilled in a particular situation."[57]

However, the question has to be raised if the only valid alternative is the emphasis on the Spirit to the exclusion of reason, even "illumined reason,"[58] as Bockmuehl seems to propose. This apparent "either—or" of reason or Spirit as the guide for ethical decision is questionable since it one-sidedly defines guidance as a supranatural process. A more balanced view of guidance can be found in Schlatter who maintains that the Holy Spirit does not change the form of our thinking and volition but, instead, renews the content of our thinking. And even if the work of the Holy Spirit takes place as a spiritual miracle, it does not destroy nature but rather orientates it toward God and is, hence, aimed at the development of the creational capacities for God.[59] The advantage of this concept of the work of the Spirit is that, rather than suggesting that the Holy Spirit becomes the subject of our actions, the "Christ-in-us," as Bockmuehl does,[60] it takes into account the promise of an ongoing process of renewal of our minds and hearts given to each Christian. This process of transformation by the Spirit encompasses the will, motivations, and feelings, and also the rational faculty.

It is interesting to note that Bockmuehl seems to employ the phrase "mind of Christ" (1 Cor 2:16) at times interchangeably with guidance of the Spirit, yet without discussing the place of human renewed reason in the process of guidance.[61] However, when speaking about the guidance

56. *LG*, 35.
57. *SU*, 20; cf. *Gospel*, 54; *GG*, 518.
58. Cf. *Gospel*, 54.
59. Cf. Schlatter, *Ethik*, 53; Neuer, *Dogmatik*, 209.
60. *GG*, 308.
61. It is interesting in this context to remind ourselves that Bockmuehl considers guidance to be verbal: "God's guidance always comes by word; he is not silent, not speechless. He guides, not as we might guide a child by the hand or a horse by the

Part Three—A Critical Appraisal

of the Spirit he does take it for granted that this includes some kind of involvement of the mind, if not while listening, certainly while testing the received guidance. Such observation indicates that the neglect of the role of reason in guidance obvious in Bockmuehl's writings is due to his attempt to redress the balance by bringing the Spirit, the long forgotten factor in ethics, back into focus. However, it could be argued that Bockmuehl does not safeguard sufficiently against an unbalanced view of the relationship between reason and Spirit due to his endeavor to recover active, supranatural guidance by the Holy Spirit that cannot be traced back to rational reflection as its source. The danger, therefore, remains that an overemphasis on supernatural, direct guidance to the expense of rational reflection can lead to arbitrariness and subjectivism, as Higgins points out: "Christians often think of the Spirit's guidance in terms of sudden inspiration or direct prompting to perform particular courses of action. I do not dispute that the Spirit may guide us in this way. But I believe that he is also lending his help to us when we are engaged in the midst of serious reflection on moral issues and sustained analysis of them. Christians who resolve their dilemmas in an inconsistent manner and on spurious grounds should not abdicate responsibility by claiming direct dependence on the Spirit."[62]

An important aspect in this context, which Bockmuehl does not mention, is the importance of the Spirit's revelatory role with regard to personal knowledge of one's true self and of God as love in order to be able to truly discern his guidance.[63] This we shall explore in a later chapter.

---

reins, but through the instructions he speaks—instructions that we hear and then act upon" (*LG*, 83). However, when equating guidance by the Spirit with "mind of Christ," Bockmuehl seems to use the term in a wider sense than purely verbal.

62. Higginson, *Dilemmas*, 233.

63. With regard to the juncture of mind and Spirit, see Munzinger, *Discerning the Spirits*, 145–47, 156–57, 170.

6

A Response: Spirit as the Loving Presence of God—Toward a Relational Concept of the Spirit in Christian Ethics

The Spirit as the Loving Presence of God: a Relational Concept of the Spirit

BOCKMUEHL'S INVALUABLE CONTRIBUTION TO the Christian world lies in his insistence upon the importance of the Holy Spirit for Christian ethics. This chapter attempts to build upon Bockmuehl's insights with regard to the Holy Spirit and Christian ethics toward the end of his life and to weave them together with a relational concept of the Holy Spirit and Christian ethics. Instead of Bockmuehl's concept of guidance by the Holy Spirit as the main missing piece in Christian ethics, we propose that the aim and foundation of Christian ethics is living in the loving presence of God, enabling the Christian to live in loving relationship with God, self, others, and the whole of creation.

The Spirit as the Loving Presence of God

When referring to the Spirit as the presence of God indwelling the believer, several issues arise that are important for our current study and need to be looked at in more depth. How should the Spirit as the *presence of God* indwelling the believer be understood? Closely related is the

Part Three—A Critical Appraisal

question how the *indwelling of the Spirit* as the presence of God should be comprehended.

Goldingay, for instance, observed with view to the Old Testament that "talk of the spirit of God is one of a number of ways of referring to the presence and activity of God."[1] *Ruach* is used to denote the universal, creative presence of God as the breath of life (cf. Gen 2:7; Job 33:4; 34:14–15; Ps 139:8) as well as the particular presence of God, which Wenk also describes as "the favourable presence of the Lord, expressed by the revealing, wisdom-giving and empowering activity of the Spirit"[2] (cf. Num 27:18; 1 Sam 16:13–14; Ps 51:11; cf. Exod 33:13–16). To be cast away from the presence of God and to have the Holy Spirit taken away (cf. Psalm 51:11) implies not being able to enjoy close fellowship with God.[3]

Furthermore, in Ezekiel and Jeremiah, we find the promises that God would put his own Spirit in them, that he would give them a new heart and move them to obey his law; that his dwelling-place will be with them (cf. Ezek 36:26–27; 37:6, 14, 26–28; Jer 31:31–34). These promises link the Spirit of God directly to the presence of God, pointing toward a time in which God himself will indwell his people corporately as well as individually in a new way by his Spirit.[4] Hence, a new kind of fellowship between God and his people is promised. That these promises are not limited to Israel alone, as the context might suggest, can be inferred from Joel, where an outpouring of God's Spirit is promised "on all people" (Joel 2:28).

According to the New Testament, these promises were fulfilled with the giving of the Holy Spirit at Pentecost. Since then, as Fee states, "[t]he church, corporately and individually, is the place of God's own personal presence, by the Spirit. This is what marks God's new people off from 'all the other people on the face of the earth.'"[5] One image that links the Spirit and the presence of God particularly clearly is the Old Testament image of the tent/temple as a dwelling-place for God, his glory/name or his Spirit (cf. 2 Sam 7:6; 1 Kgs 8:11–12, 29; Isa 63:9–14) that Paul takes up and

---

1. Goldingay, "Was the Holy Spirit Active in Old Testament Times?," 18. Cf. Turner, *The Holy Spirit*, 168, 171.

2. Wenk, *Community-Forming Power*, 115.

3. Cf. Haberer, *Living the Presence of the Spirit*, 61.

4. Cf. Fee, *God's Empowering Presence*, 6–7. For the corporate aspect, see Ezek 36:28; Jer 31:33; for the individual aspect, see especially Jer 31:34.

5. Ibid., 8; cf. Turner, *Power from on High*, 439; Haberer, *Presence*, 130; Welker, *God the Spirit*, 241; Charry, *By the Renewing of Your Minds*, 46–47; Oden, *Life in the Spirit*, 60.

A Response

applies to the indwelling of the Holy Spirit in believers (cf. 1 Cor 3:16–17; 6:19; 2 Cor 6:16).[6]

When looking at contemporary pneumatologies, we find that different concepts have been employed to explain the Spirit as the presence of God indwelling the believer. Of paramount importance, however, when considering the Spirit as the presence of *God* is what key model of God is being applied. Brümmer rightly points to the overarching significance of the respective key model of God for the mode of relating to God. He, for instance, asserts that "beliefs about the nature of God are existential in the sense that they are always directly connected with the ways in which we relate to God. For this reason all the metaphors and models employed in God-talk are primarily relational: they are intended to indicate the ways in which we are to relate to God."[7]

If God, as present in this world by his Spirit, is first and foremost seen as sovereign Lord, as Bockmuehl seems to suggest, therein following Karl Barth,[8] the primary way of relating to God is likely to be one of master-servant relationship as we have found to be the case with regard to Bockmuehl's ethics, particularly his concept of guidance. Though this kind of relationship can indeed be found in the NT, for instance, when Paul calls himself the "servant of Christ" (e.g., Rom 1:1), the more foundational relationship that was made possible through Christ is that of Father-son or Father-daughter (cf. Rom 8:14–15; Gal 3:26—4:7, 31; cf. John 1:13). Yet, even this has to be qualified further in order to capture the true nature of this filial relationship. For this, we need to look at how Scripture portrays God the Father. According to 1 John, "God is love" (1 John 4:8); the greatness of the Father's love is made manifest in the fact that the believers should not only be *called* his children but *are* his children (cf. 1 John 3:1).[9] When turning to the Gospels, we find the same fact expounded in the parable of the prodigal son (cf. Luke 15:11–32; particularly v. 20). In Romans 8:15 and Galatians 4:6, Paul declares that believers can address God as "*Abba*, Father" through the Spirit of Christ, the Son. Since this was, according to the Gospel of Mark, Jesus' own way of addressing his Father in the garden of Gethsemane (cf. Mark 14:36), these passages suggest that through the Spirit the believers share in the filial, loving relationship that Christ has with his Father. This is similarly affirmed in John 17, where,

6. Cf. Fee, *God's Empowering Presence*, 7–8.
7. Brümmer, *The Model of Love*, 19.
8. Cf. Henning, *Die evangelische Lehre*, 98.
9. Cf. Lütgert, *Ethik der Liebe*, 240.

according to John, Jesus makes clear that to the same extent as the Father loves him, the Father also loves those that believe in him (cf. John 17:20, 23).

All these passages point to the conclusion that it is the love of God, particularly revealed in Christ's life, death, and resurrection, that ultimately qualifies the nature of the filial relationship between God and the believer. When mediating the presence of God to the believers by indwelling them, the Holy Spirit mediates God's love in a special way (cf. Rom 5:5). Hence, it is precisely due to the indwelling of the Holy Spirit that "God's love, played out to the full in Christ, is an experienced reality in the 'heart' of the believer"[10] since he is the loving presence of God.

Several questions arise at this point. What notion of love do we employ? How does the love of God have to be understood? To these issues we now turn our attention.

The Relational Concept of Love of God

When examining the Christian tradition of the interpretation of God's love, it is of interest to note that "the classical paradigm that saw God's love in terms of divine sovereignty, that is, in terms of God's ability unilaterally to will and to do good,"[11] i.e., his benevolence, has been seriously challenged, particularly in the last decades. One of the criticisms brought forward was that love, instead of being understood in a relational way, was taken to be an attitude or an attribute.[12] This, according to Brümmer, "can probably be explained by the fact that western thought has suffered from a systematic blind spot for relations."[13] He suggests that "love should be interpreted as an interpersonal relationship rather than as an attitudinal or emotional attribute of persons, as has traditionally been done. Such a relational concept of love will enable us to show how the various attitudes which in the Christian tradition have been proposed as answers to the question 'what is love?', are connected with each other since all of them are in one way or another involved in the relationship."[14]

In regaining the central relational aspect of love, Brümmer, however, has the tendency to move too far in the other direction when he at times

10. Fee, *God's Empowering Presence*, 496.
11. Vanhoozer, "Introduction," 7; cf. 10.
12. Cf. ibid., 2, 7–13, 18–19; Brümmer, *Love*, 156; Fiddes, *Creative Suffering*, 17.
13. Brümmer, *Love*, 33.
14. Ibid., 34.

A Response

identifies love with relationship. This, then, seems to exclude the notion of loving one's enemies, as Vanhoozer has pointed out.[15] Yet, Brümmer does make clear that love, in distinction to beneficence, "wants to be returned, requited, and in this way fulfilled in a relationship of mutual love. Of course this does not exclude the possibility of unrequited love."[16]

For Brümmer, the main characteristic of loving, personal relationships is not "agreements of rights and duties" but, instead, "mutual fellowship,"[17] into which each partner enters freely. Each partner is irreplaceable and has the value and interest of the other person at heart.[18] With a view to the assertion that God loves the world, this implies that he seeks, above all, to have fellowship with his creatures. In this context, it is worthwhile listening to Nygren, who in his seminal book *Agape and Eros* contended: "In the Gospels, Agape and fellowship with God belong inseparably together, so that each implies the other. We cannot speak of love without speaking of fellowship with God, nor of fellowship with God without speaking of love. It is Agape that distinguishes the new fellowship with God which Christianity brings, a fellowship not governed by law but by love."[19]

According to Nygren, the aim of Jesus' life on earth was to enable people to enter into a new fellowship with God characterized by *agape* love. Hence, the next question to ask is: What are the characteristics of this new kind of loving fellowship with God? Nygren particularly highlights the fact that Christ called *sinners*, not the righteous, into fellowship with God.[20] Hence, he rightly points out that the basis of our relationship with God is not our own righteousness, holiness, or even our repentance but purely God's love, his forgiveness, his undeserved grace through Christ's life, death, and resurrection.[21] However, Nygren's concept of *agape* as entirely "unmotivated," "indifferent to value" and "creative"[22] (i.e., it creates the worth of the human being but is not motivated by it) is questionable, since it neglects the doctrine of creation with its affirmation that human

---

15. Vanhoozer, "Introduction," 19.
16. Brümmer, *Love*, 155; cf. Vanhoozer, "Introduction," 18–19.
17. Brümmer, *Love*, 164; cf. Sarot, *God*, 83.
18. Cf. Brümmer, *Love*, 165–66; Sarot, *God*, 83–84.
19. Nygren, *Agape*, 146.
20. Ibid., 68.
21. Cf. ibid., 80, 113. Cf. Watson, "Translator's Preface," xii–xiii; Brümmer, *Love*, 128.
22. Nygren, *Agape*, 75, 77, 78.

beings were made in the image of God.²³ This can be traced back to the rather rigid and insufficiently differentiated distinction so prominent in Nygren between *agape*, or "gift-love," as the true Christian love and *eros*, or "need-love," as human egocentric love. For, as Wadell pointed out, "[i]t is one thing to say God loves us regardless of what we do, but it is another thing to say God loves us regardless of who we are."²⁴ In order to safeguard that God's love is not conditioned by our behavior and cannot be earned in any way, it is not necessary, as Nygren seemed to assume, to go as far as to deny any worth on the part of the creature. Such universal, unmotivated love is, in fact, in danger of becoming impersonal, since it does not presuppose any knowledge on God's part of the individual, unique person.²⁵ That is also one of the main criticisms brought forward against equating love with benevolence since it is possible to be benevolent toward someone yet at the same time treat that person as an object without being truly interested in them personally and in their friendship.²⁶ According to Paul, acts of mercy can be performed without being truly loving (cf. 1 Cor 13:3).²⁷

Furthermore, the distinction between *agape* and *eros* as employed by Nygren leaves no room for the following suggestion by Fiddes: "God does not 'need' the world in the sense that there is some intrinsic necessity in his nature, binding his free choice . . . but he does need the world in the sense that he has freely chosen to be in need."²⁸ This chosen "need" refers not to a selfish need in God but to God's desire and his longing for us to experience his love and to love him in return, to enter into fellowship with him. Nevertheless, although God the Father is a sovereign and powerful God, he restrains himself from coercing us into a relationship with him that would bring about our happiness, thus respecting our freedom of choice.²⁹ As Julian of Norwich phrased it, "[h]e stands all alone and waits for us, continuously, sorrowfully and mournfully, until we come and He makes haste to have us with Him. For we are His joy and His delight, and

---

23. Cf. Vacek, *Love*, 164–67, 309; Badcock, "The Concept of Love," 35, 45–46; Brümmer, *Love*, 128–29, 237.

24. Wadell, *Friendship*, 89.

25. Cf. ibid., 89–90.

26. Cf. Brümmer, *Love*, 240; Mohrlang, "Love," 577; Sarot, *God*, 85.

27. Cf. Berdyaev, *The Destiny of Man*, 107.

28. Fiddes, *Creative Suffering*, 74; cf. 66–68. Hart, "How Do We Define the Nature of God's Love?," 109; Vacek, *Love*, 123.

29. Cf. Moltmann, *The Trinity and the Kingdom of God*, 119; Sarot, *God*, 88; Berdyaev, *The Meaning of History*, 57.

A Response

He is our salvation and our life."[30] He also goes in search of us, he woos us, he pleads with us, but this does not happen in a manipulative or aggressive way, for otherwise the relationship with him would be characterized by fear, not by love (cf. 1 John 4:18).[31] Hence, as Brümmer highlighted, "[t]his divine longing is accompanied by infinite restraint ... God does not coerce or oblige us to return his love, but has infinite patience in waiting on us to do so. He never gives up his willingness to forgive those who turn to him."[32] Forgiveness implies that, if sinners come home, God is willing to suffer the injury that was caused through their sinful action in order to restore the fellowship that was broken.[33]

The Importance of Suffering Love

These thoughts inevitably challenge the classic doctrine of God's impassibility, since "[t]his divine offer of love$_1$ renders God vulnerable: vulnerable not only to rejection by the beloved, but also to whatever negative factors may be afflicting the beloved"[34] and therefore reveal another characteristic of God's love that has not always been maintained, that of suffering love.[35] In recent years, however, as Goetz states, "the rejection of the ancient doctrine of divine impassibility has become a theological commonplace."[36] Nevertheless it is worth investigating the suffering love of God in some depth.

LaCugna, for instance, asserts that "the suffering and death of Jesus Christ must condition all assertions about God's love. It is inconceivable that the God ... whose whole existence is tied up with the redemption and liberation of the creature, would not suffer with the creature, that the God who is Love Itself (*Ipsum Amore*) would not suffer on account of this love."[37] Nevertheless, LaCugna admits that "we are unable to say what it

30. Julian of Norwich, *The Revelation of Divine Love*, ch. 79, 202.
31. Cf. Pinnock, *Flame*, 157.
32. Brümmer, *Love*, 226; cf. Lütgert, *Ethik der Liebe*, 210.
33. Cf. Brümmer, *Love*, 185; Volf, *Exclusion and Embrace*, 125. Bonhoeffer similarly points out that "[f]orgiveness is the Christlike suffering which it is the Christian's duty to bear" (Bonhoeffer, *The Cost of Discipleship*, 80).
34. Sarot, *God*, 85. Sarot differentiates between "love$_b$," i.e., love as benevolence and "love$_1$," i.e., love as "relation of mutual fellowship" (ibid., 83; cf. 156).
35. Cf. Bauckham, *God Crucified*, 79; Brümmer, *Love*, 227–28; Augsburger, *The Robe of God*, 215.
36. Goetz, "The Suffering God," 385.
37. LaCugna, *God For Us*, 398.

means for God to suffer as God."[38] What we can say is that "the *crucified Jesus is the 'image of the invisible God'*"[39] (cf. Col 1:15), as Barth pointed out, since, according to Hebrews, "[t]he Son is the radiance of God's glory and the exact representation of his being" (Heb 1:3) who for our sakes "was despised and rejected by mankind, a man of suffering, and familiar with pain" (Isa 53:3) in order to bring reconciliation. Hence, Christ participated in human suffering and thereby redeemed it, effecting healing, as had been promised with a view to the Messiah: "by his wounds we are healed" (Isa 53:5; cf. 1 Pet 2:24).[40] Accordingly, Bonhoeffer contended that suffering "is the only path to victory. The cross is his triumph over suffering."[41] By taking on himself the ultimate and deepest suffering of the world, which is God-forsakenness, Christ overcame it by the power of the Holy Spirit (cf. Heb 9:14), by the power of love, thereby revealing the "redemptive efficacy"[42] of his own suffering.[43]

Furthermore, what immense benefit the believer derives from the sufferings of Christ is spelt out, for instance, in Hebrews 4:15: "For we do not have a high priest who is unable to empathize with our weaknesses, but we have one who has been tempted in every way, just as we are—yet he did not sin." Due to Christ's own vicarious sufferings, his ability to identify with our painful experiences, his sympathy, and empathy take on a soteriological dimension, which aids our redemption by demonstrating God's mercy and grace.[44] Hence, since Christ suffered and died for us, he is now able to sympathize, to "suffer-with" us.[45] In fact, Matthew 25 suggests that Christ identifies with those in need to such an extent that by serving those in need we serve Christ himself.[46]

After this investigation of the significance of Christ's suffering and death, we now turn to the question of its relationship to *God the Father's*

---

38. Ibid., 296.

39. Barth, *Church Dogmatics* 2/2:123; cf. Moltmann, *Trinity*, 31–32; Moltmann, *The Crucified God*, 202–3; Wolterstorff, "Suffering Love," 227.

40. Cf. Olthuis, "Dancing Together," 146.

41. Bonhoeffer, *The Cost of Discipleship*, 81; cf. Bonhoeffer, *Letters and Papers from Prison*, 361.

42. Bonhoeffer, *The Cost of Discipleship*, 82.

43. Cf. Bauckham, "Only the suffering God Can Help," 12; Moltmann, *Crucified God*, 46.

44. Cf. Grässer, *An die Hebräer*, 252–53; Bruce, *The Epistle to the Hebrews*, 115–16; Lane, *Hebrews 1–8*, 114; Gärtner, "Suffering," 723–24.

45. Olthuis, *Beautiful Risk*, 45; cf. Fiddes, *Creative Suffering*, 16.

46. Cf. Stott, *The Cross of Christ*, 335.

A Response

suffering love. First, it needs to be pointed out that, since Christ is the ultimate self-revelation of God, "the very nature of the triune God is reflected on the cross of Christ. Inversely, the cross of Christ is etched in the heart of the triune God; Christ's passion is God's passion."[47] Even though the way of suffering was different between Father and Son since the Father did not take on bodily form, the Father shared in the suffering of Christ in as much as the suffering of Christ reflects the Father's suffering.[48] This suffering can be understood, for instance, as the willingness to open his arms toward the prodigal sons and daughters in order to embrace them and receive them home regardless of how much they have hurt him. These "open arms suggest the pain of other's absence and the joy of the other's anticipated presence."[49] Furthermore, since the price for these open arms was the cross, and due to the Father's love and compassion for his son and his oneness with him—not understood in a modalist sense but in the sense of a "reciprocal immanence"[50]—the Father cannot be thought of as having been untouched by his son's suffering and death. Instead, he must have grieved over it and shared in it, and thereby shared in the pain and suffering of the world (Matt 3:17 et al.; John 10:38; Rom 5:8; 1 John 4:8–10).[51] Galot, therefore, rightly pointed out that "[i]n the suffering face of the Saviour we must also see the suffering face of the Father. Jesus' human suffering enables us to enter into the mystery of the Father's divine suffering."[52] Hence, God's love shines through the love of Christ that, according to the New Testament, encompassed utmost suffering with, and on behalf of, humanity, enabling him to sympathize, to "suffer-with" his people even till now.[53]

That God "suffers with" his people can even be substantiated from the Old Testament where it says of the LORD in Isaiah 63:9: "In all their [Israel's] distress he too was distressed." In fact, the Old Testament contains many "anthropopathisms" with regard to the representation of God that, according to Bauckham, "are not to be set aside as rather crude ways of

---

47. Volf, *Exclusion and Embrace*, 127; cf. Moltmann, *Trinity*, 21–22.

48. Cf. Moltmann, *Crucified God*, 203; Stott, *The Cross of Christ*, 331, 334–35; Sarot, *God*, 91–96.

49. Volf, *Exclusion and Embrace*, 141.

50. Galot, *Abba*, 139.

51. Cf. Stott, *The Cross of Christ*, 334; Moltmann, *Crucified God*, 203, 205, 216, 243; Moltmann, *Trinity*, 81; Volf, *Exclusion and Embrace*, 126, 129; Barth, *Church Dogmatik* 4/2:357; Kitamori, *Theology of the Pain of God*, 115.

52. Galot, *Abba*, 139; Wong, "Holy Spirit," 70–71.

53. Cf. Galot, *Abba*, 140; Duffey, *Be Blessed*, 103.

speaking of God which are not really appropriate to the reality of God, but should be seen as central hermeneutical key to the prophetic theology."[54] God is, indeed, portrayed as engaging and responding emotionally with and to his people (cf. Hos 11:8).

We have so far suggested that an important aspect of the love of God the Father and the Son is their suffering with (solidarity/sympathy), suffering for (substitution/vicariousness), and suffering because of (vulnerability/forgiveness) his wayward people. Yet, what role does the third person of the Trinity, the Holy Spirit, play with regard to the suffering love of God? Moltmann, for instance, poses the following question with regard to the effect of Christ's suffering on the Holy Spirit: "How does the Spirit experience Jesus' living and his dying? This question is seldom asked."[55] By way of paralleling the Holy Spirit with the Old Testament/rabbinic concept of God's *Shekinah*, he arrives at the following answer: "if the Spirit 'leads' Jesus, then the Spirit accompanies him as well. And if the Spirit accompanies him, then it is drawn into his sufferings, and becomes his *companion* in suffering. The path the Son takes in his passion is then at the same time the path taken by the Spirit, whose strength will be proved in Jesus' weakness. The Spirit is the transcendent side of Jesus' immanent way of suffering. So the '*condescendence*' of the Spirit leads to the progressive *kenosis* of the Spirit, together with Jesus."[56]

Since the Holy Spirit not only strengthened and empowered[57] Christ in his sufferings but also participated in them by accompanying him to the cross, the Spirit of power is at the same time revealed as the Spirit of the passion, of the cross. Hence, Torrance drew attention to the fact that when the Spirit came to the believers at Pentecost, it was not only as the Spirit of God the Father, but as the Spirit of Jesus "mediated through the human nature and experience of the Incarnate Son . . . And therefore he came not as isolated and naked Spirit, but as Spirit charged with all the experience of Jesus as he shared to the full our mortal nature and weakness, and endured its temptation and grief and suffering and death, and with the experience of Jesus as he struggled and prayed, and worshipped and obeyed, and poured out his life in compassion for mankind."[58]

54. Bauckham, "Only the Suffering God Can Help," 9; cf. 10.
55. Moltmann, *Spirit*, 62.
56. Ibid.
57. Cf. McFarlane, *Christ and the Spirit*, 178.
58. Torrance, *Theology in Reconstruction*, 246–47; cf. Gorman, *Cruciformity*, 60; Moltmann, *Spirit*, 62, 64; 67–68. In this context the groaning of the Spirit might be illuminating. Cf. Rom 8:23, 26.

A Response

Similarly, as the Spirit of God the Father, the Spirit participated in the Father's grief and suffering with regard to his son's death and with regard to his "absent" and hurting people. As Moltmann points out, "[t]he surrender through the father and the offering of the Son take place 'through the Spirit'. The Holy Spirit is therefore the link in the separation. He is the link joining the bond between the Father and the Son, with their separation."[59] What implications this has for the believer's life shall be explored in more depth on pages 219-35.

This suffering, cruciform love "does not make God a helpless victim of evil, but is the secret of his power and his triumph over evil."[60] As revealed in Jesus, it encompasses deep concern and affection for his people, solidarity with sufferers, sympathy, compassion,[61] empathy with their weaknesses, vulnerability to the pain of rejection, openness to the joy of acceptance, active involvement and participation in their suffering to the point of self-sacrifice in order to overcome the pain of God-forsakenness.[62] Hence, suffering love has at its aim the restoration of the broken relationship between God and human beings, mutual fellowship and intimacy.

The Nature of the Loving Relationship with God

In order to qualify further the nature of this communion, it has been compared to several types of interpersonal relationships such as father/mother-child, friend-friend or lover-lover relationship, all of which are referred to in Scripture.[63] Yet, since human relationships of these types have been corrupted due to the fallenness of humankind and are, therefore, only to varying degrees truly loving, they can only insufficiently reflect a relationship in which a perfectly and unconditionally loving God is

---

59. Moltmann, *Trinity*, 82.

60. Bauckham, "Only the Suffering God Can Help," 12.

61. "The givenness of Jesus Christ surely demands that we try to understand that the love of God is not condescension but compassion" (Jenkins, *The Glory of Man*, 106); cf. Bauckham, "Only the Suffering God Can Help," 10.

62. Cf. Bauckham, "Only the Suffering God Can Help," 12.

63. Here we are not interested in the question to what degree and which of these relationships have to be seen as metaphors (McFague), models (Brümmer), or actuality (like Father—child; friend—friend; cf. Bockmuehl, *CW*, 41), but rather what they contribute to an understanding of the divine-human loving relationship. Cf. Vanhoozer, "Introduction," 16, 18; McFague, *Models of God*, chs. 4-6; Brümmer, *Love*, 29-30; *CW*, 39-41.

involved. This can be seen in Isaiah 49:15, where the question is posed by "God" if a mother could ever "forget the baby at her breast." The expected answer seems to be "no," but instead the text actually continues: "Though she may forget, I will not forget you!" Therefore, God's love, though comparable to motherly love in that he has compassion on his children (cf. Isa 49:15), comforts them (cf. Isa 66:13), is gentle and cares for his children (cf. 1 Thess 2:7), and nurtures them, goes far beyond it.[64] Hence, as Hart correctly states, "God's love both is and yet is not like ours."[65] That this also applies to the parental love of God (cf. Luke 11:11–13; Heb 12:10) is particularly important due to the fact that our early image of God is influenced to a great degree by our experience of the "significant others" in our lives. Though positive experiences can help one to grasp God's motherly or fatherly love, human experiences will always be a distorted representation of God's perfect love, some to a greater, some to a lesser extent. Hence, the ultimate example for genuinely loving father/mother–child relationships can only be found by looking at God's relationship with his children. One of the most remarkable description of God's fatherly love can be found in Jesus' parable of the Father's Love (a more appropriate name than "Parable of the Prodigal Son")[66] told in Luke 15:11–32. The parable reveals God's love as being "outrageously" greater than human love since it is hardly conceivable of a first-century father that he would ever have acted in such a loving, compassionate, gracious, and self-humiliating way.[67] The aim of God's love is for a (re-)union, a close intimacy with his children, as the image of the embrace and the kiss signify.[68]

64. *CW*, 39. Cf. Bauckham, "Only the Suffering God Can Help," 10.
65. Hart, "God's Love," 100.
66. Cf. Jeremias, *The Parables of Jesus*, 128; *CW*, 40.
67. For instance, that the Father "ran to his son" (Luke 15:20) implies, according to Bailey, that he was "shaming himself publicly," since a slow pace of walking was seen as being dignified (cf. Bailey, *The Cross*, 67). Cocksworth, in fact, states that Jesus "describes God as Father in his teaching but in a way which smashes the contemporary stereotypes of fatherhood in his culture" (*Holy, Holy, Holy*, 20).
68. Other passages particularly describing God's fatherly love can be found in: Deut 1:31 ("as a father carries his son"); Deut 14:1–2 (chosen as treasured possession); Ps 103:13 (compassion); Prov 3:12 (discipline, delights in children); Jer 31:9, (leading Israel to place of refreshment); Hos 11:1–4, 8 (parent—teaching to walk, taking by arms, "I led them with cords of human kindness, with ties of love" (4), feeding, not giving them up); 1 Thess 2:11–12: (Paul, like a Father, encouraged, comforted, and urged the Thessalonians to lives worthy of God; Paul's love reflects God's own love; cf. 1 Thess 1:6).

A Response

Whereas the image of mother is used as a metaphor for God's love, the New Testament makes it clear that God is not just *like* a father but he *is* in actuality our father by our receiving the Spirit of sonship (cf. Rom 8:15; 1 John 3:1; 2 Cor 6:18). The same is true for the relationship friend-friend, since in Christ God is our friend. Indeed, Jesus was "a friend of tax collectors and sinners" (Luke 7:34), and to his disciples Jesus made it clear that he regarded them not as servants but as friends (cf. John 15:15). The friendship is not restricted to Jesus but is true for God as well, since, in a parable, Jesus compared God to a friend we can boldly go to at any time if in need (cf. Luke 11:5-8). Similarly, Moses and Abraham were referred to as God's friends (cf. Ex 33:11 for Moses; 2 Chr 20:7; Jas 2:23 for Abraham).

In comparison to the other two relationships previously discussed, the distinct characteristic of a friendship is the freedom of choice and mutuality, or reciprocity. Whereas children cannot choose their parents, friends have the freedom to choose who they want to be friends with. Furthermore, whereas a parent-child relationship does not depend on the child's response to her/his parents' love, since parental love is described as being primarily nurturing, supporting, i.e., giving, the nature of a friendship is far more one of a mutual relation. Vacek correctly points out that "philia is marked by a bond that essentially includes reciprocity."[69] Since a friendship cannot be forced upon someone without losing the character of a loving friendship, it depends on the willingness of both partners to establish and maintain the relationship. This includes refraining from the temptation to oblige, manipulate, or force someone to return one's love as this would destroy the freedom of the other person.[70] Furthermore, due to the mutual character of friendship, "[t]he ability to receive, and not just the ability to give"[71] is of paramount importance. The depth of friendship depends on the willingness to accept and return love, for instance, to participate in each other's lives. This participation can be further described as "a unity-in-difference, a form of sharing in the life of persons or groups who remain *other* than myself."[72] This encompasses knowing the other and being known by the other through spending time in each other's company and honestly sharing one's joys and sorrows, one's concerns and interests.[73] Hence, "[c]lose relationships . . . require considerable knowledge—of

---

69. Vacek, *Love*, 284; cf. 303.
70. Cf. Brümmer, *Model*, 160; D. D. Williams, *Spirit*, 116.
71. Vacek, *Love*, 25.
72. Ibid., 296-97.
73. Cf. Wadell, *Friendship*, 86, 134.

ourselves and of those with whom we relate."[74] For without knowing ourselves at least to a certain degree, it is difficult to reveal ourselves to our friends. Yet without relational knowledge of our friends, we do not know how to truly participate in their lives and make their concerns our own.[75] Lafollette captures the reciprocal relationship between self-knowledge and friendship well when he suggests that "[e]nhanced self-knowledge will promote deeper personal relationships, which will enhance self-knowledge, etc."[76] Two other important components of close friendships besides knowledge are honesty and trust. In fact, "complete honesty is essential for ideal intimacy."[77] Honesty in a friendship encourages trust for each other, just as trust facilitates honesty.[78]

Describing our relationship with God as one of friendship implies that it is a mutual relationship into which God as well as we enter freely. However, it was God who first chose us to be his friends (John 15:16). Nevertheless, the establishment of the friendship itself depended on our choosing in freedom to enter into a relationship with God by receiving his love for us and returning it. How extraordinary the possibility of entering into a friendship with God is can be seen by the fact that, though we are by no means God's equals, he still longs for a mutual, intimate relationship with us due to his unconditional, gracious love for us.[79] Yet, how can our relationship with God be one of mutuality and reciprocity? Vacek suggests the following: "In and through the love relation between God and humans, each party receives the other and is modified . . . Each party becomes what it can be through participating in the other. One of God's personal gifts to us is to let us be significant to God's own life."[80]

When comparing our friendship with God to human friendships, it should be noted that God is an absolute perfect friend, whose love and commitment for us never wavers. Furthermore, he is perfect not only *vis-à-vis* love but also *vis-à-vis* knowledge, honesty, and trust. Therefore, he is the only friend whose friendship can truly meet all our needs, since the friendship with him enables us to enter into and remain in his

74. Lafollette, *Personal Relationships*, 19–20.

75. Cf. ibid., 134–35; D. D. Williams, *Spirit*, 121.

76. Lafollette, *Personal Relationships*, 134–35. Cf. Vacek, *Love*, 47–48; D. D. Williams, *Spirit*, 121.

77. Lafollette, *Personal Relationships*, 125. Cf. Brümmer, *Love*, 181.

78. Cf. Lafollette, *Personal Relationships*, 211. Berdyaev, *Slavery and Freedom*, 254.

79. Cf. Vacek, *Love*, 299; Lütgert, *Ethik der Liebe*, 195.

80. Vacek, *Love*, 25.

A Response

unconditional, never-ending love. In order to deepen the friendship with us, God's Spirit unveils those things that hinder this friendship.

The Spirit as the Loving Presence of God the Father and the Son

We have already noted above that, since Pentecost, the believers individually as well as corporately have become the temple, the home, for God himself due to the indwelling of the Holy Spirit. Furthermore, we have established that the main characteristic of God is love that greatly surpasses any human love and that has, above all, as its aim a close, intimate, loving relationship with his people.

In this chapter, therefore, we want to demonstrate that the principal activity of the Holy Spirit lies in establishing and deepening a loving, intimate relationship with God the Father and the Son, before then going on to explore the importance of the relational work of the Holy Spirit for Christian ethics in the following section.[81] In order to do this, we have to turn our attention to the significant fact that since the New Testament the Spirit is not only referred to as the Spirit of God, i.e., the Father, but also as the Spirit of Christ. What implications does this fact have for the understanding of the Spirit as indwelling the believer?

According to Moltmann, due to the Spirit's accompanying of Jesus Christ till his death on the cross, "the eternal Spirit of God becomes 'the Spirit of Christ' (Rom. 8.9)."[82] Hence, the Spirit indwelling the believer, though proceeding from the Father as his origin, displays the characteristics of Christ as well since he was the bearer of the Spirit during his time on earth.[83] Moreover, it is by means of the Spirit that the believer is related to and united with Christ who is now at the right hand of God. This encompasses a new, intimate relationship with Christ "that constitutes and controls all that as Christians we are and do. We live his life, we die his death, we share his suffering and his victory."[84] It is the Spirit who effects

---

81. Cf. Rabens, "Power," 152–53.

82. Moltmann, *Spirit*, 68; cf. 62.

83. Cf. Fee, *God's Empowering Presence*, 6, 837; Moltmann, *Spirit*, 68, 70; Dunn, *Epistle to the Galatians*, 221.

84. Smail, *Spirit*, 58; cf 40. Fee states that "when Paul in Gal 2:20 . . . speaks of Christ living in him, he almost certainly means 'Christ lives in me *by His Spirit*', referring to the ongoing work of Christ in his life that is being carried out by the indwelling Spirit" (*God's Empowering Presence*, 838); cf. Reed, *Genesis of Ethics*, 127.

PART THREE—A Critical Appraisal

the *koinonia*, a profound union of love with Christ through which the believer participates in the life of Christ (cf. 1 Cor 1:9; John 15:5), whereby the believer is "being transformed into his image" (2 Cor 3:18).[85] Thomas Merton describes this fellowship in the following way: "The union of the Christian with Christ is not just a similarity of inclination and feeling, a mutual consent of minds and wills. It has a more radical, more mysterious and supernatural quality: it is a mystical union in which Christ Himself becomes the source and principle of divine life in me. Christ Himself, to use a metaphor based on Scripture, 'breathes' in me divinely in giving me His Spirit."[86]

This *koinonia*, this fellowship with Christ can be further qualified as a close friendship with all the above mentioned characteristics, since Christ himself said to his disciples in John 15:15 "I no longer call you servants, because a servant does not know his master's business. Instead, I have called you friends, for everything that I learned from my Father I have made known to you." His desire to share everything with us, to be united to us so as to dwell in our hearts was the reason for laying down his own life for us (1 John 3:16)—and thereby to create access to the Father (Eph 2:18).[87] For through being united with Christ by the Spirit, the believer at the same time participates in the filial, loving relationship that Christ has with his Father.[88] This can be seen by the fact that, according to Paul, the believer is given the "Spirit of sonship" (Rom 8:15), the Spirit of Christ, who enables the believer to address God in an intimate way as "Abba, Father" (cf. Gal 4:6).[89] According to the Gospel of Mark, this was Jesus' own way of addressing his Father in the garden of Gethsemane (cf. Mark 14:36). Therefore, Galot suggests that Jesus "wanted to communicate his own divine sonship to his disciples so that they might be children of the Father in his likeness."[90] He did so by sharing with them his filial, intimate relationship with his Father. This was, and still is, accomplished

---

85. Cf. Smail, *Spirit*, 186; Oden, *Life in the Spirit*, 206; Wainwright, "The Holy Spirit," 293–94.

86. Merton, *New Seeds*, 159.

87. Cf. ibid., 153–54; Gunton, *The Christian Faith*, 177.

88. Cf. Wong, "Holy Spirit," 85; Grenz, "Holy Spirit," 11; Pinnock, *Flame*, 46, 153–54 ; Smail, *Spirit*, 205–6; Bennema, *Power*, 135; Gaybba, *The Spirit of Love*, 156–57.

89. Cf. Rabens, *Spirit*, 224–28. Grenz, "Holy Spirit," 11, 13.

90. Galot, *Abba*, 65. Galot suggests that Jesus habitually addressed his Father as "Abba," since "the Greek forms of the name 'Father' correspond to the Aramaic 'Abba'" and therefore, when teaching his disciples the Lord's Prayer, invited them to use the same invocation as he did. Galot, *Abba*, 58; cf. 64.

A Response

through the Spirit, who unites believers with Christ, drawing them into a new profound intimacy with the Father, and thus gives them a new status and identity as children of God and co-heirs with Christ (cf. Rom 8:17).[91] One of the most outstanding characteristics of this new relationship is that the Father loves the believer as he loves his Son (cf. John 17:20, 23, 26). That this divine love has as its aim an intimate, mutual relationship can be seen by the following prayer of Jesus in John 17:23, 26: "I in them and you in me—so that they may be brought to complete unity. Then the world will know that you sent me and have loved them even as you have loved me . . . I have made you known to them, and will continue to make you known in order that the love you have for me may be in them and that I myself may be in them."

In Johannine language, therefore, this new relationship with God is expressed in terms of one-ness (cf. John 10:30; 17:11, 21-23) and mutual indwelling of the Father, Son, and the believer (cf. John 14:19-20; 17:11, 21). When turning to the Spirit's role in bringing about this mutual indwelling, this new intimacy, it is worth quoting Romans 5:5, where Paul states that "God's love has been poured out into our hearts through the Holy Spirit, who has been given to us." It is only through the presence of the Holy Spirit dwelling in the heart of the believer that the love of God becomes experienced reality. For it is only through the Holy Spirit, as God's loving presence, that we can be intimately related to the Son and through him to the Father. Therefore, Vanhoozer is correct in stating that "we can know the love of God only as we come to participate in it."[92] This implies that we can experience God's compassionate, suffering, patient, forgiving, healing love only through the relational work of the Holy Spirit drawing us into a loving relationship with God.

The Experience of the Spirit's Relational Work

Thus far we have established that the Spirit is the one enabling the loving, intimate relationship between the believer and God the Father and the Son. The next question, however, that has to be answered is how the relational work of the Spirit is experienced by the believer. Important in

---

91. Cf. Dunn, "Spirit Speech," 91; LeRon Shults and Sandage, *Transforming Spirituality*, 100; Grenz, "Holy Spirit," 11; Pinnock, *Flame*, 153–54; Barron, *And Now I See*, 217.

92. Vanhoozer, "Introduction," 24–25; cf. Fee, *God's Empowering Presence*, 495, 497–98.

PART THREE—A Critical Appraisal

this context is the Spirit's activity of revealing knowledge to human beings (John 14:26; 16:13f; 1 John 2:20, 27). Gunton rightly states that this "knowledge . . . is not primarily prepositional or factual knowledge, but personal knowledge, like the knowledge we have of someone we love."[93] And since, as in every relationship, personal or relational knowledge grows through spending time with the beloved, the Holy Spirit enables an encounter with the Father and the Son.[94] Smail captures well the role of the Spirit in this encounter: "When the encounter is actually taking place it is the Son and his Father who fill our awareness; it is from them that we receive and to them that we respond. It is only when we disengage from the immediacy of the encounter and, as it were, stand back and reflect on it, that we become aware of the hidden and mysterious action of the Spirit in making it all possible for us. The presence and work of the Spirit is an essential factor in the situation, because it could not happen without him."[95]

For only by the Spirit who "stands with us on our side of the encounter with the Father and Son"[96] are we able to accept and receive God's undeserved self-giving love and thereby enter into a love relationship with him and so give ourselves back to God.[97] Yet, even though it is the indwelling Spirit who makes this response of faith possible, he does not do it without our participation. Rather, as Turner states, it is "a matter of *not resisting* the Spirit,"[98] of letting ourselves be led into an ever deeper love relationship with the Father through the Son by the Spirit. Hence, we truly need to believe *for* ourselves, but not without the aid of the Holy Spirit.[99] However, our hearts do often resist true love since the known feels safer than the unknown, slavery feels safer than freedom.[100] In fact, we oftentimes flee from true love since it implies a kind of painful death to our "false self," which Merton describes in the following way: "Every one of us is shadowed by an illusory person: a false self. This is the man that I want myself to be but who cannot exist, because God does not know

---

93. Gunton, *The Christian Faith*, 177; cf. Bennema, *Power*, 126–29; Munzinger, *Discerning the Spirits*, 156–57.

94. Cf. Ziesler, *Pauline Christianity*, 48.

95. Smail, *Spirit*, 30.

96. Ibid.

97. Cf. Smail, *Reflected Glory*, 29–30.

98. Turner, *Power*, 410.

99. Cf. Smail, *Spirit*, 110–11, 205–6; Rabens, *Spirit*, 251–52.

100. Cf. Merton, *New Seeds*, 15–16.

anything about him. And to be unknown to God is altogether too much privacy. My false and private self is the one who wants to exist outside the reach of God's will and God's love—outside of reality and outside of life."[101]

Hence, not resisting the Spirit means, therefore, letting oneself be wooed by the Spirit to enter into the Father's embrace, into the Father's love, to trust in his goodness and mercy.[102] In fact, this implies letting go of the attempt to earn God's love since this would only prevent us from accepting and experiencing his undeserved, gracious love. Yet again, even this dying to the false self and the rising to the new self, the letting go of resistances to God's love, is made possible by the Spirit himself through mediating God's love to us and his desire for a love relationship with us.[103] That this is an ongoing process can be seen by the fact that "when we begin to accept this relationship, we come to realize how far we are from full intimacy with God. When we allow ourselves to feel loved by God, we are able to let go of our defenses and see both our evil and our good."[104] And the more we, through the activity of the Spirit, "grasp how wide and long and high and deep is the love of Christ" (Eph 3:18), the more our desire grows to enter deeper into this love, into the relationship with the Father and the Son. And the more we enter into this love relationship, the more we will realize that the "[u]nion with the eternal was not a human achievement: it was the gift of God. It came, not by any spiritual exercises, but by God's self-revelation, God's self-impartation."[105] Without the Spirit's relational work, this loving, intimate relationship with God could never be experienced.

The Ethical Life as the Fruit of Living in the Loving Presence of God

After having established that the chief role of the Holy Spirit as the loving presence of God is to draw the believer into an intimate love-relationship with God the Father and the Son, our next aim is to delineate the implications this has for Christian ethics. First, we will take a closer look at the goal of ethical life, i.e., to live in loving relationships; secondly, we will

101. Merton, *New Seeds*, 34.
102. Cf. Pinnock, *Flame*, 157.
103. Cf. Rom 8:13–17.
104. Vacek, *Love*, 324.
105. Stewart, *A Man in Christ*, 164.

investigate the relationship between living in the loving presence of God and ethical life, before, thirdly, focusing on the obstacles that hinder a life lived in loving relationship with God, self, and others.

Ethical Life: Living in Loving Relationships

When turning to the issue of the goal of Christian ethical life, we first need to clarify the employment of the term *Christian ethics*. However, in face of the diversity of ethical concepts proposed by Christian ethicists in the last decades, let alone centuries, this proves to be a rather difficult task. For not only is there disagreement over the question of what makes an ethic *Christian*, i.e., what distinguishes a Christian ethic from a non-Christian one, but also over the question of an appropriate approach to, and main focus of, Christian *ethics*.[106] With regard to the latter question, there have been a range of diverse and, at times, competing approaches such as deontological (natural) law or rule ethics,[107] virtue ethics,[108] teleological, for instance, utilitarian[109] and situation ethics,[110] to name only a few, and various combinations of these approaches. And even each of these approaches presents itself in a variety of ways.[111] This diversity can be traced back to the difference of focus: if the emphasis is mainly on right/wrong or good/bad behavior and action, the subject matter of ethics will be to a great extent the establishment of principles, norms, goals etc. that determine the rightness or goodness of our conduct. Whereas if the focus is mainly on the virtue or goodness of the moral agents themselves, the subject matter of ethics will be the establishment and development of character virtues and motives that determine the virtue of the agents' character or being.[112] If the emphasis, however, is mainly on the appropriateness of an action in a particular situation, the subject matter of ethics will be the establishment of principles or criteria that determine the appropriateness of a decision and subsequent action.

---

106. Cf. Miller, *Living Ethically in Christ*, 232–44; cf. Robinson, *Groundwork*, 145–47; Fairweather and McDonald, *Quest*, 126–32.

107. Cf. Fairweather and McDonald, *Quest*, 3–37.

108. Cf. Darwall, "Introduction," 1–4.

109. Fairweather and McDonald, *Quest*, 38–55.

110. Cf. Wogaman, *Christian Ethics*, 230–33.

111. For the various forms of virtue ethics, see Porter, "Virtue ethics," 107.

112. Cf. Hollinger, *Choosing the Good*, 46.

A Response

Of great importance for the particular shape of a Christian ethic is also whether, first, a heteronomous or autonomous approach,[113] or a combination of both, secondly, an individual, communitarian, or collective approach,[114] thirdly, a rational or revelatory approach is implemented.[115]

Since a comprehensive discussion of these different approaches to Christian ethics is beyond the limits of our current study, we have to confine ourselves to a brief sketch of the concept of Christian ethics, which will serve as a basis for further discussion. We shall propose that *Christian ethics differs from other ethics because at its heart lies a love relationship between the believer and the triune God, who is love himself*. This approach is therefore "unabashedly theocentric and relational,"[116] as Grenz concludes for his own theonomous approach, which he prefers to a heteronomous or autonomous one: "The theonomous, in contrast, begins with humans-in-relationship. Above all it views us as persons who continually live before the Creator and with whom God has chosen to enter into covenant. As those who stand in a moral relationship with God, we are also called to cultivate proper relationships with each other and even with all creation. For this reason the ethical life is always life-in-relationship."[117]

Horrell, in fact, maintains that this relational nature of ethics can be found in Pauline ethics, since Paul is "concerned precisely with this 'structuring' of community life and with the *relational* pattern of morality which this requires."[118] Similarly, Motyer contends with regard to the "fruits of the Spirit" that all have "relational qualities . . . which are both emotional states and strategies for action in relationship."[119]

As to its content, this ethics of life-in-relationship shares many concerns of a character ethic. Hence, it is worth mentioning the main issues of a character ethic as summarized by Burtness:

> Character ethicists argue that morality is not a matter having to do with universal moral obligations (deontology), or with

---

113. Cf. Robinson, *Groundwork*, 148–70.

114. Robbins, *Methods in the Madness*, 8–10; Robbins, "Something in common?," 313–39, esp. 336–39.

115. Cf. Wogaman, *Christian Ethics*, 271.

116. Grenz, *Quest*, 252. Fairweather and McDonald, similarly, believe that "Christian ethics requires a relational model" (*Quest*, 243).

117. Grenz, *Quest*, 252. It is worth mentioning in this context that Neuer describes Schlatter's ethics as a "deeply theocentric-personal ethics." Neuer, *Zusammenhang*, 298.

118. Horrell, "Restructuring Human Relationships," 321.

119. Motyer, "Not Apart from Us," 236.

appropriate deeds in specific situations (situationism), or with future goods to be worked for in the present (teleology). Morality, character ethicists say, does not find its focus in the act at all, but rather in the actor. The focus is on character rather than conduct, on being rather than behaving, on who one is rather than on what one does. Morality is a matter, one could say, of the heart. Morality has to do not so much with what appears on the outside of a person, but with what is on the inside.[120]

However, while we whole-heartedly agree with the primacy of the actor over against the act, with the implications of this for ethics, and particularly with the notion of morality being a matter of the heart, we need to maintain the main focus on the relationship with God as the foundation and aim of Christian ethics and thus on the relational work of the Holy Spirit. Hence, we fully concur with Hauerwas that "the ethical issue is not just what we do but what we are and how what we are is formed by our fundamental convictions about the nature and significance of Christ,"[121] and, we might add, of the Father. Furthermore, Hauerwas rightly points out that "[c]haracter makes clear how fundamental a change must occur in the self if beliefs are to gain significance in our actual behavior and action."[122] We suggest, however, that by emphasizing the growing, deepening love relationship with God enabled by the relational work of the Spirit and resulting in changed relationships with self, others, and creation, we bridge the gap between the convictions of faith and ethical life.[123] The remolding of the character is part of this process of transformation enabled by the relational work of the Spirit but is not its ultimate goal. We will now examine in more depth the relationship between the relational work of the Spirit and ethical life.

Ethical Life as the Fruit of Living in the Loving Presence of God

The main emphasis here is on ethical life, i.e., living in loving relationships, as the *fruit* of living in the loving presence of God.[124] This implies

---

120. Burtness, *Consequences*, 83–84. Cf. Hollinger, *Choosing the Good*, 46.
121. Hauerwas, *Character*, 230.
122. Ibid., 227.
123. For a critique of Hauerwas's understanding of the role of the church in forming character, see Robbins, "Something in common," 336–37.
124. Cf. Fairweather and McDonald, *Quest*, 243.

A Response

that growth in ethical life is not something that we can bring about by ourselves. The following verse from 1 John 4:19 puts this thesis in a nutshell: "We love because he first loved us." God's love for us, therefore, always precedes our love and is the direct source of our ability to love.[125] But why is it that so often this truth seems to remain a "theological reality" rather than a "practical reality"? Chan, for instance, remarks tellingly: "At one level the relationship between justification and sanctification is quite straightforward: sanctification is a fruit of justification . . . But this theological reality does not always transform itself into practical reality. As many Christians have learned (more often sooner than later), the changed relationship that justification brings about does not automatically translate into a changed life."[126]

What in theory sounds so "straightforward" turns out to need a closer examination with a view to the practical applicability to everyday life. Even though we shall do this in more depth in the following chapter, it is worth pointing out the main reason why so often the growth of the ethical life is not experienced as taking place naturally and automatically despite one's living in loving relationship with God. The clue to this is the phrase "loving relationship"—since it is the extent to which we ourselves truly know ourselves to be loved by God which, as mentioned above, is the basis for our ability to love. However, it is not enough to have a prepositional or rational knowledge of God's love, as mentioned in the previous chapter. What is needed, instead, is an experiential, relational, personal knowledge of God—who is in his very essence love (1 John 4:16)— that reaches into the depths of our heart and enables true intimacy and ethical transformation. Rabens summarizes this poignantly when he draws attention to the fact that "it is primarily through deeper knowledge of, and an intimate relationship with, God, Jesus Christ and with the community of faith that people are transformed and empowered by the Spirit for religious-ethical life."[127] This "deeper knowledge" encompasses, first and foremost, the knowledge of the new filial relationship between the believer and God the Father, as mentioned in the previous chapter. It is this relational, felt knowledge that enables and brings forth ethical transformation since, as Dunn remarks, "the reality of God's adoption/acceptance reaches to the motivating and emotive center of the person."[128] This "reality" is brought

---

125. Cf. Lonsdale, *Eyes to See*, 63–64; Rabens, "Johannine Perspectives," 120–21.
126. Chan, *Spiritual Theology*, 79–80.
127. Rabens, *Spirit*, 123.
128. Dunn, *Epistle to the Galatians*, 219–20; cf. Rabens, *Spirit*, 230.

about by the Holy Spirit's relational work, enabling an encounter with the Father and the Son and thereby drawing us into an intimate relationship with God who is perfect love. Within this relationship we experience God's grace, forgiveness, and compassion, not as ideals, but as concrete realities due to the suffering love of the Father and the son uniquely revealed at the cross of Christ.[129] It is this love relationship that is the basis for transformation, as Fairweather and McDonald rightly contend: "the Christian's behaviour is a fruit of that relationship with the divine which is continually renewed."[130]

It is important to point out in this context that in order for the relationship with God to be truly loving it needs to encompass all one's faculties, including one's emotions. With a view to the latter, Vacek comments that "[a]n emotional acceptance of being loved is essential to a full Christian life."[131] He emphasizes especially the aspect of the emotions in this context in order to rebalance the often one-sided emphasis he observes in Western philosophy on the "intellect in dogma and the will in morality as obedience to God's will."[132] Particularly with the view to the work of the Spirit, Holotik, similarly, affirms that the Spirit reaches the very depths of our being, inlcuding our emotions, if we open ourselves up to the Spirit's work.[133]

In this context, it is worth mentioning that although Bockmuehl did attempt to break out of that mold by emphasizing guidance by the Spirit, he, nevertheless, neglected to properly draw attention to the role of our emotions and "the core of our being,"[134] with its, at times, unconscious drives and compulsions, deepest desires and longings. Bockmuehl did attempt to recover the importance of the works of supererogation as works done out of love and compelled by the Spirit. However, to be compelled by love (cf. 2 Cor 5:14), which is the fruit of living in a loving, intimate relationship with God, should not be limited to works that go beyond the law but to the whole of one's life. Drengson, for instance, points out that "[i]t is easy to think that it does not matter what we feel so long as we *act* in the right ways. And this is true as far as the law goes. But how we

---

129. Cf. D. D. Williams, *Spirit*, 5.
130. Fairweather and McDonald, *Quest*, 243; cf. Hauerwas, *Character*, 215.
131. Vacek, *Love*, 128.
132. Ibid., 6; cf. Lonsdale, *Dance to the Music*, 120.
133. Cf. Holotik, *Pneumatologie*, 164; cf. Holmes, *Becoming More Human*, 101.
134. Vanier, *Becoming Human*, 132.

A Response

feel determines how we are spiritually and vice versa."[135] Our underlying motives, desires, emotions, and passions are, indeed, of great importance, since they have direct bearing upon our ability to truly live in loving relationship with God, self, and creation. Stassen and Gushee, therefore, argue that we need to become aware of our passions in case they need transformation, since they play a significant moral role.[136] Since, as Harak suggests, "our passions can be morally praise- or blameworthy," it is important to find ways how to transform the blameworthy ones and how to cultivate the praiseworthy ones.[137] This transformation of our emotions and passions is brought about through the relational work of the Spirit, through the intimate love-relationship with God.[138] Hence, it is crucial to understand how we can grow in loving relationship with God, self, and others.

Growing in Loving Relationship with God, Self, and Others

Since living in loving relationship with God, self, and others lies at the heart of Christian ethics, it is worth exploring in more detail how it is possible to grow in these relationships and what the obstacles are that prevent us from living in this way.[139] However, writing about growing in loving relationship with God, self, and others is a difficult endeavor due to the fact that it is nearly impossible to separate these different relationships from each other. Olthuis rightly points out that "[a]ll these connections are intimately interrelated . . . The way to wholesome connection with self is via good connection with others, and affirming connections with others comes via affirming connection with self . . . The goal, pure and simple, is increased intimacy with self, others, and God. A healthy person is neither a separated self in grand isolation nor a fused self without boundaries;

---

135. Drengson, "Compassion and Transcendence," 39.

136. Cf. Stassen and Gushee, *Kingdom Ethics*, 63; Hursthouse, *On Virtue Ethics*, 108–20. Hursthouse even suggests that emotions are "a part of our rational nature" since "the emotions involve ideas or images (or thoughts or perceptions) of good and evil" (ibid., 109, 111).

137. Harak, *Virtuous Passions*, 2; cf. Vacek, *Love*, 9–10, 16.

138. Cf. Wadell, *Friendship*, 24–25.

139. With this chapter we are attempting to integrate Christian ethics into spirituality, as mentioned above, and will therefore include literature dealing with the issues of spirituality and spiritual formation.

PART THREE—A Critical Appraisal

rather, he or she is a cohesive, bounded self in wholesome connections, interdependent with other selves, the earth, and God."[140]

This interrelatedness of the different relationships can be traced back to the fact that the human heart longs, above all, for real, deep communion without which it cannot find peace.[141] This thirst for true communion can only be filled by the experience of our being loved by and loving God, self, and others. In fact, the more we truly know ourselves to be loved just as we are, the more we are able to love others since, as Daniel D. Williams suggests, "[t]he discovery that we are loved does have a causally efficacious power which creates through that experience the transformation of the self."[142] Similarly, Lafollette suggests that this knowledge "will also increase the opportunities for personal and moral growth."[143]

It is, therefore, of importance to at least attempt an outline of the obstacles that keep us from knowing ourselves to be loved by God, self, and others, not only because they impede us in our ability to truly love others, but, more importantly, because only in communion with God, self, and others can we find "life, and have it to the full" (John 10:10), as Jesus promised. In this context it is worth quoting Merton, who observes that "[i]t is a curious fact that in the traditional polemic between action and contemplation, modern apologists for the 'contemplative' life have tended to defend it on pragmatic grounds—in terms of action and efficacy. In other words, monks and nuns in cloisters are not 'useless', because they are engaged in a very efficacious kind of spiritual activity."[144] This reminds us of the early Bockmuehl with his tendency to emphasize relationship with God in order to be equipped for service. Instead, what is needed is an approach to ethics and spirituality that avoids "the habit of acting out of the profit-and-results mode of thinking."[145] Only when we focus on our communion with God as the goal of our Christian life and existence can we grow in loving and serving others as well. Similarly, Nouwen points out: "Here we are touching the profound spiritual truth that service is an

---

140. Olthuis, *Beautiful Risk*, 102.

141. Cf. Nouwen, *Here and Now*, 43; Vanier, *Our Journey Home*, 49–50; Augustine, *Confessions* 1.1 (21).

142. D. D. Williams, *Spirit*, 120.

143. Lafollette, *Personal Relationships*, 199.

144. Merton, *Contemplation*, 173.

145. Beumer, *Henri Nouwen*, 126.

A Response

expression of the search for God and not just of the desire to bring about individual or social change."[146]

When turning to the question of the obstacles that prevent us from living in loving relationship with God, self, and others, we need to face the truth about the world's fallenness and subsequent brokenness. For, as Vanier maintains, "[l]ittle by little, we human beings discover our inability to fulfill our deep thirst for communion. This inability springs from our fear of love, which finds its source in our own wounded and broken hearts and in the wounded and broken hearts of others."[147] This brokenness often leads to a "dividedness"[148] of the heart, to the "[d]isconnection from one's authentic self," which results in an estrangement from oneself, from one's own heart, which is "the very place we meet others and God." Alienation from God and others as well as the experience of desolation are the predictable consequences.[149]

Hence, in order for us to be able to live in loving relationship with God, self, and others we need to embark upon a journey of self-discovery, the discovery of our hearts, and simultaneously the discovery of true love—from God and from others.[150] This journey is a journey that does not stay on the surface but explores the depths of our hearts.

This journey toward love is directly linked to the relational work of the Spirit since it is the Spirit as the loving presence of God who enables this journey toward true loving communion with God, self, and others, hence, toward true freedom, integration, and wholeness. With regard to this journey, Crane observes that "*[t]he beginning of this risky and pain-filled journey comes when the dissonance between what is held intellectually and what is really believed in the hidden parts of the soul is exposed.*

There is a shift in the interior landscape which announces the movement of the Spirit, a kind of earthquake, a tremor which shakes the surface of life. It is the movement towards integration and integrity, the gifts of God."[151]

146. Nouwen et al., *Compassion*, 29; cf. Merton, *Contemplation*, 178.
147. Vanier, *Our Journey Home*, 50.
148. C. Williams, *Singleness of Heart*, 15.
149. Olthuis, *Beautiful Risk*, 166.
150. Keane believes that "[t]he more one can know one's deepest self, know the core of one's existence, the more apt one's moral judgements are likely to be. Here again we see that moral theology involves a deeper vision of reality, a vision which may be significantly enriched by the power of the Holy Spirit" ("The Role of the Holy Spirit," 99).
151. Crane, *Forgiving God*, 6.

PART THREE—A Critical Appraisal

This movement toward integration will in time include the facing of the painful memories and the walls and habits of protection since the latter, though once necessary for survival, keep even true, perfect love out.[152] For these wounds of the heart at times result in the feelings of intense shame, guilt, anger, and fear, leading the wounded person to have a negative image of themselves. This aspect of the possible negative image of oneself and the influence of the wounds upon one's in-/ability both to discern God's voice and to carry out Jesus' double commandment of love was not sufficiently recognized and explored by Bockmuehl. Yet, it is important to take this issue into account since, as Lonsdale remarks, "we are habitually, though often unconsciously, unable to accept ourselves as we really are."[153] The consequence often is that we have a distorted image of ourselves and doubt our own worth, especially in comparison to others.[154]

However, the problem is that discovering the disintegration of our hearts can be very difficult indeed, since we often resist facing the hidden things in our lives, such as the real motives and desires that influence our actions.[155] Daniel D. Williams describes this dividedness of the heart in the following way: "What needs to be emphasized is that in this fall within the self some sort of *self-betrayal* is involved. It is not—notice—that we betray our *best* self; that is a moralistic way to put it. We betray our *real* self, with its struggling, its hopes and fears. We refuse to trust ourselves in our real relation to anything. We refuse to believe that life is good and worthy for us as we really are, that our small margin of freedom with all its risks makes the difference between fulfilling life and destroying it."[156]

Without the Spirit as the loving, gracious presence of God, this uncovering of our brokenness and our true motives would be unbearable. Only in the presence of God's grace can we face our own brokenness and the hurts this brokenness causes others.[157] McGrath describes the relationship between God's grace and human agency in the following way: "The sun is always radiating its illumination. Nevertheless, for that light to

152. Cf. ibid., 3, 19; Vanier, *Our Journey Home*, 67.
153. Lonsdale, *Dance to the Music*, 123.
154. Cf. ibid.
155. Cf. C. Williams, *Singleness of Heart*, 15. Williams draws our attention to the fact that "if we are not aware of our unconscious motives, they will control us" (ibid., 19).
156. D. D. Williams, *Spirit*, 150–51.
157. Sell rightly points out that "[w]e do not first see our sins and then become aware of God's grace. Rather, 'We never see the face of sin so ugly, as in the glass of God's free love' (William Bridge)" (*Spirit*, 15).

A Response

enter into and illuminate a room in the house, a shutter must be opened. The opening of that shutter does not cause the sun to shine, in that this is already happening. Rather, the opening of the shutter is the means by which that light enters and illuminates the house . . . In the same way, human beings can remove obstacles to God's grace, so that they may develop and progress in the spiritual life."[158]

However, even for the removal of the obstacles we are dependent on the Spirit's work in us, helping us to face our wounds, our painful emotions, and our protective walls. Moreover, we also need God's love to be mediated to us by the Spirit through other human beings since their presence can be immensely supportive on this journey of self-discovery.[159] If this relationship is a truly loving, "life-giving" one, then it can become "the very medium of healing."[160] For, as Olthuis maintains, "[t]here is no Band-Aid for the bruising of the spirit, no elixir for hurting souls, no magic potion for broken hearts. Only experiencing love can heal a bruised spirit, a hurting soul, and a broken heart."[161] It is the relationship itself, the connection of love, the experience of being welcomed, accepted, wanted, and affirmed in one's totality, including the seemingly "shameful" and "bad" parts, that enables self-acceptance and self-love and thereby "the renewal and rebirth of the self."[162] Baumann also points to this close connection between being loved by others and self-love when he asserts that self-love is directly dependent on the experience of being loved by others.[163] The importance of other relationships for our ability to experience love and to love was, unfortunately, not spelt out enough in Bockmuehl's ethics. Holmes, in contrast, remarks that "[a]t a relational level, since it is relationships that have made us sick, it needs to be relationships, that help give us our wholeness."[164] This, however, indicates the problem: the more we have negative experiences with regard to relationships, the more we will find it difficult to truly trust another person, including God.[165] However, even though it might seem inconceivable for some people to learn

---

158. McGrath, *Christian Spirituality*, 46.
159. Cf. Lonsdale, *Dance to the Music*, 133.
160. Olthuis, *Beautiful Risk*, 103.
161. Ibid., 66.
162. Ibid., 103.
163. Cf. Baumann, *Liquid Love*, 80.
164. Holmes, *Becoming More Human*, 106.
165. Sell, for instance, believes that "the sincere sinner often knows that believing is the one thing that he, unaided, cannot do" (*Spirit*, 15).

Part Three—A Critical Appraisal

to trust again, for instance, deeply traumatized people, we concur with Fairweather and McDonald that no one is beyond redemption. It is possible for these people to have a "moment of truth"[166] when they discover that they are loved unconditionally, even if they do not feel worthy of it. In fact, as Merton expresses it, "the discovery that worthiness is of no special consequence (since no one could ever, by himself, be strictly worthy to be loved with such a love) is a true liberation of the spirit" and is brought about through the "[r]evelation of the mercy of God."[167]

This brings us to the crucial issue of the importance of our image of God for our journey toward love. Reed argues in the foreword to her book *The Genesis of Ethics: On the Authority of God as the Origin of Christian Ethics* that "[t]he genesis of Christian ethics is found in the authority of God. For many, the authority of God is the problem of Christian ethics, not its answer. Indeed, it may yet prove to be that, if authority is associated in Christian theory and polity with authoritarianism, patriarchy and legalism." In contrast, she advocates that "God's authority can be equated with divine grace, and it is here that we find the generative principles of Christian ethics."[168] Different from Bockmuehl, she suggests that "this authority is not of a controlling or hegemonic kind but of the dialogic, answerable kind, which draws human persons into relationship."[169]

When turning to the concept of "obedience" to God, which Bockmuehl emphasizes as the primary response to God's will, it is important to safeguard against an authoritarian interpretation of the word in order to avoid the notion of fear. According to 1 John 4:18 (cf. Rom 8:15), love and fear are mutually exclusive: "There is no fear in love. But perfect love drives out fear, because fear has to do with punishment. The one who fears is not made perfect in love." Hence, any fear or anxiety in us with regard to God is an indication of our brokenness and points to the fact that we still need to discover the healing love of God in a way that will truly inspire us with love and confidence rather than fear.

In this context, it is worth pointing out the crucial role of imagination, since it is through imagination that we can make God present in our mind.[170] Oswald Chambers even claimed that "[i]magination is the

---

166. Fairweather and McDonald, *Quest*, 243.
167. Merton, *New Seeds*, 75.
168. Reed, *Genesis of Ethics*, xxiii.
169. Ibid., xxiv.
170. Cf. Boyd, *Seeing is Believing*, 72–73.

A Response

greatest gift God has given us."[171] Rather than just having to wait passively for God, we can actively use our imagination to visualize those images of God that convey his love to us. This could, for instance, be the image of God the Father running toward us, welcoming us home. How closely imagination and transformation are connected can be seen in the following interpretation of 2 Corinthians 3:18 by Rabens: "the Spirit-enabled beholding of the glory of the Lord works transformation, because one (almost naturally) changes more and more into the likeness of the object of contemplation."[172]

Only the contemplation of a God who loves us unconditionally and graciously can lead us to true freedom—freedom from fear of rejection, from toxic guilt and shame, and from destructive anger. It is only when we can believe that God's love toward us does not in any way depend on our "goodness" or our performance and can, therefore, never be lost, can we be truly free to be our authentic selves (cf. Rom 8:38–39). The best example for God's completely unconditional forgiveness can be found in the parable of the Prodigal Son (Luke 15).

However, Tournier points to the paradoxical nature of our response to grace when he describes how we keep resisting the free offer of salvation while at the same time deeply longing for it.[173] The acceptance of grace will always include some kind of dying to the exterior, false self, as Merton highlights. The more our identity is linked to this exterior self, the more we will try and resist this process. Yet, we can learn to choose those things that free us from our exterior self and that open up new ways for us to be.[174] This death of the exterior self, this letting go of our attempt to earn God's love, can be extremely painful since it involves a process of grieving our desire for self-righteousness and admiration. For this process to happen we need to take time to let this gracious love reach our minds and our hearts in the here and now so that it can become an experience of transformation. Pinnock, for instance, admits that he neglected the affective side of his faith by mainly focusing on intellectual analysis. He describes how he "substituted the knowledge of the Bible for the skills of interacting with God himself. I did not trust personal experience but have relegated

---

171. Chambers, *My Utmost for His Highest*, 48 (Feb. 11). Regarding the Ignatian "imaginative contemplation," see Lonsdale, *Eyes to See*, 85.

172. Rabens, "Transforming Relationships," 11; cf. Rabens, *Spirit*, 184–203; Boyd, *Seeing is Believing*, 152.

173. Cf. Tournier, *Guilt and Grace*, 195.

174. Merton, *New Seeds*, 15–16; cf. Kierkegaard, *Either/Or*, 253–54; Nouwen, *Reaching Out*, 20.

matters of the heart to an inferior place . . . Fortunately, I was touched by God in many contexts of renewal, and the Lord has drawn me higher up and deeper into his trinitarian love, which embraces us all."[175]

Furthermore, accepting God's gracious love will always feel like a risk due to the fact that others did not always react in a gracious way toward us. Often it is the case that the less grace we experienced in our lives, the more we feel wounded. Through experiencing true gracious love, which often involves grieving for the love we did not receive, we are enabled to lower the barriers we erected around our wounds. Yet, however painful the process of letting go might be, it is truly freeing to receive grace. The more we are conscious of God's unconditional acceptance, the less we need to strive to gain other people's approval and esteem. Indeed, as Clifford Williams claims: "Grace liberates us from our apprehensive and uneasy striving to vindicate ourselves."[176]

Hence, we do not need to hide parts of ourselves before God even if we think they are unacceptable. Only through acknowledging our seemingly "bad" parts, including our addictions and compulsions, which have been rejected and hidden for so long, and bringing them into the light of God's gracious love can they lose their power over us.

Furthermore, Vanier is convinced that "God touches us in the core of our being, deeper than our compulsions for power and admiration or our fears of rejection and feelings of guilt. God reveals the uniqueness and preciousness of our being just as we are."[177] This he does by helping us accept and love ourselves, as Nouwen points out: "[w]hen you befriend your true self and discover that it is good and beautiful, you will see Jesus there. Where you are most human, most yourself, weakest, there Jesus lives. Bringing your fearful self home is bringing Jesus home."[178] It is, therefore, important to learn to keep staying connected to the place of love, to our heart, which often entails grieving the pain of rejection and the pain of the brokenness of this world.

In this context we need to point to the significance of suffering love, particularly to the suffering and death of Jesus Christ on the cross and the suffering of the Father. We fully agree with Pinnock and Brow that what is needed is an additional "relational understanding of the cross, in which we frame the problem as broken relationships, not divine anger and honor.

175. Pinnock, "Foreword," 7.
176. C. Williams, *Singleness of Heart*, 44.
177. Vanier, *Becoming Human*, 132.
178. Nouwen, *The Inner Voice of Love*, 41.

A Response

God is healing relationships through his action. He is drawing wayward children home and re-creating right family relations."[179] It was on the cross that God took upon himself our sin with all its consequences, all the pain and hurt. By deciding not to retaliate but, instead, to forgive, he opens the way to redemption and reconciliation. Yet, this comes at a high price, as Pinnock and Brow point out: "The pain of the cross is the cost to God of restoring the broken relationship."[180] The cross is the place where we can see to what immense degree God values our hearts and longs for our communion with him—so much so that he was prepared to give up his son and his life out of love for us.

Furthermore, the cross is the place where we can find release from our anger. The cross can stop the cycle of either self-harm and self-destruction, if the anger at being hurt was turned inward,[181] or of harming others in the case of outward aggression. The true, astounding nature of God's suffering love is revealed in the fact that God wants us to rather wound him than to destroy ourselves or others. He is prepared to die at our hands in order that we might experience that love is stronger than our "badness," than our anger, than our hatred. Through turning the other cheek, through enduring our anger, God can free us from our fear of ourselves—the fear of being "too bad" and, therefore, the fear of rejection. By, for instance, facing our worst emotions and exposing them to the light of God's gracious, forgiving love, we can experience that truly nothing "will be able to separate us from the love of God that is in Christ Jesus our Lord" (Rom 8:39).[182] This experience of forgiveness teaches us true humility toward others. Reinhold Niebuhr maintains that in order to extend love and

---

179. Pinnock and Brow, *Unbounded Love*, 103.

180. Ibid.

181. Crane writes about the anger of the victim of abuse: "The anger is her only witness to the invisible crimes against her, and the only defendant of the inward place that could never be reached by the invasion of another" (cf. *Forgiving God*, 8).

182. Crane describes this experience of anger directed at the cross from the perspective of someone who has suffered in childhood: "Her fury has no bounds. There, she cries, now you know what it is like. Now you suffer too and I am glad. She reaches, as it were, for the whips, and joins in the scourging of his body. Now you suffer and I am glad. It is what you deserve for making it possible for me to suffer, not just me but millions of other children, millions of adults . . . The anger which has defended her for so long, but which has also entrapped her in the past, is released. At the same moment she is horrified. This is not what a 'nice' person does. This is not how a faithful Christian person responds to the suffering of Christ. Her first reaction, of empathy with the suffering Christ, and of gratitude to him—those were the correct responses. Where has all this hatred come from? Could it be that she is not the 'good' person she has always tried to be?" (Crane, *Forgiving God*, 23).

Part Three—A Critical Appraisal

forgiveness in situations of conflict, we need to have acknowledged our own need for forgiveness due to our sinfulness. Only when we accept that, before God, our own righteousness is woefully inadequate are we willing to forgive others, including our enemies.

Moreover, the cross also uniquely reveals to us the sym-pathy of God, the "suffering-with" character of God's love, as shown above.[183] Olthuis points out that

> [r]emaining true to self, God suffers-with the creation, enters into our brokenness in the Word Made Flesh in solidarity with our pain, and holds us fast in the Spirit's healing love. A way opens for a ministry of compassion and suffering love. In a life bent by suffering, broken by sin and evil, the *with* character of love intensifies, showing its face as suffering-with. Compassion takes on brokenness and evil in order to contest, defy, and overcome it. As God suffers with those who suffer, as God mourns with those who mourn, we are called to suffer-with and to mourn-with those who suffer and mourn. In voluntary suffering-with—distinct from the involuntary suffering-from that we all undergo—there is the liberating power not only to resist suffering, but also to redeem creation.[184]

It is through experiencing the suffering, forgiving, empathizing love of God, often through communion with others, that the Spirit heals our wounds and enables us to become "wounded healers,"[185] a phrase coined by Nouwen. This means that we can become people who, despite our own brokenness, share God's compassion with a fallen and hurting world. Even though this does include taking "compassionate action"[186] in solidarity with the oppressed, the needy, the hurting, the emphasis for Nouwen, in contrast to Bockmuehl,[187] is on the aspect of *being* rather than *doing*: "[O]ur real gift is not so much what we can do, but who we are. The real question is not 'What can we offer each other?' but 'Who can we be for each other?'"[188] This is closely linked to the aspect of *becoming* who God created us to be since we are on a journey to becoming our authentic, compassionate selves in loving relationship with God, self, and others.

---

183. Cf. pages 207–11.
184. Olthuis, *Beautiful Risk*, 45.
185. Cf. Nouwen, *The Wounded Healer*.
186. Nouwen et al., *Compassion*, 114.
187. Cf., for instance, Bockmuehl, "Leiblichkeit," 41.
188. Nouwen, *Life of the Beloved*, 90.

A Response

Even though this journey might at times lead "through the darkest valley" (Ps 23:4), our hope rests in the fact that the Spirit as the loving presence of God is *guiding us home*. "Through the Spirit we come 'home' to the divine life the Father intends for us—and freely shares with us—in the Son."[189]

---

189. Grenz, "Holy Spirit," 12.

Conclusion

This study set out to offer an introduction to Bockmuehl's theology and in particular an analysis of the role of the Holy Spirit in his Christian ethics. We discovered that one of Bockmuehl's greatest contributions to ethics can be found in his attempt at recovering the crucial role of the Holy Spirit for *specific Christian ethics*: first and foremost, with regard to its foundation, i.e., for regeneration and transformation, by indwelling believers and realizing the lordship of God in their lives; second, with regard to *redemption ethics* with its main features of love for God, spirituality, mission, including Christian service, and sanctification; thirdly, with regard to *differential ethics* by offering personal and situational guidance to the individual believer. As I have shown, it was particularly the neglect of this latter aspect of the role of the Spirit in the history of Christian ethics that Bockmuehl lamented time and again since he believed that an ethic without the aspect of guidance by the Spirit tends toward legalism, which, in turn, might breed an antinomian reaction.[1] Bockmuehl himself was convinced that only by holding together the double principle of law and Spirit can a Christian ethic avoid the dangers of either legalism or antinomianism. Hence, with regard to the question mentioned in the introduction of this book, "How do we know what God's will is in a particular situation?" Bockmuehl's answer is to point to the double principle of law and Spirit, and, more precisely, the guidance of the Spirit within the framework of Scripture.

Even though I evaluated positively Bockmuehl's rediscovery of the importance of the Holy Spirit for Christian ethics, I went on to critique his emphasis on the guidance by the Spirit as the main function of the Spirit in Christian ethics and, instead, proposed that the relational function of the Spirit should be central. Rather than focusing mainly on the informative function of the Spirit, I emphasized that the primary role of the Holy Spirit is to draw believers into an intimate love-relationship with the Father and

1. Cf. *GG*, 521.

the Son by mediating God's loving presence. This avoids the tendency toward functionalism and task-orientation apparent particularly in the early Bockmuehl due to his view of the furtherance of the kingdom of God as the sole horizon, purpose, and aim of Christian life. Instead, I suggested that it is the union and communion with God that is the foundation and aim of the Christian life and that ethical life, defined as living in loving relationships, is the *fruit* of living in this loving presence of God. This raised the question of how it is possible to grow in these loving relationships and what the obstacles are that prevent us from living in this way, which are dealt with in the last section of the study.

It would be interesting to further explore some of the questions raised in this study from a psychological angle. For instance, it could be worthwhile to compare and potentially integrate our findings with attachment theory. There is also scope for further research with regard to the corporate aspect of the Spirit's transformation. Due to Bockmuehl's own emphasis on the individual's search for God's will and his solution of guidance by the Spirit, the study did not explore further how the Spirit's transforming work can be experienced corporately and what role the community plays within it.

The significance of this study lies not only in the fact that it is the first in-depth study on Bockmuehl, but also in the fact that it explores and answers relevant questions such as how to experience the Spirit's inner transformation that leads to a greater ability to live in loving relationships and how to know God's will in one's life. These questions lie at the heart of the Christian faith and life and are of concern to theologians and lay people alike.

I hope that in this book I have been able to mine some of the theological, ethical, and spiritual riches in Bockmuehl's theology and to take my reader on a Spirit-filled journey toward a deeper understanding and experience of a "love so amazing, so divine"[1] that empowers us to truly live in loving relationship with God, self, others, and the whole of creation.

---

1. From the fourth verse of Isaac Watts's hymn *When I survey*.

Bibliography

Works Cited

Adeney, Bernard T. *Strange Virtues: Ethics in a Multicultural World*. Leicester: Apollo, 1995.
Althaus, Paul. *The Ethics of Martin Luther*. Philadelphia: Fortress, 1965.
———. *Gebot und Gesetz: zum Thema "Gesetz und Evangelium."* Beiträge zur Förderung christlicher Theologie 46/2. Gütersloh: Bertelsmann, 1952.
———. *The Theology of Martin Luther*. Philadelphia: Fortress, 1966.
Amstutz, J. *Charles de Foucauld in Tamanrasset. Forscher, Politiker, Mönch und Missionar*. Romero-Haus-Protokolle 56. Lucerne, Switzerland: Romero-Haus, 1993.
Augsburger, Myron S., *The Robe of God. Reconciliation, the Believers Church Essential*. Scottdale, PA: Herald, 2000.
Augustine. *Confessions*. Harmondsworth, UK: Penguin, 1961.
———. *Letters of Saint Augustine, Bishop of Hippo*. Vol. 6/1. Edited by Marcus Dods. Edinburgh: T. & T. Clark, 1872.
Badcock, Gary D. "The Concept of Love: Divine and Human." In *Nothing Greater, Nothing Better. Theological Essays on the Love of God*, edited by Kevin J. Vanhoozer, 30-46. Grand Rapids: Eerdmans, 2001.
Bailey, Kenneth E. *The Cross and the Prodigal: Luke 15 through the Eyes of Middle Eastern Peasants*. Downers Grove: IVP, 2005.
Balthasar, Hans U. von. *ABC des Christentums*. Heidelberg: Evangelisches Studentenpfarramt Heidelberg, 1967.
———. *The Christian State of Life*. Translated by Sister Mary F. McCarthy. San Francisco: Ignatius, 1983.
———. *Cordula oder Der Ernstfall*. Einsiedeln: Johannes, 1966.
Barnette, Henlee H. *Introducing Christian Ethics*. Nashville: Broadman, 1961.
———. "The New Ethics: 'Love Alone.'" In *The Situation Ethics Debate*, edited by Harvey Cox, 121-40. Phildelphia: Westminster, 1968.
———. *The New Theology and Morality*. Philadelphia: Westminster, 1967.
Barron, Robert. *And Now I See . . . A Theology of Transformation*. New York: Crossroad, 1998.
Barth, Karl. *Church Dogmatics*. 2/2: *The Doctrine of God*. Edited by G. W. Bromiley and T. F. Torrance. Translated by G. W. Bromiley et al. Edinburgh: T. & T. Clark, 1957.

Bibliography

———. *Church Dogmatics*. 3/1: *The Doctrine of Creation*. Edited by G. W. Bromiley and T. F. Torrance. Translated by J. W. Edwards et al. Edinburgh: T. & T. Clark, 1958.

———. *Church Dogmatics*. 3/4: *The Doctrine of Creation*. Edited by G. W. Bromiley and T. F. Torrance. Translated by A. T. Mackay et al. Edinburgh: T. & T. Clark, 1961.

———. *Church Dogmatics*. 4/2: *The Doctrine of Reconciliation*. Edited by G. W. Bromiley and T. F. Torrance. Translated by G. W. Bromiley. Edinburgh: T. & T. Clark, 1958.

———. *Church Dogmatics*. 4/3.2: *The Doctrine of Reconciliation*. Edited by G. W. Bromiley and T. F. Torrance. Translated by G. W. Bromiley. Edinburgh: T. & T. Clark, 1962.

———. *Church Dogmatics*. 4/4: *The Doctrine of Reconciliation*. Edited by G. W. Bromiley and T. F. Torrance. Translated by G. W. Bromiley. Edinburgh: T. & T. Clark, 1969.

———. "Concluding Unscientific Postcript on Schleiermacher." In *The Theology of Schleiermacher: Lectures at Göttingen, Winter Semester of 1923/24*, edited by Dietrich Rischl, translated by Geoffrey W. Bromiley, 261–79. Edinburgh: T. & T. Clark, 1982.

———. *The Epistle to the Romans*. Translated by Edwyn C. Hoskyns from the 6th ed. London: Oxford University Press, 1968.

———. *How I Changed My Mind*. Introduction and epilogue by John D. Godsey. Edinburgh: St. Andrew, 1969.

———. *The Humanity of God*. Translated by Thomas Wieser et al. London: Collins, 1961.

———. *The Theology of John Calvin*. Translated by Geoffrey W. Bromiley. Grand Rapids: Eerdmans, 1995.

Bauch, H. *Die Lehre vom Wirken des Heiligen Geistes im Frühpietismus*. Hamburg: Reich, 1974.

Bauckham, Richard. *God Crucified: Monotheism and Christology in the New Testament*. Carlisle: Paternoster, 1998.

———. "'Only the Suffering God Can Help': Divine Passibility in Modern Theology." *Themelios* 9, no. 3 (1984) 6–12.

———. "Stewardship and relationship." In *The Care of Creation: Focusing Concern and Action*, edited by Robert J. Berry, 99–106. Leicester: IVP, 2000.

Bauman, Zygmunt. *Liquid Love. On the Frailty of Human Bonds*. Cambridge: Polity, 2003.

Belmans, Theo G. *Der objektive Sinn menschlichen Handelns: zur Ehemoral des heiligen Thomas*. Vallendar, Germany: Patris, 1984.

Bennema, Cor. *The Power of Saving Wisdom: An Investigation of Spirit and Wisdom in Relation to the Soteriology of the Fourth Gospel*. Wissenschaftliche Untersuchungen zum Neuen Testament 2/148. Tübingen: Mohr/Siebeck, 2002.

Berdyaev, Nicolas. *The Destiny of Man*. 2nd ed. London: Bles, 1945.

———. *The Meaning of History*. London: Bles, 1936.

———. *Slavery and Freedom*. London: Bles, 1943.

Beumer, Jurjen. *Henri Nouwen. A Restless Seeking for God*. New York: Crossroad, 1997.

Beyerhaus, Peter. Letter to Bockmuehl, March 10, 1970. Unpublished manuscript in the Bockmuehl archives in St. Chrischona.

Beyreuther, Erich. "Vorwort." In *Selbstzeugnisse August Hermann Franckes*, edited by Erich Beyreuther, 7–12. Marburg: Francke-Buchhandlung, 1963.

Bibliography

Biggar, Nigel. "Barth's trinitarian ethic." In *The Cambridge Companion to Karl Barth*, edited by John Webster, 212-27. Cambridge: Cambridge University Press, 2000.

Bloch, Ernst. *Atheismus im Christentum: Zur Religion des Exodus und des Reichs*. Frankfurt: Suhrkamp, 1968.

Bockmuehl, Klaus, "After Lausanne—What?" *Christianity Today* 19 (March 14, 1975) 67-68.

———. "Die Aktualität des Pietismus." In *Denken im Horizont der Wirklichkeit Gottes. Schriften zur Dogmatik und Theologiegeschichte*, edited by Rainer Mayer, 291-333. BWA 2/1. Giessen, Germany: Brunnen, 1999.

———. *Atheismus in der Christenheit: Anfechtung und Überwindung*. Vol. 1, *Die Unwirklichkeit Gottes in Theologie und Kirche*. 3rd ed. Giessen, Germany: Brunnen, 1985.

———. "Die Beurteilung der Abtreibung in der Frühzeit der christlichen Kirchen." In *Leben nach dem Willen Gottes. Schriften zur Materialethik*, edited by Rainer Mayer, 63-75. BWA 2/3. Giessen, Germany: Brunnen, 2006.

———. "Certificate of attendance at lectures at The London School of Economics," issued June 19, 1956. Unpublished private manuscript in the Bockmuehl archives in St. Chrischona.

———. *The Challenge of Marxism: A Christian Response*. 2nd ed. Colorado Springs: Helmers & Howard, 1986.

———. "Christ an der Universität." Bockmuehl's manuscript for a lecture given in Caux. Unpublished manuscript in the Bockmuehl archives in St. Chrischona.

———. "The Christian as Lawyer." *Quaterly—Christian Legal Society* 2, no. 1 (1981) 10-11, 33-35.

———. "Christianity has a Moral Backbone." *Christianity Today* 23 (Oct. 6, 1978) 54-55.

———. *The Christian Way of Living: An Ethics of the Ten Commandments*. Vancouver: Regent College Bookstore, 1994.

———. Circular letter written on December 1967. Unpublished manuscript in the Bockmuehl archives in St. Chrischona.

———. Circular letter written on December 12, 1977. Unpublished manuscript in the Bockmuehl archives in St. Chrischona.

———. Circular letter written December 26, 1979. Unpublished manuscript in the Bockmuehl archives in St. Chrischona.

———. Circular letter to his friends on June 29, 1985 (English). Unpublished manuscript in the Bockmuehl archives in St. Chrischona.

———. Circular letter in January 1986. Unpublished manuscript in the Bockmuehl archives in St. Chrischona.

———. Circular letter written on December 5, 1988. Unpublished manuscript in the Bockmuehl archives in St. Chrischona.

———. *Conservation and Lifestyle*. Translated by Bruce N. Kaye. Bramcote, UK: Grove, 1977.

———. "Curriculum vitae." Written April 6, 1959 in Basel. Unpublished private manuscript in the Bockmuehl archives in St. Chrischona.

———. "Curriculum Vitae." Written January 14, 1977 in Basel (english). Unpublished private manuscript in the Bockmuehl archives in St. Chrischona.

Bibliography

———. "Der Dienst der Theologie." In *Denken im Horizont der Wirklichkeit Gottes. Schriften zur Dogmatik und Theologiegeschichte*, edited by Rainer Mayer. BWA 2/1, 75–80. Giessen, Germany: Brunnen, 1999.

———. "Destroyer or Provider." *Christianity Today* 19 (June 6, 1975) 49–50.

———. "Die Diskussion über Homosexualität in theologischer Sicht." *EvTh* 24 (1964) 242–266.

———. "Dogmatisches zur Tauffrage." In *Denken im Horizont der Wirklichkeit Gottes. Schriften zur Dogmatik und Theologiegeschichte*, edited by Rainer Mayer, 3–11. BWA 2/1. Giessen, Germany: Brunnen, 1999.

———. "Eindrücke von der Arbeit." 1966. Unpublished manuscript in the Bockmuehl archives in St. Chrischona.

———. "Der einzelne und die Gemeinschaft (1 Kor 1,10)." In *Wer hört, wird leben, St. Chrischona-Predigten*, edited by Edgar Schmid, 57–64. Giessen, Germany: Brunnen, 1975.

———. "Erneuerung (Johannes 21, 15–17)." *Glaubensbote, Pilgermission St. Chrischona* 96, no. 11 (1973) 204–5.

———. "Erziehung in einem Zeitalter der Revolution." *Informationsdienst der Moralischen Aufrüstung* 20, no. 24 (1968) 104–5.

———. "Ethics/Spiritual Life, Introduction." In *The Best in Theology*, edited by James I. Packer, 1:237–8. Carol Stream, IL: Christianity Today, 1987.

———. "European Evangelicals: Seeking a Reformation." *Christianity Today* 21 (Nov. 19, 1976) 61–62.

———. "Evangelical Assertions on Social Change." *Christianity Today* 20 (May 21, 1976) 45–46.

———. *Evangelicals and Social Ethics: A Commentary on Article 5 of the Lausanne Covenant*. Translated by David T. Priestley. Outreach and Identity 4. Downers Grove: IVP, 1979.

———. "Das Evangelium in der Begegnung mit dem Menschen unserer Zeit." In *Denken im Horizont der Wirklichkeit Gottes. Schriften zur Dogmatik und Theologiegeschichte*, edited by Rainer Mayer, 122–42. BWA 2/1. Giessen, Germany: Brunnen, 1999.

———. *Frank Buchmans Botschaft und ihre Bedeutung für die protestantischen Kirchen*. Bern: Haupt, 1963.

———. "Frank Buchman's Message and its Significance for the Protestant Churches." Translated by M. Fleischmann. Unpublished manuscript in the Bockmuehl archives in St. Chrischona.

———. "Friendship with Jesus." *Crux* 15, no. 2 (1979) 2–4.

———. "Gebote, Zehn." In *Evangelisches Gemeindelexikon*, edited by Helmut Burkhardt et al., 187–8. Wuppertal, Germany: Brockhaus, 1978.

———. "Die Geburt des neuen Menschen aus dem Glauben—Antwort an die Zukunftsmacher in Ost und West." *OJC Frbrief* 46, no. 1 (1976) 13–17.

———. "Eine Geschichte der Lehre von der Kirche." Unpublished manuscript in the Bockmuehl archives in St. Chrischona.

———. *Gesetz und Geist. Eine kritische Würdigung des Erbes protestantischer Ethik*. Vol. 1, *Die Ethik der reformatorischen Bekenntnisschriften*. Giessen, Germany: Brunnen, 1987.

———. "God and Other 'Forgotten Factors' in Theology." *Christianity Today* 26 (Feb. 19, 1982) 48–49.

Bibliography

———. *Gott im Exil? Zur Kritik der "Neuen Moral."* Wuppertal, Germany: Aussaat, 1975.
———. "The Great Commandment." In *With Heart, Mind and Strength. The Best of Crux 1979-1989*, edited by Donald M. Lewis, 1:9-26. Langley, BC: Credo, 1990.
———. *Das größte Gebot*. TuD 21. Giessen, Germany: Brunnen, 1980.
———. *Grundlagen christlicher Sexualethik*. Wuppertal, Germany: Aussaat, 1965.
———. "Homosexuality in Biblical Perspective." *Christianity Today* 17 (Feb. 16, 1973) 12-18.
———. "How Did Jesus Decide His Actions?" *Crux* 17, no. 4 (1981) 2-4.
———. "Humanism and the Kingdom of God." *ERT* 3 (1979) 206-24.
———. "India Report" (Shillong, 6th May 1970). Unpublished manuscript in the Bockmuehl archives in St. Chrischona.
———. "Introduction to the Theology of the (Nineteenth and) Twentieth Century." [Word-for-word notes by Bockmuehl's assistant Rory Randall taken during Bockmuehl's lectures from January 30 until April 24, 1986 at Regent College Vancouver.[1]] Unpublished manuscript in the Bockmuehl archives in St. Chrischona.
———. "Is Christianity a Counterculture?" *Christianity Today* 23 (Aug. 17, 1979) 52.
———. "Is there a Christian 'Life-style'?" *Christianity Today* 21 (May 20, 1977) 48-49.
———. "Journals." Unpublished private manuscripts in the Bockmuehl archives in St. Chrischona.
———. "Josef, der Ernährer (Christ und Wirtschaft)." Transcribed Radio-speech, Evangeliums-Rundfunk, Wetzlar, Dec. 17, 1982. Unpublished manuscript in the Bockmuehl archives in St. Chrischona.
———. "Karl Barth 1886-1986: An Evangelical Appraisal." *Crux* 22 (3/1986) 28-32.
———. "Keeping His Commandments." *ERT* 6 (1982) 85-99.)
———. "Kirche und soziale Verantwortung. Zum Thema Christentum und Sozialismus." *Theologie und Lebensführung. Gesammelte Aufsätze* 2, 130-145. Giessen, Germany: Brunnen, 1982.
———. "Klaus Bockmuehl." In *Anstiftungen. Chronik aus 20 Jahren OJC*, edited by Horst-Klaus Hofmann and Irmela Hofmann, 28. Moers: Brendow, 1988.
———. "Der Kommunismus auf der Suche nach dem neuen Menschen." *Reformatio* [Zeitschrift für Evangelische Kultur und Politik, Zürich: Verlag Reformatio] 12 (1963) 550-66.
———. "Kopfloser Pietismus." *OJC Frbrief* 143 (2/1993) 61-64.
———. "The Latter Letters of Barth." *Christianity Today* 20 (Aug. 27, 1976) 37.
———. "Law and the Spirit: Situation Ethics With a Difference." *Christianity Today* 22 (Febr. 24, 1978) 47, 49.
———. "Lean Years—Abundant Opportunity." *Christianity Today* 26 (Nov. 26, 1982) 68.
———. "Leben aus dem Evangelium." In *Leben mit dem Gott, der redet*, edited by Horst-Klaus Hofmann, 1-75. BWA 1/6. Giessen, Germany: Brunnen, 1998.
———. "Lebenslauf Klaus Erich Bockmuehl." Written in Lörrach/Baden, May 21, 1955. Unpublished private manuscript in the Bockmuehl archives in St. Chrischona.
———. "Die Leiblichkeit des Menschen in biblischer Sicht." In *Denken im Horizont der Wirklichkeit Gottes. Schriften zur Dogmatik und Theologiegeschichte*, edited by Rainer Mayer, 28-49. BWA 2/1. Giessen, Germany: Brunnen, 1999.

---

1. This information is from Burkhardt, "Einführung des Herausgebers." *VG*, xi.

Bibliography

———. *Leiblichkeit und Gesellschaft. Studien zur Religionskritik und Anthropologie im Frühwerk von Ludwig Feuerbach und Karl Marx*. 2nd rev. ed. with new epilogue. Giessen, Germany: Brunnen 1980.

———. Letter to the Professors and Lecturers at the Theological Faculty in Basel on September 28, 1963.

———. Letter to Karl Barth, October 26, 1963. Unpublished manuscript in the Bockmuehl archives in St. Chrischona.

———. Letter to Mr. Halfenberg, December 19, 1963. Unpublished manuscript in the Bockmuehl archives in St. Chrischona.

———. Letter to P. Engelbert Heller and Martin-Eckart Fuchs, March 5, 1965. Unpublished manuscript in the Bockmuehl archives in St. Chrischona.

———. Letter to Reinhard (Kuster), June 23, 1965. Unpublished manuscript in the Bockmuehl archives in St. Chrischona.

———. Letter to Wilhelm Busch, April 13, and May 30, 1966. Unpublished manuscript in the Bockmuehl archives in St. Chrischona.

———. Letter to Hans Urs von Balthasar, June 14, 1966. Unpublished manuscript in the Bockmuehl archives in St. Chrischona.

———. Letter to Rainer Klein, December 9, 1967, Heidelberg. Unpublished manuscript in the Bockmuehl archives in St. Chrischona.

———. Letter to Martin-Eckart Fuchs, Horst-Klaus Hofmann and Willi Dammerboer, March 29, 1968. Unpublished manuscript in the Bockmuehl archives in St. Chrischona.

———. Letter to Michael Herwig, March 23, 1968. Unpublished manuscript in the Bockmuehl archives in St. Chrischona.

———. Letter to Marienschwesternschaft, July 2, 1968. Unpublished manuscript in the Bockmuehl archives in St. Chrischona.

———. Letter to H. Eißler, the chairman of the ABH-Association, March 13, 1970. Unpublished manuscript in the Bockmuehl archives in St. Chrischona.

———. "Let Us Be Listeners." *Crux* 25, no. 2 (1989) 3–7.

———. *Listening to the God who speaks. Reflections on God's Guidance from the Scripture and the Lives of God's People*. Colorado Springs: Helmers & Howard, 1990.

———. *Living by the Gospel: Christian Roots of Confidence and Purpose*. Colorado Springs: Helmers & Howard, 1986.

———. "Macht und Ohnmacht der Ideologien." In *Denken im Horizont der Wirklichkeit Gottes. Schriften zur Dogmatik und Theologiegeschichte*, edited by Rainer Mayer, 143–58. BWA 2/1. Giessen, Germany: Brunnen, 1999.

———. "The Marxist Critique of Religion and the Historicity of the Christian Faith." *Crux* 26, no. 1 (1980) 19–24.

———. *Der Mensch auf der Suche nach Menschlichkeit*. TuD pamphlet 5. Giessen, Germany: Brunnen, 1979.

———. "Mit Christus dienen." *ThBeitr* 20 (1989) 6–22.

———. "Nachwort zur 3. Auflage." In *Atheismus in der Christenheit*, Vol. 1, *Die Unwirklichkeit Gottes in Theologie und Kirche*, 3rd rev. ed., 160–61. Giessen, Germany: Brunnen, 1985.

———. "Natural Law." *Christianity Today* 21 (Nov. 18, 1977) 59–60.

———. "Der neue Mensch und die ideologischen Systeme." Unpublished manuscript in the Bockmuehl archives in St. Chrischona.

———. "On Wealth and Stewardship." *Christianity Today* 22 (June 23, 1978) 48, 50.

Bibliography

---. "Ostern 1975—Berechtigte Hoffnung." *Caux-Information* 27, no. 3 (1975) 1.
---. "Perimeters of Change. The Realism of Christian Conversion in the Light of Marxism and Some Modern Theology." Translation of *Konkrete Umkehr. Die christliche Lehre von der Bekehrung zwischen Marxismus und moderner Theologie*, TuD 56 (Giessen, Germany: Brunnen, 1989). Unpublished manuscript in the Bockmuehl archives in St. Chrischona.
---. "Das Problem der Ethik im Protestantismus." In *Theologie und Lebensführung*, 67–84. Gesammelte Aufsätze 2. Giessen, Germany: Brunnen, 1982.
---. "Das Problem einer evangelikalen Sozialethik." In *Leben nach dem Willen Gottes. Schriften zur Materialethik*, edited by Rainer Mayer, 192–205. BWA 2/3. Giessen, Germany: Brunnen, 2006.
---. "Predigt: Lukas 15, 1-3.11–24 (Das Gleichnis vom verlorenen Sohn)." In *Vorträge und Ausarbeitungen von Klaus Bockmuehl*, chapter 12. Unpublished book in library of theological seminary of St. Chrischona (Signature B 6 103/1).
---. "Pre-Suppositions in Contemporary Theological Debate." In *The Conciliar-Evangelical Debate: The Crucial Documents, 1964–1976: expanded edition of Eye of the Storm, The Great Debate in Mission, Including Documents on Bangkok and Nairobi*, edited by Donald A. McGavran, 350–59. South Pasadena, CA: William Carey Library, 1977.
---. "Protestant Ethics: The Spirit and the Word in Action.'" *ERT* 12 (1988) 101–15.
---. "Quiet Holidays." *Quarterly Bulletin* [Regent College Vancouver] 12, no. 3 (1982) n.p.
---. "The Raison d'Etre of Our Calling." *Christianity Today* 24 (Feb. 22, 1980) 54–55.
---. "'Real Humanism': Marxism as a Critique of Christianity." *Crux* 21, no. 2 (1985) 3–9.
---. "Recovering Vocation Today." In *With Heart, Mind and Strength. The Best of Crux 1979–1989*, edited by Donald M. Lewis. 1:81–99. Langley, BC: Credo, 1990.
---. "Reifezeugnis" from 1951. Unpublished private manuscript in the possession of Horst-Klaus Hofmann, Reichelsheim.
---. "Revolution of Ethics and Ethics of Revolution." *International Reformed Bulletin* 44–55 (1971) 52–72.
---. *Säkularismus und christlicher Glaube. Gottesherrschaft oder Selbstherrschaft des Menschen?* Porta-Studien 8. Marburg: SMD, 1985.
---. "Der Säkularismus und die Folgen." In *Denken im Horizont der Wirklichkeit Gottes. Schriften zur Dogmatik und Theologiegeschichte*, edited by Rainer Mayer, 159–89. BWA 2/1. Giessen, Germany: Brunnen, 1999.
---. "Saint for Our Day: Charles de Foucauld." *Christianity Today* 23 (Jan. 5, 1979) 55–56.
---. "Sanctification." In *New Dictionary of Theology*, edited by Sinclair B. Ferguson et al., 613–16. Leicester: IVP, 1988.
---. "Sanctification and Christian Mission." In *Bilanz und Plan: Mission an der Schwelle zum Dritten Jahrtausend, Festschrift für George W. Peters*, edited by Hans Kasdorf et al., 54–64. Bad Liebenzell, Germany: VLM, 1988.
---. "Scheidung, Festigung und Sendung—Überlegungen zum Thema Kirche und Welt." In *Denken im Horizont der Wirklichkeit Gottes. Schriften zur Dogmatik und Theologiegeschichte*, edited by Rainer Mayer, 12–27. BWA 2/1. Giessen, Germany: Brunnen, 1999.

Bibliography

———. "Secularism and Theology." In *With Heart, Mind and Strength. The Best of Crux 1979-1989*, edited by Donald M. Lewis, 1:39-54. Langley, BC: Credo, 1990.

———. "Secularization and Secularism: Some Christian Considerations." *ERT* 10 (1986) 50-73.

———. "Der sendende Herr—die neue Schöpfung." In *Was heißt heute Mission? Entscheidungsfragen der neueren Missionstheologie*, edited by Helmuth L. Egelkraut, 179-99. BWA 1/3. Giessen, Germany: Brunnen, 2000.

———. "Serving with Christ." English translation of the German article "Mit Christus dienen." Translated by M. W. Fleischmann, August 1987. Unpublished manuscript in the Bockmuehl archives in St. Chrischona.

———. *Sinn und Unsinn der neuen Moral: Kritik und Selbstkritik*. TuD 1. 2nd ed. Giessen, Germany: Brunnen, 1974.

———. "The Socialist Ideal: Some Soul-Searching Constraints." *Christianity Today* 24 (May 23, 1980) 53, 56.

———. "Der Streit um die 'Grundwerte'. Eine Auseinandersetzung um den *primus usus legis*." In *Theologie und Lebensführung*, 85-105. Gesammelte Aufsätze 2. Giessen, Germany: Brunnen, 1982.

———. "The Task of Systematic Theology." In *Perspectives on Evangelical Theology*, edited by Kenneth S. Kantzer and Stanley N. Gundry, 3-14. Grand Rapids: Eerdmans, 1979.

———. "Tendenzen der Theologie 1968." In *Vorträge und Ausarbeitungen von Klaus Bockmuehl*, chapter 5. Unpublished book in library of theological seminary of St. Chrischona (Signature B 6 103/1).

———. "The Ten Commandments: Are They Still Valid?" *The Christian Way of Living: An Ethics of the Ten Commandments*, 125-36. Vancouver: Regent College Bookstore, 1994.

———. "Theology as Servant." *Christianity Today* 20 (Feb. 27, 1976) 45-46.

———. "Theorie und Praxis, Änderung des Menschen und Änderung der Strukturen. Über Marxismus und Christentum und ihre Wege zur Weltgestaltung." In *glauben und handeln. Beiträge zur Begründung evangelischer Ethik (Gesammelte Aufsätze)*, 104-127. Giessen, Germany: Brunnen, 1975.

———. "Three Horizons for Theology." *ERT* 11 (1987) 5-20.

———. "'. . . to live soberly, righteously, and godly in the present age.' A Meditation on Titus 2:12." *Crux* 21, no. 4 (1985) 2-5.

———. "Toward a Spirituality of the Kingdom." *Christianity Today* 25 (Feb. 6, 1981) 42.

———. "Über die Geltung der Zehn Gebote heute. Eine Ortsbestimmung des Dekalogs." In *glauben und handeln. Beiträge zur Begründung evangelischer Ethik (Gesammelte Aufsätze)*, 50-59. Giessen, Germany: Brunnen, 1975.

———. "Überlegungen zum Thema 'Einfacher Lebensstil'." *Theologie und Lebensführung*, 106-29. Gesammelte Aufsätze 2. Giessen, Germany: Brunnen, 1982.

———. "Under the Perspective Of Eternity." *Christianity Today* 21 (Feb. 18, 1977) 64-65.

———. *The Unreal God of Modern Theology. Bultmann, Barth, and the Theology of Atheism: a Call to Recovering the Truth of God's Reality*. Translated by Geoffrey W. Bromiley. Colorado Springs: Helmers & Howard, 1988.

Bibliography

———. *Verantwortung des Glaubens im Wandel der Zeit. Protestantische Theologie im 19. und 20. Jahrhundert.* Edited by Helmut Burkhardt. BWA 3/3. Giessen, Germany: Brunnen, 2001.

———. "Vorbereitungen für Nairobi." In *Was heißt heute Mission? Entscheidungsfragen der neueren Missionstheologie*, edited by Helmuth L. Egelkraut, 172-78. BWA 1/3. Giessen, Germany: Brunnen, 2000.

———. "Vorwort des Herausgebers." In *Die Aktualität der Theologie Adolf Schlatters*, 1-4. Giessen, Germany: Brunnen, 1988.

———. "Die Wahrnehmung der Geschichte in der Dogmatik Adolf Schlatters." In *Die Aktualität der Theologie Adolf Schlatters*, 93-112. Giessen, Germany: Brunnen, 1988.

———. "Was heißt Glaube? Über die Voraussetzung christlichen Handelns." In *Denken im Horizont der Wirklichkeit Gottes. Schriften zur Dogmatik und Theologiegeschichte*, edited by Rainer Mayer, 50-74. BWA 2/1. Giessen, Germany: Brunnen, 1999.

———. *Was heißt heute Mission? Entscheidungsfragen der neueren Missionstheologie.* Edited by Helmut Egelkraut. BWA 1/3. Giessen, Germany: Brunnen, 2000.

———. "Die Wende im Spätwerk Karl Barths." In *Denken im Horizont der Wirklichkeit Gottes. Schriften zur Dogmatik und Theologiegeschichte*, edited by Rainer Mayer, 280-90. BWA 2/1. Giessen, Germany: Brunnen, 1999.

———. "Das Werk des Hl Geistes in der Heiligung." Lecture. Unpublished manuscript in the Bockmuehl archives in St. Chrischona.

———. "Wiedergeburt und Neuschöpfung." Unfinished habilitation dissertation. Unpublished manuscript in the Bockmuehl archivess in St. Chrischona.

———. "Wie lebt ein Christ an der Universität? Der Heidelberger Studentenpfarrer, Dr. Klaus Bockmühl, spricht in Caux." *Informationsdienst der Moralischen Aufrüstung* 18, nos. 1-2 (/1966) 6.

———. "Wie treffe ich eine Entscheidung?" *Caux-Information* 25, no. 15 (1973) 4-5.

———. "Zum Tode Frank Buchmans." *KiZ* 16, no. 9 (1961) 389-91.

———. "Zur Frage nach der Maßgeblichkeit der Bibel für die Ethik. Über die Quelle christlicher Handlungsnormen." In *glauben und handeln. Beiträge zur Begründung evangelischer Ethik (Gesammelte Aufsätze)*, 30-49. Giessen, Germany: Brunnen, 1975.

———. "Zur Hermeneutik Martin Luthers." In *Denken im Horizont der Wirklichkeit Gottes. Schriften zur Dogmatik und Theologiegeschichte*, edited by Rainer Mayer, 250-79. BWA 2/1. Giessen, Germany: Brunnen, 1999.

Bockmuehl, Markus. "To Love God Is to Wait for Him: Reflections on a Theme of Biblical Spirituality." In *Gott lieben und seine Gebote halten—Loving God and Keeping His Commandments: in Memoriam, Klaus Bockmuehl*, edited by Markus Bockmuehl and Helmut Burkhardt, 39-48. Giessen, Germany: Brunnen, 1991.

Bockmuehl, Markus, and Helmut Burkhardt. "Preface." In *Gott lieben und seine Gebote halten—Loving God and Keeping His Commandments: in Memoriam, Klaus Bockmuehl*, edited by Markus Bockmuehl and Helmut Burkhardt, 7. Giessen, Germany: Brunnen, 1991.

Bonhoeffer, Dietrich. *The Cost of Discipleship.* Translated by Reginald H. Fuller. London: SCM, 1959.

———. *Ethics.* Edited by Eberhard Bethge. Translated by Neville H. Smith. London: SCM, 1960 (1955).

Bibliography

———. *Letters and Papers from Prison*. Edited by Eberhard Bethge. Translated by Reginald Fuller et al. London: SCM, 1971.
Bormuth, K. H. Review of *Gott lieben und seine Gebote halten*, edited by Markus Bockmuehl and Helmut Burkhardt. *JETh* 7 (1993) 230-31.
Bosch, David J. *Transforming Mission. Paradigm Shifts in Theology of Mission*. Maryknoll, NY: Orbis, 1996.
Boyd, Gregory A. *Seeing is Believing. Experience Jesus through Imaginative Prayer*. Grand Rapids: Baker, 2004.
Brown, David. *Choices: Ethics and the Christian*. Oxford: Blackwell, 1983.
Brown, Dale W. *Understanding Pietism*. Grand Rapids: Eerdmans, 1978.
Bruce, Frederick F. *The Epistle to the Hebrews*. NICNT. Grand Rapids: Eerdmans, 1990.
Brümmer, Vincent. *The Model of Love: A Study in Philosophical Theology*. Cambridge: Cambridge University Press, 1993.
Brunner, Emil. *Die Kirchen, die Gruppenbewegung und die Kirche Jesu Christi*. Berlin: Furche, 1936.
———. "Meine Begegnung mit der Oxforder Gruppenbewegung." In *Ein offenes Wort. Vorträge und Aufsätze 1917-1962*, 1:268-88. Zürich: Theologischer Verlag Zürich, 1981.
———. *Vom Werk des Heiligen Geistes*. Tübingen: Mohr/Siebeck, 1935.
Buchman, Frank N. D. *Remaking the World. The Speeches of Frank N.D. Buchman*. London: Blandford, 1961.
Bühler, H. "Der Marxismus auf der Suche nach dem neuen Menschen." *Glaubensbote, Pilgermission St. Chrischona* 96, no. 9 (1973) 166-67.
Bultmann, Rudolf. "Bultmann Replies to his Critics." In *Kerygma and Myth: A Theological Debate*, edited by Hans W. Bartsch, 1:191-211. London: SPCK, 1972.
———. "The Case for Demythologizing." In *Kerygma and Myth: A Theological Debate*, edited by Hans W. Bartsch, 2:181-94. London: SPCK, 1972.
———. *The Gospel of John. A Commentary*. Edited by George R. Beasley-Murray. Philadelphia: Westminster, 1971.
———. *Jesus Christ and Mythology?* New York: Scribner's Sons, 1958.
———. "New Testament and Mythology." In *Kerygma and Myth: A Theological Debate*, edited by Hans W. Bartsch, 1:1-44. London: SPCK, 1972.
———. "A Reply to the Theses of J. Schniewind." In *Kerygma and Myth: A Theological Debate*, edited by Hans W. Bartsch, 1:102-23. London: SPCK, 1972.
———. "What does it Mean to Speak of God?" In *Faith and Understanding*, edited by Robert W. Funk, translated by Louise P. Smith, 1:53-65. London: SCM, 1969.
Burkhardt, Helmut. *The Biblical Doctrine of Regeneration*. Translated by Olaf R. Johnston. Outreach and Identity 2. Downers Grove: IVP, 1978.
———. *Christ werden. Bekehrung und Wiedergeburt—Anfang des christlichen Lebens*. Giessen, Germany: Brunnen, 1999.
———. "Einführung des Herausgebers." In *Christliche Lebensführung. Eine Ethik der Zehn Gebote*. By Klaus Bockmuehl, edited by Helmut Burkhardt, xiv-xv. BWA 3/2. Giessen, Germany: Brunnen, 2000.
———. "Einführung des Herausgebers." In *Verantwortung des Glaubens im Wandel der Zeit. Protestantische Theologie im 19. und 20. Jahrhundert*, by Klaus Bockmuehl, edited by Helmut Burkhardt, x-xv. BWA 3/3 Giessen, Germany: Brunnen, 2001.
———. *Einführung in die Ethik. Grund und Norm sittlichen Handelns*. Giessen, Germany: Brunnen, 1996.

Bibliography

———. "Gott ehren mit Dank. Erinnerung an K. Bockmuehl." *Arbeitskreis für evangelikale Theologie* (Nov. 1989) 1-2, 7.

———. "Handeln aus dem Hören auf Gott. Zum 10. Todestag eines ungewöhnlichen, aus dem Pietismus kommenden evangelischen Ethikers: Klaus Bockmühl." *ideaspektrum* 24 (1999) 28.

———. "Mission im Zeichen des Säkularismus. Klaus Bockmühls Beitrag zur Missionstheologie." *ThBeitr* 23, no. 4 (1992) 214-22.

———. "Zur Einführung." *JETh* 3 (1989) 5-7.

Burrell, David B. "11. The Spirit and the Christian Life." In *Christian Theology: An Introduction to Its Traditions and Tasks*, edited by Peter C. Hodgson and Robert H. King, rev. ed., 302-27. Minneapolis: Fortress, 1994.

Burtness, James H. *Consequences: Morality, Ethics, and the Future*. Minneapolis: Fortress, 1999.

Busch, Eberhard. *Karl Barth: His Life from Letters and Autobiographical Texts*. Translated by John Bowden. London: SCM, 1976.

———. *Karl Barth und die Pietisten: Die Pietismuskritik des jungen Barth und ihre Erwiderung*. Munich: Kaiser, 1978.

Busch, Wilhelm. *Jesus unser Schicksal*. 5th ed. Gladbeck, Germany: Schriftenmission, 1971.

———. *Man muß doch darüber sprechen: Kleine Erzählungen*. 2nd series. Stuttgart: Quell, 1950.

———. *Variationen über ein Thema: Kleine Erzählungen*. 3rd series. 21st rev. ed. Stuttgart: Quell, 1990.

Calvin, John. *Institutes of the Christian Religion* [1559]. Edited by John T. McNeill. Translated by Ford L. Battles. LCC 20-21. Philadelphia: Westminster, 1960.

Carrouges, Michel. *Soldier of the Spirit: the Life of Charles de Focauld*. Translated by Marie-Christine Hellin. London: Gollancz, 1956.

Chambers, Oswald. *My Utmost for His Highest*. Worcester: Oswald Chambers Publication Assoc., 1995.

Chan, Simon. *Spiritual Theology: A Systematic Study of the Christian Life*. Downers Grove: IVP, 1998.

Charry, Ellen T. *By the Renewing of Your Minds: The Pastoral Function of Christian Doctrine*. Oxford: Oxford University Press, 1997.

Cocksworth, Christopher. *Holy, Holy, Holy: Worshipping the Trinitarian God*. Trinity & Truth. London: Darton, Longman & Todd, 1997.

Crane, Judith. *Forgiving God*. Grove Spirituality Series 90. Cambridge: Grove, 2004.

Cullmann, Oscar. *Salvation in History*. London: SCM, 1967.

Darwall, Stephen. "Introduction." In *Virtue Ethics*, edited by Stephen Darwall, 1-4. Malden, MA: Blackwell, 2003.

Dietz, Thorsten. "Mystik ist alles. Name ist Schall und Rauch." *Ichtys* 15, no. 29 (1999) 74-82.

Dubay, Thomas, S.M. *Authenticity: A Biblical Theology of Discernment*. Rev. ed. San Francisco: Ignatius, 1997.

Dintaman, Stephen F. *Creative Grace: Faith and History in the Theology of Adolf Schlatter*. New York: Lang, 1993.

Dominian, Jack, *A Guide to Loving: For Young and Old*, London: Darton, Longman & Todd Ltd, 2005.

Bibliography

Drengson, Alan R. "Compassion and Transcendence of Duty and Inclination." *Philosophy Today* 25 (1981) 34–45.
Duffey, Michael K. *Be Blessed in What You Do: The Unity of Christian Ethics and Spirituality*. Mahwah, NJ: Paulist, 1988.
Dunn, James D. G. *The Epistle to the Galatians*. Black's New Testament Commentary. London: Black, 1993.
———. "Spirit Speech: Reflections on Romans 8:12–27." In *Romans and the People of God: Essays in Honor of Gordon D. Fee on the Occasion of is 65th Birthday*, edited by S.K. Soderlund et al., 82–91. Grand Rapids: Eerdmans, 1999.
Ebeling, Gerhard. "Die Beunruhigung der Theologie durch die Frage nach den Früchten des Geistes." *Zeitschrift für Theologie und Kirche* 66, no. 3 (1969) 354–68.
Egelkraut, Helmuth. "Einführung." In *Was heißt heute Mission? Entscheidungsfragen der neueren Missionstheologie*, by Klaus Bockmuehl, edited by Helmut Egelkraut, xi–xviii. BWA 1/3. Giessen, Germany: Brunnen, 2000.
Engelbrecht, Edward. *Friends of the Law: Luther's Use of the Law for the Christian Life*. Saint Louis: Concordia, 2011. Online: http://www.cph.org/pdf/124393.pdf.
Ekman, Gösta. *Experiment with God: Frank Buchman reconsidered*. London: Hodder & Stoughton, 1972.
Erb, Peter C. "Foreword." In *Pietists: Selected Writings*, edited by Peter C. Erb, xiii–xiv. London: SPCK, 1983.
Fairweather, Ian C. M., and James I. H. McDonald. *The Quest for Christian Ethics: An Inquiry into Ethics and Christian Ethics*. Edinburgh: Handsel, 1984.
Fee, Gordon D. *God's Empowering Presence: The Holy Spirit in the Letters of Paul*. Peabody, MA: Hendrickson, 1994.
Fiddes, Paul S. *The Creative Suffering of God*. Oxford: Clarendon, 1988.
Fletcher, Joseph. *Moral Responsibility: Situation Ethics At Work*. London: SCM, 1967.
———. *Situation Ethics: The New Morality*. London: SCM, 1966.
———. "What's in a Rule?: A Situationist's View." In *Norm and Context in Christian Ethics*, edited by Gene H. Outka et al., 325–49. London: SCM, 1969.
Foucauld, Charles de. *Wasser aus der Wüste: Impulse für eine neue Spiritualität des Dienstes. Worte aus dem Leben Charles de Foucauld*. Edited by Reinhard Frische. 3rd ext. ed. Basel: Brunnen, 1995.
Francke, August Hermann. "From the Autobiography 1692." In *Pietists: Selected Writings*, edited by Peter C. Erb, 99–107. London: SPCK, 1983.
———. "Short Course of Instructions on How Holy Scripture Ought to Be Read For One's True Edification." *Crux* 25, no. 1 (1989) 2–4.
Frank, Karl S. "Jesus Christus, XIII. Religiöse Gemeinschaften." *Lexikon für Theologie und Kirche*, 3rd ed., edited by Walter Kasper, 5:844–45. Freiburg: Herder, 1996.
Frische, Reinhard. "Gott lieben und seinen Willen tun. Verähnlichung mit Christus im Leben von Charles de Foucauld." In *Gott lieben und seine Gebote halten—Loving God and Keeping His Commandments: in Memoriam, Klaus Bockmuehl*, edited by Markus Bockmuehl and Helmut Burkhardt, 122–41. Giessen, Germany: Brunnen, 1991.
———. *Theologie unter der Herrschaft Gottes*. TuD 15. Giessen, Germany: Brunnen, 1979.
———. "Zur Bockmühl-Werk-Ausgabe." In *Leben mit dem Gott, der redet*, by Klaus Bockmuehl, edited by Horst-Klaus Hofmann, ix–xi. BWA 1/6. Giessen, Germany: Brunnen, 1998.

Gärtner, Bertil. "Suffering." In *The New International Dictionary of New Testament Theology*, edited by Colin Brown, 719-26. Exeter: Paternoster, 1978.
Galot, Jean. *Abba, Father, We Long to See Your Face: Theological Insights into the First Person of the Trinity*. New York: Alba House, 1992.
Gasque, W. Ward. "The Promise of Adolf Schlatter." *ERT* 4 (1980) 20-30.
Gaybba, Brian. *The Spirit of Love: Theology of the Holy Spirit*. London: Chapman, 1987.
Gensichen, Hans-Werner. "'Dienst der Seelen' und 'Dienst des Leibes' in der frühen pietistischen Mission." In *Der Pietismus in Gestalten und Wirkungen: M. Schmidt zum 65. Geburtstag*, edited by H. Bornkamm et al., 155-78. Bielefeld, Germany: Luther, 1975.
Glaw, Annette. "BOCKMUEHL, Klaus." In *Biographisch-bibliographisches Kirchenlexikon*, edited by Friedrich W. Bautz et al., 19:58-68. Herzberg: Bautz, 2001.
Goessel, Hans H. von. *Die Moralische Aufrüstung im Blickfeld des Neuen Testaments*. Berlin: Christlicher Zeitschriftenverlag, 1956.
Goetz, Ronald. "The Suffering God: the Rise of a New Orthodoxy." *The Christian Century* 103 (1986) 385-89.
Goldingay, John. "Was the Holy Spirit Active in Old Testament Times? What Was New About the Christian Experience of God?" *Ex Auditu* 12 (1996) 14-28.
Gollwitzer, Helmut. Letter to Bockmuehl, January 26, 1970. Unpublished manuscript in the Bockmuehl archives in St. Chrischona.
Gordon, Anne W. *Peter Howard. Life and Letters*. London: Hodder & Stoughton, 1969.
Gorman, Michael J. *Cruciformity: Paul's Narrative Spirituality of the Cross*. Grand Rapids: Eerdmans, 2001.
Grässer, E., *An die Hebräer (Hebr 1-6)*. EKK 17/1. Zürich: Benziger, 1990.
Grenz, Stanley J. "The Holy Spirit: Divine Love Guiding Us Home." *Ex Auditu* 12 (1996) 1-13.
———. *The Moral Quest: Foundations of Christian Ethics*. Leicester: Apollos, 1997.
Greshake, Gisbert. "Foucauld, Charles-Eugene Vicomte de." *Lexikon für Theologie und Kirche*, 3rd ed., 3:1372-73. Freiburg: Herder, 1995.
Gunton, Colin E. *The Christian Faith: An Introduction to Christian Doctrine*. Oxford: Blackwell, 2001.
———. "Salvation." In *The Cambridge Companion to Karl Barth*, edited by John Webster, 142-58. Cambridge: Cambridge University Press, 2000.
———. *The Triune Creator: A Historical and Systematic Study*. Edinburgh: Edinburgh University Press, 1998.
Haacker, Klaus, et al. "In Memoriam Klaus Bockmühl." *ThBeitr* 20 (1989) 169.
Haberer, Jack. *Living the Presence of the Spirit*. Louisville: Geneva, 2001.
Haizmann, Albrecht. "Eine Ethik der Liebe? Zur Bedeutung des Liebesgebotes für die Ethik P.J. Speners." In *Gott lieben und seine Gebote halten—Loving God and Keeping His Commandments: in Memoriam, Klaus Bockmuehl*, edited by Markus Bockmuehl and Helmut Burkhardt, 87-106. Giessen, Germany: Brunnen, 1991.
———. *Erbauung als Aufgabe der Seelsorge bei Philipp Jakob Spener*. Göttingen: Vandenhoeck & Ruprecht, 1997.
———. "Klaus Bockmühl und der Pietismus." Paper presented at the Klaus Bockmuehl-Symposion *Spiritualität und Humanität*, Schloss Reichenberg, Germany, Feb. 27–Mar. 1, 1998.

Bibliography

Hanacek, Andreas. "Archive in der Bundesrepublik Deutschland. Archive der evangelischen Kirche." 1995-2000. Online: http://home.bawue.de/~hanacek/info/darchi18.htm.

Harak, G. Simon. *Virtuous Passions: The Formation of Christian Character*. New York: Paulist, 1993.

Harrington, Donal. *What is Morality? The Light through Different Windows*. Dublin: Columba, 1996.

Harrison, N. V. "The Holy Spirit and Ethics: A Response to Philip S. Keane." *Proceedings of the Catholic Theological Society of America* 51 (1996) 114-19.

Hart, Trevor. "How Do We Define the Nature of God's Love?" In *Nothing Greater, Nothing Better. Theological Essays on the Love of God*, edited by Kevin J. Vanhoozer, 94-113. Grand Rapids: Eerdmans, 2001.

———. "Revelation." In *The Cambridge Companion to Karl Barth*, edited by John Webster, 37-56. Cambridge: Cambridge University Press, 2000.

Hauerwas, Stanley. *Character and the Christian Life: A Study in Theological Ethics*. San Antonio: Trinity University Press, 1975.

Henning, Christian. *Die evangelische Lehre vom Heiligen Geist und seiner Person: Studien zur Architektur protestantischer Pneumatologie im 20. Jahrhundert*. Gütersloh: Kaiser 2000.

Herrmann, Wilhelm. *Ethik*. 5th ed. Tübingen: Mohr, 1921.

Higginson, Richard. *Dilemmas. A Christian Approach to Moral Decision-Making*. London: Hodder & Stoughton, 1988.

Hoffman, John C. "Pietism." *New Catholic Encyclopedia*, 11:355-56. Washington, DC: Catholic University of America Press, 1968.

Hofmann, Horst-Klaus. "Geglückter Neuanfang. Der 1. Band der Bockmühl-Werk-Ausgabe ist endlich da!" *OJC* 177, no. 6 (1998) 242-44.

———. "Nachfolge Christi im Ringen um die Zukunft." In *Gott lieben und seine Gebote halten—Loving God and Keeping His Commandments: in Memoriam, Klaus Bockmuehl*, edited by Markus Bockmuehl and Helmut Burkhardt, 142-48. Giessen, Germany: Brunnen, 1991.

———. "Revolutionär für Gottes Plan. Freundschaftliche Erinnerungen an Klaus Bockmuehl." *OJC* 172, no. 1 (1998) 17-32.

Hollatz, David, *Examen theologicum acroamaticum (1707)*. Vol. 1, *Prolegomena*. 1707. Facsimile ed. Darmstadt: Wissenschaftliche Buchgesellschaft, 1971.

Holmes, Peter R. *Becoming More Human: Exploring the Interface of Spirituality, Discipleship and Therapeutic Faith Community*. Milton Keynes: Paternoster, 2005.

Holotik, Gerhard. *Pneumatologie und Spiritualität*. Theologische Berichte 16. Zürich: Benziger, 1987.

———. *Die pneumatologische Note der Moraltheologie: Ein ergänzender Beitrag zu gegenwärtigen Bemühungen im Rahmen der katholischen Sittlichkeitslehre*. Wien: Verband der wissenschaftlichen Gesellschaften Österreichs, 1984.

Honecker, Martin. "Zur ethischen Diskussion der 80er Jahre." Review article, among others, on *Gesetz und Geist: Eine kritische Würdigung des Erbes protestantischer Ethik I*, by Klaus Bockmuehl. *Theologische Rundschau* 56, no. 1 (1991) 55-79.

Horrell, David G. "Restructuring Human Relationships. Paul's Corinthian Letters and Habermas's Discourse Ethics." *Expository Times* 110, no. 10 (1999) 321-25.

Bibliography

Houston, James M. "Foreword." In *Listening to the God who speaks: Reflections on God's Guidance from the Scripture and the Lives of God's People*, by Klaus Bockmuehl, ix–xi. Colorado Springs: Helmers & Howard, 1990.

———. *The Heart's Desire: A Guide to Personal Fulfillment*. Oxford: Lion, 1992.

———. "In Memory of Klaus Bockmuehl (1931–1989)." *Crux* 25, no. 2 (1989) 2.

———. "Reflections on Mysticism. How Valid is Evangelical Anti-Mysticism?" In *Gott lieben und seine Gebote halten—Loving God and Keeping His Commandments: in Memoriam, Klaus Bockmuehl*, edited by Markus Bockmuehl and Helmut Burkhardt, 163–81. Giessen, Germany: Brunnen, 1991.

———. *The Transforming Friendship: a guide to prayer*. Oxford: Lion, 1989.

Howard, Peter. *Frank Buchman's Secret*. London: Heinemann, 1961.

———. *The World Rebuilt. The True Story of Frank Buchman and the men and women of Moral Re-Armament*. London: Blandford, 1951.

Hursthouse, Rosalind. *On Virtue Ethics*. Oxford: Oxford University Press, 1999.

Hynson, Leo O. "Christian Ethics and the Holy Spirit." *Evangelical Journal* 14 (1996) 25–45.

idea. "Für biblische Erneuerung der Theologie. Der Theologe Klaus Bockmühl erhält Johann-Tobias-Beck-Preis. Auszeichnung für Veröffentlichung über protestantische Ethik." *idea-spektrum* 21 (1988) 8.

idea. "Theologische Woche: An der Autorität der Bibel festhalten. Von 'prophetischer' Theologie eines pietistischen Theologen lernen." *idea-Pressedienst* 76 (1991) 13.

Janz, Manuel. "Zwischen Norm und Situation. Eine Ethik der Verheißung als Ausgleich zwischen unveränderlichem Gebot und veränderlicher Situation." *Ichtys* 18 (1994) 2–18.

Jenkins, David E. *The Glory of Man*, London: SCM, 1967.

Jeremias, Joachim. *The Parables of Jesus*. Rev. ed. London: SCM, 1963.

Jüngel, Eberhard. "Summary of Klaus Bockmuehl's article 'Kirche und soziale Verantwortung. Zur Frage Kirche und Sozialismus.'" In *Kirche und Sozialismus*, edited by Helmuth Flammer, 112–13. Gütersloh: Gütersloher, 1981.

Julian of Norwich. *The Revelation of Divine Love*. Translated by M. Lucy del Mastro. 2nd ed. Tunbridge Wells, UK: Burns & Oates, 1994.

Keane, Philip S. "The Role of the Holy Spirit in Contemporary Moral Theology." *Proceedings of the Catholic Theological Society of America* 51 (1996) 97–113.

Kierkegaard, Søren. *Either/Or*. Part II. Edited by Howard V. Hong and Edna H. Hong. Kierkegaard's Writings 4. Princeton: Princeton University Press, 1987.

Kirste, Reinhard. *Das Zeugnis des Geistes und das Zeugnis der Schrift: Das testimonium spiritus sancti internum als hermenutisch-polemischer Zentralbegriff bei Johann Gerhard in der Auseinandersetzung mit Robert Bellarmins Schriftverständnis*. Göttingen: Vandenhoeck & Ruprecht, 1976

Kitamori, Kazoh. *Theology of the Pain of God*. London: SCM, 1966.

Krusche, Werner. *Das Wirken des Heiligen Geistes nach Calvin*. Forschungen zur Kirchen- und Dogmengeschichte. Göttingen: Vandenhoeck & Ruprecht, 1957.

LaCugna, Catherine M. *God For Us: The Trinity and Christian Life*. New York: Harper Collins, 1991.

Lafollette, Hugh. *Personal Relationships: Love, Identity, and Morality*. Oxford: Blackwell, 1996.

Lage, Dietmar. *Martin Luther's Christology and Ethics*. Lampeter, UK: Mellen, 1990.

Lane, William L. *Hebrews 1–8*, World Biblical Commentary 47A. Dallas: Word, 1991.

Bibliography

Lawson, John. *The Biblical Theology of Saint Irenaeus*. London: Epworth, 1948.

Lean, Garth. *On the Tail of a Comet: The Life of Frank Buchman*. Colorado Springs: Helmers & Howard, 1988.

Lee, Jung Young. *God Suffers For Us: A Systematic Inquiry Into a Concept of Divine Passiblity*. The Hague: Nijhoff, 1974.

Lehmann, Martin E. *Luther and Prayer*. Milwaukee: Northwestern, 1985.

Leith, John H. *John Calvin's Doctrine of the Christian Life*. Louisville: Westminster John Knox, 1989.

LeRon Shults, L., and Stephen J. Sandage. *Transforming Spirituality. Integrating Theology and Psychology*. Grand Rapids: Baker Academic, 2006.

LeRoy Long, Edward, Jr. *A Survey of Christian Ethics*. 4th ed. New York: Oxford University Press, 1977.

Liebschner, Siegfried. "Die Bedeutung des Heiligen Geistes für die Ethik." In *Gott lieben und seine Gebote halten—Loving God and Keeping His Commandments: in Memoriam, Klaus Bockmuehl*, edited by Markus Bockmuehl and Helmut Burkhardt, 337–43. Giessen, Germany: Brunnen, 1991.

———. "The Experience of Guidance by the Holy Spirit." In *Christian Experience in Theology and Life*, edited by I. Howard Marshall, 159–74. Edinburgh: Rutherford House, 1988.

Little Sister Magdeleine of Jesus. *He took me by the hand: The Little Sisters of Jesus following in the footsteps of Charles de Foucauld*. London: New City, 1991.

Lohse, Bernhard. *Martin Luther's Theology. Its Historical and Systematic Development*. Minneapolis: Fortress, 1999.

Lonsdale, David. *Dance to the Music of the Spirit: The Art of Discernment*. London: Darton, Longman & Todd, 1992.

———. *Eyes to See, Ears to Hear: An Introduction to Ignatian Spirituality*. London: Darton, Longman & Todd, 1990.

Loos, Andreas. "Human Embodiment and the Spirit of God. Klaus Bockmühl's Challenge to the Unreality of God in modern Theology." Master of Christian Studies thesis, Regent College Vancouver, 1999.

———. "Spiritualität und Leiblichkeit bei Klaus Bockmühl." Paper presented at the commemoration of Klaus Bockmuehl's 75th birthday, St. Chrischona, Switzerland, April 28, 2006.

Lorenz, E. "Wiederentdeckung des Heiligen Geistes." Review of *Leben mit dem Gott, der redet* and *Denken im Horizont der Wirklichkeit Gottes*, by Klaus Bockmuehl. *Zeitwende* 1 (2000) 52–53.

Lütgert, Wilhelm. *Ethik der Liebe*. Gütersloh: Bertelsmann, 1938.

Luther, Martin. "Admonition to Peace, A Reply to the Twelve Articles of the Peasants in Swabia, 1525." Edited and revised by Robert C. Schultz. Translated by Charles M. Jacobs, Robert C. Schlutz, and Frederick C. Ahrens. In *Luther's Works: American Edition*, edited by Jaroslav Pelikan and Helmut T. Lehmann, 46:17–43. Philadelphia: Fortress, 1967.

———. "Against the Heavenly Prophets in the Matter of Images and Sacraments, 1525." Edited by Conrad Begendoff. Translated by Earl Beyer, Conrad Bergendoff, and Bernhard Erling. In *Luther's Works: American Edition*, edited by Jaroslav Pelikan and Helmut T. Lehmann, 40:79–223. Philadelphia: Muhlenberg, 1958.

———. "Appeal for Prayer Against the Turks, 1541." Edited by Gustav K. Wiencke. Translated by Martin H. Bertram et al. In *Luther's Works: American Edition*, edited

Bibliography

by Jaroslav Pelikan and Helmut T. Lehmann, 43:213-41. Philadelphia: Fortress, 1968.

———. "Confession Concerning Christ's Supper." Edited and translated by Robert H. Fischer. In *Luther's Works: American Edition*, edited by Jaroslav Pelikan and Helmut T. Lehmann, 37:151-372. Philadelphia: Muhlenberg, 1961.

———. "Galatians—1519." Edited by Jaroslav Pelikan, with Walter A. Hansen. Translated by Richard Jungkuntz. In *Luther's Works: American Edition*, edited by Jaroslav Pelikan and Helmut T. Lehmann, 27:151-410. Saint Louis: Concordia, 1964.

———. "How Christians Should Regard Moses, 1525." Edited and revised by E. Theodore Bachmann. Translated by Charles M. Jacobs et al. In *Luther's Works: American Edition*, edited by Jaroslav Pelikan and Helmut T. Lehmann, 35:155-74. Philadelphia: Muhlenberg, 1960.

———. *Lectures on Genesis. Chapters 15-20*. Edited by Jaroslav Pelikan, with Daniel E. Poellot. Translated by George V. Schick. Vol. 3 of *Luther's Works: American Edition*, edited by Jaroslav Pelikan and Helmut T. Lehmann. Saint Louis: Concordia, 1961.

———. *Luther's Works: American Edition*. Edited by Jaroslav Pelikan and Helmut T. Lehmann. 55 vols. St. Louis: Concordia and Philadelphia: Muhlenberg and Fortress, 1955-1986.

———. "On the Councils and the Church." Edited by Eric W. Gritsch. Translated by Charles M. Jacobs. In *Luther's Works: American Edition*, edited by Jaroslav Pelikan and Helmut T. Lehmann, 41:3-178. Philadelphia: Fortress, 1966.

———. "The Large Catechism (1529)." In *The Book of Concord: The Confessions of the Evangelical Lutheran Church*, edited by Theodore G. Tappert, 357-461. Philadelphia: Muhlenberg, 1959.

———. "A Simple Way To Pray." Edited by Gustav K. Wiencke. Translated by Martin H. Bertram et al. In *Luther's Works: American Edition*, edited by Jaroslav Pelikan and Helmut T. Lehmann, 43:193-211. Philadelphia: Fortress, 1968.

———. "The Smalcald Articles (1537)." In *The Book of Concord: The Confessions of the Evangelical Lutheran Church*, edited by Theodore G. Tappert, 287-318. Philadelphia: Muhlenberg, 1959.

———. "Theses Concerning Faith and Law, 1535." Edited by Helmut T. Lehmann and Lewis W. Spitz. Translated by Lewis W. Spitz. In *Luther's Works: American Edition*, edited by Jaroslav Pelikan and Helmut T. Lehmann, 34:105-32. Philadelphia: Muhlenberg, 1960.

Lyon, David. "The Challenge of Marxism." In *Essays in Evangelical Social Ethics*, edited by David F. Wright, 105-28. Exeter: Paternoster, 1978.

Kant, Immanuel. *Critique of Pure Reason*. Translated by John M. D. Meiklejohn. London: Dent & Sons, 1934.

Knobloch, Otto. "Karl Barth und 'unsere Gemeinschaftsleute.'" In *Antwort: Karl Barth zum Siebzigsten Geburtstag am 10. Mai 1956*, edited by Ernst Wolf et al., 399-408. Zürich: Evangelischer Verlag, 1956.

MacIntyre, Alistair. "God and the Theologians." In *The Honest to God Debate*. Edited by David L. Edwards, 215-28. London: SCM, 1963.

Marx, Karl. *Critique of Hegel's "Philosophy of Right."* Edited by Joseph O'Malley, translated by Annette Jolin and Joseph O'Malley. Cambridge: University Press, 1970.

Bibliography

Mayer, Rainer. "Einführung." In *Denken im Horizont der Wirklichkeit Gottes: Schriften zur Dogmatik und Theologiegeschichte*, by Klaus Bockmuehl, edited by Rainer Mayer, xiv-xxiv. BWA 2/1. Giessen, Germany: Brunnen, 1999.

———. "Einführung." In *Leben nach dem Willen Gottes: Schriften zur Materialethik*, by Klaus Bockmuehl, edited by Rainer Mayer, xiii-xxvi. BWA 2/3. Giessen, Germany: Brunnen, 2006.

———. "Ethik ohne Normen? Herkunft, Wesen und Kritik der Situationsethik." In *Begründung ethischer Normen*, edited by Helmut Burkhardt, 147-67. Wuppertal, Germany: Brockhaus et al., 1988.

McFague, Sallie. *Models of God: Theology for an Ecological Nuclear Age*. London: SCM, 1987

McFarlane, Graham W. P. *Christ and the Spirit: The Doctrine of the Incarnation to Edward Irving*. Carlisle: Paternoster, 1996.

McGrath, Alister E. *Christian Spirituality: An Introduction*. Oxford: Blackwell, 1999.

Merton, Thomas. *Contemplation in a World of Action*. New York: Image, 1973.

———. *New Seeds of Contemplation*. New York: New Directions, 1972.

Miller, Mark C. *Living Ethically in Christ: Is Christian Ethics Unique?* New York: Lang, 1999.

Mohrlang, Roger. "Love." In *Dictionary of Paul and His Letters*, edited by Gerald F. Hawthorne et al., 575-78. Leicester: IVP, 1993.

Moltmann, Jürgen. *The Crucified God: The Cross of Christ as the Foundation and Criticism of Christian Theology*. London: SCM, 1974.

———. *The Spirit of Life: a Universal Affirmation*. London: SCM, 1992

———. *The Trinity and the Kingdom of God: The Doctrine of God*. London: SCM, 1981.

Motyer, Stephen. "'Not Apart from Us' (Hebrews 11:40): Physical Community in the Letter to the Hebrews." *Evangelical Quarterly* 77 (2005) 235-47.

Moule, Charles F. D. "Obligation in the Ethic of Paul." In *Christian History and Interpretation: Studies Presented to John Knox*, edited by William R. Farmer et al., 389-406. Cambridge: Cambridge University Press, 1967.

Mueller, David L. *Karl Barth*. Makers of the Modern Theological Mind. Edited by Bob E. Patterson. Dallas: Word, 1972.

Munzinger, André. *Discerning the Spirits: Theological and Ethical Hermeneutics in Paul*. Cambridge: Cambridge University Press, 2007.

Neuer, Werner. *Adolf Schlatter: A Biography of Germany's Premier Biblical Theologian*. Translated by R.W. Yarbrough. Grand Rapids: Baker, 1995.

———. *Adolf Schlatter: Ein Leben für Theologie und Kirche*. Stuttgart: Calwer, 1996.

———. "Bockmühl, Klaus (1931-1989)." *Evangelisches Lexikon für Theologie und Gemeinde*, 1:287-88. Wuppertal, Germany: Brockhaus, 1992.

———. *Der Zusammenhang von Dogmatik und Ethik bei Adolf Schlatter: Eine Untersuchung zur Grundlegung christlicher Ethik*. Giessen, Germany: Brunnen, 1986.

———. "Einführung." In *Der Dienst des Christen: Beiträge zu einer Theologie der Liebe*, by Adolf Schlatter, edited by Werner Neuer, 7-18. Giessen, Germany: Brunnen, 1991.

———. "Einführung." In *Die Gründe der christlichen Gewissheit: Das Gebet*, by Adolf Schlatter, edited by Werner Neuer, 5-17. Giessen, Germany: Brunnen, 1998.

———. "Für eine Theologie aus Liebe zu Gott. Prof. Klaus Bockmühl: Die Autorität der Bibel anerkennen." *idea-spektrum* 24 (1989) 28.

## Bibliography

———. "Naturtheologie als Basis einer ökologischen Ethik. Adolf Schlatters Beitrag zu einem verantwortlichen Umgang mit der Natur." In *Gott lieben und seine Gebote halten—Loving God and Keeping His Commandments: in Memoriam, Klaus Bockmuehl*, edited by Markus Bockmuehl and Helmut Burkhardt, 243–59. Giessen, Germany: Brunnen, 1991.
———. Review of *Gesetz und Geist: Eine kritische Würdigung des Erbes protestantischer Ethik I*, by Klaus Bockmuehl. *AGORA* 15, no. 3 (1989) 37–39.
———. "Schlatter, Adolf (1852–1938)." *TRE* 30 (1998) 135–43.
———. "Schöpfung und Gesetz bei Adolf Schlatter." In *Begründung ethischer Normen*, edited by Helmut Burkhardt, 115–30. Wuppertal, Germany: Brockhaus, 1988.
———. "Die Weite im Denken Klaus Bockmühls." Paper presented at the commemoration of Klaus Bockmuehl's 75th birthday, St. Chrischona, Switzerland, April 28, 2006, 1–6. Online: http://new.chrischona.ch/files/1884.pdf.
Nicholls, Bruce J. "The WEFT Theological Comission 1969–1986." *ERT* 26, no. 1 (2002) 4–22.
Niebuhr, Reinhold. *Love and Justice: Selections from the Shorter Writings of Reinhold Niebuhr*. Edited by D. B. Robertson. Louisville: Westminster John Knox, 1957.
Noll, Mark. "Foreword." In *Adolf Schlatter: A Biography of Germany's Premier Biblical Theologian*, by Werner Neuer, translated by R. W. Yarbrough, 7–8. Grand Rapids: Baker, 1995.
Nouwen, Henry J. M. *Here and Now: Living in the Spirit*. New York: Crossroad, 1994.
———. *The Inner Voice of Love: A Journey Through Anguish To Freedom*. London: Darton, Longman & Todd, 1997.
———. *Life of the Beloved: Spiritual Living in a Secular World*. London: Hodder & Stoughton, 1992.
———. *Reaching Out: The Three Movements of the Spiritual Life*. London: Collins Fount, 1980.
———. *The Wounded Healer: Ministry in Contemporary Society*. New York: Doubleday, 1972.
Nouwen, Henry J. M., Donald P. McNeill, and Douglas A. Morrison. *Compassion: A Reflection on the Christian Life*. Rev. ed. London: Darton, Longman & Todd, 2008.
Nygren, Anders. *Agape and Eros*. London: SPCK, 1953.
Oden, Thomas C. *Life in the Spirit: Systematic Theology*, Vol. 3. New York: HarperSanFrancisco, 1992.
O'Donnell, John. *Hans Urs von Balthasar*. London: Chapman, 1992.
OJC. "Our Roots." Online: http://www.ojc.de/en/reichenberg-fellowship/roots-history.html.
Olthuis, James H. *The Beautiful Risk: A New Psychology of Loving and Being Loved*. Grand Rapids: Zondervan, 2001.
———. "Dancing Together in the Wild Spaces of Love: Postmodernism, Psychotherapy, and the Spirit of God." *Journal of Psychology and Christianity* 18 (1999) 140–52.
The Oxford Group, editors. *The Oxford Group and its Work of Moral Re-Armament*. With a Foreword by Sir Lynden Macassey. London: Lowe & Brydone, 1954.
Oyen, Hendrik van. Letter to Bockmuehl, July 6, 1968. Unpublished manuscript in the Bockmuehl archives in St. Chrischona.
———. "'New Morality' und christliche Ethik." In *Verantwortung und Freiheit*, 147–56. Gütersloh: Mohn, 1972.

Bibliography

———. "Verantwortung und Norm im Hinblick auf die Situationsethik." In *Verantwortung und Freiheit*, 157-69. Gütersloh: Mohn, 1972.

Packer, James I. "Evangelical Foundations for Spirituality." In *Gott lieben und seine Gebote halten—Loving God and Keeping His Commandments: in Memoriam, Klaus Bockmuehl*, edited by Markus Bockmuehl and Helmut Burkhardt, 149-62. Giessen, Germany: Brunnen, 1991.

———. "Introduction." In *The Best in Theology*, edited by James I. Packer, 4:vii-xiv. Carol Stream, IL: Christianity Today, 1990.

———. "Klaus Bockmuehl's Rich Legacy." *Christianity Today* 34 (Febr. 19, 1990) 9.

Palakeel, Joseph. *The Use of Analogy in Theological Discourse: An Investigation in Ecumenical Perspective*. Tesi Gregoriana, Serie Teologia 4. Rome: Gregorian University Press, 1995

Pannenberg, Wolfhart. *Das Glaubensbekenntnis: Ausgelegt und Verantwortet vor den Fragen der Gegenwart*. Hamburg: Siebenstern, 1972.

Parsons, Michael. "Man Encountered by the Command of God: The Ethics of Karl Barth." *Vox Evangelica* 17 (1987) 49-65.

Parzany, Ulrich. *Im Einsatz für Jesus: Programm und Praxis des Pfarrers Wilhelm Busch*. Neukirchen-Vluyn: Aussaat, 1995.

———. "Pietismus und soziale Verantwortung." Paper presented at the Klaus Bockmuehl-Symposion *Spiritualität und Humanität*, Schloss Reichenberg, Germany, Feb. 27-Mar. 1, 1998.

Pfander, Martin. "Vorgeschichte und Anfangsjahre des Albrecht-Bengel-Hauses in Tübingen." In *Die Hoffnung festhalten: Festgabe für Walter Tlach zum 65. Geburtstag von Lehrern und Studenten des Albrecht-Bengel-Hauses in Tübingen und seinen Freunden dargebracht*, edited by Gerhard Maier, 167-209. Stuttgart: Hänssler, 1978.

Pinnock, Clark H., and Robert C. Brow, *Unbounded Love. A Good News Theology for the 21st Century*. Downers Grove: IVP, 1994.

Pinnock, Clark H. *The Flame of Love: A Theology of the Holy Spirit*. Downers Grove: IVP, 1996.

———. "Foreword." In *Authentic Spirituality: Moving Beyond Mere Religion*, by Barry L. Callen, 7-8. Grand Rapids: Baker Academic, 2001.

Porter, Jean. "Virtue ethics." In *The Cambridge Companion to Christian Ethics*, edited by Robin Gill, 96-111. Cambridge: Cambridge University Press, 2001.

Rabens, Volker. *The Holy Spirit and Ethics in Paul: Transformation and Empowering for Religious-Ethical Life*. Wissenschaftliche Untersuchungen zum Neuen Testament 2/283. 2nd ed. Tübingen: Mohr/Siebeck, 2013.

———. "Johannine Perspectives on Ethical Enabling." In *Rethinking the Ethics of John: "Implicit Ethics" in the Johannine Writings*, edited by Jan G. van der Watt and Ruben Zimmermann, 114-39. Contexts and Norms of New Testament Ethics 3. Tübingen: Mohr/Siebeck, 2012.

———. "Power from In Between: The Relational Experience of the Holy Spirit and Spiritual Gifts in Paul's Churches." In *The Spirit and Christ in the New Testament and Christian Theology: Essays in Honor of Max Turner*, edited by I. Howard Marshall, Volker Rabens, and Cornelis Bennema, 138-55. Grand Rapids: Eerdmans, 2012.

———. "Transforming Relationships: The Spirit's Empowering for Religious-Ethical Life According to the Apostle Paul." Paper presented at the 18th British New Testament Conference, London, 2000.

Bibliography

Reed, Esther. *The Genesis of Ethics: On the Authority of God as the Origin of Christian Ethics*. London: Darton, Longman & Todd, 2000.
Reimer, Ingrid. "Moralische Aufrüstung." *Evangelisches Kirchenlexikon: Internationale Theologische Enzyklopädie*, edited by Erwin Fahlbusch, 3rd rev. ed., 3:541–3. Göttingen: Vandenhoeck & Ruprecht, 1992.
Riesner, Rainer. "Militia Christi und Militia Caesaris. Tertullian und Clemens Alexandrinus als paradigmatische Positionen in der Alten Kirche." In *Gott lieben und seine Gebote halte—Loving God and Keeping His Commandments: in Memoriam, Klaus Bockmuehl*, edited by Markus Bockmuehl and Helmut Burkhardt, 49–72. Giessen, Germany: Brunnen, 1991.
Plathow, Michael. "Der Geist hilft unserer Schwachheit. Ein aktualisierender Forschungsbericht zu M. Luthers Rede vom heiligen Geist." *KuD* 40 (1994) 143–69.
Robbins, Anna M. *Methods in the Madness. Diversity in Twentieth-Century Christian Social Ethics*. Carlisle: Paternoster, 2004.
———. "Something in common? The human person as moral agent in individual and corporate expression." *Evangelical Quarterly* 78, no. 4 (2006) 313–39.
Robinson, John A. T. *Christian Freedom in a Permissive Society*, London: SCM, 1970.
———. *Honest to God*. London: SCM, 1963.
Robinson, Norman H. G. *The Groundwork of Christian Ethics*, London: Collins, 1971.
Rommen, Edwad. "Das Problem des usus politicus legis angesichts des Phänomens der Säkularisierung." In *Begründung ethischer Normen*, edited by Helmut Burkhardt, 169–183. Wuppertal, Germany: Brockhaus, 1988.
Rüttgardt, Jan O. "Speners Wiedergeburtslehre in der Forschung." In *Schriften. 7/1: Der hochwichtige Articul von der Wiedergeburt (1969) 1715. Predigten 1–34*, by Philip J. Spener, edited by Erich Beyreuther, 1–11. Hildesheim, Germany: Olms, 1994.
Russel, Arthur J. *For Sinners Only*. London: Hodder & Stoughton, 1932.
Sarot, Marcel. *God, Passibility and Corporeality*. Kampen, Netherlands: Kok Pharos, 1992.
Schaeder, Erich. *Das Geistproblem der Theologie: Eine systematische Untersuchung*. Leipzig: Deichertsche, 1924.
Schäfer, H. Letter to Bockmuehl, November 19, 1963. Unpublished manuscript in the Bockmuehl archives in St. Chrischona.
Schlatter, Adolf. *Adolf Schlatters Rückblick auf seine Lebensarbeit*. Edited by Theodor Schlatter. Gütersloh, Germany: Bertelsmann, 1952. .
———. *Atheistische Methoden in der Theologie mit einem Beitrag von Paul Jäger*. Edited by H. Hempelmann. TuD 43. Wuppertal, Germany: Brockhaus, 1985
———. *Briefe über das Christliche Dogma*. 2nd ed. Stuttgart: Calwer, 1978.
———. *Die christliche Ethik*. 5th ed. Stuttgart: Calwer, 1986.
———. *Die Gabe des Christus: Eine Auslegung der Bergpredigt*. TuD 30. 2nd ed. Giessen, Germany: Brunnen, 1982.
———. *Das christliche Dogma*. 4th ed. Stuttgart: Calwer, 1978.
———. *Der Dienst des Christen: Beiträge zu einer Theologie der Liebe*. Edited by Werner Neuer. Giessen, Germany: Brunnen, 1991.
———. *Der Evangelist Matthäus*. 3rd ed. Stuttgart: Calwer, 1948.
———. *Do We Know Jesus? Daily Insights for the Mind and Soul*. Translated by Andreas J. Köstenberger and Robert W. Yarbrough. Grand Rapids: Kregel, 2005.

Bibliography

———. *Erläuterungen zum Neuen Testament*. Vol. 7, *Die Briefe an die Galater, Epheser, Kolosser und Philemon. Ausgelegt für Bibelleser*. Rev ed. Stuttgart: Calwer, 1963.
———. *Metaphysik. Eine Skizze. Mit einer Einführung von Werner Neuer*. Zeitschrift für Theologie und Kirche, Beiheft 7. Tübingen: Mohr/Siebeck, 1987.
———. "Natur, Sünde, und Gnade." In *Gesunde Lehre. Reden und Aufsätze*, 49-68. Velbert, Germany: Freizeiten, 1929.
———. *Paulus der Bote Jesu: Eine Deutung seiner Briefe an die Korinther*. 5th ed. Stuttgart: Calwer, 1985.
Schleiermacher, Friedrich. *Der christliche Glaube nach den Grundsätzen der evangelischen Kirche im Zusammenhange dargestellt*. 2nd ed. Berlin: G. Reimer, 1830-31.
———. *Lectures on Philosophical Ethics*. Edited by Robert B. Louden. Cambridge: Cambridge University Press, 2002.
Schmidt, Kurt D. *Gesammelte Aufsätze*. Edited by Manfred Jacobs. Göttingen: Vandenhoeck & Ruprecht, 1967.
Schmidt, Martin. "Spener und Luther." In *Luther Jahrbuch 1957*, edited by Franz Lau, 102-29. Berlin: Lutherisches Verlagshaus, 1957.
———. *Wiedergeburt und Neuer Mensch: Gesammelte Studien zur Geschichte des Pietismus*. Arbeiten zur Geschichte des Pietismus 2. Witten, Germany: Luther, 1969.
Schuman, Robert. "Préface." In *Refaire le monde*, by Frank Buchman, vii-viii. Paris: La Compagnie du Livre, 1949.
Sell, Alan P. F. *The Spirit Our Life: Doctrine and Devotion*. Shippenburg, PA: Ragged Edge, 2000.
Six, Jean-François. *Charles de Foucauld—Der geistliche Werdegang*. Munich: Neue Stadt, 1978.
———. *Das Leben von Charles de Foucauld*. Freiburg: Herder, 1966.
Smail, Tom. *The Giving Gift: The Holy Spirit in Person*, London: Darton, Longman & Todd, 1994.
———. *Reflected Glory: The Spirit in Christ and Christians*. London: Hodder & Stoughton, 1975.
Søe, Niels H. "The Personal Ethics of Emil Brunner." In *The Theology of Emil Brunner*, edited by C. W. Kegley, 247-61. New York: Macmillan, 1962.
Spener, Philipp J. "On Hindrances to Theological Studies." In *Pietists: Selected Writings*, edited by Peter C. Erb, 65-70. London: SPCK, 1983.
———. *Pia Desidera*. Translated and edited by Theodore G. Tappert. Philadelphia: Fortress, 1964.
———. *Schriften. 7/1: Der hochwichtige Articul von der Wiedergeburt (1969) 1715. Predigten 1-34*. Edited by Erich Beyreuther. Hildesheim, Germany: Olms, 1994.
———. *Theologische Bedencken, Und andere Brieffliche Antworten auff geistliche sonderlich zur erbauung gerichtete materien*. Vol. 3. Halle, Germany: Waysen-Haus, 1715.
Spiegel-Schmidt, Friedrich. *Kirche ohne Geist? Der Pietismus als Frage an die Gegenwart*. Witten, Germany: Luther, 1965.
Spoerri, Pierre. "Moralische Aufrüstung." *Lexikon für Theologie und Kirche*, 7:452. Freiburg: Herder, 1998.
Spoerri, Theodor. *Dynamic out of Silence: Frank Buchman's Relevance Today*. London: Grosvenor, 1976.
Stassen, Glen H., and David P. Gushee. *Kingdom Ethics: Following Jesus in Contemporary Context*. Downers Grove: IVP, 2003.

Bibliography

Stewart, James S. *A Man in Christ: The Vital Elements of St. Paul's Religion.* London: Hodder & Stoughton, 1938.
Stoeffler, F. Ernest. *German Pietism during the Eighteenth Century.* Leiden: Brill, 1973.
———. "Pietism." *The Encyclopedia of Religion,* 11:324-6. New York: Macmillan, 1987.
———. "Preface." In *Pietists: Selected Writings,* edited by Peter C. Erb, ix-xi. London: SPCK, 1983.
———. *The Rise of Evangelical Pietism.* Leiden: Brill, 1971.
Störig, Hans J. *Kleine Weltgeschichte der Philosophie.* Frankfurt: Fischer Taschenbuch, 1993.
Stott, John R. W. *The Cross of Christ.* 2nd ed. Leicester: IVP, 1989.
Swarat, Uwe. "Gesetz und Geist. Zu Klaus Bockmuehls theologischem Vermächtnis." *ThBeitr* 21 (1990) 35-39.
Taber, Charles R. *The World Is Too Much with Us: "Culture" in Modern Protestant Mission.* Macon, GA: Mercer University Press, 1991.
Tappert, Theodore G. "Introduction." In *Pia Desideria,* by Philip J. Spener, edited by Theodore G. Tappert, 1-28. Philadelphia: Fortress, 1964.
Thomas, Arthur D. "The Spirituality of Klaus Bockmuehl: Part One: The Influences Upon His Practice of Listening to God." *Crux* 24, no. 1 (1993) 2-10.
———. "The Spirituality of Klaus Bockmuehl: Part Two: His Practice Of Discerning The God Who Speaks." *Crux* 24, no. 2 (1993) 28-34.
Thornhill, Alan. *The Forgotten Factor.* London: Blandford, 1954.
Tillich, Paul. *Systematic Theology.* Vol. 3. London: Nisbet, 1964.
———.*Writings in Social Philosophy and Ethics/Sozialphilosophische und Ethische Schriften.* Main Works/Hauptwerke 3. Edited by Erdmann Sturm. New York: de Gruyter, 1998.
Torrance, Thomas F. *Theology in Reconstruction.* Grand Rapids: Eerdmans, 1965.
Tournier, Paul. *Guilt and Grace: A Psychological Study.* London: Hodder & Stoughton, 1974.
Tsanoff, Radoslav A. *The Great Philosophers.* 2nd ed. New York: Harper & Row, 1964.
Turner, Max. *The Holy Spirit and Spiritual Gifts: Then and Now.* Carlisle: Paternoster Press, 1996.
———. *Power from on High: The Spirit in Israel's Restoration and Witness in Luke-Acts.* Sheffield: Sheffield Academic, 1996.
Ulrich, Hans G. "Grundlinien ethischer Diskussion. Ein Literaturbericht." *Verkündigung und Forschung* 20, no. 2 (1975) 53-99.
Vacek, Edward C. *Love, Human and Divine: The Heart of Christian Ethics.* Washington, DC: Georgetown University Press, 1994.
Vanhoozer, Kevin J. "Introduction: The Love of God." In *Nothing Greater, Nothing Better. Theological Essays on the Love of God,* edited by Kevin J. Vanhoozer, 1-29. Grand Rapids: Eerdmans, 2001.
Vanier, Jean. *Becoming Human.* London: Darton, Longman & Todd, 1999.
———. *Our Journey Home: Rediscovering a Common Humanity Beyond our Differences.* London: Hodder & Stoughton, 1997.
Voillaume, Rene. *Seeds of the Desert: Like Jesus at Nazareth.* Translated by W. Hill. Wheathampstead, UK: Clarke Books, 1972.
Volf, Miroslav. *Exclusion and Embrace: A Theological Exploration of Identity, Otherness, and Reconciliation.* Nashville: Abingdon, 1996.
Vorländer, Wolfgang. *Der Heilige Geist und die Kunst zu leben.* Neukirchen-Vluyn: Aussaat, 1991.

Bibliography

Wadell, Paul J. *Friendship and the Moral Life*. Notre Dame: University of Notre Dame Press, 1989.
Wainwright, Geoffrey. "The Holy Spirit." In *The Cambridge Companion to Christian Doctrine*, edited by Colin E. Gunton, 273-96. Cambridge: Cambridge University Press, 1997.
Wallmann, Johannes. *Philipp Jakob Spener und die Anfänge des Pietismus*. 2nd ed. Tübingen: Mohr/Siebeck, 1986.
Watson, Philip S. "Translator's Preface." In *Agape and Eros*, by Anders Nygren, vii–xvii. London: SPCK, 1953.
Webster, John. "The Legacy of Barth and Bultmann." *Evangel* 1, no. 1 (1983) 8-11.
Welker, Michael. *God the Spirit*, Minneapolis: Fortress, 1994.
Wenk, Matthias. *Community-Forming Power: The Socio-Ethical Role of the Spirit in Luke-Acts*. Sheffield: Sheffield Academic, 2000.
Williams, Clifford. *Singleness of Heart: Restoring the Divided Soul*. Grand Rapids: Eerdmans, 1994.
Williams, Daniel D. *The Spirit and the Forms of Love*. Digswell Place, UK: Nisbet, 1968.
Willis, Robert E. *The Ethics of Karl Barth*. Leiden: Brill, 1971.
Wingren, Gustaf. *Theology in Conflict: Nygren, Barth, Bultmann*. Edinburgh: Oliver & Boyd, 1958.
Wogaman, J. Philip. *Christian Ethics. A Historical Introduction*. London: SPCK, 1994.
Wong, Joseph H. P. "The Holy Spirit in the Life of Jesus and of the Christian." *Gregorianum* 73 (1/1992) 57-95.
Wolterstorff, Nicholas. "Suffering Love." In *Philosophy and the Christian Faith*, edited by T. V. Morris, 196-237. Notre Dame: University of Notre Dame Press, 1988.
Woodruff, M. J. "In Memoriam." *Quarterly: Christian Legal Society* 10 (1989) 25.
Yarbrough, Robert W. "Translator's Preface." In *Adolf Schlatter. A Biography of Germany's Premier Biblical Theologian*, by Wener Neuer, translated by R. W. Yarbrough, 9-12. Grand Rapids: Baker, 1995.
Yeide, Harry, Jr. *Studies in Classical Pietism: The Flowering of the Ecclesiola*. New York: Lang, 1997.
Ziesler, John. *Pauline Christianity*. Rev. ed. Oxford: Oxford University Press, 1990.
Zimmerling, Peter. "Christliche Maßstäbe für das Wirtschaftsleben bei Zinzendorf und der Herrnhuter Brüdergemeine." In *Gott lieben und seine Gebote halten—Loving God and Keeping His Commandments: in Memoriam, Klaus Bockmuehl*, edited by Markus Bockmuehl and Helmut Burkhardt, 107-21. Giessen, Germany: Brunnen, 1991.

Bibliography

List of Klaus Bockmuehl's Works

Publications

1957

"Sinn und Ziele der Christlichen Studentenbewegung." *Communio, Schweizerische Christliche Studentenbewegung/Mouvement Chretien D'Etudiants eu suisse* 13 (1957) 174-76.

1960

Review of *Feuerbach und die Religion*, by W. Schilling. *Zeitschrift für evangelische Ethik* 4, no. 1 (1960) 58-61.

Review of *Soziologie der Kirchengemeinde*, edited by Dietrich Goldschmidt et al. *KiZ* 15, no. 9 (1960) 320-22.

"Wichtige Veröffentlichungen zum Werk Johannes Calvins 1950-1959." In *Calvin-Studien 1959*, edited by Jürgen Moltmann, 173-75. Neukirchen: Neukirchener Verlag, 1960.

1961

Leiblichkeit und Gesellschaft. Studien zur Religionskritik und Anthropologie im Frühwerk von Ludwig Feuerbach und Karl Marx. Göttingen: Vandenhoeck & Ruprecht, 1961. 2nd rev. exp. ed. Giessen, Germany: Brunnen, 1980.

Review of *Religion und christlicher Glaube*, by Hendrik Kraemer. *KiZ* 16, no. 9 (1961) 369-70.

Review of *Theologie der missionarischen Verkündigung. Evangelisation als ökumenisches Problem*, by Hans J. Margull. *KiZ* 16, no. 5 (1961) 178-80.

"Zum Tode Frank Buchmans." *KiZ* 16, no. 9 (1961) 389-91.

1962

"Die Gottesbeweise der Philosophie." Review of *Der ontologische Gottesbeweis. Sein Problem und seine Geschichte in der Neuzeit*, by Dieter Henrich. *Verkündigung und Forschung* (1960/1962) 143-48.

Review of *Begegnungen der Christen. Studien evangelischer und katholischer Theologen*, edited by Maximilian Roesle and Oscar Cullmann. *MPTh* 51 (1962) 265-67.

1963

Frank Buchmans Botschaft und ihre Bedeutung für die protestantischen Kirchen. Bern: Haupt, 1963 (reprint in *DH*, 193-226).

"Die Kirche vor der Existenzfrage. Gegen eine Reduzierung des Christentums." *Informationsdienst der Moralischen Aufrüstung* 17, no. 18 (1963) 67-68, 70.

"Der Kommunismus auf der Suche nach dem neuen Menschen." *Reformatio* [Zeitschrift für Evangelische Kultur und Politik, Zürich: Verlag Reformatio] 12 (1963) 550-66. (Reprint in *anruf* [Magazin des Deutschen EC-Verbandes. Kassel: Born] 67, no. 5 [1971] 18-22, and 69, nos. 7-8 [1971] 20-22.)

Review of *Der Atheismus im Dialektischen Materialismus*, by Peter Ehlen. *Abschaffung Gottes? Das Buch über den Atheismus*, by Hans-Gerhard Koch. *Atheismus. Gespräch mit Atheisten*, by Aurel von Jüchen. *Historischer und Dialektischer Materialismus. Ein Quellenheft*, by Erich Thier. *KiZ* 18, no. 6 (1963) 267-71.

Bibliography

Review of *Deutsche Schriften*, by Martin Bucer, edited by Robert Stupperich. *ThZ* 19 (1963) 148–49.
Review of *Ehe und Familie*, by Joseph Höffner. *MPTh* 52 (1963) 241.
Review of *Die Lehre über den heiligen Geist bei Tertullian*, by Wolfgang Bender. *ThZ* 19 (1963) 146–47.

1964

"Die Diskussion über Homosexualität in theologischer Sicht." *EvTh* 24 (1964) 242–66. (Rev. reprint in *Homosexualität in evangelischer Sicht*, edited by Klaus Bockmuehl, 26–61. Wuppertal, Germany: Aussaat, 1965. Reprint in *LWG*, 1–33. Reprint of extract as "Homosexualität in evangelischer Sicht." In *Brennpunkt Seelsorge. Beiträge zur biblischen Lebensberatung*, Reichelsheim: Christen in der Offensive e.V. 3 [1979] 6. French translation in *La Revue Réformée* 2 [1965] 1–25.)
"Die neue Moral—Fakten und Argumente." *Erziehung—Spiegel unserer Zeit oder Gestaltung der Zukunft?* Bericht einer Studientagung in Bern, Jan. 1964, 3–8. (Reprint in *"unter uns." CVJM Württemberg* 7 [1965] 156–59. French translation in *La Revue Réformée* 4 [1964] 12–17.)
Die neuere Missionstheologie. Eine Erinnerung an die Aufgabe der Kirche. Arbeiten zur Theologie 1/16. Stuttgart: Calwer, 1964. (Rev. and exp. reprint in *Was heißt heute Mission?* 1974.)
Review of *Offenbarung als Geschichte*, edited by W. Pannenberg et al. *ThZ* 20 (1964) 294–97.

1965

Grundlagen christlicher Sexualethik. Wuppertal, Germany: Aussaat, 1965. (Reprint in *LWG*, 34–50. French translation in *La Revue Réformée* 68 [1966] 24–37.)
(Editor.) *Homosexualität in evangelischer Sicht*. Wuppertal, Germany: Aussaat, 1965.
"Die Leiblichkeit des Menschen in biblischer Sicht." In *Die Leiblichkeit des Menschen in einer anthropologischen Medizin*. IX. Internationales Seminar des International Medical Congress, 21–38. Vienna: Selbstverlag, 1965. (Rev. reprint in *gh*, 60–80; *DH*, 28–49).
"Die Wiedertrauung Geschiedener—nach evangelikalem Verständnis." *Die Glocke* 19, no. 2 (1965) 15–18. (Reprint in *LWG*, 51–59.)

1966

"Vorbemerkung des Übersetzers." In *Ein Staatsmann namens Paulus*, by Paul Campbell and Peter Howard, translated by Klaus Bockmuehl, 9–11. Lucerne: Caux, 1966.
"Wie lebt ein Christ an der Universität? Der Heidelberger Studentenpfarrer, Dr. Klaus Bockmühl, spricht in Caux." *Informationsdienst der Moralischen Aufrüstung* 18, nos. 1–2 (1966) 6.
"Ziele der Christenheit." *"unter uns." CVJM Württemberg* (1966) 10–12. *Nordbund CVJM-Zeitschrift* (1966) 4–6. (Reprint as "Ziele der Christenheit. Ein Manifest." Pamphlet. [Bensheim/Bergstrasse]: Offensive Junger Christen, c. 1968. Reprint in *LWG*, 344–47).

1967

"Die Maßgeblichkeit der Bibel für die Ethik." *BuG* 67, no. 2 (1967) 122–39. (Reprint in *BuG* 94, no. 3 [1994] 28–45. Rev. reprint: "Zur Frage nach der Maßgeblichkeit der Bibel für die Ethik." In *gh*, 30–49).

Bibliography

1968

"Die biblische Idee der Humanität und ihr Verhältnis zum Strafrecht des Staates." In *Sittenstrafrecht im Umbruch: Erwägungen zu einem neuen Strafgesetz*, edited by Wendelin Reichert, 57–76. Stuttgart: Radius, 1968. (Reprint in *gh*, 81–103.)

"Erziehung in einem Zeitalter der Revolution." *Informationsdienst der Moralischen Aufrüstung* 20, no. 24 (1968) 104–5.

"Röm. 8,4: Gesetz und Geist. Eine Skizze." *Themelios* [published by IFES] 5, no. 1 (1968) 3–7.

"Ungelöste Probleme nach Uppsala. Über die Aufgabe der Kirche—Mission und Revolution—Ein Spiegelbild vielfältiger Meinungen." *Rhein-Neckar-Zeitung*, June 25, 1968. (Reprint in *Informationsbrief der Bekenntnisbewegung* 16 [Sept. 1968] 4–7. Reprint in *WM*, 168–71).

"Warum demonstrieren die Studenten?" *Persönliche Mitteilungen der Pfarrer-Gebetsbruderschaft* 46 (1968) 5–7.

1969

Atheismus in der Christenheit: Anfechtung und Überwindung. Vol. 1, *Die Unwirklichkeit Gottes in Theologie und Kirche*. Wuppertal, Germany: Aussaat, 1969. 2nd rev. ed.: Wuppertal, Germany: Aussaat, 1970. 3rd ed. with new epilogue: Giessen, Germany: Brunnen, 1985. (English translation of the 3rd ed. with a new introduction and without the epilogue: *The Unreal God of Modern Theology. Bultmann, Barth, and the Theology of Atheism: a Call to Recovering the Truth of God's Reality*. Translated by Geoffrey W. Bromiley. Colorado Springs: Helmers & Howard, 1988. Italian Translation: *Ateismus Dal Pulpito: l'irrealità di Dio nella teologia e nella chiesa*, Roma: GBU, 1981. Also translated into Finnish and Danish.)

"Klaus Bockmuehl." In *Sorge um Deutschland* 18 (1969) 5. (Reprint in *Anstiftungen: Chronik aus 20 Jahren OJC*, edited by Horst-Klaus Hofmann and Irmela Hofmann, 28. Moers, Germany: Brendow, 1988).

"Revolution ohne Gewalt." In *John Wesley—Modell einer Revolution ohne Gewalt*, by Garth Lean, 5–9. Giessen, Germany: Brunnen, 1969.

"Über die Geltung der Zehn Gebote heute." *Brüderliche Handreichung* 50 (1969) 46–52. (Reprint in *gh*, 50–59. Reprint in *Glaube, der sich sehen läßt. Christsein im Spannungsfeld ethischer Entscheidungen*, edited by Christoph Morgner, 27–36. Giessen, Germany: Brunnen, 1993. Rev. English translation: "The Ten Commandments: Are They Still Valid?" *Crux* 15, no. 4 [1979] 20–25. Reprint in *With Heart, Mind and Strength. The Best of Crux 1979–1989*, edited by Donald M. Lewis, 1:27–37. Langley, BC: Credo, 1990. Reprint in *CW*, 125–36.)

1971

Review of *Mensch—Gott—Welt. Eine Orientierung*, by Joerg Gutzwiller. *ThBeitr* 2 (1971) 188–91.

"Revolution der Ethik und Ethik der Revolution." *ThBeitr* 2 (1971) 63–90. (Also published as separate print. Basel: Brunnen, 1972. Reprint of pp. 82–84 in "Sexualität und zielbezogene Ethik." *Porta* 16 (1973) 25–26. And in *LWG*, 60–75. English translation of the whole article: "Revolution of Ethics and Ethics of Revolution." *International Reformed Bulletin* 44–55 (1971) 52–72. Translated into French.)

Bibliography

1972

"Die Beurteilung der Abtreibung in der Frühzeit der christlichen Kirchen." *ThBeitr* 3 (1972) 34-43. (Reprint in *LWG*, 63-75.)

"Theorie und Praxis. Änderung des Menschen und Änderung der Strukturen. Zur Diskussion der marxistischen Hauptthese." *BuG* 72, no. 4 (1972) 268-86. (Reprint in *ThBeitr* 4 [1973] 12-31 and in *gh*, 104-27).

Review of *Wiedergeburt und neuer Mensch. Arbeiten zur Geschichte des Pietismus*, vol. 2, by Martin Schmidt. *ThBeitr* 3 (1972) 81-86.

"Was heißt glauben? Hebräer 11." *Glaubensbote, Pilgermission St. Chrischona* 95, no. 5 (1972) 84-85. (Reprint as "Was heißt Glaube? Über die Voraussetzung christlichen Handelns." In *gh*, 5-29 and in *DH*, 50-74.)

1973

"Erneuerung (Johannes 21, 15-17)." *Glaubensbote, Pilgermission St. Chrischona* 96, no. 11 (1973) 204-5.

"Glaube (Matth. 8, 5-13)." *Glaubensbote, Pilgermission St. Chrischona* 96, no. 4 (1973) 64-65.

"Homosexuality in Biblical Perspective." *Christianity Today* 17 (Feb. 16, 1973) 12-18.

"Der Kampf um den 'neuen Menschen' in der marxistischen Welt." Supplement to *Caux-Information* 25, no. 4 (1973) 1-4.

"Sexualität und zielbezogene Ethik." *Porta* 16 (1973) 25-26.

Sinn und Unsinn der neuen Moral: Kritik und Selbstkritik. TuD 1. Giessen, Germany: Brunnen, 1973. 2nd ed.: 1974. (Norwegian tranaslation: *Den nye moral. Kritikk og Selvkritikk*. Oslo: Lunde Forlag og Bokhandel A/S, 1977. Also translated into French.)

"Wie treffe ich eine Entscheidung?" *Caux-Information* 25, no. 15 (1973) 4-5. (Rev. reprint in *Geschäftsmann und Christ* 15, no. 3 (1975) 22-29. And as "Wie entscheidet Jesus sein Handeln?" *Glaubensbote, Pilgermission St. Chrischona* (Swiss edition) 98, no. 11 (1975) 236-37. And in *TuL*, 146-53. English translation of rev. reprint: "How Did Jesus Decide His Actions?" *Crux* 17, no. 4 (1981) 2-4.

1974

"Evangelicals Without Theology." *Christianity Today* 19 (Dec. 20, 1974) 34.

"Ohnmacht des Menschen—Gottes Kraft." *Glaubensbote, Pilgermission St. Chrischona* 97, no. 11 (1974) 204-5.

"Le problème de l'éthique dans le protestantisme." *La Revue Réformée* 100 (1974) 176-89. German original published as "Das Problem der Ethik im Protestantismus."[2] In *TuL*, 67-84.

Review of *Heinrich Heine und die Abschaffung der Sünde*, by Dolf Sternberger. *ThBeitr* 5 (1974) 97-99.

"Scheidung, Festigung und Sendung. Überlegungen zum Thema Kirche und Welt." In *Berufung und Bewährung/Vocation and Victory. An International Symposium. Presented in Honour of Erik Wickberg*, edited by Jürgen H. Winterhager and Arnold Brown, 29-41. Giessen, Germany: Brunnen, 1974. English translation in the same book: "Christians in the Secular World—Disengagement, Identity and Mission." 42-51 (Reprint in *DH*, 12-27).

---

2. Speech given by Klaus Bockmuehl in Bochum/Germany on December 14, 1971. Cf. *TuL*, 158.

Bibliography

"Vorwort." In *Wilberforce—Lehrstück christlicher Sozialreform*, by Garth Lean. TuD 3:5-6. Giessen, Germany: Brunnen, 1974.
Was heißt heute Mission? Entscheidungsfragen der neueren Missionstheologie. Giessen, Germany: Brunnen, 1974. (Reprint, including other articles, in BWA 1/3. Edited by Helmut Egelkraut. Giessen, Germany: Brunnen, 2000.)

1975
"After Lausanne—What?" *Christianity Today* 19 (March 14, 1975) 67-68.
"Bekenntnis und Vergebung (Ps 32,1-5)." In *Wer hört, wird leben, St. Chrischona-Predigten*, edited by Edgar Schmid, 28-37. Giessen, Germany: Brunnen, 1975.
"Destroyer or Provider." *Christianity Today* 19 (June 6, 1975) 49-50.
"Der einzelne und die Gemeinschaft (1 Kor 1,10)." In *Wer hört, wird leben, St. Chrischona-Predigten*, edited by Edgar Schmid, 57-64. Giessen, Germany: Brunnen, 1975.
Evangelikale Sozialethik: Der Artikel 5 der Lausanner Verpflichtung. TuD 9. Giessen, Germany: Brunnen, 1975. (English translation: *Evangelicals and Social Ethics: A Commentary on Article 5 of the Lausanne Covenant*. Translated by David T. Priestley. Outreach and Identity 4. Downers Grove: IVP, 1979.)
"Gefährdete Umwelt." *ThBeitr* 6 (1975) 223-32. (Review article of M. Mesarovic/E. Pestel, *Menschheit am Wendepunkt. Zweiter Bericht des Club of Rome*; J. B. Cobb, *Der Preis des Fortschritts. Umweltschutz als Problem der Sozialethik*; F. A. Schaeffer, *Das programmierte Ende. Umweltschutz aus christlicher Sicht*; A. Günter, *Schöpfung am Abgrund. Die Theologie vor der Umweltfrage*; T. S. Derr, *Ecology and Human Liberation. A theological critique of the use and abuse of our birthright*).
glauben und handeln. Beiträge zur Begründung evangelischer Ethik (Gesammelte Aufsätze). Giessen, Germany: Brunnen, 1975.
[The individual articles of *glauben und handeln* are (first publication date in brackets):
"Was heißt Glaube? Über die Voraussetzung christlichen Handelns." (1965) 5-29 (Reprint in *DH*, 50-74.)
"Zur Frage nach der Maßgeblichkeit der Bibel für die Ethik. Über die Quelle christlicher Handlungsnormen." (1967) 30-49.
"Über die Geltung der Zehn Gebote heute. Eine Ortsbestimmung des Dekalogs." (1969) 50-59.
"Die Leiblichkeit des Menschen in biblischer Sicht. Über den Leib als Mittel unseres wirkenden Tuns." (1965) 60-80.
"Die biblische Idee der Humanität und ihr Verhältnis zum Strafrecht des Staates. Über die Stellung christlicher Ethik zu Recht und Gesetz." (1968) 81-103.
"Theorie und Praxis, Änderung des Menschen und Änderung der Strukturen: Über Marxismus und Christentum und ihre Wege zur Weltgestaltung." (1973) 104-27.]
Gott im Exil? Zur Kritik der „Neuen Moral." Wuppertal, Germany: Aussaat, 1975. 2nd ed. Giessen, Germany: Brunnen, 1984.
"Jesus Christus befreit und eint. Eine kritische Studie zu den Vorbereitungspapieren des Ökumenischen Rates der Kirchen für die Fünfte Vollversammlung des ÖRK in Nairobi, Kenia." *idea*, special edition 41 (1975) i-iv. (Reprint in *Glaubensbote, Pilgermission St. Chrischona* (Swiss edition) 98, no. 11 (1975) 245-48. Reprint as "Vorbereitungen für Nairobi." In *WM*, 172-78).

Bibliography

"Der Marxismus auf der Suche nach dem 'neuen Menschen.'" *ThBeitr* 6 (1975) 93–105. (Reprint In *Die beiden Hände Christi. Perspektiven zur Evangelisation und sozialer Verantwortung*. Edited by Klaus Bockmuehl et al., 20–45. Wuppertal, Germany: Aussaat Verlag, 1977. In parts identical with chapter 4 of *Herausforderungen des Marxismus*, 1977. Article edited by H. Bühler and published as "Auszug aus einem Referat von Pfarrer Dr. Klaus Bockmühl, das er anlässlich der Delgierten-Konferenz des Verbandes unabhängiger evangelischer Kirchen und Körperschaften in der Schweiz ['Aarauer Verband'] in Langnau i.e., hielt." *Glaubensbote Pilgermission St. Chrischona* 96, no. 9 [1973] 132–33.)

"The Marxist New Man." *Christianity Today* 20 (Dec. 5, 1975) 53–54.

"Ostern 1975—Berechtigte Hoffnung." *Caux-Information* 27, no. 3 (1975) 1.

"Pre-Suppositions in Contemporary Theological Debate." In *Defending and Confirming the Gospel: the report of the 1975 Consultation of the Theological Commission of the World Evangelical Fellowship*, edited by Bruce S. Nicholls, 36–43. New Delhi: WEF Theological Commission, 1975. (Reprint in *The Conciliar-Evangelical Debate: The Crucial Documents, 1964–1976: expanded edition of Eye of the Storm, The Great Debate in Mission, Including Documents on Bangkok and Nairobi*, edited by Donald A. McGavran, 350–59. South Pasadena, CA: William Carey Library, c1977).

Die Produktion des neuen Menschen: Wege und Irrwege der Zukunftsmacher in Ost und West. Glauben und Denken. Wetzlar: Evangeliumsrundfunk, 1975. 2nd ed.: Wuppertal, Germany: Brockhaus, 1976. (English translation: "Production of the New Man. Efforts and Failures of the Future-makers in East and West." *New World News for Moral Re-Armament* 23, no. 10 [1975] 1–4.)

Review of *Schüler fragen nach Jesus. Modell einer christlichen Schülergruppe*, by Manfred Vonier. *ThBeitr* 6 (1975) 272.

"Der sendende Herr—die neue Schöpfung." *Porta* 20 (1975) 11–26. (Rev. reprint, *Der sendende Herr—die neue Schöpfung. Mission als Aufgabe*, TuD pamphlet 2, Giessen, Germany: Brunnen, 1976. And in *Was heißt heute Mission? Entscheidungsfragen der neueren Missionstheologie*, edited by Helmuth Egelkraut, 179–99. BWA 1/3. Giessen, Germany: Brunnen, 2000).

Umweltschutz—Lebenserhaltung. Vom Umgang mit Gottes Schöpfung. TuD 6. Giessen, Germany: Brunnen, 1975. (Reprint of pp. 5–10 and pp. 37–51 in *Rechte und Pflichten des Menschen im Kosmos*. Glaube und Denken. Giessen, Germany: Brunnen, 1976. Reprint of extract as "Eine aktuelle Anfrage." In *Anstiftungen zu gemeinsamem Christenleben*, OJC Frbrief 132, no. 3 (1991) 99–100. Unabridged reprint in *LWG*, 76–114. Rev. English translation: *Conservation and Lifestyle*. Translated by Bruce N. Kaye. Bramcote: Grove, 1977. Translated into Finnish in 1980.)

"WCC—Needs at Nairobi." *Christianity Today* 19 (Sept. 12, 1975) 77.

1976

Bücher—wozu? Möglichkeiten christlicher Literaturarbeit. 1st and 2nd ed. Giessen, Germany: Brunnen, 1976. 3rd ed.: 1977. (English translation: *Books—God's Tools in the History of Salvation*. Vancouver: Regent College, 1986.)

"Der Dienst der Theologie für die Gemeinde." *ThBeitr* 7 (1976) 1–5. (Reprint in *Der Dienst der Theologie*. TuD pamphlet 1. Giessen, Germany: Brunnen 1976. In *TuL*, 5–11. In *DH*, 75–80. Shortened translation: "Theology as Servant." *Christianity Today* 20 (Feb. 27, 1976) 45–46.)

"European Evangelicals: Seeking a Reformation." *Christianity Today* 21 (Nov. 19, 1976) 61–62.
"Evangelical Assertions on Social Change." *Christianity Today* 20 (May 21, 1976) 45–46.
"Die Geburt des neuen Menschen aus dem Glauben—Antwort an die Zukunftsmacher in Ost und West." In *Die Wiederentdeckung des Menschen: Biologie, Psychologie, Pädagogik und Theologie in der Auseinandersetzung um das Menschenbild*, edited by Dietrich Busch and Siegfried Großmann, 120–43. Wuppertal, Germany: Oncken, 1976. (Shortended version in *OJC Frbrief* 46, no. 1 [1976] 13–17).
"The Latter Letters of Barth." *Christianity Today* 20 (Aug. 27, 1976) 37.
Review of *Das Religionsverständnis von Karl Marx. Abhandlungen zur Philosophie und Psychologie der Religion*, by Johannes Kadenbach. *ThBeitr* 7 (1976) 126–26.
Review of *Gesamtausgabe 6, Briefe 1961–1968*, by Karl Barth. *Christianity Today* 20 (Aug. 27, 1976) 37.

1977

Herausforderungen des Marxismus. Giessen, Germany: Brunnen, 1977. 2nd ed. 1979. (Reprint *Herausforderungen des Marxismus. Verdrängte Hintergründe und bleibende Anfragen*, edited by Rainer Mayer. BWA 1/4. Giessen, Germany: Brunnen, 2002. English translation: *The Challenge of Marxism: A Christian Response*. Downers Grove: IVP, 1980. 2nd ed. Colorado Springs: Helmers & Howard, 1986.)
"Is there a Christian 'Life-style'?" *Christianity Today* 21 (May 20, 1977) 48–49.
"Natural Law." *Christianity Today* 21 (Nov. 18, 1977) 59–60.
"Das Problem einer evangelikalen Sozialethik." In *Gott für die Welt—wir sagen es weiter*, edited by Kurt Heimbucher, 139–54. Denkendorf, Germany: Gnadauer, 1977. (Reprint as "Der Versuch einer evangelikalen Sozialethik. Zwischenbilanz und Arbeits-Impulse." In *OJC Frbrief* 55, no. 5 (1977) 115–22. And in *Anstiftungen. Chronik aus 20 Jahren OJC*, edited by Horst-Klaus and Irmela Hofmann, 304–17. Moers, Germany: Brendow, 1988. Reprint under original title in *LWG*, 192–205.)
"Reich Gottes und Humanismus." In *Das Himmelreich hat schon begonnen*, edited by Klaas Runia and John R. W. Stott, 12–30. Wuppertal, Germany: Brockhaus, 1977. (Reprint in *TuL*, 43–66. English translation: "Humanism and the Kingdom of God." *Crux* 15, no. 1 [1979] 7–15. Reprint in *ERT* 3 [1979] 206–24. French translation: "Le Royaume de Dieu et l'humanisme." *Hokhma, Revue de reflexion theologique* 4 [1977] 18–37).
"The Ten Commandments." *Christianity Today* 21 (Aug. 26, 1977) 43.
"Under the Perspective Of Eternity." *Christianity Today* 21 (Feb. 18, 1977) 64–65.

1978

"Die Argumente für die Existenz Gottes. Eine Wiedererwägung ihres Zwecks." *ThBeitr* 9 (1978) 194–204. (Reprint in *TuL*, 30–42. And in *DH*, 91–104).
"Christianity has a Moral Backbone." *Christianity Today* 23 (Oct. 6, 1978) 54–55.
"Eigentum, Besitz." In *Evangelisches Gemeindelexikon*, edited by Helmut Burkhardt et al., 135–37. Wuppertal, Germany: Brockhaus, 1978. (Reprint in *LWG*, 206–9.)
"Gebote, Zehn." In *Evangelisches Gemeindelexikon*, edited by Helmut Burkhardt et al., 187–88. Wuppertal, Germany: Brockhaus, 1978.
"Law and the Spirit: Situation Ethics With a Difference." *Christianity Today* 22 (Febr. 24, 1978) 47, 49.

Bibliography

"On Wealth and Stewardship." *Christianity Today* 22 (June 23, 1978) 48, 50.
Die Stellung des Pietismus zur Separation. Gnadauer Materialdienst nr. 3. Dillenburg, Germany: Gnadauer Verband, 1978. (Reprint in *DH*, 227–49).
Review of *Herrschaft Gottes—Freiheit des Menschen. Biblische Perspektiven zur Neugestaltung der Gesellschaft*, by Michael Herwig. *ThBeitr* 9 (1978) 93–94.

1979

"Bringing Theology Back Down To Earth." *Christianity Today* 23 (April 20, 1979) 54–55.
"Einfacher Lebensstil—biblisch-theologische Bemerkungen." In *Einfacher Lebensstil im Dienst von Evangelisation und sozialer Gerechtigkeit: Referate und Thesen der 1. Konferenz des AfeT, 6-8. Juni 1977 in Tübingen*. Published by AfeT. (Reprint as "Überlegungen zum Thema 'Einfacher Lebensstil.'" In *Einfacher Lebensstil—ein neuer Maßstab? Thesen zur Evangelisation und sozialer Gerechtigkeit*, edited by Helmut Burkhardt, 7–29. Wuppertal, Germany: Aussaat, 1981. Reprint in *TuL*, 106–29. And in *LWG*, 264–85.)
"Friendship with Jesus." *Crux* 15, no. 2 (1979) 2–4.
"Gott lieben und den Nächsten wie sich selbst." *Porta* 26 (1979) 3–18. (Reprint in *Das größte Gebot*. TuD 21, 25–46. Giessen, Germany: Brunnen, 1980. And in *LWG*, 210–48. English translation: "The Great Commandment." *Crux* 23, no. 3 [1987] 10–20. Reprint in *With Heart, Mind and Strength. The Best of Crux 1979-1989*, edited by Donald M. Lewis, 1:9–26. Langley, BC: Credo, 1990).
"Is Christianity a Counterculture?" *Christianity Today* 23 (Aug. 17, 1979) 52.
Der Mensch auf der Suche nach Menschlichkeit. TuD pamphlet 5, Giessen, Germany: Brunnen, 1979.
"Saint for Our Day: Charles de Foucauld." *Christianity Today* 23 (Jan. 5, 1979) 55–56.
"Selig sind, die Gottes Gebote halten." *Porta* 26 (1979) 23–37. (Reprint in *Das größte Gebot*, TuD 21, 7–24. Giessen, Germany: Brunnen, 1980. Rev. reprint of second part as "Das Halten der Gebote. Die biblische These." *Brennpunkt Seelsorge* 1 [1981] 39–44. English translation: "Keeping His Commandments." *Crux* 17, no. 3 [1981] 17–25. Reprint in *ERT* 6 [1982] 85–99.)
"The Task of Systematic Theology." In *Perspectives on Evangelical Theology*, edited by Kenneth S. Kantzer and Stanley N. Gundry, 3–14. Grand Rapids: Eerdmans, 1979. German translation: "Aufgaben der systematischen Theologie heute." *TuL*, 12–29. (Reprint in *DH*, 105–21.)

1980

Das größte Gebot. TuD 21. Giessen, Germany: Brunnen, 1980. (Translated into Finnish in 1981.)
Leiblichkeit und Gesellschaft. Studien zur Religionskritik und Anthropologie im Frühwerk von Ludwig Feuerbach und Karl Marx. 2nd rev. ed. with an epilogue. Giessen, Germany: Brunnen 1980.
"The Marxist Critique of Religion and the Historicity of the Christian Faith." *Crux* 26, no. 1 (1980) 19–24. (Translated into Portugese: "A Crítica Marxista à Religiao e a historicidade da fé Crista." In *Marxismo e Fé Crista: O Desafio Mútuo*, edited by Paul Freston, 13–26. Sao Paulo: Abu [Livros Para Gente Que Pensa], 1988.)
"New Testament Studies: Giving in to God." *Christianity Today* 24 (Oct. 24, 1980) 76.
"The Raison d'Etre of Our Calling." *Christianity Today* 24 (Feb. 22, 1980) 54–55.

Review of *Friedrich Engels über Religion und Freiheit*, edited by Klaus Peters. *ThBeitr* 11 (1980) 289-90.
Review of *The Intellectual Life*, by Antonin G. Sertillanges. *Crux* 16, no. 3 (1980) 31-32.
"The Socialist Ideal: Some Soul-Searching Constraints." *Christianity Today* 24 (May 23, 1980) 53, 56.

1981

Auf dem Weg. Anweisungen für die Nachfolge. Giessen, Germany: Brunnen, 1981. (Reprint in *LWG*, 286-311. Translated into Dutch in 1982.)
"The Christian as Lawyer." *Quaterly—Christian Legal Society* 2, no. 1 (1981) 10-11, 33-35.
"*Gott und wir—was gibt er uns, was erwartet er? Ein Referat zum Thema 'Leben aus dem Evangelium', gehalten auf der Pfingsttagung des Gnadauer Verbandes am 12. und 13. Juni 1981 in Siegen.*" *idea-Doku* 28 (1981) 1-18. (Reprint in *Leben aus dem Evangelium*. TuD 29. Giessen, Germany: Brunnen, 1982. Reprint of extract as "Der Ratgeber." *OJC Frbrief* 138, no. 3 [1992] 88-92.)
"Kirche und soziale Verantwortung." In *Kirche und Sozialismus*, edited by Helmuth Flammer, 98-111. Gütersloh: Gütersloher, 1981. (Reprint in *TuL*, 130-45. And in *LWG*, 249-63.)
"Toward a Spirituality of the Kingdom." *Christianity Today* 25 (Feb. 6, 1981) 42.
"Zum Streit um die Grundwerte. Eine Debatte über den primus usus legis." *ThBeitr* 12 (1981) 206-20. (Reprint in *TuL*, 85-105.)

1982

"God and Other 'Forgotten Factors' in Theology." *Christianity Today* 26 (Feb. 19, 1982) 48-49.
"Lean Years—Abundant Opportunity." *Christianity Today* 26 (Nov. 26, 1982) 68.
"Marxism and Education: A Survey Report." *The Challenge of Marxist and Neo-Marxist ideologies for Christian scholarship*, edited by John C. Vander Stelt, 210-44. Sioux Center, IA: Dordt College Press, 1982. *Leben aus dem Evangelium*. TuD 29. Giessen, Germany: Brunnen, 1982. Translation into English (extended version): *Living by the Gospel: Christian Roots of Confidence and Purpose*. Colorado Springs: Helmers & Howard, 1986. German translation of the English version: *Leben mit dem Gott, der redet*. Edited by Horst-Klaus Hofmann. BWA 1/6, 1-75. Giessen, Germany: Brunnen, 1998. Reprint of pp. 60-75 in "Die Verkündigung." *OJC* 177, no. 6 (1998) 244-56.
Theologie und Lebensführung. Gesammelte Aufsätze 2. Giessen, Germany: Brunnen, 1982.
[The individual articles are (first publication date in brackets):
"Der Dienst der Theologie." (1976) 5-11.
"Aufgaben der systematischen Theologie heute." (English 1979) 12-29.
"Die Argumente für die Existenz Gottes. Eine Erwägung ihres Zwecks." (1978) 30-42.
"Reich Gottes und Humanismus." (1977) 43-66.
"Das Problem der Ethik im Protestantismus." (French 1974) 67-84.
"Der Streit um die 'Grundwerte'. Eine Auseinandersetzung um den *primus usus legis*." (1981) 85-105.
"Überlegungen zum Thema 'Einfacher Lebensstil.'" (1981) 106-29.

"Kirche und soziale Verantwortung. Zum Thema Christentum und Sozialismus." (1981) 130-45.
"Wie entscheidet Jesus sein Handeln? Eine Betrachtung über Johannes 5,30." (1981) 146-53]
"Quiet Holidays." *Quarterly Bulletin* [Regent College Vancouver] 12, no. 3 (1982) n.p.

1983

"Aufbruch der Evangelikalen—in die Zersplitterung?" *idea-spektrum* 39 (1983) 15-17. (Reprint in *OJC Frbrief* 89, no. 1 [1984] 34-35. And in *Anstiftungen, Chronik aus 20 Jahren OJC*, edited by Horst-Klaus Hofmann and Irmela Hofman, 717-20. Moers, Germany: Brendow, 1988.)

"'Freies Werk in der Kirche'—ein aktuelles Modell. Kirche und Pietismus müssen die Kleingruppe neu entdecken." *idea-spektrum* 47 (1983) 13-14. (Rev. reprint as "Kirche im Pietismus." In *Die Aktualität des Pietismus*, 11-14. TuD 45. Giessen, Germany: Brunnen, 1985).

"Nicht rechts, nicht links, sondern geradeaus. Profil und Identität müssen das zentrale Thema werden." *Idea-spektrum* 42 (1983) 16-17. (Rev. reprint as "'Aufbruch der Evangelikalen'—wohin?" In *Die Aktualität des Pietismus*, 9-10. TuD 45. Giessen, Germany: Brunnen, 1985).

"Secularism and Theology." *Crux* 19, no. 2 (1983) 6-14. (Reprint in *With Heart, Mind and Strength. The Best of Crux 1979-1989*, edited by Donald M. Lewis, 1:39-54. Langley, BC: Credo, 1990.)

Editor. *Verkündigung und soziale Verantwortung. Eine evangelische Verpflichtung. Gemeinsame Veröffentlichung des Lausanner Komitees für Weltevangelisation und der Evangelischen Welt-Allianz*, edited and introduced by Klaus Bockmuehl, 5-8. TuD 33. Giessen, Germany: Brunnen, 1983.

"Die Wende im Spätwerk Karl Barths." *ThBeitr* 14 (1983) 180-88. (Reprint in *DH*, 280-90.)

1984

"Allein der Glaube macht noch keinen Christen aus—Die Aktualität des Pietismus: Das Thema Heiligung." *idea-spektrum* 9 (1984) 14-15. (Rev. reprint as "Das Thema 'Heiligung.'" In *Die Aktualität des Pietismus*, 26-30. TuD 45. Giessen, Germany: Brunnen, 1985).

"Angst ist der Preis des Säkularismus—Die Bedeutung des Pietismus im Protestantismus." *idea-spektrum* 4 (1984) 14-15. (Rev. reprint as "Konzentration auf Jesus." In *Die Aktualität des Pietismus*, 19-22. TuD 45. Giessen, Germany: Brunnen, 1985).

"Das Evangelium in der Begegnung mit dem modernen Menschen." In *Schritte zu den Menschen*, edited by Kurt Heimbucher, 40-52. Dillenburg, Germany: Gnadauer, 1984. (Reprint in *Das Evangelium und die Ideologien*, 7-24. And in *DH*, 122-42.)

"Für eine theologische Alternative—Unglückliches Verhältnis: Der Pietismus und die Theologie." *idea-spektrum* 47 (1984) 13-14. (Rev. reprint as "Der Pietismus und die Theologie." In *Die Aktualität des Pietismus*, 38-41. TuD 45. Giessen, Germany: Brunnen, 1985).

"Macht und Ohnmacht der Ideologien—eine christliche Stellungnahme." In *Schritte zu den Menschen*, edited by Kurt Heimbucher, 94-103. Dillenburg, Germany: Gnadauer, 1984. (Reprint in *Das Evangelium und die Ideologien*, 25-37.)

"Die pädagogische Schwäche des Protestantismus—Von den Vätern des Pietismus lernen." *idea-spektrum* 40 (1984) 14-15. (Rev. reprint as "Der pädagogische Beitrag des Pietismus." In *Die Aktualität des Pietismus*, 35-37. TuD 45. Giessen, Germany: Brunnen, 1985.)

Review of *Essays in Evangelical Social Ethics*, edited by David F. Wright. *Transformation* 1, no. 1 (1984) 29.

"'Verkirchlichung' freier Werke schadet der Weltmission—Was hat das missionarische Engagement des deutschen Pietismus so geschwächt?" *idea-spektrum* 25 (1984) 15-17. (Rev. reprint as "Der Pietismus und die Mission." In *Die Aktualität des Pietismus*, 31-34. TuD 45. Giessen, Germany: Brunnen, 1985.)

1985

Die Aktualität des Pietismus. TuD 45. Giessen, Germany: Brunnen, 1985 (articles published in *idea-spektrum* in 1983-1984. Reprint in *DH*, 291-333.)

"Bekehrung und Wiedergeburt: 'Andere können dieselbe bei uns gewahr werden...' Zur Aktualität des Pietismus." *idea-spektrum* 14 (1985) 16-17. (Rev. reprint as "Bekehrung und Wiedergeburt." In *Die Aktualität des Pietismus*, 23-26. TuD 45. Giessen, Germany: Brunnen, 1985.)

"'...fehlende Vertrautheit im Umgang mit der Bibel'—Der Pietismus und die Heilige Schrift." *idea-spektrum* 6 (1985) 15-16. (Rev. reprint as "Der Pietismus und die Bibel." In *Die Aktualität des Pietismus*, 14-19. TuD 45. Giessen, Germany: Brunnen, 1985.)

"Nachwort." In *Atheismus in der Christenheit: Die Unwirklichkeit Gottes in Theologie und Kirche*, 3rd rev. ed. with new epilogue, 160-61. Giessen, Germany: Brunnen, 1985.

"Ein Neubeginn des sozialen Engagements. Der Pietismus und die Sozialethik: Von Anbeginn an dabei." *idea-Pressedienst* 31 (15 April 1985) iii-iv. (Rev. reprint as "Der Pietismus und die Sozialethik." In *Die Aktualität des Pietismus*, 46-51. TuD 45. Giessen, Germany: Brunnen, 1985.)

Säkularismus und christlicher Glaube. Gottesherrschaft oder Selbstherrschaft des Menschen? Porta-Studien 8. Marburg: SMD, 1985. (Partly identical with "Secularism and Theology." *Crux* 19, no. 2 (1983) 6-14).

"Der Säkularismus und seine Folgen für die Ethik. Referat des evangelikalen Theologen Dr. Klaus Bockmühl auf dem Zweiten Christlichen Medienkongreß vom 16. bis 18. April 1985 in Böblingen." *idea-Doku* 13 (1985) 1-21. (Reprint as "Der Säkularismus und die Folgen." In *Das Evangelium und die Ideologien*, 38-60. TuD 48. Giessen, Germany: Brunnen, 1986. In *OJC Frbrief* 102, no. 2 (1986) 53-68. In *Anstiftungen, Chronik aus 20 Jahren OJC*, edited by Horst-Klaus Hofmann and Irmela Hofmann, 347-73. Moers, Germany: Brendow, 1988. In *DH*, 159-89).

"Secularization and Secularism: Some Christian Considerations." *ERT* 10 (1986) 50-73. (Reprint in *Christian Faith and Practice in the Modern World*, edited by Mark A. Noll and David F. Wells, 263-84. Grand Rapids: Eerdmans, 1988. Shortend reprint in *The Best in Theology*, edited by James I. Packer, 1:177-87. Carol Stream, IL: Christianity Today, 1987.)

"'Real Humanism' Marxism as a Critique of Christianity." *Crux* 21, no. 2 (1985) 3-9. (Reprint as "Karl Marx's Negation of Christianity: A Theological Response" in *ERT* 9, no. 3 (1985) 251-63.)

"Die Seele der Barmherzigkeit—Chancen und Gefahren für die Diakonie der Gegenwart." *idea-spektrum* 2 (1985) 10-11. (Rev. reprint as "Der diakonische

Auftrag." In *Die Aktualität des Pietismus*, 42-46. TuD 45. Giessen, Germany: Brunnen, 1985.)

"'... to live soberly, righteously, and godly in the present age.' A Meditation on Titus 2:12." *Crux* 21, no. 4 (1985) 2-5.

1986

Das Evangelium und die Ideologien. TuD 48. Giessen, Germany: Brunnen, 1986.
[The individual articles are (first publication date in brackets):
"Das Evangelium in der Begegnung mit dem Menschen unserer Zeit." (1984).
"Macht und Ohnmacht der Ideologien." (f1984).
"Der Säkularismus und die Folgen." (1985).
(reprint of all three articles in *DH*, 122-89)].

"Karl Barth 1886-1986: An Evangelical Appraisal." *Crux* 22, no. 3 (1986) 28-32.

1987

"Ethics/Spiritual Life, Introduction." In *The Best in Theology*, edited by James I. Packer, 1:237-8. Carol Stream, IL: Christianity Today, 1987.

Gesetz und Geist. Eine kritische Würdigung des Erbes protestantischer Ethik. Vol. 1, *Die Ethik der reformatorischen Bekenntnisschriften*. Giessen, Germany: Brunnen, 1987. (2nd ed.: BWA 1/5. Edited by Reinhard Slenczka. Giessen, Germany: Brunnen, 2009. Reprint of extract as "Gott spricht auch noch heute." In *Gotteswort im Menschenwort? Zum Verstehen und Auslegen der Bibel*, edited by Sven Grosse and Jochen Walldorf, 80-82. Porta Studien 30. Marburg: SMD, 1999.)

"Mit Christus dienen." *Die Diakonie Schwester: Neue Folge der Blätter aus dem Evangelischen Diakonieverein und aus dem Zehlendorfer Verband für Evangelische Diakonie*. [Berlin: Christlicher Zeitschriftenverlag] 83, no. 9 (1987) 159-67. (Reprint in *ThBeitr* 20 (1989) 6-22. Shortened reprint in *Reformiertes Forum, Schweizerischer Evangelischer Pressedienst* [Basel: Friedrich Reinhardt AG] 28, no. 1 (1987) 1-3. Unabridged reprint in *LWG*, 324-43.)

Review of *Jüdische Ethik anhand der Patristischen Perikopen. Jerusalemer Vorlesungen*, by Shalom Ben-Chorin. *ThBeitr* 18 (1987) 269-70.

"Three Horizons for Theology." *ERT* 11 (1987) 5-20.

1988

Editor. *Die Aktualität der Theologie Adolf Schlatters*. Giessen, Germany: Brunnen, 1988. ["Vorwort des Herausgebers." 1-4. "Die Wahrnehmung der Geschichte in der Dogmatik Adolf Schlatters." 93-112. (Reprint of latter article in *DH*, 334-54.)]

"Ethics/Spiritual Life, Introduction." In *The Best in Theology*, edited by James I. Packer, 2:263-5. Carol Stream, IL: Christianity Today, 1988.

"Gesetz und Geist. Eine Anfrage an das Erbe protestantischer Ethik." *ThBeitr* 19 (1988) 5-22. English translation: "Protestant Ethics: The Spirit and the Word in Action." *ERT* 12 (1988) 101-15.

"Klaus Bockmuehl." In *Anstiftungen. Chronik aus 20 Jahren OJC*. Edited by Horst-Klaus Hofmann and Irmela Hofmann, 28. Moers, Germany: Brendow, 1988.

"Recovering Vocation Today." *Crux* 24, no. 3 (1988) 25-35. (Reprint in *With Heart, Mind and Strength: The Best of Crux 1979-1989*, edited by Donald M. Lewis, 1:81-99. Langley, BC: Credo, 1990.)

Review of *On the Tail of a Comet—The life of Frank Buchman*, by Garth Lean. *For A Change* 1, no. 9 (1988) 18.

Bibliography

Review of *Protestant Thought in the 19th Century*, 2 vols., by Claude Welch. *Crux* 24, no. 3 (1988) 36-37.
"Sanctification." In *New Dictionary of Theology*, edited by Sinclair B. Ferguson et al., 613-16. Leicester: IVP, 1988.
"Sanctification and Christian Mission." In *Bilanz und Plan: Mission an der Schwelle zum Dritten Jahrtausend, Festschrift für George W. Peters*, edited by Hans Kasdorf et al., 54-64. Bad Liebenzell, Germany: VLM, 1988. (German summary of english article: "Heiligung und Mission." 65-68. German translation of english article in *LWG*, 312-23. Translated by H. Ottinger, 312-23.)
"Von der Anstössigkeit der 'hässlichen Protestanten' (I)—Braucht die Kirche den Pietismus?—Warum der heutige Pietismus Aschenputtel der Theologie ist." *idea-spektrum* 28 (1988) 15-16.
"Zurück zu den Anfängen: Buße und Wiedergeburt (II)—Die Stunde des Pietismus— Ein Schuh, in dem das Evangelium durch die Welt laufen kann." *idea-spektrum* 29 (1988) 17-18. (Reprint of (I) and (II) as "Kopfloser Pietismus." *OJC Frbrief* 143, no. 2 (1993) 61-64.)

1989

"Ethics/Spiritual Life, Introduction." In *The Best in Theology*, edited by James I. Packer, 3:189-92. Carol Stream, IL: Christianity Today, 1989.
Konkrete Umkehr. Die christliche Lehre von der Bekehrung zwischen Marxismus und moderner Theologie. TuD 56. Giessen, Germany: Brunnen, 1989. (Reprint of chap. 3 as "Die biblische Lehre von der Bekehrung." *Brennpunkt Seelsorge* 1 [1991] 4-9.)
"Let Us Be Listeners." *Crux* 25, no. 2 (1989) 3-7. German translation: "Laßt uns Hörer sein, Ansprache bei der Abschlußfeier ('convocation') des Regent College, Vancouver/Kanada am 15. Mai 1989." *JETh* 3 (1989) 8-18.

1990

Listening to the God who speaks. Reflections on God's Guidance from the Scripture and the Lives of God's People. Colorado Springs: Helmers & Howard, 1990. (German translation: *Hören auf den Gott, der redet.* Translated by Elisabeth Bockmuehl. Giessen, Germany: Brunnen, 1990. (Reprint in *Leben mit dem Gott, der redet*, edited by Horst-Klaus Hofmann, 77-180. BWA 1/6. Giessen, Germany: Brunnen, 1998. Reprint of extracts: "Hören auf den Gott, der redet." *Brennpunkt Seelsorge* 4 (1990) 75-81. "Bernhard von Clairvaux." *OJC Frbrief* 143, no. 2 (1993) 70. "Augustinus" *OJC* 144, no. 3 (1993) 118-9. "Franz von Assisi." *OJC Frbrief* 145, no. 4 (1993) 159). Swedish translation: *Lyssna till Gud*. Kumla: HFs, 1992).

1993

Christliche Lebensführung, Eine Ethik der Zehn Gebote. Edited by Helmut Burkhardt. Giessen, Germany: Brunnen, 1993. 2nd ed.: 1995. (Reprint *Christliche Lebensführung, Eine Ethik der Zehn Gebote.* Edited by Helmut Burkhardt. BWA 3/2. Giessen, Germany: Brunnen, 1999). English translation: *The Christian Way of Living: An Ethics of the Ten Commandments.* Vancouver: Regent College Bookstore, 1994.

Bibliography

1998
Leben mit dem Gott, der redet: Leben aus dem Evangelium. Hören auf den Gott der redet. Edited by Horst-Klaus Hofmann. BWA 1/6. Giessen, Germany: Brunnen, 1998.
[Reprint of extract as "Die Verkündigung." *OJC Frbrief* 177, no. 6 (1998) 244–56.]

1999
Denken im Horizont der Wirklichkeit Gottes. Schriften zur Dogmatik und Theologiegeschichte. Edited by Rainer Mayer. BWA 2/1. Giessen, Germany: Brunnen, 1999.
[The individual articles are (first publication date in brackets):
"Dogmatisches zur Tauffrage." (first publ.) 3–11.
"Scheidung, Festigung und Sendung—Überlegungen zum Thema Kirche und Welt." (1974) 12–27.
"Die Leiblichkeit des Menschen in biblischer Sicht." (1975) 28–49.
"Was heißt Glaube?" (1975) 50–74.
"Der Dienst der Theologie." (1976) 75–80.
"Zur Frage des Glaubensbekenntnisses im Gottesdienst." (first publ.) 81–90.
"Die Argumente für die Existenz Gottes." (1978) 91–104.
"Aufgaben der systematischen Theologie heute." (1982) 105–21.
"Das Evangelium in der Begegnung mit dem Menschen unserer Zeit." (1986) 122–42.
"Macht und Ohnmacht der Ideologien." (1986) 143–58.
"Der Säkularismus und die Folgen." (1986) 159–89.
"Frank Buchmans Botschaft und ihre Bedeutung für die protestantischen Kirchen." (1963) 193–226.
"Die Stellung des Pietismus zur Separation." (1978) 227–49.
"Zur Hermeneutik Martin Luthers." (first publ.) 250–79.
"Die Wende im Spätwerk Karl Barths." (1983) 280–90.
"Die Aktualität des Pietismus." (1985) 291–333.
"Die Wahrnehmung der Geschichte in der Dogmatik Adolf Schlatters." (1988) 334–54.]

2000
Was heißt heute Mission? Entscheidungsfragen der neueren Missionstheologie. Edited by Helmuth L. Egelkraut. BWA 1/3. Giessen, Germany: Brunnen, 2000.
[The individual articles are (first publication date in brackets):
"Was heißt heute Mission?" (1964/1974) 1–167.
"Ungelöste Probleme nach Uppsala." (1968) 168–71.
"Vorbereitungen für Nairobi." (1975) 172–78.
"Der sendende Herr—die neue Schöpfung." (1975/6) 179–99.
(Helmut Egelkraut, "Epilog: Die weitere missionstheologische Fragestellung im 20. Jahrhundert." 200–29)].

2001
Verantwortung des Glaubens im Wandel der Zeit. Protestantische Theologie im 19. und 20. Jahrhundert. Edited by Helmut Burkhardt. BWA 3/3. Giessen, Germany: Brunnen, 2001.

Bibliography

2006
Leben nach dem Willen Gottes. Schriften zur Materialethik. Edited by Rainer Mayer. BWA 2/3. Giessen, Germany: Brunnen, 2006.
[The individual articles are (first publication date in brackets):
"Die Diskussion über Homosexualität in theologischer Sicht." (1964) 1–33.
"Grundlagen christlicher Sexualethik." (1965) 34–50.
"Die Wiedertrauung Geschiedener nach evangelischem Verständnis." (1965) 51–59.
"Sexualität und zielbezogene Ethik." (1971/1973) 60–75.
"Die Beurteilung der Abtreibung in der Frühzeit der christlichen Kirchen." (1972) 63–75.
"Umweltschutz—Lebenserhaltung. Vom Umgang mit Gottes Schöpfung." (1975) 76–114.
"Evangelikale Sozialethik. Der Artikel 5 der Lausanner Verpflichtung." (1975) 115–55.
"Bücher—wozu? Möglichkeiten christlicher Literaturarbeit." (1976) 156–91.
"Das Problem einer evangelikalen Sozialethik." (1977) 192–205.
"Eigentum/Besitz." (1978) 206–9.
"Das größte Gebot." (1980) 210–48.
"Kirche und soziale Verantwortung: Zum Thema Christentum und Sozialismus." (1981) 249–63.
"Überlegungen zum Thema 'Einfacher Lebensstil.'" (1981) 264–85.
"Auf dem Weg. Anweisungen für die Nachfolge." (1981) 286–311.
"Heiligung und Mission." (1988) 312–23.
"Mit Christus dienen." (1987) 324–43.
"Ziele der Christenheit: Ein Manifest." (1968) 344–47.]

2009
Gesetz und Geist. Eine kritische Würdigung des Erbes protestantischer Ethik. 2nd ed. BWA 1/5. Edited by Reinhard Slenczka. Giessen, Germany: Brunnen, 2009.

Unpublished manuscripts[3]

"Die Bedeutung des Kreuzes Christi." Referat, gehalten an der Konferenz "Ziel für Deutschland" in Castrop-Rauxel am 16. April 1965. [An address delivered at the conference "Objective for Germany" in Castrop-Rauxel on April 16, 1965.]
"Christ an der Universität." [Bockmuehl's manuscript for a lecture given in Caux; a shortened version published as "Wie lebt ein Christ an der Universität? Der Heidelberger Studentenpfarrer, Dr. Klaus Bockmühl, spricht in Caux." *Informationsdienst der Moralischen Aufrüstung* 18, nos. 1–2 (1966) 6].
"Certificate of attendance at lectures at The London School of Economics," issued June 19, 1956.
"Curriculum vitae." Written in Basel, April 6, 1959.
"Curriculum Vitae." Written in Bettingen (Basel) on January 14, 1977 (english).

---

3. In the Bockmuehl archives in St. Chrischona unless otherwise stated.

Bibliography

"Education in an Age of Revolution." Speech, Moral Re-armament Conference: "New Horizons for Education," Caux, Switzerland, August 2, 1968. [German version published 1968.]

"Eindrücke von der Arbeit." 1966.

"Evangelikale ohne Theologie."

"Frank Buchman's Message and its Significance for the Protestant Churches." Translated by M. Fleischmann.

"Eine Geschichte der Lehre von der Kirche."

"Grundvoraussetzungen in der gegenwärtigen theologischen Debatte." Incomplete manuscript.

"India Report."

"Introduction to the Theology of the (Nineteenth and) Twentieth Century." [Word-for-word notes by Bockmuehl's assistant Rory Randall taken during Bockmuehl's lectures at Regent College Vancouver. German translation by Elisabeth Bockmuehl published in VG, chs. 1–7.]

"Josef, der Ernährer (Christ und Wirtschaft)." Evangeliums-Rundfunk, Wetzlar/Giessen, 17.12.1982. [Transcribed Radio-speech, Evangeliums-Rundfunk, Wetzlar, Dec. 17, 1982.]

"Journals."

"Lebenslauf Klaus Erich Bockmuehl." Written in Lörrach/Baden, May 21, 1955.

"Der neue Mensch und die ideologischen Systeme."

"Perimeters of Change. The Realism of Christian Conversion in the light of Marxism and Some Modern Theology." [Unpublished translation of *Konkrete Umkehr. Die christliche Lehre von der Bekehrung zwischen Marxismus und moderner Thelogie.* 1989]

"Reifezeugnis" [equivalent to A-level] from 1951. [In possession of Horst-Klaus Hofmann, Reichelsheim.]

"Serving with Christ." [English translation by M.W. Fleischmann in August 1987 of "Mit Christus dienen." *ThBeitr* 20 (1989) 6.]

Vorträge und Ausarbeitungen von Klaus Bockmühl. Unpublished book in the library of the Theological Seminary of St. Chrischona (Signature B 6 103/1):

1) "Die Religionskritik des Marxismus."
2) "Der Marxismus auf der Suche nach dem 'neuen Menschen.'" [Published in 1975.]
3) "Herausforderung des Marxismus + Quellenzitate zu den Vorträgen."
4) "Die Stellung des Pietismus zur Separation." [Published in 1978.]
5) "Tendenzen der Theologie 1968."
6) "Scheidung, Festigung und Sendung (Überlegungen zum Thema Kirche und Welt)." [Printed in 1974].
7) "Über die Geltung der Zehn Gebote heute." [Published in 1969.]
8) "Die Wiedertrauung Geschiedener—nach evangelischem Verständnis." [Published in 1965.]
9) "Dogmatisches zur Tauffrage (Ein Bericht)." [Published in *DH*, 1999.]
10) "Predigt: Psalm 32, 1–5 (Bekenntnis und Vergebung)" [Published in 1975.]
11) "Predigt: 2. Kor. 10, 4–5 (Die Indienstnahme des Denkens)."
12) "Predigt: Lukas 15, 1–3.11–24 (Das Gleichnis vom verlorenen Sohn)."
13) "Neuere Theologiegeschichte (1770–1940)."
14) "Datenüberblick zur Kirchengeschichte (1.–20. Jahrhundert) von Frau Bockmühl."

Bibliography

"Vortrag von Dr. Klaus Bockmühl, Heidelberg, am 22. Juli 1965 bei einer Tagung der Aktion SORGE UM DEUTSCHLAND. Mutterhauskapelle der Evangelischen Marienschwesternschaft Darmstadt-Eberstadt—unkorrigierte Abschrift vom Tonband" [Lecture by Dr. Klaus Bockmuehl, Heidelberg, July 22, 1965 at a conference of CONCERN FOR GERMANY. Chapel of the mother house of the Protestant Sisterhood of Mary in Darmstadt-Eberstadt—uncorrected transcript from an audio tape"]
"Was können wir tun?" Nachschrift der Einleitung Pastor Dr. Klaus Bockmuehls, Basel, am 5. Dezember 1964 in Darmstadt-Eberstadt zur ersten Planungsbesprechung für eine kommende Aktion: SORGE UM DEUTSCHLAND. [Transcript of the introduction by Klaus Bockmuehl, Basel, at the first planning meeting of CONCERN FOR GERMANY on Dec. 5, 1964 in Darmstadt-Eberstadt.]
"Das Werk des Hl Geistes in der Heiligung." Lecture.
"Wiedergeburt und Neuschöpfung." [Unfinished postdoctoral dissertation (*Habilitation*).]

Private Correspondence[4]

Letter to Karl Barth, September 27, 1963.
Letter to Karl Barth, October 26, 1963.
[Letter from H. Schäfer to Bockmuehl, November 19, 1963.]
Letter to Mr. Halfenberg, December 19, 1963.
Letter to the professors and lecturers at the theological faculty in Basel on September 28, 1963.
Letter to Jörg Gutzwiler and Alfred Kunz, March 1, 1965.
Letter to P. Engelbert Heller and Martin-Eckart Fuchs, March 5, 1965.
Letter to Reinhard (Kuster), June 23, 1965.
Letter to Pfarrer Lindenmeyer, September 12, 1965.
Letter to the "Sekretariat Charles de Foucauld," February 8, 1966.
Letter to Dieter Reiher, April 11, 1966.
Letter to Wilhelm Busch, April 13, and May 30, 1966.
Letter to Hans Urs von Balthasar, June 14, 1966.
Letter to Professor Eichrodt, November 21, 1966.
Letter to Pfarrer Lindenmeyer, November 21, 1966.
Letter to Fromund Helmes, January 15, 1967.
Letter to Rainer Klein, December 9, 1967.
Circular letter written by Bockmuehl December 1967.
Letter to "Guy," December 7, 1967 (English).
Letter to Michael Herwig, March 23, 1968.
Letter to Martin-Eckart Fuchs, Horst-Klaus Hofmann, and Willi Dammerboer, March 29, 1968.
Circular letter written by Bockmuehl April 18, 1968.
Letter to Marienschwesternschaft, July 2, 1968.
[Letter from Hendrik van Oyen to Bockmuehl, July 6, 1968.]

---

4. Correspondence in German unless otherwise noted.

Bibliography

Letter to the "europäische Pfarrermannschaft," February 10, 1970. [Includes a report on the consultations with the "Pfarrermannschaft" ("team of pastors") in London end January 1970.]
[Letter from Helmut Gollwitzer to Bockmuehl, January 26, 1970. Review of *Atheismus in der Christenheit*.]
Letter to H. Eißler, the chairman of the ABH-Association, March 13, 1970.
[Letter from Beyerhaus to Bockmuehl, March 10, 1970.]
Letter to "Landesbischof" (regional bishop Hans-Wolfgang Heidland), November 26, 1974.
Circular letter written by Bockmuehl on December 12, 1977.
Circular letter written by Bockmuehl on December 26, 1979.
Circular letter written by Bockmuehl to his friends on June 29, 1985 (English).
Circular letter written by Bockmuehl to his friends in January 1986.
Circular letter written by Bockmuehl to his friends on December 1, 1988.
Circular letter written by Bockmuehl to his friends on December 5, 1988 (English).

Reviews of Bockmuehl's Works[5]

1961
Fischer, H. Review of *Leiblichkeit und Gesellschaft*. In *ThLZ* 87 (1962) 453-54.
Gollwitzer, Helmut. Review of *Leiblichkeit und Gesellschaft*. In *Verkündigung und Forschung* 2, no. 3 (1962) 201-9.
Oelmüller, W. Review of *Leiblichkeit und Gesellschaft*. In *Philosophische Rundschau* 12, no. 1-2 (1964) 98-100.
Wiesner, W. Review of *Leiblichkeit und Gesellschaft*. In *ThZ* 19, no. 1 (1963) 65-67.
Review of *Leiblichkeit und Gesellschaft*. In *Lutherische Rundschau / Literatur-Umschau* 12, no. 2 (1962) n.p.
English translation:
Review of *Leiblichkeit und Gesellschaft*. In *Lutheran World / Literature Survey* (1962) n.p.
Review of *Leiblichkeit und Gesellschaft*. In *Politisch-soziale Korrespondenz* 13, no. 10 (1964).
1963
Ellenberger, W. Review of *Frank Buchmans Botschaft*. In *Der Säemann, Monatsblatt der Bernisch-Reformierten Landeskirche* 80, no. 4 (1964) 44.
Gaßmann, G. Review of *Frank Buchmans Botschaft*. In *Deutsches Pfarrerblatt* (1964) 394.
Neidhart, W. Review of *Frank Buchmans Botschaft*. In *Evang. Missionsmagazin* 108, no. 1 (1964) 41-42.
Review of *Frank Buchmans Botschaft*. In *Das Neueste, Buchberichte* [Stuttgart: Vereinigung Evangelischer Buchhändler e.V.] 13, no. 1-2 (1964) 18.
Weiser, G. Review of *Frank Buchmans Botschaft*. In *Kirchenblatt für die Reformierte Schweiz* 120, no. 11 (1964) 174.
Werner, P. Review of *Frank Buchmans Botschaft*. In *CVJM Berlin* (1964) 16.

---

5. Listed according to date of publication of Bockmuehl's works.

Bibliography

1964
Enklaar, I. H. Review of *Die neuere Missionstheologie*. In *Nederlands Theologisch Tijdschrift* [Wageningen] 20 (1965/1966) 78.
Gruhn, K. Review of *Die neuere Missionstheologie*. In *Deutsches Pfarrerblatt* 65, no. 1 (1965) 23.
Holsten, W. Review of *Die neuere Missionstheologie*. In *ThLZ* 91 (1966) 312–3.
Müller, J. Review of *Die neuere Missionstheologie*. In *Zeitschrift für Missions- und Religionswissenschaft* 49, no. 2 (1965) 134.
Plenter, J. D. Review of *Die neuere Missionstheologie*. In *Kerk en Theologie* 16, no. 2 (1965) 188.

1965
Bieneck, E. Review of *Grundlagen christlicher Sexualethik*. In *"unter uns." Württemberg CVJM* 12 (1965) 314.
Bovet, Theodore. Review of *Grundlagen christlicher Sexualethik*. In *EHE. Zentralblatt für Ehe- und Familienkunde* 3 (1966) 159–61.
Hutten, Kurt. Review of *Grundlagen christlicher Sexualethik*. In *Materialdienst. Längsschnitt durch die geistigen Strömungen und Fragen der Gegenwart* 29, no. 6 (1966) 145.
"Und schuf sie beide . . ." Review article of, among others, *Grundlagen christlicher Sexualethik*. In *Unser Auftrag, Handreichung für Mitarbeiter in der Gemeinde* [Munich : Evang. Presseverband] 11 (1965) 206–7.

Bieneck, E. Review of *Homosexualität in evangelischer Sicht*, edited by Klaus Bockmuehl. *"unter uns." CVJM Württemberg* 12 (1965) 314–15.
Bovet, Theodore. Review of *Homosexualität in evangelischer Sicht*, edited by Klaus Bockmuehl. *EHE. Zentralblatt für Ehe- und Familienkunde* 3 (1966) 70–71.
Walter, K. H. Review of *Homosexualität in evangelischer Sicht*, edited by Klaus Bockmuehl. *Der Büchertisch, Literatur-Beilage zur Zeitschrift "Die Gemeinde"* 2 (1966) 3.

1969 (1988)
Benktson, B.-E. Review of *Atheismus in der Christenheit*. In *Svensk Teologisk Kvartalskrift* 46, no. 3 (1970) 202–5.
Burkhardt, Helmut. Review of *Atheismus in der Christenheit*. In *ThBeitr* 1 (1970) 36–38.
Eber, Jochen. Review of *Atheismus in der Christenheit*. In *Ichhtys* 3, no. 4 (1987) 70.
Cedergren, R. "De Beredde Vägen för 'Gud är Död-Teologin.'" Review of *Atheismus in der Christenheit*. In *Dagen* (Stockholm), 20 Nov. 1969, 4.
Cedergren, R. "Karl Barth och Gudsförhållandet." Review of *Atheismus in der Christenheit*. In *Dagen* (Stockholm), 21 Nov. 1969, 4.
Cilleruelo, L. Review of *Atheismus in der Christenheit*. *Estudio Augustiniano* 6 (1971) 316.
Jones, G. V. Review of *Atheismus in der Christenheit*. In *Scottish Journal of Theology* 24, no. 2 (1971) 223–6.
Jüngel, Eberhard. Review of *Atheismus in der Christenheit*. In *EvTh* 30, no. 10 (1970) 570.
Review of *Atheismus in der Christenheit*. In *Verkündigung, Theologisches Blatt der "Lutherischen Stunde"* 8, no. 2 (1970) 19–20.

Bibliography

Review of *Atheismus in der Christenheit*. In *Informationen aus der Kirchlichen Erziehungskammer für Berlin* 1 (1970) 35.
Schmid, H. Review of *Atheismus in der Christenheit*. In *Kirchenblatt für die reformierte Schweiz* 126, no. 16 (1970) 242–44.

Buchanan, M. Review of *The Unreal God of Modern Theology*. In *Crux* 25, no. 1 (1989) 27–28.
Bromiley, Geoffrey W. Review (Recommendation/Advertisement) of *The Unreal God of Modern Theology*. In *Theology Today* 46, no. 1 (1989) 99.
Drew, G. Review of *The Unreal God of Modern Theology*. In *CBRF-Journal* 120 (1990) 41–43.
Hamersveld, M. Van. Review of *The Unreal God of Modern Theology*. In *Reformed Review* 43 (1990) 234–35.
Morrison, J. D. Review of *The Unreal God of Modern Theology*. In *Journal of the Evangelical Theological Society* 35 (1992) 115–17.
Wallace, M. I. Review of *The Unreal God of Modern Theology*. In *The Journal of Religion* 71 (1991) 107.
Weaver, G. R. Review of *The Unreal God of Modern Theology*. In *Christian Scholar's Review* 20, no. 4 (1991) 430–32.
Witmer, J. A. Review of *The Unreal God of Modern Theology*. In *Bibliotheca Sacra* 147 (1990) 238.

1973
Bormuth, K. H. Review of *Sinn und Unsinn der "neuen Moral."* In *ThBeitr* 6 (1975) 220–21.

1974
Knöpfel, E. Review of *Was heißt heute Mission?* In *Porta* 20 (1975) 99.
Peters, H.-J. Review of *Was heißt heute Mission?* In *Ichthys* 3, no. 5 (1987) 54–56.
Triebel, J. Review of *Was heißt heute Mission?* In *ThBeitr* 6 (1975) 180–82.

1975
Kirk, J. Andrew. Review of *Evangelicals and Social Ethics Evangelicals and Social Ethics: A Commentary on Article 5 of the Lausanne Covenant*. In *Churchman: a quarterly journal of Anglican theology* 94, no. 4 (1980) 375–76.
Gutsche, F. Review of *glauben und handeln, Beiträge zur Begründung evangelischer Ethik*. In *Mitarbeiterhilfe der CVJM* 34, no. 2 (1979) 46.
Gutsche, F. Review of *glauben und handeln, Beiträge zur Begründung evangelischer Ethik*. In *Porta* 26 (1979/1980) 56.
Jonker, W. D. Review of *Gott im Exil? Zur Kritk der "Neuen Moral."* In *Ned Gereff Teologiese Tydskrif* 18, no. 3 (1977) 287.
Liebschner, S. Review of *Gott im Exil? Zur Kritik der "Neuen Moral."* In *ThBeitr* 7 (1976) 40–43.
Kanitz, H. Review of *Gott im Exil? Zur Kritik der "Neuen Moral."* In *idea-spektrum* 18 (1985) 20.

Fieres, H. Review of "Der Marxismus auf der Suche nach dem 'neuen Menschen.'" In *Porta* 24 (1977/1978) 72.

Burkhardt, Helmut. Review of *Umweltschutz—Lebenserhaltung*. In *ThBeitr* 9 (1978) 282.

1976
Gutsche, F. Review of *Bücher—wozu? Möglichkeiten christlicher Literaturarbeit*. In *Porta* 24 (1977/1978) 69.

1977 (1980)
Neuer, Werner. Review of *Herausforderung des Marxismus*. In *ThBeitr* 10 (1979) 238-39.
Holtmann, Wilhelm. Review of *Herausforderung des Marxismus*. In *Reformierte Kirchenzeitung* 120 (July 15, 1979) 191-92.

Bourdeaux, M. Review of *The Challenge of Marxism: A Christian Response*. In *Religion in Communist Lands* 10 (1982) 351-52.
Feuvre, P. Le. Review of *The Challenge of Marxism: A Christian Response*. In *Journal of Theology for Southern Africa* 40 (1982) 76-77.
Hibma, J. Review of *The Challenge of Marxism: A Christian Response*. In *Reformed Review* 38 (1985) 164.
Hollenweger, W. J. Review of *The Challenge of Marxism: A Christian Response*. In *Expository Times* 92 (1981) 283-84.
Hug, J. E. Review of *The Challenge of Marxism: A Christian Response*. In *Theology Today* 38 (1981) 266-67.
Kirk, J. A. Review of *The Challenge of Marxism: A Christian Response*. In *Churchman: a quarterly journal of Anglican theology* 95, no. 4 (1981) 368-69.
Kubricht, P. Review of *The Challenge of Marxism: A Christian Response*. In *Christian Scholar's Review* 10, no. 4 (1981) 356-59.
Leckrone, T. L. Review of *The Challenge of Marxism: A Christian Response*. In *Christianity Today* 26 (Jan. 22, 1982) 46.
Lyon, D. Review of *The Challenge of Marxism: A Christian Response*. In *Evangelical Quarterly* 54 (1982) 62-64.
Macdonald, M. H. Review of *The Challenge of Marxism: A Christian Response*. In *Eternity* 33, no. 1 (1982) 40-41.
Mulayinkal, T. Review of *The Challenge of Marxism: A Christian Response*. In *Indian Missiological Review* 3, no. 3 (1981) 248-50.
Newberg, E. Review of *The Challenge of Marxism: A Christian Response*. In *Journal of the American Scientific Affiliation* 35, no. 2 (1983) 116-17.
Roodkowsky, N. D. Review of *The Challenge of Marxism: A Christian Response*. In *"America"* 144 (1981) 351-52.
Smolik, J. Review of *The Challenge of Marxism: A Christian Response*. In *Journal of Ecumenical Studies* 20, no. 1 (1983) 157.
Young, W. Review of *The Challenge of Marxism: A Christian Response*. In *Journal of the Evangelical Theological Society* 24, no. 3 (1981) 379.

1980
Burkhardt, Helmut. Review of *Das größte Gebot*. In *ThBeitr* 12 (1981) 239.
Roll, D. Review of *Das größte Gebot*. In *Mitarbeiterhilfe der CVJM* 37, no. 4 (1982) 44-45.

Bibliography

1982 (1986)
Frische, Reinhard. Review of *Leben aus dem Evangelium*. In *ThBeitr* 13 (1982) 277-79.

Blanch, S. Review of *Living by the Gospel*. In *The European Christian Bookseller* (June 1990).
Herrick, J. A. Review of *Living by the Gospel*. In *Eternity* 38, no. 6 (1987) 46-47.
Orde, K. v. Review of *Theologie und Lebensführung*. In *ThBeitr* 20 (1989) 47-49.
Sibley, L. "Roots and Branches of Christian Living." Review of *Living by the Gospel*. In *Christianity Today* 31 (April 3, 1987) 33.

1983
Eber, Jochen. Review of *Verkündigung und soziale Verantwortung*, edited by Klaus Bockmuehl. *Informationsbrief der Bekenntnisbewegung Kein anderes Evangelium* 102 (1984) 38.
Orde, Klaus v. Review of *Verkündigung und soziale Verantwortung*, edited by Klaus Bockmuehl. *ThBeitr* 20 (1989) 49-50.

1985
Sorg, Theo. Review of *Die Aktualität des Pietismus*. In *ThBeitr* 18 (1987) 325.

Kohler, C. Review of *Säkularismus und christlicher Glaube. Gottesherrschaft oder Selbstherrschaft des Menschen?*. In *Porta* 36 (1985) 55.

1986
Becker, W. Review of *Das Evangelium und die Ideologien*. In *AGORA* 15, no. 3 (1989) 34-36.
Rommen, E. Review of *Das Evangelium und die Ideologien*. In *ThBeitr* 18 (1987) 325-26.

1987
Birmelé, A. Review of *Gesetz und Geist: Eine kritische Würdigung des Erbes protestantischer Ethik I*. In *Revue d'Histoire et de Philosophie Religieuses* 68, no. 4 (1988) 506.
Bormuth, K. H. Review of *Gesetz und Geist: Eine kritische Würdigung des Erbes protestantischer Ethik I*. In *JETh* 2 (1988) 154-56.
Fagerberg, H. Review of *Gesetz und Geist: Eine kritische Würdigung des Erbes protestantischer Ethik I*. In *ThLZ* 114 (1989) 222-24.
Honecker, Martin. "Zur ethischen Diskussion der 80er Jahre." Review article, among others, on *Gesetz und Geist: Eine kritische Würdigung des Erbes protestantischer Ethik I*. In *Theologische Rundschau* 56, no. 1 (1991) 55-79.
Neuer, Werner. Review of *Gesetz und Geist: Eine kritische Würdigung des Erbes protestantischer Ethik I*. In *AGORA* 15, no. 3 (1989) 37-39.
Puttkammer, D. Review of *Gesetz und Geist: Eine kritische Würdigung des Erbes protestantischer Ethik I*. In *Das missionarische Wort, Zeitschrift für Verkündigung und Gemeindeaufbau* 4 (1989) 159-60.
Swarat, Uwe. "Gesetz und Geist: Zu Klaus Bockmühls theologischem Vermächtnis." Review artice on *Gesetz und Geist: Eine kritische Würdigung des Erbes protestantischer Ethik I*. In *ThBeitr* 21 (1990) 35-39.

Bibliography

1988

Frische, Reinhard. Review of *Die Aktualität der Theologie Adolf Schlatters*, edited by Klaus Bockmuehl. *JETh* 4 (1990) 233-39.

Hafner, H. Review of *Die Aktualität der Theologie Adolf Schlatters*, edited by Klaus Bockmuehl. *ThBeitr* 20 (1989) 206-7.

Marschner, R. Review of *Die Aktualität der Theologie Adolf Schlatters*, edited by Klaus Bockmuehl. *ThLZ* 114 (1989) 760-61.

1989

Burkhardt, Helmut. Review of *Konkrete Umkehr: Die christliche Lehre von der Bekehrung zwischen Marxismus und moderner Theologie*. In *JETh* 3 (1989) 211-13.

Neuer, Werner. Review of *Konkrete Umkehr: Die christliche Lehre von der Bekehrung zwischen Marxismus und moderner Theologie*. In *ThBeitr* 23, no. 6 (1992) 343-44.

1990

Blanch, S. Review of *Listening to the God Who Speaks*. In *The European Christian Bookseller* (1990).

Buis, H. Review of *Listening to the God Who Speaks*. In *Reformed Review* 44 (1991) 261-62.

Houston, G. Review of *Listening to the God Who Speaks*. In *Scottish Bulletin of Evangelical Theology* 15 (1997) 67-68.

Stewart, D. Review of *Listening to the God Who Speaks*. In *Crux* 28, no. 2 (1992) 43-44.

Becker, W. Review of *Hören auf den Gott, der redet*. In *AGORA* 23, no. 11 (1990) 36.

Diener, D. Review of *Hören auf den Gott, der redet*. In *JETh* 7 (1993) 238-41.

Heimowski, U. Review of *Hören auf den Gott, der redet*. In *dran* 1 (1999) 28-30.

Zimmerling, Peter. Review of *Hören auf den Gott, der redet*. In *ThBeitr* 22 (1991) 49-51.

1993 (1999)

Berger, K. R. Review of *Christliche Lebensführung: Eine Ethik der Zehn Gebote*. In *JETh* 14 (2000) 263.

Neuer, Werner. Review of *Christliche Lebensführung: Eine Ethik der Zehn Gebote*. In *ThBeitr* 25 (1994) 344-46.

Parzany, Ulrich. Review of *Christliche Lebensführung: Eine Ethik der Zehn Gebote*. In *Schritte* (1994) 50.

Seiferth, A. Review of *Christliche Lebensführung: Eine Ethik der Zehn Gebote*. In *AGORA* 31, no. 6 (1994) 29-30.

1998

Lorenz, E. Review of *Leben mit dem Gott, der redet* and *Denken im Horizont der Wirklichkeit Gottes*. In *Zeitwende* 1 (2000) 52-53.

Wünch, H.-G. Review of *Leben mit dem Gott, der redet*. In *JETh* 13 (1999) 158-59.

1999

Glaw, Annette. Review of *Denken im Horizont der Wirklichkeit Gottes*. In *JETh* 14 (2000) 232.

Lorenz, E. Review of *Leben mit dem Gott, der redet* and *Denken im Horizont der Wirklichkeit Gottes*. In *Zeitwende* 1 (2000) 52-53.

Bibliography

Müller, W. Review of *Denken im Horizont der Wirklichkeit Gottes*. *European Journal of Theology* 11, no. 2 (2002) 150–51.

Glaw, Annette. Review of *Bockmühl-Werk-Ausgabe (BWA)*. *Ichthys* 30 (2000) 74–79.

Author Index

Althaus, Paul, 32, 33, 111, 116, 140, 141, 174
Amstutz, J. 75, 76
Augustine, Aurelius, 26–29, 191, 226

Bailey, Kenneth E., 212
Balthasar, Hans U. von, 78–79
Barnette, Henlee H., 136, 187–88
Barth, Karl, xii, 7, 9, 26, 31, 46, 52, 54, 57, 64–72, 91–92, 94–95, 112, 119–31, 143, 147, 161, 167, 181, 188, 192–93, 203, 208–9
Bauckham, Richard, 137, 207–12
Belmans, Theo G., 78
Bennema, Cor, 216, 218
Berdyaev, Nicolas, 206, 214
Beyerhaus, Peter, 13, 94
Bloch, Ernst, 46
Bockmuehl, Markus, 8
Bonhoeffer, Dietrich, 140, 168, 207–8
Bosch, David, 49–51
Boyd, Gregory A., 230–31
Brown, Dale W., 43, 47, 49, 51–52
Brümmer, Vincent, 203–7, 211, 213–14
Brunner, Emil, 52, 62–63, 86, 130, 144, 168, 188
Buchman, Frank N. D., 4–5, 8, 21, 79, 80–88, 113, 158, 161–62, 171–74, 195–96

Bultmann, Rudolf, 46, 54, 57, 91–92, 119–31, 167, 188
Burkhardt, Helmut, 10, 17, 19, 21, 40, 43, 45, 62, 65, 92, 102, 143, 145–47, 161, 165, 178–79, 181
Burtness, James H., 221–22
Busch, Eberhard, 66–67
Busch, Wilhelm, 4–5, 9, 38–41, 88

Calvin, John, 28, 30–31, 33–38, 42, 112–14, 149, 157–58, 173, 182
Carrouges, Michel, 74, 76
Chambers, Oswald, 230–31
Chan, Simon, 2, 185, 223
Crane, Judith, 227, 233
Dubay, Thomas, S.M., 191–92, 198
Dintaman, Stephen F., 53–55
Drengson, Alan R., 224–25
Dunn, James D. G., 215, 217, 223

Ebeling, Gerhard, 188
Ekman, Gösta, 82–84
Erb, Peter C., 41, 44

Fairweather, Ian C. M., 130, 220–22, 224, 230
Fee, Gordon D., 202–4, 215, 217
Fiddes, Paul S., 204, 206, 208
Fletcher, Joseph, 45, 129–36
Foucauld, Charles de, 73–78, 239
Francke, August Hermann, 40, 42–44, 46, 49–52

Author Index

Frische, Reinhard, 47–48, 62, 73–75, 77, 88

Galot, Jean, 209, 216
Glaw, Annette, vii, 6
Goldingay, John, 202
Grenz, Stanley J., x, 3, 216–17, 221, 235
Gunton, Colin E., 70, 129, 192–93, 216, 218

Haizmann, Albrecht, 41–43, 46–48, 52
Harak, G. Simon, S.J., 225
Hart, Trevor, 123, 206, 212
Hauerwas, Stanley, 125–26, 131, 222, 224
Henning, Christian, 124, 127–28, 203
Herrmann, Wilhelm, 142
Higginson, Richard, 200
Hoffman, John C., 42, 49
Hofmann, Horst-Klaus, 3–7, 9–12, 14–15, 17–18, 37, 39–40, 65, 72, 89, 110–11
Holmes, Peter R., 224, 229
Holotik, Gerhard, 187, 224
Honecker, Martin, 190–91
Horrell, David G., 221
Houston, James M., 8, 16, 19–21, 150, 198
Howard, Peter, 80–81, 83–88
Hynson, Leo O., 187

Janz, Manuel, 190
Jeremias, Joachim, 6, 212
Jüngel, Eberhard, 153
Julian of Norwich, 19–20, 206–7

Keane, Philip S., 227
Kierkegaard, Søren, 122, 231

LaCugna, Catherine M., 207
Lafollette, Hugh, 214, 226
Lean, Garth, 4, 80–84, 87

Lohse, Bernhard, 34, 111
Lonsdale, David, 223–24, 228–29, 231
Loos, Andreas, 71, 156–57, 184, 192–95, 198
Lütgert, Wilhelm, 203, 207, 214
Luther, Martin, xiii, 26, 28, 30–31, 33–38, 40, 42, 59, 68, 87, 94, 110–12, 114–17, 140–43, 154, 158, 161–62, 196, 239

Kant, Immanuel, 56, 120, 142

MacIntyre, Alistair, 130, 135
Marx, Karl, xi, 7, 95, 97–98, 119–20
McDonald, James I. H.
    See Fairweather, Ian C. M.
McFarlane, Graham W. P., viii, ix, 210
McGrath, Alister E., 228–29
Merton, Thomas, 216, 218–19, 226–27, 230–31
Moltmann, Jürgen, 8, 53, 149, 175, 206, 208–11, 215
Motyer, Stephen, 221
Munzinger, André, 200, 218

Neuer, Werner, x, 1–3, 17, 35, 38, 53–60, 62–63, 72, 88–89, 160, 179, 188–89, 192, 199, 221
Niebuhr, Reinhold, 233
Nouwen, Henry J. M., 226–27, 231–32, 234
Nygren, Anders, 205–6

OJC, xiii, 11
Olthuis, James H., ix, 208, 225–27, 229, 234
Oyen, Hendrik van, 7, 9–11, 131, 134

Packer, James I., 21, 38, 52, 88, 90, 102
Pannenberg, Wolfhart, 175–76

Author Index

Parzany, Ulrich, 38–40
Pinnock, Clark H., 193–94, 207,
   216–17, 219, 231–33

Rabens, Volker, ix–x, 215–16, 218,
   223, 231
Reed, Esther, 215, 230
Riesner, Rainer, 14–15, 17
Robbins, Anna M, 221–22
Robinson, John A. T., 45, 129–32,
   135

Sarot, Marcel, 205–7, 209
Schlatter, Adolf, 17, 38, 52–63, 144,
   160, 179, 192–93, 199, 221
Schleiermacher, Friedrich, 142, 240
Schmidt, Martin 42–43, 52
Sell, Alan P. F., 228–29
Six, Jean-François, 73–76
Smail, Tom, 215–16, 218
Søe, Niels H., 52, 63
Spener, Philipp J., 17, 40–43,
   45–48, 50–52
Spoerri, Theodor, 4–5, 81–83, 86
Stoeffler, F. Ernest, 41–47, 49, 166
Stott, John R. W., 16, 163, 208–9
Swarat, Uwe, 52, 61, 178

Thomas, Arthur D., 3–4, 7–8, 10,
   12, 16–20, 30, 35, 38–40, 51,
   72, 80, 88–89, 105, 157
Tillich, Paul, 130, 142
Torrance, Thomas F., 210
Tournier, Paul, 231
Turner, Max, 202, 218

Vacek, Edward C., S. J., 206,
   213–14, 219, 224–25
Vanhoozer, Kevin J., 204–5, 211,
   217
Vanier, Jean, 224, 226–28, 232
Voillaume, Rene, 74–76
Volf, Miroslav, 207, 209
Vorländer, Wolfgang, 197

Wadell, Paul J., C.P., 206, 213, 225
Williams, Clifford, 227–28, 232
Williams, Daniel D., 213–14, 224,
   226, 228
Wingren, Gustaf, 122–23, 126, 140,
   144
Wogaman, J. Philip, 220–21
Wolterstorff, Nicholas, 208

Subject Index

Abba (Father), 203, 209, 216, 251
abortion, 29, 90
acceptance, 44, 97, 152, 211, 223–24, 229, 231–32
activism, 2, 20, 69, 72, 159, 195, 197
Adenauer, Konrad, 83–84
adoption, 223
agape, agapeic, 133, 205–6, 257, 262
Ambrosius, Aurelius, 29
Anabaptist, 37, 94–95, 111, 113, 183, 188
analogy/analogia, 120, 122–24
anger, 228, 231–33
Anglican, 143
(St.) Ansgar, missionary to Scandinavia, 27
anthropological, 121–21, 127–28, 136
antinomian, vii, 33, 35, 142, 189, 191, 237
antinomianism, 104, 133, 135, 144, 178, 189, 237
Apostle, 34, 49, 55, 61, 182
Aquinas, Thomas, 139
arbitrariness, 115, 133, 173, 200
atheism, 12, 13, 16, 40, 46, 66, 67, 78, 106, 119, 128
  in ethics, 106, 119, 128
  practical, 98, 135,
authority, 61, 91, 94, 109, 111, 130, 136, 141–42, 230
  of Scripture, 17, 30, 52, 57, 98

autonomous, 94, 126, 142, 221
autonomy, 91–92, 122, 125, 130–31, 135–36, 142, 147, 149, 152, 181
avoidance
  ethic of, 116, 180

Baader, Franz von, 54, 59–60
Basel (Switzerland), 6–7, 9–10, 13, 18, 54, 64
Beck, Johann Tobias, 19, 54
behavior, 159, 190, 206, 220, 222, 224
Bernard of Clairvaux, 26–27
biblical, 3, 6, 9, 31–32, 39, 41, 51–52, 54–55, 60–62, 67, 91, 106, 116, 121–22, 127, 134, 136, 139, 154, 160, 165, 167–69, 174, 180, 184, 188–89
  ethics, 32
birth, 117
  new birth 46, 49, 96, 100, 167
  rebirth, 44, 46, 96, 100, 169, 229
Bockmuehl, Elisabeth, x, 6–8, 17, 28, 30
body, 49, 100–101, 125, 150, 164, 197, 233,
Bovet, Theodor, 10
brokenness, 227–28, 230, 232, 234

Catholic, 67
catechism, 76, 174
  Large Catechism, 33, 114, 117

291

Subject Index

Caux, Switzerland, 5, 7–8, 13, 18, 79, 83–84, 86–87
change, 5, 14, 45, 48, 66–67, 81–82, 84, 86, 96–97, 101, 120–21, 124–25, 127, 131, 149, 152, 160, 165, 171, 194, 197, 222
  of lordship, 97, 147, 150, 152
  moral/ethical, 32, 44, 126, 129, 153, 188, 195–96
  personal, 14, 83
  practical, 119, 126
  social, 47, 129, 165, 227
character, 36, 58–59, 115, 120, 122–27, 130, 140–41, 153, 177, 179, 196, 213, 220, 222, 234
  ethic/ethicist, 221–22
charismata, 101, 116–17, 162, 165, 170, 176
  See also spiritual gifts
child, children, 3, 8, 40, 54, 163, 171, 193, 197, 199, 203, 211–13, 216–17, 233
(St.) Chrischona, x, 6, 13, 15–18, 28
Christ, 20, 40, 45, 68, 74, 76, 79, 81, 86, 93, 94, 98–99, 105, 124–26, 129, 132, 136, 138, 141, 143, 150, 157, 160–61, 174, 203, 205, 207–10, 213, 215–16
  cross of, 81, 86–87, 93, 97–98, 121, 126, 208–10, 215, 224, 232–34
  communion/fellowship with, 159, 216
  Jesus Christ, 40, 58, 65, 86, 88, 123, 149, 152, 211, 215, 223, 232–33
  lordship of, 94, 166
  love for, 197, 209
Chrysostomos, John, 29
church, vii–viii, 3–4, 7, 9–10, 12–16, 18–19, 25, 27, 29, 31–32, 40–41, 47–49, 54–55, 59, 61–62, 65–67, 79–80, 85, 87–95, 102, 106, 109, 111, 113, 116, 141–43, 150, 153, 161–65, 182–84, 194, 197, 199, 202, 222
  church-building activities, 29, 35, 48, 103, 110, 115, 162, 166, 176, 182, 188
  Church Dogmatics (Karl Barth), 52, 66–72, 122–23, 126, 143, 208–9
  Church Fathers, 26, 29, 72, 139
  Confessing Church ("*Bekennende Kirche*"), 39
  contemporary church, vii–viii, 86–87
  Evangelical Church in Germany (EKD), 3, 7–9, 11, 30, 41
  Protestant church, 14, 29, 79, 86, 157, 162, 189
  Reformed Church, 9, 30–31, 183
Clement of Alexandria, 29
commandment, 29, 34, 38–39, 63, 70, 77, 102, 105, 115, 126, 132–33, 153, 156, 169–70, 173–77, 189–91, 194
  divine/God's, 9, 47, 49, 51, 63, 141, 199
  double commandment of love, 26, 47–48, 103–6, 134, 141, 145, 154, 156, 158, 161, 168, 170, 177, 228
  Ten Commandments (*see also* Decalogue), 30, 33–35, 65, 70, 94, 103–4, 114, 117, 140–41, 144–45, 153, 174
commission, 15, 20, 26, 28, 48, 85, 116, 137, 139, 148, 156, 161–64, 174, 180, 196
  cultural, 94, 137, 139–40, 183
  ethic of, 48, 116
  Great Commission, 49–50, 68–70, 87, 116, 139, 153, 160–61, 179, 182–83, 193

Subject Index

communion, vii, 20, 103, 105, 129, 157–59, 161, 164–66, 191, 194–95, 198, 211, 226–27, 234, 238
community, 11–12, 32, 92–93, 103, 132, 145, 151, 173–74, 221, 223, 238
compassion, 77, 209–12, 224, 234
compassionate, 52, 212, 217, 234
compulsion, 144, 224, 232
Confessing Church. *See* church
confession, 44, 83, 97, 112, 152
  Augustine's Confessions, 27, 226
confessional, 31, 52, 78
conscience, 135, 141, 189, 191
conservation, conserve (the environment) 2, 16, 139
contemplation, 2, 76, 159, 226, 230–31
contemplative, 115, 121, 226
conversion, 4, 38, 40, 43–45, 49, 74, 77, 81–82, 96–97, 103, 124, 126, 152–53, 160, 167, 169
  See also birth, new birth/rebirth
core of being, 224, 227, 232
corporeal, 99, 127
corporeality, 7, 99–101
counseling, counselor, 10, 12, 89, 154, 158, 163
covenant, 71, 95, 170, 221
creation, 32, 54, 68, 71, 94–96, 99, 103, 138–40, 144–45, 175–76, 180–81, 187, 193–94, 205
  creation ethic/ethics, 32, 68–70, 95, 103–4, 137, 140–41, 144–47, 174–76, 178–80, 183, 189, 191–92, 194
  and redemption, 71, 92, 95, 192–93, 197
  creator, 183, 193–194, 221
  laws of, 140, 145, 147
  new creation, 93, 151–53
criterion/criteria, 42, 91, 132–35, 139, 154, 173, 220

Cremer, Hermann, 55
cross, 4–5, 7, 197
  See also Christ, cross of Christ
cultural mandate, 32, 69, 103, 137, 140, 144, 147, 174, 179
culture, 16, 98, 102, 143, 145, 212
  See also commission, culture commission

Decalogue, 33–35, 47–48, 70, 104, 107, 114–16, 118, 140–45, 159, 169, 173, 175–78, 180–81, 183, 189
  See also commandment, Ten Commandments
decision, 13–14, 16–17, 56, 127, 129, 131–35, 188, 195, 199, 220
decision-making, 1, 5–6, 70, 117, 126, 131–32, 135, 147, 169, 194–95, 199
demythologization, demythologize, 121, 127, 130
deontology, 221
  deontological ethics, 220
desire, 14, 18, 20, 76–77, 97, 125, 206, 216, 219, 224–25, 227–28, 231
development, 7, 9, 11, 13–15, 30, 40-41, 48, 68, 71, 118, 149, 152, 174, 199, 220
diakonia, 43, 48, 103, 110, 164, 180
  See also social action
  See also service, Christian service
dialectic, dialectical, 62, 66, 95, 122, 126, 130, 137, 167, 181, 188
differential
  "differential" principle, 70, 103, 114–16, 169
  differential ethics, 35, 70, 103–4, 147, 169, 175–78, 182–83, 237
differentiation, 33, 110, 169–170

293

Subject Index

dignity, 20, 99, 162, 197
discernment, 17, 118
discipleship, 73, 197
dissertation, 9–10, 54,
dogmatics/Dogmatics, 11, 15, 56–57, 61, 99, 127
dualism, 92–93, 199
duty, 11, 29, 60, 138, 142, 162, 170, 177–78, 180, 182, 190–91, 207

earth, 67, 92, 101–2, 122–24, 137–38, 149, 184, 193, 202, 205, 215, 226
ecological ethics, 103, 189
economy, 3, 126, 139
education, 8, 43, 96
efficacious, efficacy, 208, 226
Eichrodt, Walther, 6, 9
embodiment, 71, 127
emotion, emotional, 104, 135, 154, 157, 204, 210, 221, 224–25, 233
empathy, 208, 211, 233
encounter, 4, 38, 40, 63, 100, 181, 218, 224
Enlightenment, 49, 56, 120
environment, environmental, 2, 90, 103, 107, 139, 179
  environmental ethics, 16, 189
epistemological, 99, 115, 118
eschatology, 96, 149
eternal, eternity, 34, 104, 122, 141, 142, 148, 149, 215, 219
ethics. *See* biblical, creation, deontological, differential, ecological, environmental, evangelical, kingdom, Lutheran, Marxist-Leninist, Pauline, pneumatic, Protestant, redemption, Reformation, salvation, situation, social, teleological, trinitarian, utilitarian, virtue

  See (ethics of) avoidance, commission, involvement, love, preservation, restoration, the (Holy) Spirit
ethicist, 11, 53, 136, 188, 220–22
euthanasia, 197
evangelical, 16, 40–41, 88
  Christians, 18, 44
  ethics, 16
Evangelicals, 41, 44, 50, 88, 146, 150, 165
Evangelical Church in Germany (EKD). *See* church
evangelism, Evangelicalism, 35, 40, 49–50, 62, 76, 82, 103, 160, 162–63
evangelist, 38–39, 80, 163
evil, 8, 60, 93–94, 131, 145, 152, 174, 211, 219, 225, 234
existential, 97, 121–22, 125, 127–28, 130, 203
experience, vii, ix, 1, 5–6, 14, 21, 41, 44–45, 49, 52, 55, 57–58, 62, 74, 81, 85–87, 91, 98–100, 105, 126, 152–53, 155, 166, 181, 198, 208, 210, 212, 217, 226–27, 229, 231, 233, 238
  of guidance, 27–28, 83, 110–11, 171–72
experiential, 92, 119, 168, 223
exposition, vii, 26, 33, 48, 61–63, 69, 90, 109, 114–15, 160, 182

faith, ix, 34, 38, 43, 45, 47, 54, 57–60, 73–74, 90, 121–23, 125, 127–28, 163, 165–66, 175, 191, 194, 197, 218, 222–23, 231
  definition of (according to Bockmuehl), 97
  Christian, 4, 14, 45, 57–58, 238
faithfulness, 136, 188
fallenness, 193, 211, 227

Subject Index

family, x, 3, 16, 32, 54, 74, 80, 117, 162, 164, 233
father, 3, 26, 38, 117, 211–13
   See also Church Fathers
   See also God as father
fear, 20, 26, 61, 207, 227–28, 230–33
feeling(s), 16, 154, 199, 216, 228, 232
fellowship, 58, 76, 93, 151, 159, 171, 197, 202, 205–7, 211, 216
Feuerbach, Ludwig, 7, 97, 119, 122
forgiveness, 38, 44, 52, 81, 83, 94, 96, 105, 146, 151–52, 155, 166, 172, 174, 194, 205, 207, 210, 224, 231, 233–34
Francis of Assisi, 27–28
freedom, 3, 27, 75, 127, 171, 177–78, 189, 193, 206, 213–14, 218, 227–28, 231
friendship, 19–21, 39, 55, 75, 85, 105, 151, 157, 198, 206, 213–16
   See also relationship
fruit, 44, 101, 150–51, 156, 219, 222–24, 238
   of the Spirit, 105, 136, 178, 188, 221
functional, functionalism, vii, 148, 193–98, 238

Gandhi, Mahatma 83
Gerhardt, Paul, 51
Germany, 3–6, 11–13, 30, 50, 55, 65, 80, 83–84, 86, 142, 162, 189
Geschichte, 120–23
gift/gifts
   of God, 191, 214, 219, 227, 231
   of the (Holy) Spirit, 20, 44, 105, 113, 152, 155, 169, 172, 178
   spiritual, 117, 162

glory, 36, 66, 81, 99, 149, 198, 202, 208, 231
God, 3, 26, 38, 117, 211–13
   deity of, 66
   as father, vii–viii, x, 3, 79, 104, 149, 159, 161, 164, 172, 176, 183, 185, 203–4, 206, 208, 209–13, 215–19, 222–24, 231–32, 235, 237
   humanity of, 66–67, 122
Gogarten, Friedrich, 98
Golden rule, 103, 141, 145, 153
Gomaringen Circle, 17, 77
Good Samaritan, 138, 180–81
goodness, 136, 188, 198, 219–20, 231
(the) gospels, 154, 203, 205, 216
grace, ix, 44, 52, 61, 112, 125, 127, 162, 192, 194, 205, 208, 224, 228–32
grief, 210–11
guidance
   of/by the Holy Spirit, 1–2, 13–14, 18, 20, 25–28, 35, 37, 43, 51–52, 59, 61–63, 68, 70, 75, 77, 80, 82, 86–87, 89, 101, 103–4, 107, 110–13, 115–18, 134–36, 149, 158–59, 162, 165, 170–73, 175–77, 181–85, 188, 190–91, 195–96, 198–201, 224, 237
   individual, 115–16, 169, 175, 177–78, 183–84
   See also inspiration, prophecy
guilt, 228, 231–232

Harnack, Adolf von, 55
healing, ix, 60, 103, 141, 171, 174, 208, 217, 229–30, 233–34
heart, 21, 41, 104–5, 129, 154, 167–68, 170, 172, 174, 191, 199, 202, 204, 209, 216–18, 222–23, 226–29, 231–33
Hegel, Georg W. F., 95

Subject Index

Heidelberg (Germany), 11–13, 30, 55, 65, 78
Heim, Karl, 38
Hellenistic, 56, 141
heritage, 9, 18, 30–31, 41–42, 44, 132, 166, 189–90
Historie, 120–21
history
    of Christian ethics, 9, 109, 237
    salvation, 98, 100, 123
holiness, 35, 77, 103, 152, 167–68, 205
    See also sanctification
Holy Spirit
    inner/inward testimony of the Holy Spirit, 27–28, 51, 112
    See also Spirit
home, ix–x, 3, 75, 101, 103, 207, 209, 215, 231–33, 235
homosexuality, 9–10
humanity, 20, 66–67, 69, 85, 91, 98, 100–3, 120, 122, 141, 144, 146, 209
humility, 74, 191, 233

identity, 18, 93, 164, 217, 231
image, 137, 202, 212–13, 225, 228
    of God, 119, 138, 152, 206, 208, 212, 230–31
    of Christ, 85, 168, 179, 193, 196, 216
imagination, 230–31
incarnation, 99
India, 14, 78, 82–84
individual guidance. *See* guidance
individualization, 33, 117
indwelling (of the Holy Spirit), 152, 177, 201–4, 215, 217–18, 237
inspiration, ix, 28, 37, 51, 85, 89, 111, 135, 164, 170–71, 178, 196, 200
integration, 95, 192–93, 227
integrity, 46, 227

intimacy, x, 211–12, 214, 217, 219, 223, 225
    See also relationship
intuition, 135–36
involvement
    ethic of, 180
(St.) Irenaeus, 140
Israel, Israelite, 83, 202, 209, 212

John (apostle), 20, 72, 136, 139, 154, 156, 161, 188, 195, 197, 203–4, 207, 209, 213–14, 216–18, 223, 226, 230
(St.) John of the Cross, 191
journey (spiritual), ix–x, 3, 80, 177, 227, 229–30, 234–35, 238
joy, 104, 136, 154, 188, 191, 206, 209, 211, 213
judgment, ix, 46–48, 96, 124, 135–36, 227
justice, 102, 134, 153, 187
justification, 46, 67–68, 96, 124–25, 127, 139, 166, 174, 223
    doctrine of, 36, 43, 78, 174
    See also righteousness

kingdom
    of God, 11, 20, 71, 77, 85, 87, 90–92, 95–97, 100–102, 105, 118, 123, 147–51, 158–59, 161, 173, 184, 193, 195–97, 238
    ethic/ethics, 103, 178, 183
    Two kingdom concept, 38, 94
knowledge, 12, 14–15, 42, 45, 52, 88, 105, 113, 124, 136, 156, 185, 200, 218, 226, 231
    experiential, 223
    of God, 52, 124, 185, 195, 223
    of God's will, 136, 156, 185, 195, 200
    of self, 124, 200, 213–14
    personal, 52, 218, 223
    relational, 214, 218, 223

Subject Index

law
  constitutional, 141–43, 145
  moral, 107, 141–43
  functions of, 33–34, 173
  natural, 2, 107, 140–44, 147, 220
  third use of, 33–35, 144–45, 174–75
legalism, legalistic, vii, 47, 104, 115, 130, 178, 189–90, 237
Lenin, Vladimir I., 138
liberalism, 16, 64
liberation, 207, 230
lifestyle, 4, 32, 36, 73, 77, 88, 139, 148
listening to God, 1, 5–6, 14, 19–21, 27, 51, 77, 79–80, 82–83, 85, 87–89, 100, 110, 149, 155–56, 159, 172, 191
  See also prayer
Løgstrup, Knud E., 144
lordship, 91, 93, 97, 136,
  of God, 92, 95, 97, 99–101, 122, 125, 147–50, 160, 163, 165, 176, 237
  of Christ, 94, 160–61, 166, 183
love
  ethic/ethics of, 47–48, 60, 153, 178, 188, 191
  for one's neighbor, 20, 26, 36, 48, 71, 79, 104–5, 132, 134, 138, 145, 151, 154, 156, 159, 164, 167, 173, 176, 195
  self-love, 229
  suffering love, 207–11, 217, 224, 232–34
  See also commandment, double commandment of love
Lutheran, Lutheranism, 30, 55, 80, 104, 143, 148, 157, 183
  Lutheran ethics, 37

Machovec, Milan, 128
man
  new man, 3, 96–97, 196

mandate. *See* cultural mandate
manifestation (of God's reality), 97, 99–100
Mann, Thomas, 6
Mary (and Martha), 159, 197
Marxism, Marxist, xi, 3, 5, 12, 13, 15, 16, 40, 44, 53, 57, 65, 90, 95, 96, 99, 119–21, 123, 148, 152, 196
  Marxist-Leninist ethics, 148
materialism, 100, 167
meditation, 51, 74, 77, 158
Melanchthon, Philipp, 36, 173
mercy, 44, 123, 134, 138, 206, 208, 219, 230
metaphor, 177, 203, 211, 213, 216
Meyer, Frederick B., 81–82
Michel, D. Otto, 6
mind of Christ, 170, 200
mission, 18, 43, 48–50, 61–62, 80, 103, 107, 110, 115–16, 118, 153–54, 157, 159, 160–68, 173, 176, 179, 181, 196
  Moravian, 49
  Danish-Halle, 49
  world, 6, 40, 49–50
Monasticism, 32, 77, 110
Moral Re-Armament/MRA, xiii, 4–8, 10, 13–14, 79–89, 158, 196, 253, 257, 268, 278
  See also Oxford Group
morality, 143, 191–92, 221–22, 224
  old, 15, 129, 136, 148, 190, 199
  new, 15–16, 40, 78, 118, 129–36, 147–48, 169, 174, 199
  See also ethics
Moravian, 49
  See also Zinzendorf, Nikolaus L. von
Moses, 213
motivation, 26, 37, 95, 127, 131, 152, 155, 159, 164, 177, 197, 199
mutuality, 213–14

Subject Index

new creation. *See* creation
new man. *See* man
new morality. *See* morality

obedience, 16, 49, 78, 97, 105, 111, 127, 136, 149–50, 154–56, 169, 197, 224, 230
obligation, 139, 221
old morality. *See* morality
orthodox, 28, 45, 49
    Lutheranism, 30, 42, 80
Orthodoxy, 41
    Lutheran, 59
    Protestant, 28, 37, 117
Oxford Group 63, 79–88, 248, 257
    See also Moral Re-Armament

pain, 20, 98, 208–9, 211, 227, 232–34
parable, 138, 213, 253
    of the Prodigal Son, 203, 212, 231
participation, 93, 97, 162, 191, 211, 213, 218
(St.) Patrick (missionary to Ireland), 27–28
Paul, Pauline, ix, 116, 127–28, 141, 160, 182, 202–3, 206, 212, 215–17, 221,
    ethics, 221
peace, 33, 136, 159, 188, 191, 226
Pentecost, 202, 210, 215
perceptibility (of God's works), 57–58, 62–63, 92, 97–98
performance, 195, 197, 231
Peter (apostle), 156
philosophy, 54, 142, 224
Pietism (German), 4, 8–9, 17–18, 38–52, 67, 88–89, 146, 156, 166
    classical Pietism, 40–43, 45, 50
    Pietist/pietistic, 38–44, 46, 48–55, 67, 88–89, 95, 166, 189, 196

pneumatic, pneumatology, 7, 52, 58–59, 61, 101, 105, 118
pneumatic ethic/ethics, 58, 90, 190–91
political, politics, 12, 126
(the) poor, 50, 75–76, 148–49, 164–65, 182
poverty, 74, 76, 170
praxis pietatis, 45, 166
prayer, ix, 4, 17, 19, 38–39, 51, 74, 76-77, 105, 111–12, 155, 157, 167, 169, 191, 197, 216–17
    listening, 16, 74–75, 105, 111–12, 158–59, 164, 172
preaching, 2, 9, 39, 46, 76, 107, 154, 165, 179
preservation, 32, 48, 95, 103, 137–39, 143, 145–46, 164, 174
    ethic/ethics of, 137, 179–80
primacy (of God/of God's love), ix, 64–65, 71, 79, 91
proclamation, 13, 50, 62, 79, 121, 131, 141, 146, 162–65, 179
prophecy, 112–13
prophet, prophetic, vii, 15, 68, 111, 161, 210
proprium of Christian ethics, 69, 104, 110, 118, 160, 179–82, 191
Protestant, 162
    milieu, 43, 51, 61
    ethics, 18, 29–30, 48, 59, 60–61, 118, 129, 142, 153, 157, 166, 175, 188–89
psychological, 122, 238

"quiet time," 5–6, 8, 11, 14, 17, 40, 77, 82–83, 85, 105, 196

rational, 135–36, 199–200, 221, 225
Rationalism, 49
reason, 117, 132, 135–36, 147, 154, 169, 189, 194, 198–200

Subject Index

reconciliation, 14, 47, 69, 74, 83, 151, 184, 208, 233
reciprocity, 141, 213–14
redemption, 97–98, 180, 207–8, 230, 233
   ethic/ethics, 58, 70, 95, 103–4, 110–18, 146, 153, 157, 166, 175, 179, 183, 192, 194, 237
   See also creation and redemption
Reformation ethics, 33, 35, 59, 61, 110–18, 138, 147, 169, 198
Reformed tradition, 31, 35–36, 42
Reformers, 28–38, 41–43, 47, 50, 68, 72, 111, 113–18, 139–40, 144, 150, 173–74, 177
regeneration, 9, 33, 43–45, 100, 124, 151–53, 160, 167, 171, 179, 88, 237
   See also conversion
Regent College Vancouver, 16–19, 21, 52, 172, 98
rejection, 115, 207, 211, 231–33
relational
   approach/concept, vii, 2, 185, 201–19, 221
   work/function of the Holy Spirit, x, 191, 193–94, 215, 219, 222, 224–25, 227, 237
relationship
   intimate, 185, 214–17, 219, 223–25, 237
   filial, 203–4, 216, 223
   mutual, 214, 217
   parent-child, 211–13
   See also intimacy
renewal, 11, 35, 41, 48, 62, 125, 164, 196, 199, 229, 231
restoration, 60, 102, 164, 179–80, 193, 211
   ethic/ethics of, 116, 179–80
resurrection, 65, 98, 121, 125–26, 131–32, 149, 152, 204–5
revelation, 51–52, 57, 62, 98, 120, 123, 143, 209, 219, 230

righteousness, righteous, 35, 60, 145, 194, 205, 231, 234
Ritschl, Albrecht, 55

sacred (and profane), 32
salvation, 48, 54, 67–68, 78, 125, 129, 152–53, 160–61, 166, 174, 181–82
   ethics, 58, 68, 70, 153, 207, 231
   history, 98, 100, 123
Samaritan. *See* Good Samaritan
Scripture
   as corrective, 57, 67, 71–72, 90–91
Schlatter, Susanna, 54
Schuman, Robert 83–84
secularization, 44, 100–101, 117, 162
secularism, 67, 77, 90–91, 94, 100–101, 128
self
   exterior, 231
   false, 218–19, 231
   new, 97, 219
   true, 200, 232
self-understanding, 91, 99, 121, 124–25
Sermon on the Mount, 95, 153
servant, 29, 74, 92, 192, 195, 197, 203, 213, 216
shame, 228, 231
sin, 8, 33–34, 44–45, 81, 83, 85–86, 98, 121, 125, 152, 167, 174, 194, 208, 228, 233–34
situation
   ethic/ethics, 52, 59, 70, 78, 130–34, 169, 188, 220
   situationism, 130, 222
slave, slavery, 26, 75, 218
social
   action, 43, 45, 164–65. *See also diakonia*
   ethics, 16, 18, 53, 91, 103, 144–46, 179, 189
   gospel, 164

Subject Index

socialism, 3, 12
sonship, 213, 216
solidarity, 210–11, 234
soul, 28, 44, 49, 104–5, 154, 164–65, 227, 229
sovereignty, 91, 136, 204
Spirit
    ethic/ethics of the (Holy) Spirit, 59, 178, 183, 187–88, 192
    See also pneumatic ethics
spirituality, vii, 2, 17, 26–27, 35, 48, 51, 72–73, 75, 80, 103, 106–7, 110, 115, 153, 157–60, 166, 176, 188, 190–91, 225–26, 237
    medieval spirituality, 41–42
standard, 42, 56, 58, 150–51
    moral/ethical standards, 83, 85–87, 99, 102, 141
station (in life), 32–33, 68, 118, 129, 182–83
stewardship, 32, 103, 137, 139
subjectivism, 173, 200
suffering, 74, 98, 207–11, 215, 232–34
sufficiency (of the law), 114, 177
Sundermeier, Karl, 4, 6
supernatural/supranatural, 199–200, 206
synecdoche, 114–15, 176

Tauler, Johannes, 26, 42
teaching, 19, 25, 35, 77, 103–4, 109, 112, 163–64, 172, 184, 212
teleological, 148
    ethics, 148, 220
    teleology, 222
temple (of the Holy Spirit), 202, 215
Ten Commandments
    as the "grammar of creation," 94, 140
    See also Decalogue

theology, theologian
    Protestant, 2, 17, 28, 35, 59, 63, 73, 113, 142–44, 154, 157, 168, 180, 189
    systematic, 7, 16, 53, 56, 90
Thomas Aquinas. *See* Aquinas, Thomas
Thomas à Kempis, 27–28,
transformation, ix, 2, 45, 82, 100–101, 107, 150, 152, 168, 188, 198–99, 222–26, 231, 237–38
Trinity/trinitarian, 109, 112, 183, 210, 232
    ethics, 104, 183
    and God, 44, 209, 221
trust, 62, 154, 157, 214, 219,
truth, 27, 73, 113, 120–21, 127, 136, 165, 188, 223, 226–27, 230
    God's, 21, 26, 61
Tübingen, 6, 13, 18, 38, 54–55

utility, utilitarian, 133–34, 169
    ethics, 220

validity (of the law/commandments), 9, 30, 33, 35, 39, 58–59, 116, 132, 141, 143, 173–74, 180, 189
virtue ethics, 220
vocation
    Christian, 68–69, 103–4, 161
    civil, 32–33, 50, 68, 116, 118, 140, 147, 161, 169, 181, 194
    special, 116

Watts, Isaac, 81, 238
Wesley, John, 52
Whitefield, George, 52
wholeness, 227, 229,
Wilhelm II, German Emperor, 55
wisdom, 72, 138, 171, 202
Wolff, Hans-Walter, 6

works of supererogation, 29, 59–60, 105, 115, 176, 181–82, 188, 224
Wuppertal (Germany), 6–8

Zacchaeus, 44, 100, 182
Zinzendorf, Nikolaus L. von, 40, 49, 51